THE DEED AND THE DOER
IN THE BIBLE

THE DEED AND THE DOER
IN THE BIBLE

David Daube's Gifford Lectures, Volume 1

David Daube

EDITED AND COMPILED BY **Calum Carmichael**

TEMPLETON FOUNDATION PRESS
West Conshohocken, Pennsylvania

Templeton Foundation Press
300 Conshohocken State Road, Suite 670
West Conshohocken, PA 19428
www.templetonpress.org

Templeton Foundation Press helps intellectual leaders and others learn about
science research on aspects of realities, invisible and intangible. Spiritual realities
include unlimited love, accelerating creativity, worship, and the benefits of purpose in persons and in the cosmos.

Designed and typeset by Kachergis Book Design

LIBRARY OF CONGRESS CATALOGING-IN-PUBLICATION DATA
Daube, David.
    The deed and the doer in the Bible / David Daube ; compiled and edited by
Calum Carmichael.
        p. cm. — (David Daube's Gifford lectures ; v. 1)
    Includes bibliographical references and index.
    ISBN-13: 978-1-59947-134-1 (pbk. : alk. paper)
    ISBN-10: 1-59947-134-5 (pbk. : alk. paper)   1. Bible—Criticism,
interpretation, etc.   I. Carmichael, Calum M.   II. Title.
    BS511.3.D365 2008
    220.6—dc22

                        2007044635

Printed in the United States of America

08   09   10   11   12   13   10   9   8   7   6   5   4   3   2   1

CONTENTS

PREFACE

David Daube delivered two sets of Gifford Lectures at the University of Edinburgh: "The Deed and the Doer in the Bible" in September and October 1962, and "Law and Wisdom in the Bible" in April and May 1964. At the time he was the Regius Professor of Civil Law at the University of Oxford, a position that King Henry VIII had established, and which had been offered to Daube in a handwritten note from the then prime minister, Winston Churchill.

Daube traced his scholarly lineage back to the eleventh-century Italian jurist Irnerius, who at the University of Bologna revived the study of Roman law and taught it along lines long established in the teaching of scripture. The pedigree is an unbroken one of teacher and pupil and contains some of the most illustrious names in European legal history. Daube's career spanned almost the entire twentieth century with roughly equal periods of time spent in Germany (where he was born February 8, 1909), Great Britain, and the United States (where he died February 24, 1999). A confluence of forces produced a scholar immediately recognizable as unique. He came out of a strictly Orthodox Jewish upbringing that from boyhood included instruction in Aramaic and Hebrew. He was immersed in the 1920s in the classical tradition of the German educational system. His rare abilities were recognized and cultivated by a number of outstanding scholars in Germany in the 1920s and in Cambridge (England) in the 1930s and 1940s. Although he gave up a commitment to an Orthodox Jewish life, its influence remained. His scholarly work grew out of his engagement with biblical, Greek, Roman, and talmudic texts, and his absorption in the intricacies of different legal traditions made him alert to elements of the law that find expression in the world of literature, be it Christian, Greek, Jewish, or Roman.

Daube was introduced to biblical criticism at the University of Göttingen by Johannes Hempel and proceeded to complete his doctorate on the biblical legal topic of blood vengeance (*Das Blutrecht im Alten Testament*). A teacher at his Freiburg synagogue told him at the time, "If you must do biblical criticism, do it like a surgeon who has to operate on his father." The looming threat of National Socialism in Germany led to Daube's moving to Cambridge in 1933 where he completed a Roman Law doctorate on damage to property (*Formalism and Progress in the Roman Law of Delict*). At Cambridge, biblical scholars S. A. Cook, C. H. Dodd, and F. S. Marsh encouraged Daube to pursue his studies in both Old and New Testament literature.

I first met Daube when he gave his 1962 series of Gifford lectures. I had been on my way from Edinburgh to study with Roy Porter at Oriel College, Oxford, but Daube suggested that I come to him at All Souls College because of my interest in biblical law. There began an increasingly close association that lasted until his death in a Californian nursing home in 1999. When Daube took on a student, he gave of himself unstintingly. It was more a relationship of master with disciple than teacher with pupil. He trained five students in addition to myself in different areas of the law: Peter Stein, who became Regius Professor of Civil Law at the University of Cambridge; Reuven Yaron, who held the Chair of Roman Law at the Hebrew University, Jerusalem; Alan Watson, who has been the holder of chairs of law in British and American universities; Alan Rodger, who is currently one of the law lords in the House of Lords in London; and Bernard Jackson, who holds a chair in Jewish Studies at the University of Manchester, England.

Daube's scholarly output is substantial by any standards, but he never published his Gifford lectures. To be sure, the preparation that went into them led to the inclusion of some of their contents into published articles. A few of the lectures he did write out, but most of them existed in the form of typescripts transcribed by a secretary in Edinburgh from a tape recorder, which, alas, can no longer be located. His strong South German accent; his use of Latin, Greek, Hebrew, and German terms; and the deficiency of the then available technology made the task a far from simple one. My own efforts in compiling them have been easier because of my familiarity with

Daube's work. To date, in a project at the School of Law, University of California, Berkeley—Daube taught there for thirty years after he left Oxford—I have supervised the publication of four volumes of his collected works.

In compiling the material of Daube's ten lectures plus a supplement that appear in this volume, and in ten currently in preparation (*Law and Wisdom in the Bible*), I have used the existing typescripts, those lectures he wrote out himself, and parts he incorporated into published items. There is some repetition which I chose not to excise, because when Daube looks at a matter again he invariably brings new insights to bear on it.

Calum Carmichael
CORNELL UNIVERSITY

ABBREVIATIONS

AB   Anchor Bible

ArOr   *Archiv Orientalni*

AV   Authorized Version

BLL   *Studies in Comparative Legal History: Collected Works of David Daube,* vol. 3, *Biblical Law and Literature*, ed. Calum Carmichael (Berkeley, 2003)

CLJ   *Cambridge Law Journal*

CLR   *California Law Review*

CSRL   *Collected Studies in Roman Law*, 2 vols., eds. David Cohen and Dieter Simon (Frankfurt am Main, 1991)

EOW   *Studies in Comparative Legal History: Collected Works of David Daube,* vol. 4, *Ethics and Other Writings*, ed. Calum Carmichael (Berkeley, 2008)

HAT   *Handbuch zum Alten Testament*

HUCA   *Hebrew Union College Annual*

ICC   International Critical Commentary

ILR   *Israel Law Review*

JJS   *Journal of Jewish Studies*

JQR   *Jewish Quarterly Review*

JR   *Juridical Review*

LQR   *Law Quarterly Review*

ABBREVIATIONS

LRB	*London Review of Books*
LXX	The Septuagint
MAL	Middle Assyrian Laws
Mekhilta	A second-century CE rabbinic commentary on the book of Exodus
NLF	*Natural Law Forum*
NT	*Novum Testamentum*
NTJ	*Studies in Comparative Legal History: Collected Works of David Daube,* vol. 2, *New Testament Judaism*, ed. Calum Carmichael (Berkeley, 2000)
RIDA	*Revue Internationale des Droits de l'Antiquité*
RJ	*Rechtshistorisches Journal*
TL	*Studies in Comparative Legal History: Collected Works of David Daube,* vol. 1, *Talmudic Law*, ed. Calum Carmichael (Berkeley, 1992)
TLR	*Tulane Law Review*
UCLALR	*University of California Los Angeles Law Review*
VT	*Vetus Testamentum*
ZAW	*Zeitschrift für die Alttestamentliche Wissenschaft*
ZNTW	*Zeitschrift für die Neutestamentliche Wissenschaft*
ZSS	*Zeitschrift der Savigny-Stiftung für Rechtsgeschichte*

THE DEED AND THE DOER
IN THE BIBLE

CHAPTER 1

CAUSATION

"Whodunit" is the question asked when a crime has been committed and the identity of the criminal is unknown. But the question may arise where the identity is known and all other facts are clear. Suppose all the archives pertaining to the First and Second World Wars are open and we ask: who caused these wars? Or, I am run over and killed by a skidding car. Is it the driver who has caused my death, or the manufacturer of the tires that were defective, or the person who asked me to lunch, but for whom I should not have been there? Where does God or fate come in? If my aunt on hearing the news gets a temperature, is wrongly treated, and dies, who or what has caused her death? We confront the problem of causation.

The Role of God. He Instructs Man; Works Inside His Mind; Instigates Him; Puts a Stumbling Block in His Way; and Uses Him as His Instrument. In the Bible, apart from God as creator and hence the cause of everything (logically worked out in late sources: e.g., Sir 33:14, 15; Rom 1:19, 20; 8:19–23[1]), he plays an enormous role, but the modalities vary. A few follow. Any event and any human undertaking depend on God admitting it—at least in advanced portions of the Bible. As with a school or an army, it is admission, not causation. The admission may be negative: there is no interference with free play except the recognition that it could be prevented or crossed at any moment. The noninterference is taken for granted; it is one way of viewing the direction of history. Some players are given free rein; others are cut off, frustrated: a prayer is not allowed to succeed, Moses is not to cross the Jordan (Deut 3:25), the prophecy that the attack on Jerusalem in the reign of Hezekiah by the Assyrians will come to nothing (2 Kgs 19:6). There is innumerable other evidence.

Express reference to admission is made above all where a boast is refuted or the mysterious purpose behind an unsatisfactory situation is stressed. Both are found in John 19:11: "Thou [Pilate] couldest have no power against me except it were given thee from above." This example reveals the problem. Admission, though not causation, may be observed: it is seen that he who could have hindered, and did not, plays a decisive role (and authorities who deny that this is early overlook the role of God). What about evil enterprises? In primitive parts of the Bible—independent of God, that is—admission is not yet general. The serpent in the Adam and Eve story is an example. The dualism never quite dies out and is dominant in some late sections. In between there are all sorts of solutions: punishment, discipline, and testing. One tendency is to deny that something will ever succeed, or succeed for long. Gamaliel in Acts 5:34–39 says that just as the leaders of certain movements, Theudas and Judas of Galilee, failed, so will the Christians fail if their cause is not of God. The position is typical of those who are successful (would not do in Russia). In the Old Testament, consciousness of admission in general is confined to major, national questions, though in the psalms we find a more individual orientation.[2] A very minute application of the notion is found in the New Testament: in Matt 10:29, no sparrow falls to the ground without the Father permitting it, and the hairs of one's head are all numbered. Similar notions appear among the Rabbis.[3]

There is also positive influence on human action. Law with its specific orders provides an example that is wide and deep. Moses constantly does "according to all that God commands him," and he "walks with God." God's will is done "on earth as in heaven." The human mirrors the divine. The relation is similar to what we today find for the master-pupil; the design is the former's, but the merit of the latter is recognized.

God may steer to misdeeds. He does so by acting inside a person, as when he hardens Pharaoh's heart (Exod 4:21; 7:3, etc.), or places a stumbling block before people (Jer 6:21), or blinds them (Isa 6:9; Mark 4:12). In the first case there is a problem of free will—but only for later theologians. Originally, in all cases, God keeps the wicked to the latter's road to punish all the more and triumph. A stubborn sinner is a demoniac, mad, and a higher force is seen to be at work. In Greek sources we have the sylleptor [literally, one that takes hold of with], the co-operator.[4]

The moral responsibility lies with the sinner, though God contributes. Ezek 3:20 shows that the problem is felt: "if a righteous man turns from his righteousness and commits iniquity, and I [God] lay a stumbling block before him, he shall die." The sinner has already turned from his righteousness. But there are other cases. God stirs David to take the census (2 Sam 24:1). Perhaps the same problem that Ezekiel felt explains why the Chronicler replaces God in 2 Sam 24:1 by Satan (1 Chr 21:1). Sometimes the specific method used by God in steering the person to misdeeds is left open. Eli's sons did not hearken to their father "because God wanted to kill them" (1 Sam 2:25). Needless to say, God may also inspire fine actions, charity, art, and so on.

Man is God's instrument, for good or evil. There are two ways in which this happens. The nation or the individual has a mandate to act as the instrument and hence is justified in so acting. The Assyrians are "the rod of my anger" (Isa 10:5), "the Lord shall hiss for the fly of Egypt and the bee of Assyria" (Isa 7:18), "I will raise up against Babylon a destroying wind" (Jer 51:1), and some nations are left to test Israel (Judg 3:1). Other times there is no mandate, hence there is no justification for their acting as they do and they are punished in the end. How does God set them in motion? Something like admission, as above, is pertinent. Within that admission, nations freely act, yet serve *Heilsgeschichte* [salvation history]. So do individuals: in the story of Samson the encounter with the Philistines is from God, admitted, although engineering is also implied. Admission proves very important in the New Testament, where inimical actions are done so that everything is fulfilled. The opponent claims to be the conscious legitimate mandatory.

I intend to make three points and one plea.[5]

I

Indirect Causation in Early Law. The first point is this. As is well known, some ancient regulations attach legal consequences only to the most direct causation, say, a man hitting his slave with a stick and the slave dying there and then.[6] It would be quite wrong to conclude that a restriction of this sort is due to a primitive incapacity for seeing through a less direct causation. The same code that contains the statute just quoted also contains one imposing liability on a man who digs a pit into which another man's animal falls.[7] It might perhaps be argued that the two statutes, though in the same code, date from different periods, the rule concerning the slave being prior to that concerning the pit. Even if correct, this would not alter the principal point here to be established: that however far back in time we go, we find a full understanding of the most lengthy and complicated chain of events linking cause and effect. The opposite view is founded on a naive belief (which captured the world of anthropology, ancient history and classics in the nineteenth century) in a progress of mankind from childishness to intelligence.

The narrative of David and Uriah is old. No murder could be less direct, yet Nathan charges David: "Uriah the Hittite thou hast smitten with the sword."[8] Actually, there is a more precise repetition at the end of the verse, perhaps a gloss to explain and insist on the ascription of the deed to David: "and him thou hast slain with the sword of the Ammonites." It is interesting that a modern commentator, Caspari,[9] finds it necessary to mitigate this in translation and make it less direct: *hast den Uria erschlagen (lassen)*. David himself had been sent into battle by Saul when the latter wanted to get rid of him without doing the actual dispatching. Saul's daughter, promised to David if he deserved her by his exploits, would, Saul hoped, be "a snare to him."[10] "Let not mine hand be upon him, but the hand of the Philistines."[11] "But Saul thought to make David fall by the hand of the Philistines."[12] In one of the earliest trials of the Bible, there is an almost formal *Gewährenzug* or *remotio criminis* [diversion of the accusation] from the accused to another delinquent named as intellectual author, and from the latter to a yet further intellectual author. "Hast thou eaten of the tree?" God asks Adam, who replies: "The woman whom thou gavest to be with me, she gave me of the tree and I did eat"—a (not very gallant)[13] shuffling off of the guilt to Eve and, indeed, in a way, to God himself whose present she was. Then God turns to Eve: "What is this that thou hast done?" "The serpent beguiled me, and I did eat."

In meting out their punishment, God begins with the serpent, proceeds to Eve, and ends with Adam.[14] The story of Abimelech and Sarah is steeped in legal language and pursues definite legal aims. Here Abimelech, having taken Sarah into his harem, tells Abraham, who has merely suppressed the fact of her being his wife, "Thou hast brought on me and my kingdom a great sin."[15]

These instances could be multiplied—let us recall one from Greek mythology: Eriphyle killed by her son in revenge for his father's death, for which she was responsible because she made him take part in the war from which he did not return. They expose the baselessness of any theory that would explain the rigidity of early statutes in the matter of causation by an inability to grasp a less obvious nexus. Nothing could be further from the truth.

Difficulties of Evidence. Why, then, do we get these narrow definitions? For practical, technical reasons, reasons of machinery; above all, because less direct causation usually does mean less certainty, and in an age without a highly organized police force, forensic laboratories, truth drugs, and so on, that uncertainty is prohibitive. The law cannot exact retribution where the evidence leaves a degree of doubt.

Take the beating to death of a slave by his master, already mentioned. Vengeance is sanctioned only "if he die under his hand," and is expressly excluded "if he continue a day or two." No such limitation is met in the provisions of the same code regarding the killing of a free man.[16] So it is not as if a less instantaneous result had not been recognized for what it was. However, the code has a very suggestive rule concerning an injury inflicted by one man on another, as a result of which the victim must take to his bed. It is laid down that "if he rise again and walk abroad upon his staff, then shall he that smote him be quit."[17] The problem here settled is one that creates enormous difficulties even in modern times. Any insurance company is familiar with the person who receives a bump, lives happily for twenty years, then develops migraine—and claims. Of course, the migraine might be due to the bump. The rule in our code fixes a time limit: once the victim has gone out, any subsequent disaster—in particular, his subsequent death—is no longer to be laid at the injurer's door. In Rome, the third chapter of the *lex Aquilia*, dealing with wounds inflicted on another man's slave or beast, adopted the rigid time limit of thirty days.[18]

Returning now to the slave beaten to death by his master, this provision comes immediately after that concerning the injured man who takes to his bed. The problem is the same—where to draw the limit in imputing consequences. True, a number of critics separate the two provisions; they place the delict of hurting a woman with child[19] between them.[20] But this is to replace the peculiar notions determining the original arrangement by what one might expect in a present-day Act of Parliament. The time, then, in the case of the slave is extremely short, a day or two. The reason? A master may beat his slave constantly. If vengeance were lawful even should death occur after weeks or months, he would be in danger whenever a slave of his died. It could always be connected with a beating. Two free men will not normally fight every day. An injury is an isolated occurrence; its development for better or worse can be watched. In the case of a slave, all this is different. Unless the law intended to make beating itself illegal, the master's liability must be confined to the most flagrant, clearest murder. (It should be noted that if the slave suffers loss of an eye or tooth, he must be freed.)[21]

On this basis, we can explain the puzzling motivation given by the code: "for he is his money"—that is, he bought him.[22] It means that any less narrow time limit would (in the circumstances of that age) break the master's power over his slave. If the slave stays alive, for however short a while, vengeance may not be exacted—for a slave is his master's property and may still be treated as such. The statute, like the others in this code which relate to slaves, is a compromise typical of a certain phase of evolution when the weaker group is guaranteed some valuable rights but the stronger still retains a great deal of its position.

Needless to say, other factors besides the need for simple, unambiguous evidence may make for the requirement, in certain contexts, of a very direct causation. After all, even in modern law, a gunsmith, for instance, or a motorcar manufacturer would never be held accountable for the catastrophes brought about by his products, though it is perfectly foreseeable, when he produces them, that a certain number of catastrophes must ensue; and the prophet Nathan (or Professor Goodhart) might tell him, "Thou art slaying thousands of innocent people." If I kill you by a blow—intentional or unintentional—there is less room for intervention by outside elements than if I shut you up and starve you to death. Nor are we denying that, once there is a tradition of insistence on direct causation, such insistence can become mechanical, a game even: lawyers are prone to elevate a means into an end. Here and there, where bloody deeds are concerned, magical ideas—even these not usually without roots in reason—play a part. But these and other reservations are of a minor nature.

Our point, that the narrowness of some ancient statutes is due to deliberate caution rather than to defective grasp, is confirmed by the fact that, whenever there is no reason for such caution, statutes of equal antiquity show no trace of the narrowness. Equal antiquity: to be taken *cum grano salis*—we do not consider such differences as exist one way or the other to be essential.

There is reason for caution where legal consequences are attached to a deed. There is no reason where people are to be warned to refrain from a deed, or where divine retribution is called down (God knows the evidence), or where a man has to declare his innocence before heaven.[23] Hence we never find a commandment "Thou shalt not smite a free man so that he take to his bed and rise not again and walk abroad," or "Thou shalt not smite a slave so that he die within one day." What we find is "Thou shalt not murder,"[24] "Thou shalt not rule over him with rigor."[25] Again, we never find a curse restricted in that meticulous fashion; what we find is "Cursed be he that smiteth his neighbor secretly," or "that perverteth the judgment of the stranger, fatherless and widow."[26] As for an avowal of innocence, if a man is found murdered in the country and his murderer cannot be traced, the elders of the nearest city have to proclaim: "Our hands have not shed this blood, neither have our eyes seen it."[27] The second half embraces any manner of participating or condoning. It would be far too wide even nowadays as a basis of earthly punishment; but, significantly, the Book of the Dead furnishes a parallel, "I have done no murder, I have not given the order for murder to be done for me." Here also, "I have not ill-treated servants," "I have not defrauded the oppressed," "I have not carried away the milk from the mouths of children."[28]

In an article on error in biblical law, I pointed out[29] that, although there is little straightforward biblical legislation on the treatment of error outside the Levitical sphere, there is a considerable amount designed to prevent error from being committed. Similarly, there is considerable legislation catching indirect causation before the result has come about. I have already alluded to the release of a slave whose eye or tooth is knocked out by his master. That master at any rate can no longer kill him, whether by a blow immediately fatal or by one fatal after an interval. In this case, the legislator may not have this particular point in mind; the slave no doubt has to be freed simply because of what has been done to him. But take the Deuteronomic injunction to make a railing around your roof.[30] It is highly unlikely that, if a man fell from your roof, whether before or after this law, vengeance would be legitimate or a court would sentence you; and we should note that what happens, in the words of this law, if anyone falls to death is that there is "blood-guilt on your house"—not on you. It may even be doubted whether the law was meant to be enforced by authority: it stands together with others—concerning a bird's nest and the mixing of different kinds of seed—which were hardly at the time under any effective public control. Nevertheless it remains true that here is a deliberate legislative effort to ensure action before it is too late. The situation in question, an unprotected roof, is a common one; its dangers are known; and it is easily definable—and easily rectifiable. So the legislator can tackle it. In a sense, a statute like that about a false witness is analogous. That the lawgiver has in mind the ultimate result to which the offense may lead is shown by the punishment: the culprit suffers that penalty which he tried to get inflicted on the other party.[31]

At one time I wondered whether the laws against witches and the like were partly intended to render punishable misdeeds that would escape the very narrow definitions of other serious crimes. They would make it possible to get at the indirect author of death or injury. I was encouraged by the close association in many systems between witchcraft and poisoning—poisoning is less direct than a blow and, moreover, the preparer of the poison would frequently not even administer it himself; it would go through several hands, maybe innocent ones. (Remember the *Trachiniae*.) The Septuagint does translate *mekhashsheph* by *pharmakos*.[32] But the position of these laws in the Hebrew text speaks against this idea. They are not placed together with penal laws carefully worded, as if to fill the gaps left by these laws, but with laws directed against heathen malpractices.

So far we have dealt with the question of why certain statutes do not go beyond the narrowest causality. It should be noted that this narrow causality is found in other, comparable domains. A solemn oath is apt to be interpreted very literally. King David, though having sworn to Shimei that "he would not kill him with the sword," deems it in order on his deathbed to charge his son Solomon with bringing about a situation in which that old enemy may be justly eliminated.[33] Heine has written a cleverly cynical poem about the king's last wishes concerning Joab. Again it would be absurd to conclude that the nature of indirect killing was not understood. David knew what he was doing, knew that he was encompassing Shimei's death. In fact, it was fully realized even that this construction put on the oath was a peculiarly formalistic one, to which there would have been a nonformalistic, honest, natural alternative.[34] But this aspect lies outside our present inquiry. I may perhaps just mention that overliteral interpretation plays a part also in the continuation of the story, that is to say, in the method Solomon chooses to execute his father's mandate.[35] On a decent, nonformalistic interpretation, the arrangement that Shimei may not cross the Kidron, on pain of death, hardly includes the case of running after some fugitive servants, a completely nonpolitical errand.

II

Causation and Intent. My next point is to draw attention to some correlation between direct causation and presence of intent and between indirect causation and absence of intent. We have seen that in a number of statutes only the closest causation is accepted as a sufficient basis for sentencing an offender. Conversely, we may now add, where I am the absolutely direct cause of your death, that may almost amount to proof of intent. In other words, those cases of homicide in which allowance is made for accident usually contain an element—however slight—of indirectness.

Take the one detailed illustration of accidental homicide supplied by biblical law: the two men hewing wood together and one unwittingly killing the other.[36] He does not do it with his hands, he does not even do it by a direct blow with the axe; but as he swings down the axe, the iron head flies from the handle and the other man is hit. (To be sure, one could translate "and the axe slips from the tree to be cut." I regard it as slightly less likely. In any case, my thesis would not be much affected.) If I kill you with my own hands, except for such special situations as a boxing contest, it will nearly always be murder. Accidental homicide does normally involve some indirectness, and in the specimen case under review, with the head of the axe coming off, the indirectness is of such a nature as to furnish practically conclusive evidence of absence of intent.

Significantly, the formulation is reminiscent of an ancient provision respecting an indirect mode of damage to property: the case of a person lighting a fire on his land.[37] The fire "makes its way out and finds, *umasa'*, the stacks or standing corn" of the neighbor. Just so, the head of the axe "flies from the wood and finds, *umasa'*, the other man." There is between the person starting off the affair and the result something approaching an animate force which, given its opportunity, does the dismal work. It is a measure of the variability of the lawgiver's point of view and his adaptability to the requirements of a situation that, whereas it is the purpose of the statute concerning fire to establish full civil-law liability despite the indirectness, the statute concerning homicide uses the indirectness in support of the mitigated criminal-law liability where there is no intent.

It is sometimes maintained that in primitive law, either you have caused death with intent or, if not, you are regarded as not having caused it at all: some other cause must be considered exclusively responsible. This, however, is a simplification which, like that I tried to discredit in the first section, is due to an underrating of the intellectual powers of people in that age. We must not forget that even today causality and planning are linked in many respects. To take again the example of the motorcar manufacturer, in normal circumstances one would not readily look on him as the major cause of a particular accident. But imagine a film starring a sadist who takes to and boosts this industry in order to satisfy his lust: on bank holiday he hovers above the A1 in a helicopter. By reason of his intent, the audience could be got to condemn him as a major cause.

In my view there was no time in history when people did not see that, if a disaster results from the head of an axe flying off, the person who swung the axe is a cause in one sense at least, namely, as having triggered the chain of events; though in another sense, as a thinking being, he is not, so that from this angle prominence must be accorded to the axe or to fate or to God. Indeed I would go as far as to contend that, where some factor outside the person is represented as the exclusive cause, we have before us, not a primitive stage, but on the contrary a rather sophisticated or technical one, with ulterior motives determining the one-sided emphasis—as when Oedipus Coloneus claims that the terrible things he is charged with are the work of others, not him. (The discussion by my brother[38] is too much in line here with orthodox classical scholarship.) In Greek law (I know we should speak only of Attic or Theban law, but let it pass) proceedings may be taken against the instrument that caused a death (cf. the English deodand). Plato, Aristotle, and Demosthenes agree in confining them to the case where no person handled the instrument or where he remains undetected.[39] Maschke argues[40] that they must have taken place also where the person is available but the deed was accidental: to the primitive mind, the instrument would appear the exclusive cause. But this is simply contrary to the sources. (It would, by the way, mean two trials before different courts: one against the person before the Palladion or perhaps Delphinion, another against the instrument before the Prytaneum.) It is relevant to note that the biblical provision about the escaping fire, with full liability (though only at civil law) of the person behind it, precedes in date that about the axe which makes itself independent, with mitigated liability (at criminal law) of him who wielded it.

At any rate, biblical law knows no proceedings against an inanimate killer. Nor does, say, Hittite law or Babylonian law—so that we cannot attribute this feature to a peculiarly Hebraic disapproval of animism. There are indeed tendencies which might have led to such proceedings: an ox that kills a man is to be stoned,[41] and I have already referred to the bloodguilt "on the house" if anyone falls to his death from it.[42] But it would be arbitrary, for the sake of what some moderns feel primitives ought to have felt, to postulate such an institution.

In the same ancient code that contains the statute about fire, accidental homicide appears as the case where "he lie not in wait but God let it happen to his hand."[43] We have not enough detail to say precisely what kind of situation is contemplated: even here, in all probability, not primarily a blow with the hand but, for example, the throwing of an object which unexpectedly hits somebody. The legislation in Numbers, insofar as it describes the manner of accidental homicide, has two cases where an instrument is involved: "he threw at him any instrument," *hishlikh 'alaw kol keli,* "or with any stone and cast it upon him," *'o bhekhol 'ebhen wayyappel 'alaw.*[44] But the first case listed is definitely the rare contingency of accidental homicide by a direct blow, without any object intervening: "and if he thrust him," *we'im hadhapho.*[45]

In the Hittite laws, in the case of accidental homicide, "only his hand transgresses."[46] (It seems that where a deliberate sin is perpetrated, "the head transgresses."[47]) A similar formulation may have existed in early Hebrew law (not necessarily dependent on the Hittite one), and the clause "and God let it happen to his hand" may be a modification of it. On the other hand, in Hebrew, where a phrase like "with a high hand" denotes deliberate action, the Hittite way of expressing accident may never have been appropriate. However this may be, the biblical statute, by ascribing the event to God who uses the person's hand, not only introduces a profound theological concept but also greatly advances a unified view of all accidents: the manifold visible agents—hand, axe, stone—are equally directed by the ultimate mover and, indeed, the case is fundamentally equated with accidents in which no human cause is discerned at all.

Here again, however, we must not jump to conclusions deriving from the notion that the authors of these laws or their addressees were simpleminded. Causation and intent, Maschke claims, are invariably combined by the primitive intellect. But the consequence of the accidental deed being attributed to the hand in Hittite law is not that the hand is called to account (that would be small comfort to its owner), and of course there is no scope for anything of the kind in the biblical regulation. On the contrary, it is for a despicable outrage that, under Deuteronomic law, a woman's hand is cut off.[48] No doubt the limbs and organs of a person were often thought of as, up to a point, forces in their own right. But it is, up to a point only: there is far more purposeful construction in these old statutes or in, say, the legal and moral arguments met in the Greek dramatists than seems commonly allowed for.

A brief comment on the emendation of *nashal* in the provision about the axe into *naphal*. It hardly affects the sense; it would be the axe "flies" or "falls" or "slips" in either case. The emendation is recommended by Rudolf Kittel's *Biblia Hebraica*,[49] mainly on the strength of 1 Kgs 6:5, where *naphal* is used of the iron coming off (but this text itself is not free from difficulty). One might add another argument: in Numbers, in the reference to accidental killing by a stone, we again find *naphal*, or rather a causative: "or with any stone and cast it upon him," literally, "and made it fall upon him," *wayyappel*.[50] Nonetheless I would not emend. I do not see why language must be uniform throughout all laws and narratives. Moreover, *nashal* is comparatively rare, hence unlikely to be substituted by a careless scribe for the commoner *naphal*. On *'inna*, "God let it happen to his hand," it may be advisable to have an excursus at the end.

Here all that remains to add is a word about Solomon's judgment.[51] It is the only nonlegal chapter in the Bible mentioning an accidental homicide, and even so, no interest in it is being evinced at all: the story would be just the same if, instead of one of the mothers overlaying her child, there had been a spontaneous heart failure. I have tried elsewhere to explain why the Bible—outside the legal portions—pays practically no attention to the accidental deed.[52] In the present context we may note three things.

First, the child's death is accepted without any thought of legal consequences. For this, there are all sorts of reasons. He is a baby, he is the son of a whore, he is killed by his mother, he is killed in a way in which presumably many babies perished, his death is an unmitigated misfortune for the person who killed him.

Second, as usual in accidental homicide, there is an element of indirectness. The mother did not kill by a blow, *hadhaph*. She overlay the child, *shakhebha 'alaw*. Though that means physical contact, it will produce death only after some while, by impeding breath and movement.

Third, the situation is such that there is no doubt as to absence of intent; neither the storyteller nor his audience would even think of this question. The mother, in her sleep, killed her treasure. Yet it is clearly seen and stated that she is the cause: "and this woman's child died in the night, on whom she lay." I refuse to believe that there was an earlier stage when, in natural speech, her causality would have been denied. This story is valuable precisely because it demonstrates the way ordinary folk would look at such a matter. Suppose, in a trial, the mother had to plead that she did not do it but her body, or a demon, or God; that would be not primitive but sophisticated, an exaggeration for a purpose. An exaggeration—that is to say, there would be some substance in it. But still a calculated exaggeration.

III

Special Interest of Lawgivers. My third point is the fact that, in the earliest biblical code interested in private law, the rules concerning damage to property exclusively contemplate damage indirectly caused: a pit dug by a man and another man's animal falling into it, a man's ox killing another man's ox, a man's cattle pasturing in another man's field, fire spreading from one man's land to another's.[53] In passing we may observe that the range of these rules is extremely narrow also in respect of the type of property damaged: it is either beasts or the produce of a field. My point, however, is that the code says nothing about the simple case of a man in person damaging another man's property, willfully or otherwise. In fact, there is no simple principle envisaging this case enunciated in the whole of the Bible. The nearest we find is a provision in a priestly religious context, that "he that smiteth any soul of man shall surely be put to death, and he that smiteth a soul of beast shall make it good, soul for soul."[54]

This conspicuous absence of simple, direct damage is not accidental, nor should it be explained away by postulating rules that have been lost. The answer is that many ancient codes regulate only matters as to which the law is dubious or in need of reform or both. The XII Tables also do not deal with direct damage by a *paterfamilias*, and even the *lex Aquilia*, some two hundred years later, deals only with the special case of damage to animate property.[55] That you are liable for damage done in person—say, you, a *paterfamilias*, yourself smash another man's cart, intentionally or unintentionally—is taken for granted; it is the more complicated cases just enumerated that engage the lawgiver's attention.

This brings us to a problem of a fundamental nature having to do with early administration of justice. At Rome, from the moment that the concept of *legis actio* is fully worked out and established, which implies that no lawsuit can be brought but one founded on a statute, this incompleteness of primitive legislation, the omission of precisely the most ordinary cases, creates enormous difficulties. It is not my task here to suggest how they were solved. In biblical law, I do not think the situation was ever equally precarious. To be sure, by rabbinic times we also find the idea that no penalty may be exacted unless it is sanctioned by Scripture. (As a matter of fact, Roman law, when it had reached a comparable stage of development, had greatly relaxed the requirements prevailing under *legis actio*.) But by rabbinic times, interpretation of Scripture was so liberal and progressive that any gaps could be filled (for example, the passage in Leviticus about killing a beast was now taken to embrace all direct damage to property); and in a previous era, as in other Oriental systems, the law was handled far less meticulously and carefully than in *legis actio*; there was *cadi* justice, there was much binding custom of diverse kinds, and so on. In other words, while at Rome, under the *legis actio*, an informal loan, for instance, was for centuries irrecoverable in the courts till a certain statute made it recoverable, I do not believe that this would ever have been so in biblical law. (On the other hand, as already remarked, at a more advanced stage things were to some extent the other way round: the Rabbis now had to find scriptural justification for any verdict, whereas the praetor could grant new remedies at his discretion.)

Dangerous Things and Actions. It is worthwhile to inspect the way in which the four cases of indirect damage in our code are construed. They fall into two groups: the pit and the ox on the one hand, the cattle and the fire on the other. In between are some provisions concerning theft.

The two groups are very different. The chief basis of liability for the pit and the ox is ownership of the object causing the damage. In both cases the word "owner," *ba'al*, occurs: "the owner of the pit shall make it good," "and his owner guard him not." ("Owner" is, of course, an unsatisfactory approximation: the German *Herr* would be nearer.) Actually, where an ox not known to be dangerous kills another ox,[56] this is the only basis. The law does not hint at any further connection between the owner and the damage done by his ox. It treats the case as a collision between two objects belonging to different owners: the loss is shared. This seems to me an eminently satisfactory regulation—with only one parallel, Laws of Eshnunna, §53, as far as I can see, in any other system—especially as it will be difficult to establish, neither of the oxen involved being known as dangerous, which of them started misbehaving. (It is different in the case of ox versus man.)

Where the owner knows his ox to be dangerous,[57] and equally in the case of the pit,[58] there is in addition to the ownership a blameworthy omission making him responsible for what happens: "and he cover it not" in the case of the pit, "and he guard him not" in that of the ox. I shall not here go into the question whether, or how far, the owner's blameworthiness had to be proved in any individual case. We might say that the basis of liability here is ownership, not just of the object causing the damage, but of a dangerous object causing damage: the pit, the ox known to have misbehaved in the past. The loss here is not shared; the guilty owner must fully replace it. (That the mention of monetary payment in the case of the pit, "and he shall give money to the owner thereof,"[59] is an addition to the original text I have argued elsewhere.)[60]

Let us go on to the second group, the cattle and the fire. The word "owner" does not occur. These are not cases of a man responsible for an object, or a dangerous object, that he owns. In both cases liability arises because of what a man does—"if he cause a field to be eaten and shall put in his cattle," "he that kindled the fire shall surely make good the loss." Certainly, he causes damage not *corpore corpori*, but through an agent: that is the problem rendering legislation necessary. And it is significant that we find the term *shillaḥ*, "he send in" the cattle, a root very prominent in all kinds of agency (though we are not implying that the "sending" of the cattle need be more than a "letting go"—no *dolus* is required); nor is the fire devoid of some sort of life, "it makes its way out and finds" its food.[61] But the fact remains that he is responsible primarily for doing something, for setting the agent to work, rather than because an object belonging to him does something or because he has not prevented a dangerous object belonging to him from doing something.

There is, of course, a good reason for the different construction. In the first group, the pit or the ox is there some time, then a disaster takes place in which the owner has no hand. (The Deuteronomic injunction to make a railing around the roof is allied to this group.) In the second group, the cattle or the fire is set in motion by a person on this particular occasion. Hence it is in this second group that causation—indirect, but active causation—is clearly given as the basis of his liability. In a way, the attitude of the XII Tables is comparable. While the action *de pauperie* [damage done by a beast] is noxal, that is, the owner of the aggressive beast has either to make good the damage or to hand over the beast, the action *de pastu pecoris* and the action on the ground of a fire that spreads into the neighbor's land are not noxal, that is, the person responsible has no choice but to make good the loss: responsibility *qua* owner over against responsibility *qua* cause behind the agent. It is interesting, as a parallel to *shillaḥ* and, for that matter, to *yabhʿer*, "he causes to be eaten" or "to be pastured," that *de pastu pecoris* is directed against him who *immisso pecore depaverit* [sent in beasts to feed]. (No provision in the XII Tables about a pit.)

I shall not dwell on the various emendations of the rules concerning cattle and fire that have been proposed in modern literature. Most of them are irrelevant to the present discussion and in any case too arbitrary to be taken seriously. One I must mention because it is recommended by the excellent dictionary of Gesenius-Buhl.[62] Georg Hoffman[63] would refer both rules to fire, one dealing with fire that spread as a result of negligence, the other with fire that spread despite normal care because there was inflammable material on the neighbor's land. This is a hypermodern distinction that has no place in an ancient code.

I hope I have been fair in making it clear that the difference in construc-

tion between the two groups can be adequately accounted for by the difference in the nature of the cases. Nevertheless I wonder whether group 2 is not
later than group 1. Years ago I tried to show that the rules concerning an ox
that kills another ox are later than those concerning an ox that kills a man.[64]
If the two had been formulated at the same time, they would stand together;
whereas in fact they are separated by the case of the pit, the older rules coming before this case, the later ones after it. Note, too, that the rules concerning an ox killing another ox use the verb *naghaph*, "to hit," which is wider
than *naghah*, "to gore," and that for full liability they require that the dangerous nature of the ox "should be known," *nodha'*, less formalistic and more
subjective than the requirement of "attestation," *hu'adh* (much, though not
absolute, assimilation in rabbinic exegesis).

By the same token, group 2, the cattle and the fire, seems to be separated
from group 1, the pit and the ox, because the cattle and the fire are of later origin. This does not mean that the following rules, about deposit and so on,[65]
must be yet later. Group 2 may well have been inserted in the present place
as an appendix to the part of the code concerned with delict, even though a
further part, about deposit and the like, was already in existence.[66]

In support, it may be suggested that the cattle and the fire perhaps presuppose a more settled phase of economy than the pit and the ox. In the
cases of the pit and the ox, the object destroyed is an animal, whereas in
those of the cattle and the fire, the damage is done to the produce of land.
The former cases might call for legislation before land was shared out in per-
manency among individual holders.

If this relative dating should be correct, it would underline what appears
to emerge from comparative law: that the idea of responsibility *qua* owner—
group 1—finds statutory expression before the idea of responsibility *qua*
indirect cause of a result, *qua* mover of an agent—group 2.

IV

Language. The Semitic Causative. Lastly, my plea. It is highly precarious to pronounce on direct and indirect causation in law without paying regard to the

manner in which these phenomena are tackled by language as such. Yet when one turns to grammars and lexica for assistance, one receives little information, and of that little a good deal is misleading. My plea is for more and accurate information.

In English or German, there are many intransitive verbs or adjectives describing a state from which causative verbs can be formed: "to fall"—"to fell," *wachen-wecken*; "to be dry, moist"—"to dry, moisten," *trocken, feucht— trocknen, befeuchten*. Often—more often in English than in German—the same verb has an intransitive meaning and a causative one: "to tire," *trocknen*. The primary reference of these causatives is usually to fairly direct causation. Indeed, when one compares a causative with a circumscription by means of "to make," "to let," "to cause to," the latter is apt to introduce an element of indirectness: "to make a tree fall" over against "to fell." That is to say, as may be expected, the simple causative establishes a closer connection between the subject and the object than the circumscription which interposes a general causative concept: the interposition has a complicating effect. There are fascinating intermediate cases, such as the verbs derived from Latin in which a word—adjective or noun—and *facere* have grown together so as to form a causative: "to sanctify," "to specify."

In Hebrew, the range of words from which causatives may be formed is considerably wider; above all, causatives may be formed even from transitive verbs—*lamadh*, "to learn"; *limmadh*, "to teach"; *'akhal*, "to eat"; *he'ekhil*, "to make eat"; *shakhah*, "to forget"; *shikkah* or *hishkiah*, "to make forget." From Egyptian and Hamitic analogies it is clear that causatives were freely employed already at the proto-Semitic stage;[67] they are certainly much older than the earliest extant laws. In fact, we meet examples in these laws. There may be a causative of a transitive verb in Exod 21:8, *wehephdah*, "and he let her redeem (herself)" or "and he let (anyone) redeem her." (Possibly also in Deut 15:3, *tashmeṭ*, "thou shalt make thy hand give up so-and-so." Of course, any number of causatives of intransitives.) If the role of the causative in language had been borne in mind, surely most of the speculations about primitive lack of insight in the field of causation would have been avoided.

But when all this is said, there do remain remarkable limitations to the causative, or certain varieties of it, and how is a legal historian to get his background right if philologists do not bother about them and, indeed, appear totally unaware? For example, I have the impression that, in Hebrew, where the basic verb is transitive, of the two conjugations serving as causatives the Piel is used less commonly than the Hiphil and, as a corollary, is seldom followed by two accusatives: *limmadh* and *shikkaḥ* are among the rare instances. Presumably the reason is that the Piel is older and less specifically causative. Its primary function is to express the intensive or the iterative. So it is only natural that the more daring and conspicuous causative, from transitive verbs, should be the domain of the later Hiphil. This is not to deny that, in individual cases, a causative formed by means of the Hiphil may precede one formed by the Piel, or at least we may have earlier evidence of the Hiphil: "to make forget" is *hishkiaḥ* in Jeremiah,[68] *shikkaḥ* only in Sirach.[69] However, for any conclusions to be valid, one would have to compare the position in other Semitic tongues.

An illustration of how our philological standard works can be positively misleading is provided by the traditional choice of *qaṭal*, "to kill," as the paradigm of the various forms of the verb. The Hiphil *hiqṭil* does not occur in the sources. This would not matter were it due to the extreme rarity of the word. But very probably, even if it were far commoner, there would still be no causative—there is none from *haragh*, "to slay." Even in postbiblical Hebrew, one would not expect to find *peloni hiqṭil* (or *heherigh*) *'eth peloni*, "A made B kill (slay) C." (I am not invoking the absence of such phraseology from modern Hebrew, where the Hiphil is in retreat anyhow.) It would lead too far afield here to attempt an explanation. Moreover it is not a lawyer's task.

Let us spare a moment, however, for a passage which, at least for postbiblical literature, seems to refute my contention, and to some extent does refute it.[70] In the Mishnah, we are told that an ox made to fight in the stadium is not to be put to death for killing a person: "for Scripture says, If an ox gore, not that they make him gore," *welo' sheyyaggihuhu*. Here we do come across a Hiphil, *higgiah*, "to make gore," which appears to justify *hiqṭil*, "to make kill." But it is a very exceptional case: the Mishnah deliberately puts a most unusual, almost impossible form—the point being that that is the form which an advocate of the contrary view (namely, that the ox of the stadium is liable) would have to show to be used by Scripture. Still, though an isolated and very special instance, it does reveal the potentialities of the Hiphil, which a legal historian interested in causation would disregard at his peril. (Incidentally, Plato's *Laws*[71] enjoin prosecution of an animal murdering a man "except if it do so in a public competition." A Mishnic rule which agrees with a Greek one may nevertheless be native. In this case, however, as the very subject matter—an ox fighting in the arena—is un-Jewish, foreign influence is not unlikely.)

The legal historian might do well to have at the back of his mind also the genesis of the Semitic causative, that is to say, what little we know of it. The Piel is universally regarded as, in essence, expressive of the intensive or the iterative. If we adopt this starting point, we might infer that, compared with the basic stem, the causative was originally felt to be more intense or, possibly, some iterative element was seen in the proceeding from cause to effect. But one cannot suppress a certain doubt about the starting point. The Piel may have been the conjugation signifying any peculiar, striking materialization of the root idea. The grammar of Gesenius-Kautzsch approaches, though it does not quite reach, this general interpretation, by saying that the Piel means "to busy oneself eagerly."[72] It may be because the Piel was associated with the striking fact that, in Hebrew, the reflexive formed by means of *t*, though at one time existing also in the Qal, became confined to the Piel: the reflexive action is always peculiar. On this basis the causative was simply one of several remarkable nuances, on the same level as, not belonging to, the intensive or the iterative.

As for the Hiphil, the prefixes employed are declared by Bauer and Leander[73] to have originally denoted something like "to make." We are not, I suppose, meant to understand that they were in the nature of verbs and that we have before us in the Hiphil a proto-Semitic forerunner of "to sanctify" or "to specify." Presumably all that the two writers wish to convey is that these prefixes had causative force—they imparted a causative sense to the stem to which they acceded—but that, of course, adds nothing at all to the initial statement that the Hiphil primarily functions as a causative. The truth is that we are in the dark concerning the prefixes. They might have had an intensive meaning, an iterative one, a generally emphasizing one to bring out something striking, or indeed a very specifically causative one—but how and why and against what background and with what antecedents nobody so far seems to be able to tell.

Excursus on 'inna

According to Exod 21:13, full criminal liability does not arise where "he lie not in wait and God let it happen to his hand." Perhaps the more prevalent rendering is "and God deliver [the victim] into his hand." Either interpretation is justifiable.

I prefer the former, adopted by the Jerusalemite Targum: "and from God did his anguish happen to his hand." For one thing, it seems a more natural development from, or contrast to, a formulation of the Hittite type, "only his hand transgresses." For another, it is in closer accord with other applications of the verb: "the Lord doth not let evil happen to them that fear him,"[74] "no evil shall be made to occur to thee,"[75] "no mischief shall be made to occur to the righteous,"[76] "he is trying to collide with me" in the sense of "he seeketh an encounter with me, an occasion for hostility against me";[77] also the relevant nouns: "he sought an encounter with the Philistines," that is, "an occasion for hostility,"[78] "her occasion" in the sense of "her heat."[79] If the particle 'eth, the accusative sign, is connected with this root, it would be a further argument in favor of "to let it encounter, happen, occur, meet."

Actually, the passage from Sirach, "the Lord doth not let evil happen to them that fear him," may well be the result of speculations in which the statute from Exodus played a prominent part. In that statute, God is represented as the author of a disaster. Sirach in this chapter combats the doctrine that evil deeds are not really the fault of man, since God is the cause of all. True, Sirach is concerned with premeditated wrong, the old statute with an accidental deed. But the problem is fundamentally one, and what I shall have to say about the rabbinic attitude to Exod 21:13 tends to confirm that this text—with others—is in the background of the passage from Sirach, if not actually in Sirach's mind. Conceivably, we may see a precursor of the passage, known to Sirach, in Prov 12:21, "no mischief shall be made to occur to the righteous." This line may not mean simply—like Ps 91:10—that the righteous will not be unfortunate; it may at the same time allude to his being preserved from sinning: 'awen, "mischief," signifies both "sorrow" and "wickedness." The idea, incidentally, reaches deep into the early strata of the Bible: it is enunciated in the tale of Abimelech and Sarah—"I know that thou didst this in the integrity of thine heart, and I also withheld thee from sinning."[80] The wrong in question is an unwitting one, committed in error.

However, if the interpretation "and God let it happen" is traceable as early as Sirach, and has the approbation of the Jerusalemite Targum, that "and God deliver [the victim]" may be found in the Septuagint, *paredoken*; Philo, *paradidosthai*;[81] Targum Onkelos, "and from God was he delivered into his hand"; and as we shall see, also in an early Amoraic discourse. For our main thesis, it is just as acceptable as the other.

That Amoraic discourse deserves closer inspection. But let us first consider the attitude of the Rabbis at large to Exod 21:13. The involvement of God (no matter whether he "let it happen" or "deliver the victim") must have created a grave difficulty. How could God act as he did? How, in particular, could he make an innocent man shed blood? It is surely significant that, with the exception of that one Amoraic utterance, there is no comment whatever. One would expect such a statement to be the starting point for many a deduction, legal or theological. There is nothing, even (with that single exception) in a work like the Mekhilta, where every little point of the code in question is subjected to the most painstaking scrutiny. Silence here argues not neglect, but profound interest coupled with reverence and caution. I have already remarked that I regard the rabbinic attitude as one more indication that somewhere behind Sir 15:13 lies a discussion of the reference to God in Exod 21:13.

The one comment preserved to us, by Simeon ben Laqish, supports the assumption that, in reality, a good deal of thought was devoted to this disquieting clause. It is transmitted in *b. Makk.* 10b and in the *Mekilta* on Exod 21:13, though the latter does not name the author. It takes the form of a proem; that is to say, a discourse is opened by associating, for the purpose of elucidation, the Pentateuchic verse Exod 21:13, "and if he lie not in wait," and so forth, with one from the Prophets, 1 Sam 24:13, "as saith the proverb of the ancients, from the wicked ones proceedeth wickedness." (To the Rabbis, the phrase "proverb of the ancients" perhaps stood for "the Torah," "the Pentateuch," so that Simeon would understand: "as saith the Torah, from the wicked ones proceedeth wickedness." Nothing depends on it for us.)

There has been so far no remotely adequate explanation of the choice of precisely this passage from 1 Samuel. Rashi on this occasion provides no real help, and modern writers do not go beyond him,[82] not even Bacher.[83]

The mystery, however, is capable of solution. Simeon ben Laqish is confident that God is absolutely just. So he will deliver over to an unwitting homicide only a man deserving death. (It should now be clear that Simeon translates "and he deliver the victim.") In other words, the man will be, say, a murderer who, owing to lack of witnesses, escaped his proper punishment. But God's justice is even more meticulous: the unwitting homicide himself is made to kill only because he in turn deserves the penalty for just such a deed, banishment. That is to say, he himself (Simeon reasons) will previously have caused another death by accident for which, again owing to lack of witnesses, he could not be banished.

I do not think it has been seen that, up to this point, the argument is not Simeon's own but far older. Philo explains that the description of God as delivering the victim to the killer implies a defense of the latter on the ground that the victim is a criminal, who by his resourcefulness evaded earthly justice. Moreover (this second part of the interpretation precludes any thought of a mere coincidence between Philo and Simeon), the unwitting killer must inevitably be guilty of some minor offense, otherwise God would not use him in this fashion; the use that God makes of him, with the resulting banishment, is his appropriate penalty. (Philo is more plausible than Simeon. According to Philo, the unwitting homicide must be guilty of some previous offense— which may be a deliberate one—and God punishes him by making him the instrument of a death so that he gets banished. According to Simeon, he must be guilty of a previous accidental killing. But, then, why was he used as an instrument on that previous occasion? Because of a yet further previous accidental killing? And why that? A *regressus ad infinitum*. The impasse is of course due to Simeon's desire to represent the punishment as scrupulously accurate.)

Two possibilities. This exegesis of Exod 21:13 is due to Philo or his milieu and at a subsequent stage reached the Rabbis. Or it reached Philo or his milieu from the Rabbis, though in rabbinic literature it remains submerged until the early Amoraic period.

Anyhow, Simeon ben Laqish's contribution is the importation into this exegesis of 1 Sam 24:13, the composition of a proem. What made this passage more suitable than many others in which God's justice or the idea that good begets good and evil begets evil is stressed?

For one thing, the word *ṣadha*, "to lie in wait," is used two verses before this passage. It is its only occurrence apart from Exod 21:13. Nor is the relation merely verbal. "Thou liest in wait," David complains to Saul, "for my soul to take it"; and God, he trusts, will judge between them. It is in view of this context that the proverb "from the wicked ones proceedeth wickedness" receives its peculiar applicability to Exod 21:13, as the Rabbis (or Philo) understand it. Here is Saul, a murderous character, who cannot be summoned before an earthly tribunal, but whom God will deliver over to vengeance. The wicked man—and only he—will end by others sinning against him.

In fact, in a way, the judgment is beginning even at this moment: Saul in the cave could easily be dispatched by David, whose men advise him: "Behold, the day of which the Lord said, I will give thine enemy into thine hand." (Remember that in Exod 21:13 God delivers the criminal into the homicide's hand.) And David himself calls out to Saul: "Thine eyes have seen how that the Lord hath given thee to day into mine hand." We may note that, in Simeon's illustration of how a murderer might be accidentally killed, he meets his fate in an inn, *pundaq* (the Greek *pandokeion*)—possibly suggested by the cave where David comes upon Saul.

In a proem we must not expect the parallel from the Prophets to be analogous to the Pentateuchic text in every detail. Some inconsistencies, however, which a casual reader might find in the combination of Exod 21:13 and 1 Sam 24:13 are more apparent than real, provided the author's personal doctrines are sufficiently studied. I am thinking above all of the fact that whereas in Exod 21:13 the criminal who at first evaded rightful punishment but now meets death is truly a murderer, Saul never accomplished his monstrous schemes. For Simeon ben Laqish, this discrepancy—in any case not too serious—would be particularly slight: it was he who emphasized the fact that Exod 2:13 calls "a wicked one" him who only raises his hand against his fellow: "and Moses said to the wicked one."[84] In fact, as it happens, the term *rasha'* used in Exod 2:13 is the same that occurs in the ancient proverb "from the wicked ones proceedeth wickedness." It is also, incidentally, the one found in the second half of Prov 12:21: "no mischief shall be made to occur to the righteous, but the wicked ones shall be filled with evil."

A final question respecting the relation of *b. Makk.* 10b and the *Mekhilta*. The latter does not name Simeon; it has only part of the proem, though, to be sure, the essential, opening bit, with the verse from 1 Samuel; but what is perhaps queerest—the part we do get contains an awkward legal excursus that distracts the attention from the point of the proem. Such a disturbance is quite unusual in this most classical of Midrashim. Elijah of Wilna (or whoever the author of *Ephat Zedeq* may have been) cuts out the excursus. But it is given by all manuscripts, and H. S. Horowitz, while admitting that it is incongruous, rightly disagrees with the erasion.[85]

The explanation is that the Tannaitic proto-*Mekhilta* did not include this proem—an Amoraic proem—at all. There was complete silence on the role of God in Exod 21:13. The comment on this verse was purely legal, so that what now perplexes and distracts as a legal excursus was perfectly in order. Probably it is to the school of R. Johanan bar Nappaha, where a redaction of the *Mekhilta* seems to have taken place,[86] that we owe the insertion of the proem of Johanan's brother-in-law. It is inserted without the author's name, just like the sayings of Johanan himself. Its insertion around a lengthy legal disquisition is awkward; but, with that disquisition already in existence, unless one was prepared to make a separate paragraph of the proem, it would not have been easy to do better. At least, the need was now felt to say something about that difficult clause in the old statute.

The New Testament. The Crucifixion: Jews and Romans.[87] I disregard the question of the historicity of the various accounts of the crucifixion. I am only looking at the issue of causation. Partly because of the context, but also to a slight extent because of a difference in conceptual thinking, different writers differ in regard to how they formulate the issue of causation. The book of Acts is interesting: the Jews are definitely held responsible for having Jesus killed. They are called murderers: "ye crucified and killed by the hand of lawless heathens."[88] The formulation is reminiscent of how the prophet Nathan accuses David of killing Uriah by the sword of the Ammonites.[89] It is also reminiscent of how Saul tried to kill David by the hand of the Philistines.[90] It is hardly direct influence, but we have the same construction.

In Matt 27:24, Pilate washes his hands of any culpability for the fate of Jesus. Already a law in Deut 21:1–9 shows a concern with indirect causation: the elders of the town nearest to a murder victim attest that their eyes "have not seen" who shed the man's blood. Despite the difference between the two situations, Pilate too dissociates himself from any indirect contribution to the fate of Jesus. Very remarkable is John. (He never, I think, uses *apollumi*, destroy; that must not be contemplated.) Jesus says in John 8:21, "Whither I go ye cannot come." The Jews respond, "Will he kill himself?" The statement is ironically true in a sense—as John 7:34 and 35 indicate how they think he will go to the dispersed among the gentiles (the Greeks?) and teach them (the Greeks?), so causing his own death. The idea is alright, but the formulation is very unusual. John is a bold writer. In Greek sources it is less unusual to find this way of thinking. Orestes says to Clytemnestra, "You are killing yourself, not I."[91]

Appendix. Daube always claimed that the crucifixion of Jesus raised insoluble problems, and hence he largely avoided discussing it in his writings (although in his lecture "Intellectual Authorship" [see chap. 6, this volume] he discussed an important aspect of it under the rubric, "The Instigator Shoulders Responsibility"). He found all the literature about it inadequate in various ways and had himself no firm conclusions to offer. "We do know that the people who actually erected the cross and put him up there were Roman soldiers. Further, we do know that some prominent Jewish circles wished to get rid of him. Beyond this, everything is uncertain. The evangelists display a tendency to shift the blame away from the Romans; and gradually, as the majority of believers become gentile, it is more and more the thing to render responsible the Jews at large. However, exactly how far the facts recorded in the Gospels have thereby been distorted is highly controversial. Jewish scholars usually try to exonerate the Jews as far as possible and therefore overplay the tendency I have mentioned. Anti-Semitic scholars (and I include in this category many who would deny being anti-Semitic) adopt the opposite stance.

"Suppose we could miraculously reconstruct all the facts. Even then the question would not be answered. Do we say that the Americans killed Martin Luther King Jr. or John or Robert Kennedy, or ill-treated the students at Santa Rita [jail in 1967]? Do we say that the French killed Joan of Arc, or the Romans Caesar, or the Greeks Socrates? And insofar as we do speak in such terms, do we draw any conclusions today as to the nations concerned (letter of January 10, 1972, on file)?"

Daube was once struck by a news article he read with the headline of "Retrying Case of Jesus" (*San Francisco Chronicle*, July 17, 1972). As he put it, "Some nut wishes the Israeli courts to resume this trial and acquit the accused. This is by no means the first attempt of this type. A few years ago a court at Athens actually did pronounce in the matter of Socrates, though only to the effect that as this philosopher had been thoroughly rehabilitated in the minds of men, there was no point in going into it all again."

Daube further commented:

> What would be interesting would be to explore the question: who, I mean what kind of person, feels so strangely involved as to go to the length of pursuing an appeal? And also what are the circumstances, the conditions of the times, which produce this kind of person? That the approach has a rather wide fascination is shown, for instance, by the fact that a copy of the *San Francisco Chronicle* was placed into my mail box by Frank Newman [colleague on law faculty, University of California, Berkeley]. I had seen the article before, but it would not have occurred to me that my colleagues might be interested. Clearly wrong, and I ought to have inferred from the mere appearance of the piece in the *Chronicle* that quite a few people do find this important in some way or other. (Personal note of July 21, 1972, on file)

CHAPTER 2

INTENT

In many cases in the Bible, a sanction—a penalty or a reduction in status—is attached to an act irrespective of whether it is done with or without intent. "He who toucheth the dead body of any man shall be unclean seven days."[1] This clearly applies even to contact involuntarily established; in the same chapter we learn that a person entering a tent wherein is a corpse automatically incurs uncleanness.[2] Again, it is laid down that "One smiting a man so that he die shall be surely put to death."[3] In the present text, there immediately follows a reservation to exempt the unwitting homicide, but the principle may well come from some code (I do not say it must) where it stood alone, admitting of no excuse. Similarly, take the two provisions: "And anyone if he smite any soul of man shall surely be put to death; and one smiting a soul of beast shall make it good, soul for soul."[4] It is most unlikely that the second provision, concerning a beast, means to confine the duty of reparation to the case where the killing is intentional. It follows, considering the identical formulation of the first provision, about a man, that quite possibly (I would not say more) we have before us a law demanding the death penalty even where you kill a man by accident. How are we to explain this indifference to the presence or absence of intent?

Let us for the moment—and only for the moment—exclude from consideration two categories. First, the obviously Levitical cases, like uncleanness, where the concern is from the outset about the state in which you are, no matter how you got into it—with intent, without intent, maybe without being active at all. An open vessel, we are told, which happens to be in a tent wherein there is a corpse is unclean,[5] and equally significant is the combination of groups in an order, like: "Put out of the camp every leper and everyone who hath an issue and whosoever is defiled by the dead."[6] Disease of a certain kind and uncleanness are on the same level: abnormal states. Second, let us exclude what we might call private law, roughly, the cases settled by replacement of a loss, like the one just quoted, "and one smiting a beast shall make it good." In this field, it is hardly surprising to find liability imposed absolutely, without reference to moral guilt: he who causes damage ought to repair it.

This leaves us with crime, with acts followed by vengeance or punishment: "One smiting a man so that he die"—or, "And anyone if he smite any soul of man—shall be surely put to death." Why this indiscriminate treatment of intentional and unintentional deed (supposing the rules do imply such treatment)? The prevalent answer is that there was a time when people were incapable of seeing or appreciating the difference between the two. But my dog knows it. Any normal person knows it from his own experience and readily transfers it to the life of his fellow man. It is difficult to believe that it could ever have been otherwise. Perhaps we should emphasize that we are not referring to the difference, far less simple, between a deed done in full knowledge of all circumstances and one done under a misapprehension, as when Oedipus slew his father. We are referring to the difference between killing intended—whether in knowledge of the circumstances or not—and killing unintended, as when I throw a stone at a bird and it hits a man. One would require the strongest historical evidence to be convinced of the correctness of the usual answer, a priori so implausible. The evidence generally relied on turns out to be illusory.

In the Bible, it seems that those rules which do differentiate between intentional and unintentional killing are the earliest extant.[7] This may indeed be due to the vagaries of transmission. Still, the clause protecting a man "if he lie not in wait but God let it happen to his hand"[8] or some of the criteria which look like having been worked out by ancient sanctuaries to which homicides fled—"And if he smite him with an instrument of iron, he is a murderer; and if he smite him with a stone wherewith one may die, he is a murderer"[9]—are very old, probably older than the principle "One smiting a man," and so forth, and certainly older than the rather artificial coordination of the killing of a man and that of a beast. However, there is no certainty; and in any case we are not denying that we must in an ancient system reckon with a strict rule of the type "One killing a man shall be put to death," unaccompanied by any exception. Only it does not mean that the difference between murder and accidental killing is not understood.

Difficulties of Evidence. We must distinguish. A difference may be disregarded because it is not seen or fully appreciated, or it may be disregarded though fully appreciated because, in a particular context, no other course is practicable. Where a very early regulation is couched in these absolute terms, "one smiting a man so that he die shall be put to death," it is done as a *pis aller* [second best]. In an ill-organized society, with means of evidence severely limited, earthly justice, if it is to function at all, can take little account of the exceptional. What happens in ninety-nine, or seventy-five, out of one hundred cases must be the basis of judgment in all. If A dies being hit by B, normally B will have acted with intent. Hence, at a very early stage, the rule must be that if B hits A and A dies, B is to suffer punishment. The alternative would be, not a differentiation at this stage far beyond what is provable or disprovable before a court, but complete resignation, allowing those aggrieved by a deed to take whatever steps they fancy. In other words, a rule of the type discussed is aimed at murder, though, to be effective, it must be indiscriminate. Being indiscriminate, it may give the impression of a lack of insight into the role of intent; but this impression is totally misleading.

It is relevant to note that the same kind of problem and the same kind of solution recur in the more advanced phase, when the unwitting homicide does receive consideration and care is taken that the full consequences of the deed should fall only on a murderer. "And if he smite him with an instrument of iron, he is a murderer." Of course, even if I kill somebody with a sword, it might be an accident; and it would be quite wrong to think that they did not know. But it is extremely unlikely to be an accident and, therefore, so long as a fairly simple test is needed, this case must be assigned to intent. A *pis aller*. (At some stage, as we hope to demonstrate, they did append the desirable reservation to the rule concerning an iron instrument;[10] and the Deutero-nomic example of accidental killing is of two men hewing wood together, and as one of them swings down the axe its iron head comes off and kills the other.[11]) Today, when we proceed from full punishability of malice afore-thought however evidenced and mitigated punishability or exemption from punishment of unintentional killing however evidenced, and when we are, in making up our minds about a case, to take note of as many exceptional cir-cumstances as may come to our attention, in the end, we are still reduced to reliance on external signposts; which means that, in the end, we shall still conclude that because, ordinarily, such and such conduct reflects such and such an attitude, it must do so in this case. "You don't bite policemen with-out intending it," recently declared a West London magistrate.[12]

The prevalent view is very hard on the primitives. On the one hand, it is said, they could not see beyond the most direct causation. This accounts for the narrowness of a statute like "One smiting a man so that he die shall be put to death": it was not realized that you might kill a man by means less direct than smiting, so anyone using a less direct means was safe. On the other hand, they could not see that you might kill a man in the most direct way, yet without intent. This explains the excessive range of the statute, its inclusion of the unwitting homicide. In reality, the statute betrays defective understanding in neither respect. Its drawbacks are dictated by technical, practical limitations; in the face of these, it gives the only feasible solution. As I discussed in my previous chapter on causation, liability is restricted to direct killing because, in the absence of modern possibilities of evidence, there is too much uncertainty about an indirect method; it would be at once too difficult and too easy to prove. Conversely, it may now be added, liabil-ity extends to unintentional killing as well as intentional because, again, it is too difficult or too easy to prove absence of intent. We should perhaps repeat what we hinted at already, that, at this stage, if such a statute were rejected as too rough-and-ready, the result would be not progress, but abdication by society in favor of unsupervised self-help of the parties.

With regard to causation, we derive strong support for our approach from the fact that, in contexts where there is no practical necessity of restriction to the direct deed, we never find it. It is necessary where earthly justice must decide about a case. It is not where a wrong is to be prohibited—"Thou shalt not murder," "Thou shalt not covet"[13]—or where divine justice takes action or avowal of sin or innocence is made before God—the prophet charges David with killing Uriah and David admits "I have sinned."[14] Now the same is true of the inclusion of the unwitting deed: it is not to be met in prohibitions or in manifestations of divine justice. "Thou shalt not murder"—the Hebrew term is *raṣaḥ*, definitely a hostile attack. It might perhaps be objected that, unless one were specifically interested in negligent behavior, there is no sense in prohibiting an unwitting deed: you can ask a man only to refrain from what he might resolve to do, that is, from an intentional act. Precisely. These prohibitions, "Thou shalt not murder" and so on, have the only sensible form; all we are contending is that the ancients were shrewd enough, human enough, to know the place of intent. As for divine justice, motive is stressed from the case of Cain, who "was very wroth" because of the preference shown by God to Abel and who "rose up against Abel his brother and slew him,"[15] to all the other cases, David and Uriah,[16] Ahab and Naboth.[17] Are we to take it that there was ever a time when a Nathan or an Elijah would have used equally strong language of condemnation if the monarch had, say, killed an elderly citizen by bumping into him in the dark? But if not, the traditional explanation of those strict laws will not do.

As a matter of fact, there is not a single instance recorded in the Bible of an unwitting homicide incurring punishment. Surely this ought to give pause to the exponents of the prevalent view, that originally people could not discriminate. What is more, in the whole of the Bible we find noted only one instance of accidental killing. The person who caused the death is not called to account; indeed, nothing of the kind is even remotely contemplated. I am referring to Solomon's judgment:[18] one of the two women before him overlaid her child. Admittedly there are several very special features of the situation that may account for this aspect, the killing, being completely disregarded. It is, for example, conceivable that, at the time, a harlot would not be molested even if she strangled her child. Still, it is of interest that, in the only biblical case of unintentional killing, the story would remain exactly the same if the victim had died from a snake bite or a heart attack. The date of the story is uncertain; recent critics consider it old,[19] and anyhow there are parallel folk tales among other Oriental peoples. No reason whatever for assuming that, as far as our problem is concerned, the story does not reflect the natural way of looking at things, which would never have been different, however far back we go.

At this point it may be observed that also in the realm of Greek mythology and saga no instance—not one—may be found of accidental killing punished. (This is particularly pertinent because we suspect that the prejudice here combated owes a good deal of its continued vigor to the corresponding doctrine of classical philologists.) In fact, much as in the biblical field, it seems impossible to adduce more than one mention of such an accident, and nothing whatever happens to the doer. Perseus—fulfilling an oracle—throws a disk in the games which hits his grandfather Akrisios. Akrisios dies, and Perseus is very sad about it: that is all. How strong the prejudice is that in early times people were unable to distinguish murder and accidental killing may be illustrated by the way in which Latte deals with the question.[20] This leading expert asserts that originally the presence or absence of intent or other secondary circumstances did not matter, and he quotes two passages by way of evidence. One from the *Iliad*,[21] where the ghost of Patroclos mournfully recalls how in early youth he slew a friend, "though I willed it not, in wrath over the dice"; for which he had to go into exile. But the fact that the passionate criminal, sobered down, feels that he did not want what happened to happen, or even the recognition by some legal systems that there is some substance in this claim, does not turn the deed into an unintentional one. *La fureur me possédait*, says Don José of his state when he killed Carmen. If nonetheless he holds himself responsible, that does not show that Merimée was unaware of the difference between intentional and unintentional killing. The other text of Latte's is from Hesiod,[22] about Hyettus who had to go into exile because he killed the seducer of his wife. Accident indeed. In the England of 1961, we might ask for his extradition and—provided he did it with a revolver—hang him. Elsewhere[23] Latte supports the current opinion by a line from Homer[24] showing, he thinks, that at that time *Falscheid* [false oath] was still looked on as *Meineid* [perjury]. Hector swears to Dolon that the latter, as reward for a risky incursion into the Greek camp he is about to undertake, will be the glorious rider of two splendid horses. But Hector, Homer adds, was swearing a false oath—for Dolon proved clumsy and cowardly in his enterprise and indeed never returned from it but was killed by Diomedes. Latte's argument rests on the use of *epiorkos*, generally denoting real perjury, for Hector's false oath. It may suffice to point out three things. First, to throw homicide and oath together is an oversimplification. No doubt any period will be characterized by certain features found throughout the entire area of human relations. But we must not overlook shades and gradations. There are very special practical reasons, not to be paralleled from homicide, for treating an oath as absolutely binding, any—or almost any—nonfulfillment as a breach. Second, an oath the fulfillment of which is prevented by unforeseen events has nothing to do with unintentional killing. The oath is taken with intent. Killing under a misapprehension—Oedipus—might be nearer, but this is not our topic in the present lecture. The two should not be confused. Third, granted that the primary meaning of *epiorkos* is *Meineid*, perjury, the passage does not show at all that in Homer's time or a thousand years before his, they looked on *Falscheid* as the same. (As may be gathered from our first point, we are not denying that in quite a few contexts the actual treatment would not be different.) Homer uses the word in an attenuated or, I should prefer to say, a deliberately ambivalent, ironic sense. Latte fails to observe that no evil consequence whatever follows for Hector. Are we to conclude that in the eyes of Homer and his contemporaries perjury—real perjury—is the done thing, not worth any further comment?

Once we postulate an initial blindness to mental attitudes in the case of a killing, we ought to do so in other cases as well. Adam and Eve were told not to eat of the tree in the middle of the garden. As this story is of considerable age, the intervention of the serpent is apparently supererogatory: the outcome (on the basis of the prevalent doctrine) would have been the same if an apple had dropped into the sleeping Adam's open mouth. But to take a province in which the law is interested—sexual intercourse without intent is certainly even rarer than killing without intent. Yet evidently, the possibility is seen and appreciated from the earliest times. We need only think, on the man's side, of Lot made so drunk by his daughter that "he perceived not when she lay down nor when she arose";[25] and on the woman's, of the nuances depicted in the stories of Dinah and Absalom's sister Tamar[26] or the section in Deuteronomy[27] exempting from punishment a betrothed girl raped in the open field because, it is assumed, "she cried and there was none to save her." Where a very early statute makes no such differentiation, it is not owing to defective insight but owing to the practical difficulties of proof: the rare exception cannot be allowed for by earthly justice. In the section just quoted, which does mark off enforced intercourse from consent, a rigid criterion is nevertheless employed on this higher level—comparable to the weapon of iron which, we saw, is declared by the law to be evidence of murderous intent. Here, if a betrothed girl is found with a man in the city, she has no defense. This by no means warrants the inference that they were too foolish to realize that she might be gagged or unconscious. Remember Lot, Dinah, Tamar. But at this stage, unless society is to leave things in the hands of the parties, a rule of thumb is inevitable. Kleist's *Marquise von O.* is misused while in a faint. But Kleist himself wrote an epigram: *Diese Geschichte ist nicht für dich, meine Tochte. Schamlose Posse! Sie hielt, weiss ich, die Augen nur zu* [This story is not for you. Rascally actress! For sure, she merely pretended a faint!]. The woman talking in the epigram refuses to believe in so extraordinary an occurrence.

Again, it stands to reason that, if there was a stage when the distinction between presence and absence of intent was not understood, that must have been so whether the deed was blameworthy or praiseworthy. We should have to conclude that, for example, Phinehas would have earned the title of one zealous for God's sake even if he had killed the Midianite woman and her Israelite's friend in an unpremeditated collision.[28] It will not do.

Disregard of Intent for the Sake of System Making or of Restoration of Balance. We must now append some major reservations. We argued that where a very early provision has the same punishment for murderer and unwitting homicide, this is an adjustment to the poor organization of the community. The same, however, cannot be maintained of all subsequent legislation. There, we may come across regulations deliberately equating the unwitting homicide with the murderer, that is, though another course would now be open. It is possible, for example, that the pair of rules "And any one if he smite any soul of man shall surely be put to death, and one smiting a soul of beast shall make it good" dates from such a period. Let us be clear: we would contend that none of these provisions where, without external necessity, full responsibility attaches to unintentional killing is primitive, in the sense of preceding the differentiation. None of them, that is, implies an inability to distinguish; they are one and all considered abstractions from guilt. How, then, do they come about?

There are many factors, rational and not so rational. Even the unwitting homicide is the cause of his victim's death, so some basis for a theory of full responsibility does exist. Further, we must not forget that as long as negligence is not taken out of the bulk of unintentional killing, the latter will include many cases where severity is not out of place. Then there is the idea that the normal order upset should be restored by some corresponding *actus contrarius*. The following two factors, however, seem of particular importance. First, a *pis aller* is apt to develop a life of its own, especially in law. Though, initially, a rule may be unsatisfactory for want of a better way, once firmly established it may become sacrosanct or be carried on mechanically long after the reason for its imperfection has gone. (I shall leave you to think of your own pet examples.) Second, there is priestly Levitical system-making, science, magic, call it what you will. Most violent deaths are brought about by the shedding of blood, and most are preceded and followed by disturbances in the society where they take place. So the shedding of blood as such, bloody killing as such, becomes an evil, exposing the doer and maybe his clan or city or land to harmful forces and requiring expiation irrespective of the moral background. At the beginning of this discussion we excluded the obviously Levitical region of uncleanness. In the system-making phase now under consideration, however, having killed a man is treated more or less along the lines of, say, leprosy or an issue. But though this phase may look uncanny, strange, even barbarous to us, far from being primeval it is doctrinaire, a conscious discounting of variety well understood for the sake of a unified picture of events, breach of the order, and remedy.

Sometimes it is easy to demonstrate the relative lateness of the rules falling in this category.[29] In the regulation repeatedly cited, "And anyone if he smite any soul of man shall surely be put to death, and one smiting a soul of beast shall make it good, soul for soul," the artificial combination under the denominator "soul" is a typical product of advanced priestly science. The covenant with Noah also quite possibly insists on full liability irrespective of the presence or absence of intent, and quite possibly at a time when a differentiation would no longer be incapable of enforcement. Significantly, here too the relevant provision is part of a highly elaborate structure: we find put together the eating of animal blood and the shedding of human. "But flesh with the life-blood thereof shall ye not eat. And surely of your life-blood will I require an account.... Whoso sheddeth man's blood, by man shall his blood be shed; for in the image of God made he man."[30] How far such system-making might go may be gathered from a statute that assimilates the slaughtering of a beast otherwise than as an offering at the tabernacle to the shedding of blood: "What man soever killeth an ox and bringeth it not unto the tabernacle, blood shall be imputed unto that man, he hath shed blood."[31] None of this is primitive in the temporal sense. Nor are all the logical consequences drawn from these sophisticated constructions; the fictitious shedder of blood, for instance, does not incur the usual punishment for murder. To cross over for a moment to a related question: as is well known, according to one version David was too busy with his wars to build a temple; according to another, God did not allow him to build a temple because of the blood shed in his wars.[32] The version that regards even the just warrior as tainted is the later of the two: advanced theology. David is rejected as "a man of wars"—in the song of the red sea "the Lord is a man of war."[33]

It is conceivable that, where the Levitical concept of defilement is central, irregular intercourse also would be treated with little regard to whether it was voluntary or brutally compelled. But this also would reflect not any primitive blindness to the distinction—there is no such thing—but elaborate, one-sided doctrine. It almost looks as if the legislation in Deuteronomy concerning a betrothed girl was directed against a doctrine of this nature. If she is raped in the open country, she is guiltless: "for as when a man riseth against his neighbor and murdereth him as to his soul, even so is this matter."[34] This clause explaining that she is like a person murdered strikes one as a protest against a more magical attitude. As a contrast, we may recall the early narrative of Sarah with the pharaoh.[35] It is owing to her own and her husband's scheming that she is taken into the harem, and the narrator clearly regards this as a great compliment to her beauty and, in a way, an honor to her husband: one is reminded of a story like that of Amphitryon, Zeus, and Alkmene.

A further reservation to our main thesis has regard to early times as well as later ones. Together with the Levitical area we also excluded private law, where the ideas of compensation, restoration of balance, approximation to the *status quo ante* are prominent. Even in our century, the notion that a man causing loss to another man should make amends no matter whether he acted with intent or without (and no matter even whether he was negligent or not) has its defenders, nor are they entirely without merit or success. It should now be observed that there were times when homicide was treated chiefly from this point of view. According to the Hittite laws,[36] if you kill somebody you have to supply his family with one or more persons. Where this attitude prevails, it is only natural for unintended killing to receive the same treatment—or essentially the same—as murder. In fact, a reformer would here be concerned, less with protecting the unwitting homicide, than with stiffening the sanction of murder; in this connection we may recall the Pentateuchic prohibition of taking ransom either from the murderer in lieu of his life or from the unwitting homicide in lieu of his exile in a city of refuge.[37] Compensation, however, is a most variable idea. It need not mean replacement to the loser, positive compensation; it might consist in the man causing the loss or his family being deprived of an equivalent—that also restores the balance, negative compensation.[38] In other words, we might find that a homicide or perhaps a member of his family is to be put to death, not so much by way of vengeance or punishment as by way of compensation. In such circumstances, again, though the settlement is not a monetary one, we must expect the unintentional deed to be placed on a very similar footing to the intentional.

But none of this is in the least suggestive of an incapacity to distinguish between the two. Actually, there are indications that even where the idea of compensation predominates and, as a result, the question of intent recedes into the background, there are limits beyond which the approach undergoes a more or less radical change. In the Hittite laws, the murderer is liable to a penalty as well as compensation: he has to supply four persons, the unwitting homicide only two. Surely, the reaction may be even stronger if the head of a clan—not just anybody—deliberately eliminates the head of another clan—not just anybody.

Let us look at damage by fire. Perhaps the earliest biblical code, the *Mishpatim*, declares you liable to restitution if fire spreads from your field into your neighbor's:[39] a typical private law regulation, and you have to repair the loss though you did not intend it. Indeed, the legislator has in mind only damage caused without intent. Certainly, you might cunningly make a fire in your own field in order to burn the adjoining one. But this complication is definitely not envisaged when the law says "If fire breaks forth"—*scil.* from the field where it was made: the prototype of unintentional damage. It follows that arson is excluded. The legislator is aware of the difference between unintentional damage by fire and arson and, what is more, marks off—by a rough-and-ready criterion—the former from the latter. We can detect no trace of a period, however remote, when people were unable to differentiate between fire spreading in a way not planned and arson; though owing to difficulties of proof, earthly justice may to some extent have to proceed indiscriminately. The Philistines fully understood the nature of Samson's deed when he sent the burning foxes into their corn.[40] So did Joab Absalom's action when the latter, in order to induce the former to visit him, made his servants set fire to a field of his.[41] It is utterly incredible that the reaction of the Philistines or of Joab would have been what it was had Samson or Absalom caused a fire by inadvertence. The XII Tables seem to have treated as capital the burning down of a dwelling or a heap of corn next to a dwelling, while ordaining restitution in the event of a fire spreading from your field to your neighbor's: the case of arson and the typical case of unintentional damage, *casus*.[42]

Some Verbs. "To sin." Some comments on vocabulary may be useful. There is the key word *ḥaṭaʾ*. It and its derivatives occur some 570 times in the Old Testament. Except for six relatively late passages, the meaning is invariably "to sin" or something allied to it; and we find a fair number of examples already in the earliest sources. Nonetheless, scholars are agreed that the original meaning is to be deduced from these six passages and that it is much the same as the original meaning—or what is taken as such—of Greek *hamartano*, namely "to miss the mark" objectively, with no regard to subjective, mental attitude. It would follow that for some reason or other the original meaning found no place anywhere in the preexilic literature preserved to us, though it did live on all the time outside it, to reemerge in the six passages.

Such a word history is not a priori unthinkable, but in this case it is. For one thing, one would be far more inclined to accept it for an uncommon word than for a word which is to be met hundreds of times and the alleged extraliterary meaning of which would be useful in many contexts. Again, the root occurs in Accadian and Ugaritic. To look at recent Hebrew dictionaries,[43] the latter might support the traditional view; but in reality, the only meaning in Ugaritic as in Accadian is "to sin." We must, then, suppose that this secondary meaning had captured the literary side already at that stage. As far as Ugaritic is concerned, of course, this aspect was not yet known to the scholars who first propounded the history here attacked. But that this history should be universally approved is astounding. (The spell of *hamartano*, no doubt. The danger of circular reasoning is plain. Professor Barr[44] quotes *ḥaṭaʾ* and *hamartano* as evidence that Hebrew semantic movement was often strikingly close to Greek, Latin, and other Indo-European languages: in both cases, he assumes, the development was from "to miss the mark" to "to sin." But what if this development in the Hebrew case is upheld chiefly in view of the—supposed—development in Greek? This is not to express disagreement with Professor Barr's main thesis.)

It becomes more so when we examine the six passages. Two, one from the second-to-last chapter of Isaiah and one from Psalms,[45] we shall discount from the outset: the so-called original meaning of *ḥaṭaʾ* can be obtained only from emendation. Another, from Job, runs as follows: "Know also that thy tent shall be in peace; and thou shalt visit thy habitation, *we loʾ teḥeṭaʾ*."[46] The concluding phrase is usually interpreted as "thou shalt not lack," that is, "thou shalt miss nothing." Maybe correct, maybe not. Apart from the fact that it is a far cry from "to miss the mark" to "to lack"—a fact too easily veiled in English by putting "to miss" in the sense of "to lack"—a comparison with other lines in Job strongly suggests that we ought to translate: "and thou shalt not sin." That is to say, among the blessings held out in this section is the peace of piety. The verbs "to visit" (or "to inspect," "examine") and "to sin" are coupled only a little further on, where Job laments: "What is man that thou shouldest visit him every morning? I have sinned."[47] And a little further on again, we find together the three concepts: "to sin," "habitation," and "peaceful" or "prosperous." This is in Bildad's speech: "Though the children have sinned against God and he has cast them away for their transgression, if thou wert pure and upright, he would make peaceful thy habitation of righteousness."[48] There is no need to list the numerous parallels from other books of the Bible where material and spiritual welfare are depicted as one, and in similar language.[49]

Next, we have Wisdom proclaiming its own praise in Proverbs: "Blessed is the man who heareth me, watching at the posts of my door; for whoso findeth me findeth life and shall obtain favor of the Lord, but whoso misseth me wrongeth his own soul, all those who hate me love death."[50] Certainly "whoso misseth me" makes sense. But so does the older translation "whoso sinneth against me."[51] This sermon does not distinguish between one who by chance hits on the right course, with luck and favor to follow, and one who by chance misses it, with disaster resulting. It distinguishes between the assiduous lover and disciple of wisdom, "watching," and him who despises it, "hating."[52] The latter is a sinner, a sinner against wisdom. This is an intellectualized notion of sin—to be expected in this book. Surely, this explanation—that a religious notion of sin is here intellectualized—is far more plausible than the sudden reappearance in this philosophical milieu of a primeval notion devoid of any reference to mental attitude. It should be noted that practically all the terms employed in this section are reminiscent of religious preaching: "blessed," "to hear," "to watch," "to find," "life," "favor," "to wrong," "to hate," "to love," "death." Transferred to the preaching of wisdom, they assume a different coloring. But there is plainly room here for "to sin."

The following quotation from Proverbs is perhaps the—relatively—most serious evidence of the meaning "to miss the mark," since the portion in which it occurs is nowadays often considered to be rather early: "Better is the poor who walketh in his integrity than he who is crooked with his lips and a fool (rich?). Also that the soul be without knowledge is not good, and he who hasteneth with his feet misseth the aim. The foolishness of man perverteth his way and his heart fretteth against the Lord."[53] This was one of the two instances of "to miss the mark" claimed by Gesenius, who may have been the originator of the idea.[54] His other one has long been given up as a bad job,[55] but as we have seen fresh passages are being dragged in to prop up the doctrine. Nowhere, once again, though "to miss the mark" is perfectly reasonable, it is difficult to see why "to sin" would not do. The fact that the picture is of one who "hasteneth with his feet" in no way speaks against it: there are ever so many texts in which piety is expressed by "to walk properly" or "to walk in the proper path," sin by "to walk wrongly" or "in the wrong path." In the very lines cited we hear of one "walking in his integrity" and one "perverting his way." The verb "to hasten" recurs three times in Proverbs. "Haughty looks and a proud heart and the splendor of the wicked are sin. The plans of the diligent tend only to plenteousness but of everyone who is hasty only to want."[56] The latter makes the same contrast as the passage under discussion between reflection and lack of it; but the former shows that—especially where the allusion is to care and recklessness in gaining wealth—we are not very remote from the contrast between righteousness and sin. "A faithful man shall abound with blessings, but he who maketh haste to be rich shall not be held innocent [or, shall not remain unpunished]."[57] It would not be surprising if the ending read "shall be sinning." "Seest thou a man who is hasty in his words? There is more hope of a fool than of him."[58] Neutral, but that your speech may involve you in sin is a commonplace in wisdom literature.[59]

Finally, for the Benjaminites in the book of Judges who would "everyone sling stones at a hair's breadth and not let miss"[60]—the verb is the causative of *ḥaṭa'*, that is, *heḥeṭi'*. There is no question that it does here signify "to allow to miss." But, in a chapter that by common consent shows close affinity to Chronicles, it is simplest to assume that this is a metaphorical application, a slight twist of the basic "to sin." Those experts would not let their missiles do the wrong thing.

This brings us to the problem of semantic evolution. Gottfried Quell is very emphatic on the unconnectedness of ḥaṭaʾ and the doer's inner qualities; he extends this dogma even to the field of "sin" proper. He argues that while "to sin" can be explained as having grown out of "to miss," the opposite development would be inexplicable.[61] But for one thing, we do not need a general explanation of "to sin" into "to miss"; we need to explain only the one expression in Judges, easy enough. For another, in a culture so preoccupied with sin as the Jewish, even if we did find that a root originally denoting "to sin" acquired the sense of "to miss," surely that would not be so astounding. Another argument put forward by Quell is the early use of ḥaṭaʾ in legal or semilegal contexts, like Jephthah telling the king of the Ammonites that "I have not sinned against thee, and thou doest wrong to war against me,"[62] or officials of the Pharaoh "sinning against their lord."[63] Why such passages, in which the reference is manifestly to hostile or treacherous conduct, should support the view that ḥaṭaʾ means a purely objective miss is not clear.

About the Greek hamartano, we shall say nothing, except that even here the postulate of a completely amoral, objective first stage[64] is backed less by solid evidence than by the preconceived opinion of a certain school of philologists as to the nature of the archaic. They seem to experience a sort of vicarious satisfaction in dwelling on that awful simplicity which goes only by the deed, unconscious as yet of the distinction between the intentional and the unintentional. This grim—gruselige—picture corresponds to no historical reality. The case of hamartano, of course, is very different from that of ḥaṭaʾ (and if biblical theology must not be imported into Homer, it would be desirable also that the conclusions of Greek experts should not be overhastily adopted by Semitists). From the available evidence it very much looks as if its meaning had from the outset been fairly wide, "to go wrong." Or rather, that was its potentiality, and therefore, according to the context, it might signify "to commit a deliberate offense," "to commit a culpable offense," "to go wrong in a neutral fashion," "to go wrong in all innocence."[65]

"To murder" and "to slay." Let us compare "to murder" and "to slay." The

former verb always implies moral condemnation: in no circumstances could a reverent person speak of God as murdering somebody. It nearly always refers to a deliberate deed—but, for example, a mother whose child is run over might say that the driver had murdered it, and she might say so even though it was not his fault at all: the verb would serve to express her rejection of him. "To slay," on the other hand, cannot be used of an unintentional act. It contains an element of wildness, battle, heroism. At the same time it does not necessarily express disapproval. God might slay his enemies. In Hebrew the two corresponding words are *raṣaḥ* and *haragh*. One asks oneself why, if in primitive times the moral character of an act remained unnoticed, *raṣaḥ* is confined in the manner outlined.

One relaxed usage may be noted. In the laws about the cities of refuge the unwitting homicide as well as the murderer is termed *roṣeaḥ*, "murderer." For example: "Ye shall appoint cities that the murderer may flee thither who killeth unintentionally. And if he smote him with an instrument of iron and he died, he is a murderer, the murderer shall surely be put to death. But if he thrust him without enmity, the congregation shall deliver the murderer out of the hand of the revenger of blood."[66] Evidently, it is only in the verse "And if he smote him with an iron, he is a murderer, the murderer must die" that *raṣaḥ* has its pregnant sense—though here it has it to the full. In the rest of the legislation, if we press it, it means just the opposite, the unwitting homicide. Part of the explanation is that, as we shall see, the code contains layers from different periods: the rule declaring the iron to be evidence of murder is older than its surroundings. But the main explanation, which accounts for the freer usage in the rest,[67] is that, as the killer to begin with appears as acting with intent, a murderer, he continues under this heading even though subsequent probing shows him to be that exceptional case, the unwitting homicide. The murderer—that is, he who prima facie looks like one—may flee into a city of refuge to have the matter investigated, and if he turns out a murderer without intent he is granted protection. This somewhat illogical usage can be amply paralleled from other branches of law, ancient or modern. Imagine a rule to the effect that so long as the contract is not in writing, there is no sale. It would not be surprising to find a continuation saying that, if in such circumstances the buyer has already paid, the vendor is to refund: in speech, the prima facie quality of buyer or vendor survives the avoidance of the sale.[68]

"To smite." The verb *hikka*, "to smite," illustrates well the futility of starting from a very narrowly circumscribed signification which expands by a gradual, logical process: it is far more likely that, within a certain area, from the beginning a word may display different facets in different contexts. The same code imposes the death penalty on "One smiting his father or his mother" and "One smiting a man so that he die."[69] The former crime consists in mere hitting—no need that the parent should have suffered death or injury. But it must mean deliberate hitting, by a son revolting against or despising a parent. Another capital offense in this code is to curse one's father or mother,[70] also clearly deliberate. Yet above we admitted the possibility that, at one time, "One smiting a man so that he die" might have included any killing, intended or unintended. So "to smite" would here have a quite different sense. In the provisions where "the smiting of a soul of man" and that "of a soul of beast" are paired off, we also held that the presence or absence of intent might be disregarded;[71] the verb denoting to "kill" no matter how. On the other hand, when we find a curse pronounced against "One smiting his neighbor in secret,"[72] while the verb again denotes "to kill," it carries the additional element of malice aforethought. It is not an accident that happens "in secret"; it is a misdeed committed by one who hopes in this way to escape the consequences—and who is here given over to divine retribution. There are several such crimes in this list of curses, and there is not one that could be done unwittingly.

Definitions of the Intentional and the Unintentional. In conclusion, some remarks on how the Bible defines the distinction between intent and absence of intent—that is to say, where it does define it instead of merely implying it. As killing normally takes place with intent, one's guess is (it is no more than a guess) that the exception was worked out first—that is, the decisive characteristic of unintentional killing was formulated before the converse characteristic of intentional.[73] At times unintentional killing is defined negatively, by the absence of the characteristic of murder; at others positively, by a criterion of the unwitting or by illustration. In one of the oldest statutes on the matter we find both: "And if a man lie not in wait but God let it happen to his hand."[74] Which of the two, if either, has priority it is impossible to say. In the Hittite laws, in the case of accidental homicide, "only the hand transgresses."[75] This is not dissimilar from the positive part of the Hebrew formulation, but I do not think it helps with the relative dating of the positive and the negative.

The statute protecting the unwitting homicide is followed by one directed against the murderer who "comes presumptuously upon his neighbor to slay him with guile"[76]—conceivably a later addition. The notion of "presumption" plays a certain part in Deuteronomic legislation, though only as presumption against God;[77] but the allied "to stand up over one's neighbor" occurs in connection with murder.[78] Again, the quality of "guile," somewhat intellectual, has affinity with *da'ath*, "knowledge," "forethought," and also with *'arabh*, "to ambush," "to lurk"—attributes of murder in Deuteronomy.[79] However, these are slight indications to go by, and it is best to keep an open mind.[80]

Toward the end of the book of Numbers we find a major piece of priestly legislation concerning homicide.[81] In the introductory section, where the institution of the cities of refuge is ordained, unintentional homicide is said to be committed "in error."[82] We are arguing in another chapter ["Error and Ignorance"] that the concept of "error," *sheghaghah*, is here transferred from the Levitical sphere to one where it is rather out of place. There follow three provisions declaring the signs by which a murderer may be recognized: it is he who kills with an iron instrument or with a weapon of stone suitable for killing or with a weapon of wood suitable for killing[83]—rough-and-ready criteria. An iron weapon speaks for itself; in the case of stone or wood, it must be of a dangerous type. These criteria may well have originated in an announcement of some sanctuary setting out who would and who would not be granted shelter. The provisions as they stand, however, are designed to enforce the rigor of the law where intent is proved. A further section equally insists on the death penalty in the event of murder, but on the basis of internal criteria: "If of hatred he thrust him, or hurl at him by laying of wait, or of enmity smite him with his hand."[84] (The "laying of wait," which we already came across in another statute,[85] is not indeed strictly internal like "hatred" and "enmity"; but it is near enough, and it is certainly remote from the rigid tests of weapons.) As a corollary, the nature of the instrument employed does not matter: actually, no instrument need be employed at all. A blow with the hand is expressly listed as capital, provided it is struck "of enmity." It is tempting to regard these direct references to attitude as later than the preceding external tests, but the temptation ought probably to be resisted. What we can say is that they must ultimately go back to a different source, since—apart from the discrepancy in style—they really detract from the meaningfulness of the external tests. But that source may be as old as the one making the decision dependent on the weapon.

Now there comes yet one more cluster of definitions, this time of the unwitting homicide. "But if suddenly, without enmity, he thrust him, or he hurl at him any instrument without laying of wait, or with any stone wherewith one may die, seeing him not, and he cast it on him and he died, and he was not his enemy neither sought him harm."[86] This section, though no doubt containing ancient elements, in its present form does seem an addendum. Its chief purpose seems to be to rectify a specific drawback in the tests according to weapons. A man may kill with a very nasty weapon, yet do so without intent. The two clauses, "he hurl at him any instrument without laying of wait" and "with any stone wherewith one may die, seeing him not," make the desirable correction in this respect to the rules that an instrument of iron or a stone of the murderous type proves murder. In truth, they abolish these rules; it is no longer necessary for the sake of security and clarity to put up with an occasional injustice such as the earlier system involved.

The attribute of suddenness is significant. Evil, destruction, the destroyer come upon man suddenly.[87] Here an innocent person's act brings death to another person and at least the threat of retribution to himself, a sudden calamity—and the very suddenness as far as his involvement is concerned exonerates him. The attribute characterizes the accidental violation of a Nazirite's vow, also in the book of Numbers.[88] A Nazirite may not come into contact with a corpse, and there are special provisions as to a sacrifice to be brought and so on "if any man die suddenly by him." Actually, the literal translation would be "on him." In English, too, if somebody else's breakdown produces disagreeable secondary consequences of which I am the passive bearer, we speak of its happening "on me": "he died on me."

The element of "not seeing" is quite natural in this context: it will be a comparatively frequent mishap for a man to throw an object that hits somebody he did not see. One of Antiphon's speeches is about a boy practicing with the javelin and another boy running into the javelin's path and being killed. The former's father says, "My son saw no one running across."[89]

In Deuteronomy the unwitting homicide is described as acting "without knowledge, deliberation, calculation,"[90] *bibheli dha'ath*, which is reminiscent of Aristotle's *paralogos* for this deed.[91] (We are not thinking of any influence one way or the other.) Moreover, he "hated him not yesterday and the day before yesterday." As an example the law gives two men hewing wood together; as one of them swings down his axe, the iron head flies off and kills the other—a case I discussed in my lecture on causation [see chap. 1]. By contrast, the murderer who may not be granted the protection of the cities of refuge is he who "hateth his neighbor and lurketh for him and riseth up against him." The criteria are flexible, no rigid tests. We have already drawn attention to the intellectualism of *dha'ath*, as also to the curious emphasis on the presumptuousness of the crime, "to rise over somebody." In origin at least, the latter feature probably has to do with the physical posture of the deliberate killer: after all, it is in an early story that we hear how "Cain rose up against Abel and slew him."[92]

Finally, there is the establishment of cities of refuge in Josh 20, represented as the execution of the scheme that had been communicated to Moses. Here the unwitting homicide is characterized by a combination of the attributes of Numbers and Deuteronomy: "error," "no calculation," "he hated him not yesterday and the day before yesterday." It is interesting that in this latest version, only the internal attributes are taken over. We find no trace either of the tests according to weapon or of the example of the two men hewing wood, this despite the fact that the chapter clearly draws on the earlier ones containing these details.

In the field of illicit intercourse, the law considers only one situation in which intent is not present: that where the woman is raped.[93] We have already referred to the story of Lot and his daughters.[94] Manifestly the distinction between the intentional and the unintentional deed means quite disparate things.

The New Testament and Rabbinic Judaism: Law and Morality. In general, in the sphere of morality, with no trial in prospect, considerable freedom is taken with the wrongs known to the law: they are apt to be more expansively conceived. *La propriété, c'est le vol*, says Proudhon, "property is theft," *Eigentum ist Raub*. It is noteworthy, however, that in the moral writings of the Romans, there is relatively little of this. Probably the most familiar ancient illustrations are from rabbinic and New Testament literature. Here, the moralist will frequently oppose his wider notion to the lawyer's narrower one. Take these extensions of adultery and murder: "Thou shalt not commit adultery[95]—not even with the eye, not even in the heart,"[96] "The eye of the adulterer waiteth for the twilight[97]—lest you should think that only he who commits adultery with his body is called an adulterer by Scripture: he also who commits adultery with his eye is called an adulterer by Scripture";[98] "Whoever looks at (or, thinks about) a woman with desire is as if he had cohabited with her";[99] "Ye have heard that thou shalt not commit adultery, but I say unto you that whosoever looketh on a woman to lust after her hath committed adultery with her already in his heart";[100] "He who puts his fellow to shame in public is like a shedder of blood";[101] "He who hates his fellow belongs to the shedders of blood";[102] "Ye have heard thou shalt not kill and whosoever shall kill shall be in danger of the judgment, but I say unto you that whosoever is angry with his brother without cause shall be in danger of the judgment."[103] Anyone guilty of the essential, wicked element of the crime is included. It may well be significant, however, that in none of these quotations do we meet a simple pronouncement, "He who desires another man's wife is an adulterer." "He who hates his fellow is a murderer." There are little reservations: "is called such and such," "is as if," "has done so and so in his heart," "is like," "belongs to those who."[104] Much prominence is given to mentality in the above, and the matter will be taken up further in the chapter "Attempt" [see chap. 7].

CHAPTER 3

ERROR AND IGNORANCE

A. ERROR

I shall begin by bringing out certain aspects of the relationship between the attitude of the Bible to acts performed in error and its attitude to acts performed by accident.[1]

Error and Accident

It may be useful, before going into the subject, to state what will be understood by these two things, acts performed in error and acts performed by accident. Roughly, if there is a flaw in your plan, in your assumptions, but the act as such is executed as intended, without anything to upset it, we speak of error; whereas if the very act goes wrong, we speak of accident. The Amalekite who killed Saul, hoping that David would treat him as his benefactor,[2] committed an error; but there was no accident. He did put Saul to death wittingly; the act as such was executed as intended, without anything to upset it. Only he proceeded from a mistaken belief: for David was not pleased, or at any rate declared that he was not. On the other hand, if a man is felling trees and the axe flies from the handle and slays a fellow worker,[3] it is a case of accident, not error. He did not want to kill his companion; what he wanted to do was to hit the tree, and it is the very act that has gone wrong. Error means that you carry out the act in full consciousness, though for a wrong reason. Accident means that you never designed the act at all, the entire situation arising unexpectedly. It is essentially the distinction made by Aristotle[4] where he explains that a man may injure his fellow without committing a wrong in the full sense, an *àdikēma*. The damage may happen unexpectedly, *paralogōs*; this is accident, *àtukhēma*. Or it may be foreseen, *mē paralogōs*, yet be done without evil intent, *mē àpo ponērias*, through ignorance *àgnoia*; this is error, *àmartēma*.

I propose, then, to draw attention to the absolute neglect, everywhere except in proper codes, of acts performed by accident, in favor of acts performed in error (I). Three reasons will be suggested: one, the far greater frequency of the latter in daily life (II), another, the slowness and inadequacy of the process by which they were brought under definite rules (III, IV), and the third, their having to do with man as a thinking being, while the former have not—at least not in the same sense (V, VI). The question will be raised why the position is rather different in actual codes (VII, VIII).

I

Interest of Poets and Interest of Lawgivers

If we compare the material on error and that on accident, a striking feature emerges; it is a feature not confined to the Bible, but recurring in all ancient sources, Eastern and Western. So soon as we go outside the legal codes in the narrowest sense, into myth, saga, drama, historiography, we find interest exclusively concentrated on acts performed in error. Acts performed by accident play no part in reflections on human fate and responsibility.

In the Bible, the role of error is considered in chapters like that of Isaac who blesses Jacob, thinking that Esau stands before him;[5] or of Jacob who lies down to sleep on holy ground, without noticing it;[6] or of Joseph's brothers who pay him homage, under the impression that he is an Egyptian nobleman;[7] or of Benjamin who is convicted of the theft of Joseph's cup on the ground of what, to him, must seem a complete misunderstanding;[8] or of Moses who prepares to approach the burning bush, unaware of the presence of the deity;[9] or of two of Aaron's sons who bring an unlawful sacrifice, ignorant of its nature;[10] or of Joshua who makes a covenant with the Gibeonite messengers, believing them to represent a distant country;[11] or of Uzzah who keeps the ark from falling, not familiar with the dangerous taboo;[12] or of Uriah who takes charge of a letter in which his own destruction is decreed, unconscious of its contents;[13] or of David who declares a ruthless thief to deserve the death penalty, little suspecting that he is that thief;[14] or of the prophet who, contrary to an order of God, dines at Beth-El, after being assured by another prophet that some angel has countermanded the prohibition;[15] or of Haman who advises the king as to how to honor a faithful friend, convinced that himself must be meant;[16] or of those who do not accept the gospel, blind to the truth and made more blind by God;[17] or of the servant who does wrong, because he has not been acquainted with his master's wishes;[18] or of the Gentiles living before the advent of Jesus who sinned, for lack of full information as to God's demands according to one view,[19] despite sufficient information according to another;[20] or of Paul who curses the High Priest, mistaking him for a minor member of the court.[21] This is only a selection of passages dealing with acts performed in error; there are many more. By contrast, the number of texts giving prominence to acts performed by accident is extremely small; there are hardly any.

The same phenomenon is to be met with throughout the ancient world. Greek literature furnishes countless examples of acts performed in error: Zeus who chooses the bones of animals offered, deceived by, Prometheus; Oedipus who kills his father and marries his mother, in all innocence; Alkmene who receives the visit of Zeus disguised as her husband; the Trojans who take hold of the wooden horse, deeming it valuable booty; the daughters of Pelias who kill their father, expecting Medea to bring him back to life rejuvenated; Croesus who goes to war, misled by an ambiguous oracle; and so on. In the Germanic field, there are Siegfried who leaves Brunhilde for another woman, having partaken of a drink that produces forgetfulness; Brunhilde who has to marry Gunther, since it is posing as Gunther that Siegfried conquered her; the tyrant who eats from a bowl made of his child's skull by Weyland the Smith; Hadubrand who, when his father Hildebrand returns from service on foreign soil, offers battle, not recognizing him (the theme comes from an early Indian legend); and numerous others. Yet, except in laws and direct comments on them, acts performed by accident are never in the center of interest.

II

What are the causes of this glaring discrepancy? One of them no doubt is the preponderance, in actual life, of acts performed in error over acts performed by accident. Of many, perhaps most, human operations, intention is an essential element; or at least, it is virtually impossible, in fact if not in theory, that they should be due to chance. Take sexual intercourse. It is true that the Bible has the narrative of Lot and his daughters,[22] to which a great German poet, Kleist, has written a fine pendant,[23] and that Talmudic legislation, for the sake of systematic accuracy, contemplates situations of this kind.[24] But, quite apart from the fact that Lot can scarcely be held to have acted at all, be it even by accident, these are highly extraordinary cases. Sexual commerce does almost necessarily presuppose intention. It follows that we cannot expect intercourse by accident to be of much importance in popular thought, and similar considerations apply to nearly all human activity.

On the other hand, it is precisely operations undertaken intentionally—that is, the majority of human operations—that admit of error. Indeed, as we know to our cost, there is no intentional operation that does not admit of error, and in innumerable ways too. To illustrate this from the same province as before, mention has already been made of the unions of Oedipus and Jocasta, with both of them unaware of their close relationship; of Alkmene and Zeus, with the former unaware of the latter's being a stranger; of Siegfried and his second wife, with both unaware of the former's alliance to Brunhilde; and of Brunhilde and Gunther, with the former unaware of the latter's lack of a proper claim to her.

But the list represents only a fraction of the variations conceivable. It is sufficient to quote, from the Bible, the stories of Pharaoh who does not know that Sarah is married[25] (the Assyrian collection, incidentally, expressly recognizes the plea of ignorance in adultery);[26] Judah who does not know of Tamar's peculiar place in his family;[27] Jacob who does not know that he is with Leah, the wrong daughter;[28] Samson's first wife and her father who, at the moment of her remarriage, do not know that she is not divorced[29] (this is the most natural interpretation of that pericope, which does not appear to have been appreciated); Amnon's sister who, when she first comes to him at any rate, does not know that he is only simulating illness;[30] and Ahasuerus who does not know that Esther is Jewish[31] (this situation we have learned to understand better in the past fifteen years). Also, from Josephus, the anecdote of the pious man smitten with the charms of an actress, but saved by being given his niece whom he mistakes for the heathen[32]—another instance of "the wrong one," though this time she is really the better of the two (one is reminded of the *Marriage of Figaro*, in which the Count commits "adultery" with his own wife); and from other literature, the folktale that leads up to the wedding of a couple of apparently unequal standing, the inferior partner later to turn out to be of princely blood—a type not without a substratum of serious, social argument. If we add the cases, particularly popular in modern writing, where sexual intercourse as a result of deception is just avoided—for example, Scott's *Redgauntlet*, but also the episode of Sarah with Abimelech, who receives timely warning from God,[33] we get some idea of the possibilities of error in an area with, as we saw, next to no room for accident.

To repeat, truly accidental deeds are rare in actual experience. But any intentional deed may be affected by error, and there is hardly any limit to the various forms that error may assume. To some extent, therefore, the sources, in dwelling on acts performed in error and disregarding acts performed by accident, simply reflect the facts of life.

III

However, this cannot be the whole explanation. For the sources present the same picture even when we go on to branches of human activity where accidental deeds do occur in everyday life. More precisely, even when we consider, for instance, homicide, though cases like that of the man felling trees whose axe hits his comrade are not unduly exceptional, yet, outside proper codes, it is never these acts performed by accident that are recorded and discussed, but only acts performed in error, such as the killing of Saul by an Amalekite too confident of David's approval. It is, indeed, amazing that the whole of the Bible, not counting the statutes, should contain one single instance of accidental homicide only, namely, in the chapter on Solomon's judgment. The one child, we are told, died through his mother lying on him.[34] Even this solitary instance is not really relevant, since, for one thing, the author presumably thinks of the mother as asleep, so that it is doubtful whether we ought to regard her as actively causing her son's death at all, and for another thing—much more significant—the narrative is not in the least concerned with the specific problem of killing by accident, not in the least concerned with the place of killing by accident in the mechanism of destiny and action. In fact, the substance of the story would remain quite intact if the child had died from a sudden disease or in an earthquake, definitely through no man's agency, or if he had been cruelly murdered by ruffians. The only point interesting the author is the method used by Solomon to discover to whom the remaining child belongs.

Homicide in error is treated very differently. Quite a few biblical specimens are preserved, and in all of them emphasis is laid on the specific position created by the error. In addition to the story of Saul's end, where the culprit's miscalculation costs him his life, and the closely analogous story of the end of his son Ishbosheth, who is murdered by two traitors also hoping for a reward from David and bitterly disappointed,[35] there is the midnight battle between Gideon and the Midianites, in which the latter, totally confused, fall upon one another.[36] (The Draconian inscription, it may be observed, specially exempted from punishment one who killed *èn polemō àgnoēsas*, i.e., one who killed a person in the war, not recognizing him as a fellow countryman.) The decisive and, for the Midianites, terrible role of the error is clearly seen; for the text says that it was the Lord who turned their swords in the wrong direction. Again, the account of Ahab's death has all the makings of a Greek tragedy. His own prophets having assured him of victory, but Micaiah having foretold his doom, he has gone into battle in the armor of a plain knight, in order that the enemy should not single him out as their main target. But he receives a mortal shot from an archer who never knew he was aiming at the Israelite king.[37] The converse error occurs in the anecdote of Eleazar Avaran. He, fighting under his brother Judas Maccabaeus, mistakenly believes that the Syrian king is sitting on a particularly splendid and well-protected elephant, slays the beast, and is himself killed.[38] Josephus discusses what would have happened had his assumption been correct. It does not matter in this connection that according to him, the outcome of the struggle would not have been greatly affected: the nature of the case is realized. Further, it would be a mistake to overlook the narrative of Susannah. For though she is saved in the nick of time, but for Daniel's intervention, she would have been executed on the basis of false witness. Manifestly, the danger of inflicting the death penalty on an innocent person in error is very much noticed; and certain divergences between the LXX and Theodotion indicate that there was more than one attempt to analyze the quality and effects of such an error. Finally, we have to list here the most famous of all cases of homicide in error: those guilty of Jesus' death "know not what they do,"[39] to which may be added the warning that a time will come when whoever kills one of his followers "will think that he doeth God service ... because they have not known the Father, nor me,"[40] and Paul's participation, while still "ignorant" and "foolish" in the execution of Stephanus.[41] It is superfluous to show that this error in all its aspects occupied the minds of the very earliest Christian theologians; it is anything but a negligible quantity in the story; its relation to the principles of fate and responsibility is vital.

These observations are fully confirmed by the non-Jewish material. There also we find acts performed in error dominating even those fields—such as homicide—in which, in daily life, acts performed by accident are by no means unheard of. The encounter between Hildebrand and Hadubrand has been mentioned above. Greek literature is full of homicide in error. Besides Oedipus and the daughters of Pelias, already referred to, we need only recall Aktaeon, hunted to death by his own dogs and friends that can see only a stag in him; Pentheus, torn to pieces by his mother and other Bacchantes, to whom he appears to be a lion; Prokris, killed by the spear of her husband, who mistakes her for a doe as she steps out from between the trees from where she thought to surprise him with his paramour; Hippolytus perishing in consequence—partly at least—of a curse of his father Theseus, who was persuaded that his son had tried to seduce Phaedra; Antigone, sentenced to death by Creon who utterly misjudges both the extent of his authority and the results of his verdict; Orestes, nearly slaughtered by Iphigeneia, before she discovers his identity; it would be easy to go on. In all these cases, the error is essential to the plot and, indeed, to the whole purpose, the philosophy, of the saga. In contradistinction, it seems impossible to glean more than one or two examples of homicide by accident. The only one, in fact, seems to be provided by Perseus, who kills his grandfather by an unfortunate throw of the disk in the games. Even here, it is noteworthy that the storytellers evidently were not content with accident: error does come in, rather unnecessarily, for things happen in such a way that Perseus and his grandfather do not recognize one another.

IV

In view of these statistics, clearly, we have to look for further reasons for the preference accorded, everywhere except in actual statutes, to acts performed in error over acts performed by accident. It is not enough to say that the former happen more often in real experience. That may be part of the explanation, but the treatment of homicide shows that there must be more behind it. So we come to another factor which helped to shape the material: a good many stories and discussions relating to error are owing to the absence or slowness of legislation on the matter.

It is a point to be observed in all literatures at all times that those departments of legal commerce the regulation of which is controversial are popular providers of subjects for saga, drama, novel, and the like. On the London stage, in these weeks, a play is showing directed against the proposed reform of the medical service.[42] Certain elements of the story of Cain and Abel no doubt date from a time when it was still necessary to advocate animal sacrifices as against vegetarian ones,[43] and the narrative of the interrupted sacrifice of Isaac, like that of Iphigeneia, from a time when it was still necessary to advocate animal sacrifices as against human ones.[44] Of the incidents of the man collecting wood on a Sabbath, and the daughters of Zelophehad, the Bible itself says that they led to the filling of gaps in the law;[45] and similarly, the account of Jesus healing on a Sabbath expressly refers to a prohibition no longer enjoying universal approval.[46] We know—and there will be occasion to go a little into this—that legislation on acts performed in error developed painfully gradually, far more gradually than legislation on acts performed by accident. Accordingly it would almost be a matter for wonder if the struggle had left no traces in the form of half-legal anecdotes and reflections.

Let us look at a few cases in point. It is quite conceivable that the story of Samson's first wife, for whom her father finds another husband under the impression that Samson has divorced her, and who is burned together with her father—it should be remembered that burning is the normal penalty for harlotry in the Old Testament[47]—was written with a view to affirming a strict practice according to which error was no excuse in such circumstances. The discussion between God and Abimelech about the analogous question of the latter's appropriation of Sarah is manifestly the work of one troubled by a reactionary law. He operates throughout with legal notions, and even the form is that of a trial, with charge and defense. To be sure, no radical reform is yet recommended, the solution being sought in a religious thesis: God will warn the innocent in time; he kept back Abimelech from touching Sarah. Similarly, the chapters of Aaron's sons who perish because they bring an unlawful sacrifice, and of the man who, well-meaning though he is, perishes on contact with the ark, may at some date have been intended to bolster up a system actually in force which, where a person was accused of trespass on the sacred domain, did not admit the plea of ignorance. The tale of Moses and the burning bush might reflect a later phase. The problem has begun seriously to worry people, and it is assumed, much as in the case of Sarah and Abimelech, that God will warn the innocent before his error produces an irremediable offense: hence "And the Lord saw that he turned aside to see, and God called unto him.... Draw not nigh hither." A still more advanced stage seems represented by the account of how Jacob, discovering to his terror that he slept on holy ground, appeases the deity by a gift—an account very possibly set down in support of legislation that prescribed a sacrifice in the event of desecration in error. In many ancient systems, at one time or another, there was a rule that if I missed an article soon after you left my house and if I pursued you at once and found the thing in your possession, you were to be treated as a thief caught in the act. That this rule may bring about condemnation of a guiltless person is fully realized in the episode of Joseph's cup in Benjamin's sack. Certainly, there is no genuine error on the former's part, but the possibilities of error are seen. Once again, no change of the law is proposed, the solution of the difficulty is theological: God, the author of the narrative assumes, would not have allowed Joseph's brothers to suffer innocently, had they not deserved just this punishment by their conduct years before. But, clearly, the ground is thus prepared for the actual cancellation of the rigid rule in question.

The story of Susannah, as has been recognized for some time, is a veritable *Rechtslegende*, legal legend. One of its objects is to oppose to the antiquated, ceremonial, collective testifying of witnesses, so easily misused for throwing dust in the eyes of the judges, the modern method of rational, cool cross-examination of each witness separately; as is well known, the Sadducees wanted to retain the former institution, the Pharisees favored the latter. At first, the accusers of Susannah lay their hands on her head, by way of solemn affirmation of the charge, tell their wicked story, and succeed in convincing the court, which sentences her to death, in error. The procedure so far has been that which prevailed in Old Testament times: we find it in two trials for blasphemy, "Bring forth him that hath cursed ... and let all that heard him lay their hands upon his head,"[48] and—this is from the case of Naboth— "And there came in two men, children of Belial ... and they witnessed against him ... in the presence of the people, saying, Naboth did blaspheme God and the king."[49] But now Daniel intervenes, urging that the court, in adhering to this procedure, has neglected the Deuteronomic provision "And the judges shall make diligent inquisition."[50] What "diligent inquisition" means he demonstrates by separating the two witnesses and probing into the consistency of their statements. This is the procedure that prevailed in Talmudic times[51] and through which incidentally, if we go by Mark, the attempt to get Jesus convicted for his utterance concerning the destruction of the temple broke down.[52] The error is discovered, Susannah acquitted, and her accusers put to death instead—also in accordance with the Pharisaic interpretation of the statute in Deuteronomy: in the view of the Sadducees, a witness, however dishonest, must not be put to death unless his testimony has actually led to the execution of his victim. Here, then, we have before us an elaborate

tale designed to justify the introduction of a new mode of dealing with witnesses, by which miscarriage of justice in error may be avoided. The change
must have been regarded as very bold at the time (an indication, possibly,
that the story is slightly older than is nowadays assumed). For Daniel's view
of the meaning of "diligent inquisition" is given as coming to him straight
from God, a usual claim in antiquity in connection with great legal innova-
tions. It is worth noting that at this period, say, 100 BC, it is not yet enough,
if you want to establish a fresh rule, to be a rabbi and reinterpret Scripture.
Appeal to Scripture there already is, but a reformer must still possess the
qualities of a prophet. That, among the masses, the concept persisted for
several more centuries is evident from the New Testament.

Again some references to error in early Christian writings may have been
made in order to counsel a certain course in organizing the church. It is not
unlikely that a passage like "Father, forgive them, for they know not what they
do" was meant to influence the attitude of the officers, the jurists, toward
converts of the type of Paul.

Things are much the same in the Greek sources. Several versions of the
Oedipus theme are concerned to supply arguments in favor of a progressive
treatment, in the law courts, of homicide in error, and even behind the repre-
sentation of Creon's error in the Antigone there loom highly acute, constitu-
tional, politico-legal problems.

V

It is safe to say, then, that the preoccupation with error in a number of cases
springs from a preoccupation with the development of the law in this field.
Nevertheless, even when we take this factor into account, we still have not
arrived at the full answer to our question. For one thing, there are too many
instances where an interest in legislation plays absolutely no part. The death
of Saul, Ishbosheth, or Ahab—or that of Pelias, Aktaeon, or Prokris—has
nothing to do with legal difficulties of the time. Nor, it may be recalled, can
these stories be accounted for by the numerical superiority in life of acts performed in error, since they are stories of homicide, and accidental homicide
is by no means rare. For another thing, we have to consider that many even

of those cases which do imply legislative tendencies are certainly not wholly the product of juridical reflection. The story of Susannah is surely an exception. An utterance like "Father forgive them, for they know not what they do" or a story like that of Oedipus, even though one of the purposes of recording it may have been that it should help to guide the laws in a certain direction, yet is principally determined by far wider interests.

It looks as if there must be yet another, more fundamental motive at work in the early authors here considered. In other words, when acts performed in error excite so much more speculation than acts performed by accident, it is not merely on account of the greater frequency of acts performed in error in everyday dealings or on account of the unsatisfactory, tortuous advance of legislation respecting such acts, but also, and maybe chiefly, on account of some inherent quality of particular significance distinguishing them. This quality, it is submitted, consists in their being connected with man as a thinking, planning, moral being in a far higher degree than are acts performed by accident.

Acts performed by accident may be most deplorable, but they are no more different, in essence, from any other kind of chance occurrence that does not originate in a human operation. There is no fundamental difference, for example, between the situation when you are felling trees and the axe flies from the handle and kills your friend, and the situation when your friend is killed by lightning. Certainly, in the former, you will be very sorry to have been even an unwilling link in the chain of events. But, if we disregard the possibility of negligence, the whole thing is just a misfortune, and nothing else. You intended no harm to him. Nevertheless he was killed, but that it happened through your axe rather than through a fishbone or earthquake does not really alter the nature of the case. Acts performed in error, on the other hand, do form a class *sui generis*. They are not at all like the ordinary sort of accident; on the contrary, they come about as the direct consequence of a man's plan. The Amalekite who killed Saul did so after careful consideration; the manner of Saul's death is far from comparable to death by lightning. This is the distinctive point in acts performed in error, one of immense importance both in practice and theory: the result is wanted, yet there is some defect in the undertaking as a whole, and the defect lies in a human mind, in the calculations on the ground of which action is taken.

In what respects is this distinctive point of such importance? It would lead too far afield to mention more than one or two. For one thing, as error, quite unlike accident, means a flaw in the consciously formed judgment of a person, one man may deliberately produce it in another; in fact, a large proportion of actual instances of error must be traceable to deception. Thus, while acts performed by accident happen somehow, just as do diseases or earthquakes, acts performed in error are among the typical situations arising out of the peculiar, social structure of human life, the pitching of intellect against intellect. This renders them considerably more arresting, dramatic and relevant from the ethical point of view. It is remarkable in how many of the cases adduced above from the Bible and other literature the error is brought about by fraud—fraud from sheer selfishness usually, as in the stories of Sarah and Pharaoh, Prometheus and Zeus and so on, but also pious fraud, as in the stories of Judah and Tamar, the uncle given his Jewish niece in the place of a heathen actress and so on. It is the battle of wits, with all its implications, that rouses the interest of an author.

There is, however, a further, even more decisive consideration. As error, quite unlike accident, means a flaw in the consciously formed judgment of a person, it brings out the impotence of man at the highest level of his existence: it is truly tragic. As I just noted, acts performed by accident happen somehow, as do diseases or earthquakes. No doubt they also express human limitations, or in the language of Herodotus, they also may prove that *to theion* is *phthonōron kai tarakhōdes* [heaven is jealous and given to trouble].[53] But they do it only in a very general way: man is constantly dependent on incalculable outside interferences, and, for that matter, not only he but all creation. Acts performed in error, on the other hand, reveal his helplessness in that specific sphere where he might hope to be free and radically superior to the rest of the world; they reveal his helplessness even where he succeeds in carrying out his purpose. If you are felling trees and the axe comes off the handle and kills your companion, as a thinking, moral being you are no more involved than if he, or you, had perished through a mishap proceeding from the most distant quarter. It is sad that fate should choose you as its instrument, but you are an instrument in no other way than lightning or an illness or a tiger might be. Essentially, there is neither a special problem nor a special tragedy: it is a case of man, or any other unit in creation, versus blind or envious forces. But the opposite is true of the Amalekite who killed Saul. He was fully involved as a thinking, moral being. He deliberately slew the king, weighing the pros and cons—as far as he could see them. The act was executed according to plan. And yet he found that he had done the wrong thing, that he had prepared for his ruin instead of his advancement. This is a case, not of man, or any unit, versus blind or envious forces, but of man, and man alone, against himself. You intentionally produce a result, but "you" means a you that is blind, incomplete, in conflict with a potentially different, enlightened, perfect you. This is a terrible situation. It is man's great tragedy and, obviously, it raises difficult, in fact, insoluble problems.

Here, it is submitted, lies the main cause of the never-ceasing attention paid by the ancient mind to acts performed in error, to the exclusion of acts performed by accident. The tragic, problematic side of the former constitutes the most fascinating and most worrying theme of all that concerns specifically human undertakings. Surely, it is this side, this terrible element, which gives significance to, or enhances the significance of, many of the cases adverted to in the course of this paper: Oedipus, the wooden horse and so forth from Greek literature; Siegfried and Brunhilde, Hildebrand and Hadubrand and so forth from Germanic; Isaac and Jacob, Haman, the crucifixion and so forth from biblical. We need only substitute accidental acts in these narratives to see the real point. What would remain of the profound tension in the epic of Isaac and Jacob if there had been no error but, say, Isaac, by a mere slip of the tongue, had uttered Jacob's name instead of Esau's? Or of the New Testament, if Jesus had been killed by the purely accidental act of a Pharisee or Roman, say, through a brick unwittingly dropped by a workman from a roof? It is a highly suggestive coincidence that, as Aristotle calls after the deed is done *ekplēktikon*, "astounding," "shattering,"[54] so in one of the earliest biblical stories quoted, of Jacob's acquisition of the blessing, Isaac, on finding out the truth, "trembled very exceedingly."[55] This is an effect absolutely alien from acts performed by accident; it is characteristic solely of acts performed in error.

VI

An observation of only indirect bearing on the topic discussed may here be inserted. Aristotle holds that a perfect tragedy must culminate in *peripeteia* and *ànagnōrisis*, "peripety, reversal of fortune, and discovery, recognition."[56] Professor Gilbert Murray comments as follows:[57] "This strikes the modern reader as a very arbitrary assumption. Reversals of Fortune of some sort are perhaps usual in any varied plot, but surely not Recognition?" He goes on to account for the theory by the origin of tragedy in the ritual of Dionysius, which is supposed to have been similar to that of Osiris, which in turn involved the finding of the god's corpse by his wife. The latter feature, Professor Murray suggests, is responsible for the role of recognition in Aristotle.

This criticism, however, is unjustified. Whether *ànagnōrisis* goes back to the ancient ritual or not—and it looks as if those beginnings of the theater were nowadays somewhat overemphasized—error is the tragic factor in human life; it is of the essence of a genuinely tragic play, and the most dramatic moment of error is, of course, its discovery, the moment when the person erring, or maybe the public, recognizes that all the proud planning and directing started from void assumptions. In his chapter on the construction of plots,[58] Aristotle explains that the tragic hero must be represented, first, as passing from happiness to misery; second, as doing so not as a result of depravity—still less as a result of mere incongruous accident[59]—but as a result of some misconception. The doctrine of *peripeteia* and *ànagnōrisis* follows from these two requirements. The most conclusive way in which a man may pass from happiness to misery is by a change of the status quo into its very opposite, *peripeteia*; the climax of an error is reached in its detection, *ànagnōrisis*.

Professor Murray's avowed failure to understand why Aristotle makes recognition one of the vital components of tragedy is typical of a period when the powers of the unaided intellect were grossly overrated, when error was regarded as a thing easily avoided by a well-trained mind, and when, indeed, a good many playwrights thought they had composed a tragedy if the curtain opened on the first stage of tuberculosis and came down on the last; if, that is, they depicted a series of unfortunate accidents. Of these plays, only those will last which do somehow bring out an error, say, an error inherent in the system of modern society. As for the unlimited trust in human judgment, we live today through an *anagnōrisis* of that very mistake, coupled, as in the ideal Aristotelian tragedy, with a fearful *peripeteia*. Admittedly, it is not necessary that the error should always be of the straightforward kind as in the cases of Jacob and Leah, Pharaoh and Sarah, Oedipus—sheer ignorance of identity, legal status or relationship. In the stories of the Amalekite who kills Saul, Haman who explains to the king how he should reward loyal service, Paul who welcomes the stoning of Stephanus, and, from Greek literature, Creon who murders Antigone, the error is much more intricate. Yet error it is that renders them tragic; the textual proof is irrefutable. The Amalekite is "like a messenger of good tidings in his eyes,"[60] Haman "thinks in his heart, To whom would the king delight to do honor more than to myself?"[61] Paul is "foolish"[62] and "verily thinks with himself that he ought to do many things contrary to the name of Jesus of Nazareth,"[63] and to and of Creon the seer Teiresias expressly says that "erring is common to all men."[64] Aristotle himself states that recognition need not be of persons, though a form like the return to reason of Don Quixote on his deathbed[65] is perhaps of a subtlety not contemplated by him. The famous tragedies would each and all collapse if we cut out error, the destructive insect attacking just that flower which we would fain preserve unspoiled.

VII

We have now to put the question why, in legal regulation, as opposed to myth, historiography, and so on, error seems somewhat in the background. In the biblical codes, for example, while we find provisions about such cases as that of a man felling trees and killing his fellow worker by an unfortunate stroke, we find none about homicide in error. True, the term *sheghaghah*, "error," does occur in two legislations concerning homicide,[66] but it does not there mean what one would expect it to mean: it refers to killing by accident.

Again, whereas there is an abundance of narratives about contracts of various kinds entered into as a result of deception, hardly any statute deals with this phenomenon. Why is error not more prominent in the actual laws?

One thing is obvious. The fact that error is more fascinating than accident from the philosophical point of view cannot move a lawgiver. A lawgiver chooses those subjects which are most in need of, and capable of, regulation. The saving from retribution of an accidental homicide, therefore, is at least as likely to be made the object of legislation as the saving of one who has killed in error. More generally, the tragic element, which accounts for a good deal of the interest taken in error by those who speculate on the destiny of man, has no influence when it comes to the enactment of statutes. For this reason alone, some discrepancy between codes in the narrow sense and all other literature is bound to exist.

There are additional factors. A lawgiver, as has just been remarked, chooses those subjects which are most in need of, and capable of, regulation. Homicide by accident is such a subject; homicide in error very much less so. As regards the need for legislation, it is true that most human deeds presuppose intention and cannot be performed by accident, sexual intercourse, for example. But it is precisely acts of destruction, killing, wounding, damage to property, which form an exception, in that they are often due to chance; and, clearly, it is precisely acts of destruction that are among the commonest and most important subjects of proceedings before the courts. Consequently, a problem like homicide by accident is apt to become urgent, in the legal sphere, at a comparatively early date.

Above all, however, as regards the possibility of legislation, we must not forget that, while it is easy to distinguish between accident and design, it is exceedingly difficult to mark off from any irrelevant error that sort and degree of error which you want to consider as exonerating a man. There would be universal agreement nowadays that one who kills a fellow countryman in the war, mistaking him for an enemy, should go unpunished. The same agreement would not prevail with regard to the Amalekite who thought he acted in accordance with the wishes of the new king in slaying Saul. What about the judges in the case of Susannah, supposing their original verdict had been carried out?

What about the judges in the cases of Jesus and Stephanus, or Creon in the *Antigone*? And what about those giving effect to sentences of this type? These latter instances involve the problem, which may arise in connection with any crime, of error as to fundamental religious tenets. How far should it excuse? The question, *mutatis mutandis*, is as urgent and baffling for the modern politician as for the ancient, though one sometimes wonders whether the latter did not approach it with deeper insight and greater courage. When we go on to other branches of the law, matters become more rather than less complicated. Should an error like Jacob's when taking Leah invalidate the union? If you decide it should, as most modern systems do, would that not be hard on the woman and, possibly, children? What about an error like that of Ahasuerus concerning the partner's religion? It might remain undiscovered for many years of married life. As for the ordinary contracts of everyday commerce, no treatment at once reasonable and consistent has ever been achieved by any system: there are too many possible nuances of error, from the most intense to the most subtle; there are too many possible causes, from a direct lie to an unavoidable oversight; there are too many interests to be considered—the party under an error, the opposite party, third persons necessarily involved (such as the children in a marriage), the public which may, or may not, rely on what has been arranged, the sanctity of the given word. In these circumstances, the paucity of precise biblical rules on error is far from surprising.

VIII

However, the matter would not be seen in the right perspective if the following five points were overlooked. First, little legislation on error does not mean little interest on the part of lawyers. Far from it. There are, as we have seen, enough semilegal stories and reflections to render it clear that the problem was tackled by the lawyers all the time.

Second, we have to reckon with the possibility of one or the other rule having got lost. It is quite conceivable in view of the narratives of Sarah with Pharaoh and Sarah with Abimelech, as well as a paragraph of the Assyrian collection already adverted to, that Hebrew law from a relatively early age did contain a provision making allowance for error in adultery.

Third, we come across an enormous amount of what may be called concealed or indirect legislation on error, in particular, legislation with the object of preventing error in time and thus mitigating the troublesome problem. Samson's first wife, we saw, is remarried by her father in the belief that she has been divorced. The custom to write a bill of divorcement[67] no doubt grew up under the influence of such cases: it was decided to eliminate the possibility of uncertainty. An immense number of rules of evidence of this and other kinds are designed to circumscribe the area in which error may occur. We need only think of the provisions intended to make sure that no innocent person should be found guilty of a crime: they are legion. If a man wounds another man and the victim recovers sufficiently to go out again, any further consequences are not imputed to him who inflicted the wound;[68] if a betrothed woman is violated in the field, where she might have cried for help without being heard, she is to be acquitted;[69] and so on. The general warning, repeated on several occasions by the Deuteronomic lawgiver to investigate capital charges with great care,[70] and the minimum requirement of two witnesses for these accusations,[71] have already been mentioned. It has also been shown that one of the purposes of the story of Susannah is to bring out the inadequacy of just this latter precaution against erroneous condemnation.

Fourth, in two departments, there does exist direct legislation on the consequences of error. The Old Testament is very strict regarding idolatry and false prophecy; error in these respects is no excuse but in itself an unforgivable crime.[72] A certain wavering, however, is noticeable. There must have been occasions when, not the leaders, but the followers of a heretical movement at least, did more or less successfully defend themselves by showing that they had acted with the best of intentions. Otherwise it would be unintelligible why the law should lay down the test that a genuine prophet must undergo—his prophecy, we are told, has to come true[73]—or why, in flagrant contradiction to this attitude, any test should be declared insufficient so long as the prophet was not a true one.[74]

The other field where legislation on error is preserved is that of Levitical commerce. Here, indeed, legislation mitigating the penalty in the case of an offense being due to error seems to have come into existence fairly early, and a technical designation for the kind of error contemplated was evolved, *sheghaghah*.[75] The reason is not far to seek. In this Levitical world, it is not an action as such which is prohibited, but an action if done by or to a person or thing belonging to a special category. It is not, for example, eating an ox or entering the sanctuary that is prohibited, but eating an ox dedicated to the temple or entering the sanctuary in an unclean state. As these special qualities making an otherwise innocuous action illicit are not, as a rule, obvious to the senses, there is plenty of scope for error, which renders some compromise highly desirable. Moreover, the error is always of the same variety, an unawareness of the relevant, Levitical attribute of a person or thing, so that a systematic, uniform regulation is not beyond the powers of an intelligent lawgiver. The solution gained by the priests in this particular corner was gradually extended to other provinces with the result that the laws of holiness had an impact far beyond their original field.[76]

Where error or ignorance leads to breach of a taboo, it takes quite long for people to be confident that heaven will refrain from or mitigate retribution. Yet perhaps the majority of these regulations are of the kind I have just described—that is, the wrongful nature of the act is far from conspicuous. You may easily not realize that you are in a state of uncleanness precluding you from entering the sanctuary; or that the food before you is withdrawn from profane use. Jacob, waking up from the famous dream of the ladder, is full of fear because he unwittingly slept on hallowed ground; luckily, the deity accepts his offering.[77] Moses is warned by God in time not to approach the burning bush.[78] It is a dangerous world. No wonder, once Levitical legislation does get properly under way, the problem receives a comprehensive solution: if you slip up in this fashion, certain sacrifices and/or payments will put things right. There is technical terminology, a verb *shaghagh* or *shaghah*, "to go astray," and even a noun, *sheghaghah*.

What renders this evolution important for the general criminal law is the fact that, in the book of Numbers,[79] the priests subsume under the heading *sheghaghah* various instances of accidental homicide, that is, homicide not from error or ignorance but, say, where you aim a stone at a bird and it hits a person. A daring feat of synthesis: henceforth, throughout the legal system, the word may denote any absence of evil intent as basis for relief. The LXX and Vulgate cannot quite keep up with it, having to distinguish between *agnoia* or *ignorantia* in the Levitical precepts[80] and *akousios* or *nolens* [against one's will] in connection with homicide. Curiously, the semantic development of German *Versehen* [to be in error] is remotely comparable to that of *sheghaghah*—maybe due to Luther's treatment of the term. But it is too complicated a matter here to pursue.

This brings us to the fifth and last point. Though there may be few traces of it in the New Testament, by the time of Jesus, in criminal law, we know that legislation had made great strides and settled a large number of cases outside the Levitical domain. Exactly how far the development had gone it is difficult to say. One pericope in Acts may be taken as reflecting the rabbinic law of the epoch—where Paul, reproached for insulting the high priest, answers that he did not know whom he had before him. This was presumably a complete defense: it is probable that the old provision "Thou shalt not revile God nor curse the ruler of thy people,"[81] which is given a rather wide meaning in our Talmudic sources,[82] was at the time still construed literally, as directed against attacks on God and the president of the Sanhedrin. Transgression of the latter part of the rule was ordinarily punished by stripes, but left unpunished if there was error. (Incidentally, the words "For it is written, Thou shalt not speak evil of the ruler of thy people" do not, as is generally considered, belong to Paul's reply, but are a comment of the author of Acts.) It should be noted, however, that while the crime in question is not Levitical in the narrow sense, it does consist in doing something to a person possessing a very special characteristic; it consists, that is, not in cursing anyone, but in cursing the president of the Sanhedrin. Like Levitical attributes such as holy and profane, or clean and unclean, this is a dignity not immediately visible; and precisely the kind of error, therefore, is possible that distinguishes Levitical offenses. Accordingly, it is only natural that the rules concerning error in the Levitical field should be applied to this crime, and we must not be tempted by the fact to jump to conclusions. More precisely, when we find that, by the period of the New Testament, *sheghaghah* was recognized as exonerating a man in this case of cursing the ruler, this does not entitle us without further evidence to assume the same for crimes of an entirely different character, say, violation of the Sabbath in a moment of forgetfulness.

B. IGNORANCE

It may be best to begin by distinguishing between two kinds of knowledge and ignorance. As a rule, knowledge means the possession of information, ignorance the lack of it. But—in Hebrew and Greek in particular—knowledge may also mean the possession of deeper understanding, insight, judgment; ignorance may mean blindness despite any amount of information. You may or may not be aware that the man you are shooting dead belongs to your own army, not to the enemy,[83] or that the road on which you are driving is closed to traffic from this direction, or that the sale of spirits to children is prohibited; in all these cases it is a question of information. But take a well-educated fascist: if we say of him that he does not really know or that he is really an ignoramus, we are referring to something beyond information, to a grasp of the meaning of life and man's position. "Know thyself," the inscription at Delphi, falls into this latter area of understanding. So do the words often given a conspicuous place on the ark or a wall in synagogues, "Know before whom thou standest."[84] So does the first prayer in the Eighteen Benedictions—which, as Montefiore stressed, is not a prayer for forgiveness or for the power to repent, but "O favor us with knowledge, understanding and discernment from thee."[85]

Admittedly, the distinction is not clear-cut. In many cases there is overlapping, not to mention the fact that understanding can perhaps be largely reduced to the simpler type of knowledge, on a different plane. However, for the moment we may rest content, and take first the problem of sinning—or shall we say, more neutrally, slipping—in ignorance of or error about relevant circumstances, in the absence, that is, of information or of correct and sufficient information.

Lack of Information

After one of his victorious battles with the Philistines, King David decided to bring the ark from Baale of Judah to Jerusalem. The ark was put on a cart drawn by oxen. As the oxen shook it and it threatened to fall down, one Uzzah held it up. For this God smote him dead there and then.[86]

We can sympathize with David who, we are told, "was displeased because the Lord had made a breach upon Uzzah." But by that time religion had reached a stage where an intrusion on sacred ground or the infringement of a sacred rule might be fatal, regardless of motive. (We are implying that this rigid attitude is not the earliest, but we cannot here inquire into its antecedents.) However unwitting the trespass, however well-meant even, it must be followed by punishment, from God or man acting for him.

Moses, when turning aside to investigate the bush which burned but was not consumed, was saved only because he was warned in time: "Draw not nigh hither, put off thy shoes, for the place whereon thou standest is holy ground."[87] Before God descended on Sinai, he commanded that the people should be kept away from the mount: "Whosoever toucheth it shall be surely put to death; whether it be beast or man, it shall not live."[88] Even a beast, then, would incur the penalty.

There was indeed little difference between an active trespass and a passive exposure to forces that should not be approached. The people present at the revelation were afraid that the sight and sounds they were witnessing would spell their death: "And they said unto Moses, Speak thou with us and we will hear, but let not God speak with us, lest we die."[89] Just so Manoah, on seeing the angel who prophesied Samson's birth ascend to heaven, said to his wife: "We shall surely die, because we have seen God."[90] And even Isaiah, when he had beheld God sitting upon a throne surrounded by the seraphim, exclaimed: "Woe is me, I am undone, for mine eyes have seen the Lord of hosts."[91]

Jonathan was unaware that his father Saul had placed under a curse anyone taking food during the battle. He ate some wild honey and, thus strengthened, wrought havoc among the enemy. When his fault was discovered, he himself admitted that he deserved death, and he would have been killed had not the people insisted on a reprieve. Nor did they refer to his innocence; what they maintained was that his success showed him to be on God's side.[92] Whether they could have done so had he knowingly contravened Saul's ban is indeed doubtful. On the other hand it is not impossible that, in an earlier version, Jonathan was saved though he had acted in open defiance.[93] A lion devoured the anonymous prophet who, charged by the Lord not to return the way he had set out, trustingly believed another prophet when he told him that the order had been countermanded.[94] Lions, too, raged among the heathen whom the king of Assyria settled in Samaria in the place of the deported Israelites and who, naturally, did not know the kind of worship that the God of the land expected.[95]

These examples of an unwitting transgressor being held liable could be multiplied. However, from the first it was possible sometimes, or even most times, to expiate the violation of a taboo by some devotional act, and gradually there grew up a definite system of sacrifices to be offered where a religious offense was committed from ignorance or error. When Jacob awoke from his dream of the ladder, "he said, Surely the Lord is in this place and I knew it not, and he was afraid, and he took the stone that he had put for his pillows and set it up for a pillar and poured oil upon it."[96] Here the expiatory process has still something spontaneous about it; it arises naturally out of the particular situation. Later there were fixed standardized directives.[97] A story like that of Jacob might be recounted partly in order to recommend the hero's conduct: it might prepare the ground for Levitical legislation.

Two things, however, should be noticed. The false worship of heathendom was not, of course, covered by the general regulations concerning unwitting sins; it was an error *sui generis*, which we have no time to discuss. Furthermore, within Judaism, even when any religious offense committed unwittingly had become capable of expiation, it still remained an offense; otherwise no sacrifice would have been requisite at all. The psalmist (at least as the Rabbis understand him) prays to be preserved or cleansed not only from deliberate sin, but also from sinning in error,[98] and the latter figures in fairly late confessions.[99] So even on this advanced level, however blameless you might be from the moral point of view, a breaking through of the sacred barrier could not be simply disregarded. The consequences were now very bearable; atonement was assured—but there was still need for atonement.

A characteristic rabbinic contribution to this province, incidentally, is the teaching that it is sometimes wiser not to enlighten a person who does not know that what he is doing is incorrect—namely, where the deed is a very minor, religious offense, and where there is considerable risk that he would go on with it even if warned not to, thus willfully repudiating God's commandments.[100] To be sure, he is guilty of some transgression even if he does not know his action to be forbidden. But the transgression is far less serious; it is committed in ignorance, ignorance of the law. You had better condone it.

In the case of transgressions affecting society, the development is very checkered. Adultery committed by a man in ignorance of the woman's status is a good example. According to an Assyrian collection of precepts of about 1250 BC, if he did not know her to be married, he is to be acquitted.[101] Three stories in Genesis are relevant.[102]

In chapter 12[103] it is recorded that Abraham in Egypt suppressed the fact that Sarah was his wife, Pharaoh took her, God sent plagues against him, he realized the truth, and Sarah was returned. No trace of Pharaoh's ignorance counting in his favor, no trace even of this disregard of his innocence being felt to be a problem.

Then we come to chapter 20. In Gerar also, Abraham concealed Sarah's status and she was brought into the king's harem. But this time God, though again sending plagues, appeared to the king before he had touched Sarah, threatened him with death—and was met by a spirited defense. To kill him, the king declared, would be contrary to the elementary principles of justice. At this point a most remarkable idea is introduced. God replied, we are told, as follows: "Yea I know that thou didst this in the integrity of thy heart, and yea I withheld thee from sinning against me, therefore suffered I thee not to touch her." So the truly pure man, however deep in error, is kept by God from defiling himself. The affinity with the well-known view that the good man escapes disease and other misfortune is unmistakable: a sin from error somewhat resembles a disease.

We cannot be certain how far the author of the story would have extended this idea beyond the specific case of adultery—say, to the killing of a fellow soldier on the mistaken assumption that he belongs to the enemy army. We may leave generalizations to modern psychoanalysis, some of whose theories, though cruder, are distinctly comparable: Oedipus would not have married his mother but for the complex. But whether the range of application of the idea was wide or narrow, it expresses a profound trust in a moral government of the world by God.

Therein, from a practical point of view, lay a danger. He who firmly believes that, so long as a man is really well-intentioned, God will somehow prevent him sinning in ignorance, may have little objection to a law that is indifferent to motive. For if a man does sin in ignorance, if he does have intercourse with another man's wife thinking her unmarried, this is proof that he is not really well-intentioned; otherwise God would have intervened. So retribution may take its course; no need to progress and admit the plea of innocence. It is the same type of attitude that, for instance, would not greatly encourage the abolition of slavery or poverty or even disease, because God will not allow anyone to be a slave or poor or sick who ought to be free or rich or healthy.

No doubt theology, ancient and recent, has found it possible to counter this reasoning and to reconcile the tenet that God will permit no injustice with the tenet that man, as far as lies in his power, must permit none. After all, there exist no more passionate indictments of unjust practices than those of the two Testaments. Nonetheless we have to admit a grain of truth in the charge, often heard, that religious trust is apt to engender a conservative if not reactionary mentality. Nor, unless it is a cover for self-interest, is this mentality anything to be ashamed of: there is a—limited—place for it.

At any rate, the story under review is significant. The problem of adultery in ignorance of the woman's status is posed as forcefully as can be: "Wilt thou slay a righteous nation?" the king answered God. "Said he not unto me, she is my sister, and she herself said, he is my brother: in the integrity of my heart and innocency of my hands have I done this." Yet the solution is not: Well, then, in these circumstances no matter how far you went, neither is heaven offended nor should any earthly tribunal pronounce against you. (We may recall the Assyrian laws, exempting such a case from punishment.) The solution is: "Therefore suffered I thee not to touch her." A magnificent assertion of God's providence. But, from the practical point of view, for one who expects a lead in this difficult matter, a dodge, an evasion. The problem is treated as nonexistent.

Historically, what makes the case even more fascinating is the possibility that, in an earlier version, the lead was given, a progressive solution was put forward. More precisely, in an earlier version of this chapter, just as in chapter 12, the king, it would seem, did take Sarah. This is strongly suggested by the way God pronounces his sentence before the defense of error cancels it: "Behold thou art a dead man for the woman thou hast taken."[104] (Similarly, in the king's defense, we find the phrase "I have done this," and his subsequent reproaches to Abraham are based on the same presupposition: "What have I offended thee, that thou hast brought on me a great sin?" So are the infliction of infertility on all the inhabitants of the palace, and the payment to Abraham of a substantial fine.) So the problem was squarely faced: the king, having taken a married woman, pleaded ignorance, and God accepted the plea, withdrew his threat.

In that version, then, God set a precedent in the enlightened treatment of a trespass committed in good faith—a precedent that could not fail, and was intended, to make an impact on the reaction of human courts to this case. How momentous an innovation it was, this acquittal on the ground of absence of moral fault, may be gauged from the fact that it had to be wrung from God, much like his reversal of collective liability in the case of Sodom and Gomorrah. There was a *Streitgespräch*; his original verdict was boldly controverted. If it was controverted by a mere human, he could appeal to those basic demands of justice that must be binding on God himself.

Of course, there was one feature about this particular episode that must have made the innovation somewhat easier. The king's error concerning Sarah's status had not just come about anyhow: it was due to deception practiced on him by precisely the two persons whom his action chiefly affected, the husband and the wife. In these circumstances, the case for exonerating the victim of error was exceptionally strong.

It must not be thought, however, that even in these circumstances the reform was at once carried to its ultimate conclusion. Though God consented to spare the king's life, he and his people still suffered some plague, and he had to pay Abraham a fine. He was still somehow in sin. He himself complained to Abraham: "What have I offended thee that thou hast brought on me and my kingdom a great sin?" We found a similar holding back in the domain of Levitical transgressions before the last consequences of a rational, perhaps overrational, approach—before the denial, that is, of any wrong at all in such a case. In modern law, by the way, a child resulting from an adulterous union would be illegitimate (discounting rules of evidence) irrespective of any good faith on the part of father or mother, and could not, while the original marriage continued, be legitimated by either party.

Later, it was considered essential to emphasize that Sarah escaped untouched. It was this concern that led to the distinctive character of the version before us. Her escape, untouched, was introduced as flowing from the king's innocence—the idea we have discussed: the good man is preserved by God from sinning in error. And the clear, progressive, practical solution of the problem of motive was sacrificed. It is curious how such a thing can happen from considerations not germane to the issue in the least.

We must still say a word about the third story in Gen 26.[105] Now it was Isaac who, in Gerar, gave out that Rebekah was his sister. In an earlier version, once again, it may well be that the king took Rebekah. When he "looked out at a window" to find Isaac sporting with her, that must have been a window giving on an inner yard of the palace; so she was living there. According to the story in its present form, the king found out the truth before anything untoward had happened. But there is no sign in this chapter that ignorance would have been considered an excuse.

The Rabbis, needless to say, reinterpret all these events in a fashion tending to make moral fault the sole basis for punishment. Of the pharaoh of chapter 12, for example, they tell us that he was plagued because Sarah, when alone with him, did reveal to him her married status and he tried to violate her though now he knew.[106] (According to the Mishnah,[107] a man who has intercourse with another man's wife in ignorance of her status is not subject to extirpation but need only bring a sin offering.) But an instance of error as to status occurring in the New Testament[108] shows best how far Jewish institutions had advanced by that time.

When the Roman chief captain summoned the high priest and his council to examine Paul, the high priest soon lost patience and ordered the servants to strike Paul in the face. Paul replied by a curse: "God shall smite thee, thou whitened wall." Now in principle, to curse the president of the Sanhedrin was a grave offense,[109] and the people present were not slow to bring the charge. Paul, however, pleaded that he had been unaware of the status of the man conducting his examination: "I wist not, brethren, that he was the high priest." This defense apparently finished the matter at once and absolutely. Not the smallest fine or the like. The historicity of the incident can hardly be called in question. For Paul's conduct, though understandable, is not consonant with the highest idealistic Jewish and Christian teaching of the period. Fiction would presumably have made it so. (But even if it were all invented, our main conclusion would not be affected: the author would still remain within the bounds of what his public accepted as possible.)

On the other hand, in the case of an unintentional killing—say, you are felling trees together with another man and your axe flies from the handle and hits him—even by New Testament times you were still deemed guilty, though in a far lesser degree than a murderer. (Strictly, this case of the axe taken from Deuteronomy[110] is to be classed as accident, not error,[111] but for the present purpose the distinction may be disregarded.) Already the Old Testament had sent the unintentional homicide into a city of refuge, and, theoretically at least, banishment remained the penalty in New Testament times also.[112] If it be asked why the old biblical ordinances were not interpreted more boldly by the Rabbis, the answer is that there were very good reasons for caution. In the vast majority of unintentional killings (whether by error or accident) there is an element of carelessness, when modern law does not hesitate to impose some sanction. The sanction is perhaps not always as strict as it ought to be; it has become rather cheap to maim or kill by means of a motored vehicle, but still we do register a protest. Considering that this entire field came under the law concerning unintentional killing, the occasions on which an injustice was done must have been rare; and they were made yet rarer by the purposefully restrictive way in which the Rabbis defined a killing. (There was a dispute even about the case of the axe, Rabbi Judah the Prince taking the view that the man wielding the axe was altogether free from responsibility.[113])

For the Jewish theologians and philosophers, however, the case presented a twofold problem respecting God's justice. First, why should the particular victim—say your fellow woodcutter who is hit by your axe—die at this moment? This was comparatively easy to answer. He deserves to die for his sins, as does any human being when God puts an end to his life. The only point we may note here is the ingenious connection that Philo established with the scriptural text.[114] Scripture says of the unintentional homicide that, far from his planning the deed, "God let it happen to his hand," or another possible translation, "God delivered the victim into his hand."[115] Philo took it in the latter sense, and he argued that this definition was intended as a partial excuse of the agent. "God delivered the victim into his hand"—that meant (Philo explained) God used the unintentional homicide as his instrument in cutting short a life that ought not to continue. (About the middle of the second century, the school of R. Ishmael explains a little linguistic peculiarity in the injunction to make a railing around your roof as indicating that, should any person fall to his death as a result of your failure to comply, that death was decreed from the Creation; but in this case there is no implication that you are to some extent excused.[116] The explanation, by the way, is in accordance with the Pharisaic opinion, outlined by Josephus,[117] as to the collaboration between fate and the individual.)

But here we come to the second aspect of the problem, subtler than the first and more immediately relevant to our topic. Your fellow woodcutter deserves death at this moment. But what about you? Why should you, who did not desire his death, find yourself the cause of it, and theoretically at least be liable to banishment as a result? Remember that carelessness was not yet worked out into a general basis of culpability, and now and then a man might indeed be convicted of unintentional killing though not even carelessness could be attributed to him. What is the explanation of God bringing guilt upon you, unwitting as you are? (If the unintentional homicide were liable only in case of negligence, there would be no difficulty. He who builds no railing around his roof is called "culpable," "wicked," by the school of Ishmael; if he causes a death, it illustrates the maxim that heaven brings about a bad thing through a bad man.[118])

Philo replied that, however innocent you might be in respect of this deed, you must previously have committed some wrong that remained undetected, unrequited; and that God now, by making you an unwitting homicide, with banishment ensuing, was sending you the punishment you merited. This reply is highly reminiscent of the idea relied on many centuries earlier by the author of Gen 20.

Of course, there are differences. For one thing, in Gen 20, a good man is preserved from an unwitting wrong; that if you do fall into an unwitting wrong you cannot be really good is only implied—in Philo it is clearly stated. For another, in Gen 20 you are preserved from the particular wrong in regard to which you are truly innocent; and it follows that if you commit a wrong, then, though appearances may be to the contrary, you cannot have been truly innocent in this particular respect. Say you were given to understand that a married woman was unmarried: if you take her, this is proof that you were not really well-intentioned in this matter. By contrast, Philo admits that the unwitting homicide may be perfectly blameless as far as this killing is concerned; it may be for a sin committed on an entirely different occasion that God punishes him by making him incur responsibility for a death.

It is obvious that this inclusion of past conduct enormously eases the task of justifying the ways of God to men. Any human being does evil at some time. (In accounting for disease, death, or a disaster, the reference to past conduct is indeed extremely old and very common. Joseph's brothers, when convicted of the theft of a cup they did not steal, accept what befalls them as the requital for their former treachery.[119] We have just remarked that, for the Rabbis, the victim of an unintentional killing dies for his sins—any sins committed in the course of his life; no doubt the same explanation would have been given in far earlier times. Philo extends this reasoning to the unintentional homicide.) Certainly, even further advances along this road are conceivable: we may, for example, think of the misfortune of one man, or

even the sin of one man considered as a misfortune, as a means of expiation of the sins of another. But though we must go on trying, every new step
of this kind inevitably brings with it its own new difficulties. No doctrine of
theodicy will ever be satisfactory. *Il faut être fou, aveugle ou lâche pour se résigner à
la peste ... Il faut admettre le scandale*.[120]

No matter where Philo's explanation originated—in Alexandria or Palestine—we meet it again in third-century Palestine, propounded by Simeon
ben Laqish.[121] But the rabbi attempts too much. He declares not, like Philo,
that the unintentional homicide must previously have committed some sin
that remained undetected, but that he must have committed another unintentional killing which remained undetected; now God makes him commit
one in the open, so that he will suffer just the right punishment he had at
first escaped. The flaws of this thesis are manifest. (To be sure, Simeon may
not have wished us to take him *au pied de la lettre*. But while bearing this in
mind, we may legitimately probe into what he actually says in order to get
at the point of his deviation from Philo.) Apart from the fact that it is simply contrary to experience that any unintentional killing detected is preceded
by one undetected, one may ask why the man was made by God to commit
the previous undetected killing. Because he had committed a yet earlier one?
But at some point we must reach his first one. This thesis is much cruder,
much more pedantic, than what we find in Philo. And yet—the crudeness
and the pedantry are admirable, since they reflect the desperate desire to represent God as absolutely just, as above the slightest arbitrariness, as treating
each individual in strictest accordance with his deserts. That the standard of
justice is taken from the written law, that Simeon assumes the penalty laid
down by the latter to be the obviously appropriate one, goes without saying.

Lack of Understanding

It is time to proceed to the relation of sin and the second kind of knowledge
or ignorance. We have seen that, as far as knowledge means information and
ignorance or error the lack or inadequacy of it, the tendency in the Bible (where
it is not counteracted, as in Gen 20, by special considerations) is to pay more
and more attention to this factor. Lack of relevant information ends by being

fully recognized as a mitigating circumstance, if not as precluding any wrong: we may recall the case of Paul. There is all the difference between a deed of this nature and one committed deliberately in full possession of all the facts.

When we pass to knowledge and ignorance in the sense of deeper understanding and blindness, it is clear that this is primarily the territory of actions undertaken by one who, in the ordinary sense, is quite *au fait*; yet he may be sinning owing to failure to appreciate the ultimate good, like David when he invited Bathsheba—no error as to status here—or Ahab when he appropriated Naboth's vineyard, or, according to the authors of the New Testament, that party who rejected Jesus' claim. Indeed, as is well known, it has been said that but for such ignorance of the ultimate good you could not sin—so that we reach the paradox: knowledge in the sense of information is essential to a sin properly so called, knowledge in the sense of understanding is incompatible with sin.

It is important to notice, however, that even where it is held, or felt, that sin proper is necessarily the result of a lack of understanding, the conclusion that it deserves to be excused is rarely drawn. On the contrary, the sinner is reproached for nothing more violently than his blindness, insanity, raving. "My people are destroyed for lack of knowledge," says Hosea;[122] and "Ephraim also is like a silly dove without heart."[123] "Shut the eyes of this people," Isaiah is bidden by God,[124] "lest they see and understand and be healed"; the passage recurs in the New Testament, quoted and reapplied by Jesus and Paul.[125] There is a Talmudic dictum that no one commits a sin unless a spirit of madness or stupidity has entered into him. But this is not meant as a defense. In origin, it is a pun on the adulteress who, Scripture says,[126] *tisṭe* "goes aside"; the Rabbis read *tishṭe*, "she acts madly." It is precisely for her "madness" that heaven will inflict terrible punishment on her. Idolaters are called "madmen," "fools." We could reformulate the paradox to which we have just drawn attention as follows: while ignorance in the ordinary sense, of lack of information, is at least a mitigating circumstance, ignorance of the more profound kind, meaning lack of understanding, blindness, madness, is the very gist of a serious charge.

John plays upon the two meanings of knowledge and ignorance.[127] So, incidentally, does Montefiore. "Knowledge," he says, and here he means learning, information, "must know her place"; here, to know is to judge, to see through.[128] Let us take John. "For judgment I am come, that they which see not—that is, the uninformed ones—might see— that is, understand— and that they which see—the informed ones—might be made blind—in the deeper sense. And the Pharisees said, Are we blind also— that is, do we, with all our learning, not understand? Jesus said, If ye were blind— that is, uninformed—ye should have no sin, but now ye say, We see— that is, you yourself admit to possession of all information and you even boast of understanding—therefore your sin remaineth." This evangelist at least is fully alive to the different senses of the terms. To appreciate the subtlety of his punning it must be remembered that, in the context, there is the further transition from physical blindness and its cure to spiritual. But what we would emphasize at this juncture is the fact that the blindness of the Pharisees, their lack of understanding, far from being an excuse, is precisely that enormity for which they stand condemned in judgment.

The best-known exception to the rule is Socrates, who did argue that, in principle, no wrongdoer might be called to account, since, but for ignorance in the sense of lack of understanding, he could not have acted as he did.[129] The murderer, the adulterer, the tyrant, the false prophet, they all were exculpated on this ground. Socrates thus claimed for ignorance in this sense— you kill a rival from envy—the same indulgence as the law (in some cases at least) had long accorded to ignorance in the sense of lack of information— you kill a soldier whom you mistake for a member of the enemy army. And he may well have been consciously drawing on and transferring the latter, more ordinary doctrine.

"Father, forgive them."

In the New Testament, though normally blindness is a crime, several passages—in Luke, Acts,[130] 1 Timothy[131]—represent the opponents of Jesus as ignorant and, therefore, less guilty. The text most illuminating in the present connection is Jesus' prayer on the cross: "Father, forgive them, for they know not what they do."[132]

As it stands in Luke, it might refer either to the Roman soldiers participating in the crucifixion or to that Jewish party who approved of it. Modern scholars are divided in their interpretation, as are already the second-
century authorities. What has not been noticed, however, is that according as
the prayer is for the Roman soldiers or the Jewish opponents, the meaning
of "they know not" is very different. If it is a prayer for the Roman soldiers,
"they know not" means that they lack information, they have never been told
who Jesus really is, they must think he is just a common criminal. Ignorance
of this kind is a defense in all mature systems of law and ethics; we may once
again recall Paul's successful plea when he had cursed the high priest. By
contrast, if the prayer is offered for the Jewish opponents, "they know not"
means that they lack understanding. They have been given every possible
information, they have been told all there is to tell, they desire Jesus' death
despite the most detailed and insistent preaching. The moral of Luke's story
of the rich man and Lazarus[133] is that even the miraculous appearance of one
risen from the dead could add nothing to what may be gathered from the
Scriptures; those not persuaded by the latter are deaf to persuasion. If such
sinners are nonetheless to be pardoned on the ground of ignorance, this is
something very much rarer than acceptance of the plea of lack of information. It is akin to the Socratic view that the sinner, the open-eyed sinner not
affected by any ordinary error, is blind to his true interests and destiny, and
that, acting from blindness, he cannot be held responsible.

There are indications that the prayer was first uttered, or thought to have
been uttered, by James, the brother of Jesus, before it was attributed to the
latter. It was James who, according to a second-century source, offered the
prayer for the Jews who were putting him to death.[134] For the Jews, so "they
know not what they do" here plainly means "they have not sufficient insight."
For our purpose it is enough that there should occur in the New Testament
and primitive Christian writings—Acts, 1 Timothy, the prayer of James, and
an early interpretation at least of the prayer of Jesus—the notion of the defiant sinner, who goes on with his crime though he has all the relevant information, deserving forgiveness, or a measure of forgiveness, because he
does not know. And the question arises whether we must assume Greek-

Hellenistic influence or whether this notion could have its roots in independent Jewish tradition.

We consider the latter to be quite possible. In the Old Testament, when, for example, the Suffering Servant is the hope of those who "like sheep have gone astray"[135]—a simile taken up in the New Testament[136]—this does imply the plea of ignorance in the sense of helplessness, loss of direction, lack of understanding; and in that *Divina Comedia* of the Old Testament, the book of Jonah, the point is made in so many words, in the final proclamation by God: "And should I not spare Nineveh, wherein are more than sixscore thousand persons that do not know between their right hand and their left hand, and also much cattle?" "They do not know" does not here signify lack of information; the wicked Ninevites had not been acting from ignorance in the ordinary sense. The phrase refers to their basic ignorance as weak, short-sighted creatures, not much wiser than their beasts; they are spared because they did not know in this deeper sense what they were doing. What makes this particular passage relevant to an investigation of Judaism in New Testament times is the fact that, almost certainly, the book of Jonah was then as today used as a lesson from the Prophets on the Day of Atonement.[137] So the words in which it culminates occupied a most prominent place in the liturgy of that period; their message must have come through. Incidentally, this role of the book of Jonah is quite overlooked by those scholars who, in view of the universalistic tendency of the work, call it the least Jewish of the Old Testament. Montefiore remonstrated against this strange prejudice.[138]

There is more evidence. According to the Epistle to the Hebrews,[139] the high priest to whom Jesus is likened procures atonement for "the ignorant and those that are out of the way"—a clear reference to that ignorance which means lack of grasp, misjudgment of one's true position and aim. Again, Eliezer the Great of the first century finds a verse in Numbers[140] on which to base the teaching that even the deliberate, presumptuous sins of the community are treated by God as sins committed in error. It is this section from Numbers by means of which nowadays the entire service of the Day of Atonement is placed under the motif of forgiveness on the ground of deeper ignorance. The very first quotation from Scripture in this service is the following: "And it shall be forgiven all the congregation of Israel and the stranger that sojourneth among them, seeing that all the people were in ignorance." In its original context, the verse envisages only sins excusable because of some real error in the ordinary sense, say, a mistake is made in the fixing of the date of a festival. But, boldly torn from that context, and placed at the opening of the Day of Atonement service which covers the case of the most desperate sinner, it becomes a prayer for and promise of pardon in view of man's ever-deficient understanding. Hermann Cohen noticed with pleasure the affinity with Socratic ethics.[141]

The prayer in Luke, then, and allied passages may well be thoroughly Judaic; this unusual notion of the wrongdoer being excused by the blindness necessarily the source of his wrong has a consistent history, independent of its Greek counterpart, from the Old Testament down to the New Testament and rabbinic faith. Maybe in both Jewish and Greek thought, what favored the emergence of this notion—as opposed to the common one of blindness as a reproach—was the encounter with another civilization (Jonah), or at least another group within the civilization (Socrates, the Rabbis, the New Testament), which, while it had to be disapproved and combated, possessed too many qualities to be utterly rejected. At any rate, in the Bible— both the Old Testament and the New—and in Rabbinism the notion tends to come to the fore where there is hope that the wrongdoer may be converted or may repent, or where conversion or repentance has taken place. The obdurate enemy—not to mention him who relapses into darkness after seeing the light—is not readily granted the defense, just as in the Socratic system a way is found to justify his punishment.

At first sight it is puzzling why a notion of such importance in itself and so prominent in the liturgy of the Day of Atonement should otherwise play a very small part in Judaism. The explanation seems to be that, if too much is made of this doctrine that the sinner deserves forgiveness because his very misdeeds prove him to be a helpless creature, the result may be a dangerous weakening of the sense of responsibility, a blurring of the distinction between right and wrong, a toleration of license. We have some experience with twentieth-century theories tending that way. It is significant that, unlike the Greek philosophers, the Rabbis never attempt to import this notion into trials confined to earthly tribunals. Socrates was more radical in this respect, and if it were the case—we have little evidence one way or the other—that this part of his teaching contributed to the impression he gave of undermining the existing social order, one could hardly wonder. In the New Testament and rabbinic sources the plea of ignorance in the deeper sense is advanced only vis-à-vis God. In a human court you must shoulder the responsibility for your actions—unless there are specific grounds of exemption or mitigation.

Perhaps, in conclusion, we should point out that the defense by reference to lack of understanding is very different from the modern defense by invoking motives of conscience. This modern defense, which would for instance be available in a case of political assassination, or euthanasia administered by a doctor who believes it to be his duty, does not stress the offender's misguidedness, creaturely helplessness, inability to see the true value. Far from it. It rests on either of two ideas—or a blend of them. One is that, as any view concerning ultimate values is basically a matter of individual conviction, we ought to respect positions which disagree with that taken up by the majority. Hence if it is a man's unorthodox position which leads him to commit a crime, he must be treated better than an ordinary criminal—not as being misguided, but on the contrary, because he represents an order that, though clashing with the prevalent one, is *au fond* equivalent. (It is chiefly this idea that underlies one method of dealing with conscientious offenses, namely, legislation to the effect that certain acts—such as refusal to comply with conscription—which would ordinarily be offenses are not to count as such if dictated by religious or philosophical conviction.) Another approach is to regard the crime from motives of conscience as a sector of the wider class of crimes not the result of a despicable disposition (*die nicht aus ehr-loser Gesinnung entspringen*), and to place it together with such cases as dueling or murdering the seducer of one's sister. Viewed in this way, the offense is not the expression of another, equivalent order; it does show misguidedness, inability to make the right decision. But it is considered less heinous than ordinary crime, not because of this misguidedness, but in spite of it—the redeeming feature being that the wrongdoer errs in a manner which, up to a point, commands our esteem.

In Germany, where the *Überzeugungsverbrecher* [one who commits a crime from conviction] enjoyed certain privileges under the Weimar Republic, it was one of Hitler's first measures to abolish them. Quite generally, as regards political crimes, there was more inclination to leniency about the turn of the century than nowadays: Western society then felt more secure and able to afford the luxury of respect for the dissenter; also it had not yet become customary for dissent to take the form of a mass organization of thugs. Happily, Britain has not succumbed to the illiberal trend. But all this has little to do with forgiveness "for they know not what they do."

Not that there are no early adumbrations of the recognition of the conscientious crime as a lesser disgrace; as one might expect, the basis of the recognition in those early cases is a respect for an honorable disposition rather than for a different order of equal standing. Something of the kind is in Paul's mind when he says:[142] "My heart's desire for Israel is that they might be saved, for I bear them record that they have a zeal of God." It is interesting that he immediately passes on to their lack of understanding, as a reproach, not as an excuse: "they have a zeal of God, but not according to knowledge, for being ignorant of God's righteousness" and so on. The Talmud distinguishes between one who eats carrion, *ṭerephah*, because he defies, despises the Law, and one who eats it from appetite, from desire.[143] Both act in full awareness, but the former from conviction, as a heretic or apostate, the latter just from weakness, from lust. What is here of relevance is the fact that, while there is unanimity as to the transgressor from appetite being untrustworthy as a legal witness, one great rabbi at least, of the first half of the fourth century, would admit the transgressor from defiance: a remarkable tribute to a man however terrible his deeds, so long as he is upright and consistent.

CHAPTER 4

PASSIONS

EARLY LAW: *Fight and Murder*

Greek writers distinguish someone who is "beside himself" in a sudden passion from someone who commits premeditated murder. There is little of this in the Bible. The legal text that started me off years ago was a law distinguishing the unwitting homicide from the murderer; the former is defined as having "thrust his victim suddenly, without enmity."[1] Here are two men with no grudge against one another, and "suddenly" one of them has killed the other. We may think of the example given in Deuteronomy of two men felling trees together, and as one of them swings his axe its head flies off and hits the other.[2] Fearful not only for the victim but also—or in a way worse—for the doer, Philo and the Rabbis indeed conclude that the doer must previously have committed some sin; otherwise God would not use him as an instrument in bringing death to another person.[3]

In Plato the same description is applied to one who kills in a fit of anger, *exaiphnes aprobouleutos*, "suddenly without evil intention," immediately repenting: again there is swift and startling disaster for both parties.[4] Quintus Curtius tells us[5] that Alexander, insulted by Cleitus during a drinking bout, "suddenly," *repentine*, leaped up and murder ensued, soon to be followed by regret, *paenitentia*. It might perhaps be asked why we ascribe to the biblical *bephetha' belo''ebha* ("suddenly without enmity," Num 35:22), a sense different from Plato's *exaiphnes aprobouleutos*. It would lead too far afield to argue the case, and I am not even certain that the Hebrew phrase at all stages of its existence (suppose it did exist outside its present context) must have meant "by accident" rather than "in a fit."

In the *Mishpatim* (Book of the Covenant, Exod 21–23), Exod 21:18 speaks of *ribh*, "to strive": "If men strive together and one smite the other with a stone, or with his fist, and he die not, but keepeth his bed, if he rise again, and walk abroad upon his staff, then shall he that smote him be quit: only he shall pay for the loss of his time, and shall cause him to be thoroughly healed." There is a limitation on liability for the one causing the initial damage. It is a typical case. If a master strikes a slave with a rod so that he dies, there is a restriction on liability depending on the time that passes before the slave dies, but otherwise no limitation is recognized despite the relationship being that of a master-slave. The master is punished for the slave's death.[6] Might there be cause for restriction on liability if a free person was murdered? Or is this case just not considered?

In Exod 21:26, 27, about a master causing the loss of a slave's eye or tooth, there is no reference to a rod being used, and the slave is given his freedom. In Exod 21:22–25, about one pushing another's pregnant wife and a miscarriage results, there is liability for payment only. It is possible that the punishment replaces a previous talionic penalty in which the offender's child is killed. In Deut 25:11–12, about a woman interfering in a struggle (verb is *naṣah*) between her husband and an assailant and grabbing the latter's genitals, the penalty is that she has her hand cut off. Here certainly there is no mitigation. In 2 Sam 14:6, in the story that the woman of Tekoah communicates to King David—it is really about Absalom and his slain brother Amnon—her sons are in the field when they "strive together" (*naṣah*), one kills the other, and the family wants to kill the offending son. In his response, David mitigates the deed certainly to the extent of granting the culprit freedom from death. If it had been murder, however, the king perhaps would not have been so easily moved. In the actual parallel, Absalom is very premeditating; it is not just a quarrel in a field. In Exod 2:13, two Hebrews "strive together" (*naṣah*). Moses tells off the one in the wrong. The judgment is neutral in regard to any emotions involved in the affray.

Killing in an outburst is rarer than in Greek sources. David has Uriah killed to cover up his adultery with Bathsheba. David's intent had been to let Uriah have his wife rather than face the consequences of his crime. There is not a single instance of a killing in an outburst of passion over a woman. One of the few quarrels we read about is in 2 Sam 3:8. After King Saul's death, Abner, Saul's commander of his forces, becomes sexually involved with Rizpah, Saul's concubine. Ishbosheth, Saul's son, tells off Abner because he regards him as an illegitimate lover, and Abner is very wroth.[7] No biblical sexual prohibition stresses passion, but an Israelite's attachment to heathen customs perhaps comes close. Deuteronomy 22:26 exempts the betrothed woman who has intercourse in the field, since it is assumed she has been raped and cannot be heard when she cries out. The lawgiver compares the situation to that of a man rising against another and murdering him. The rapist's passion is disregarded.

SOME STATES

DRUNKENNESS[8]

An extraordinary aspect of drunkenness appears in the Old Testament. In the Europe I grew up in drunkenness among Jews, even assimilated ones, was rare.[9] We were proud of this; and I remember a Yiddish song—presumably there were more of the kind—contrasting the pious, spiritual Jew with the crude, bibulous Gentile. The fact, however, was disputed by no one. Indeed, both Jews and Gentiles recognized that the distinction was of long standing.

A phenomenon of this nature would hardly be the effect of a single cause. Still, one factor seemed to me to be of particular importance: the fundamental insecurity of Jewry. For some two thousand years it had been without a home, scattered over many countries, never more than a tiny fraction in any of them, at best grudgingly tolerated, often persecuted, always in fear of having to move on. People living in this condition could not afford to let their guard down ever. A careless or stupid act which, if committed by a Gentile, was rectifiable or at any rate not too costly; if committed by a Jew it might spell disaster to him and any number of his co-religionists. It was the nation's

survival instinct among hostile hosts, I thought, that chiefly accounted for
its sobriety.

Nowadays I spend much time in American academia, where I come across
quite a few Jews with—to use a fashionable term—"a drinking problem."
Though even so, there are extremes not yet, I believe, reached. One of the
heroes of my friend Richard Stookey's novel *A Still and Woven Blue*[10] remi-
nisces about his father who

> had somehow managed to come home from the war, the first one, with a
> military airplane which he kept in the barn and cranked up only during the
> dark of the moon in order to ferry whiskey to Chicago for a local bootlegger.
> Morse, as he told of the miraculous exploits that grew out of this enterpris-
> ing sideline, became almost giddy. I chuckled along with him, finally watch-
> ing out of the corner of my eye as he raised one enormous hand to simu-
> late the flight of the ill-fated craft as it descended, full of white lightning
> but empty of gas, into the forbidding waters of Lake Michigan. Then, as the
> description of his father's damp outrage overcame him, he took off the dark
> glasses and tears of laughter began to stream down his pale cheeks. "He got
> two bottles of the stuff out before it went down, before it sank," he gasped.
> "When the fishermen found him the next morning, bobbing up and down in
> his yellow lifebelt, they thought he was dead . . . but he was only dead drunk!"
> Morse threw his head back and crowed like a rooster.

This, however, does not necessarily refute the explanation just outlined. For
one thing, in some respects, acculturation to the mainstream is more thorough in the States than it was in Europe—notwithstanding the strong, well-
organized coherence of ethnic groups, including Jewry. For another, rightly
or wrongly, American Jews have traditionally felt less threatened. The plight
of the Red Indians, on the other hand, may be said to show how harmful a
lack of that survival instinct can prove to a minority which, like European
Jewry, is considered a nuisance by those in power.

My real shaking up came before I settled in America, in the early 1960s,
when I went into crimes perpetrated in a passion for my first series of Edinburgh Gifford Lectures on "The Deed and the Doer in the Bible." I found
that, of about a dozen cases of drunkenness in the Old Testament, from
Genesis to Judith, not one involved violence, or the remotest threat of it, on

the part of the drunk, whereas in all of them the drunk suffered or narrowly escaped serious hurt: a strong indication that it did not need the dispersion for drunkenness to be viewed as primarily endangering the drunk and to be avoided in the interest of self-preservation. The dispersion and its concomitants might still play a role in perpetuating and intensifying this attitude. But, in essence, it turned out to go back to a much earlier period.

Here are the biblical incidents.

Three drunks pay at once with their lives, and the death of two of them brings ruin to their dependents. Amnon, David's eldest son, ravishes his half-sister Tamar. Her full brother Absalom invites him to a sheep-shearing festivity, makes him drunk, and has him struck down.[11] Elah, king of Israel in the first quarter of the ninth century BC, while drunk, is slain by one of his officers, Zimri, who usurps his position and exterminates his entire house.[12] From the era of the Second Temple comes the book of Judith. As the Assyrian general Holofernes is marching on Jerusalem, this beautiful widow visits him in his camp and sits next to him at a feast at which he "drank so much as he had never drunk in his life." Later she is alone with him in his bedroom, he "lying on his bed, fast asleep, being exceedingly drunk." She cuts his head off with his own sword and, since all his servants, too, are in a drunken sleep, has no difficulty in making her way out. The next day the Israelites attack the invaders who, finding their commander assassinated, panic and flee.[13]

Toward the middle of the ninth century BC a drinking bout leads to the defeat of the Syrian King Benhadad by King Ahab of Israel, though Benhadad just manages to save his person. He is encamped before Ahab's capital Samaria and so convinced of his superiority that even when negotiations for Ahab's peaceful submission break down, he does not interrupt a banquet with the thirty-two minor kings who have joined forces with him. By the time the Israelites start a sortie, he is drunk and, informed that there are men coming out from the city, gives the tipsy instruction: "If they come out for peace, capture them alive, and if they come out for war, capture them alive!" Each of the two parts of this order is senseless in itself, and together they are a characteristic product of inebriation. While his leaderless army is being routed, he gets away on a horse with the help of some companions.[14]

Next, for Nabal who, at the height of his powers, is savagely crossed while drunk and loses his life as a result within little over a week. At this point in time, Saul still reigns and David is an outlaw surrounded by a band of irregulars. Nabal is about to celebrate the shearing of his sheep. David sends messengers to him with the request for a gift—what would nowadays be called protection money: they are to remind Nabal that David's troop not only refrained from stealing his animals but also stood between them and other gangs. Nabal rudely refuses. Possibly he is drunk already: when a servant of his informs his wife Abigail, adding that her husband "is such a son of Belial—of worthlessness—that one cannot speak to him,"[15] this may be a reference to intoxication. (Hannah, whom we shall discuss below, as Eli suspects her of being drunk, says, "Count not your handmaid a daughter of Belial."[16]) At any rate, Abigail, without telling him, has a number of asses loaded with an enormous supply of food and, with a suitable retinue, hastens to bring it to David. She arrives just in time to prevent him from taking murderous vengeance on Nabal and all his men. She showers him with praise while expressing contempt and hate for her husband whom, indeed, she speaks of as if he had already come to a villain's end: "May your enemies be as Nabal," she wishes David.[17] (The news of the rebellious Absalom's death is brought to David thus: "May the enemies of my lord the King be as that young man."[18]) The latter graciously accepts her presents. She returns home the same night to find Nabal drunk at his carousal—and this time the fact is stated in no ambiguous terms.[19] So it is only in the morning that she can report her exploit. He suffers a paralytic stroke, and another, fatal one ten days later, whereupon Abigail becomes David's wife.[20]

(According to 2 Samuel,[21] their son was called *Kil'abh*, a name probably connected with that of the hero from whom Nabal was descended, *Kalebh*.[22] To honor Nabal's memory in this way would be in line with David's conduct on other occasions. He composed the greatest dirge in world literature for Saul and Jonathan, whose death secured him the kingdom;[23] and the second-greatest for Absalom, who had risen against him and lost his life when the revolt was put down.[24] He executed the murderers of Saul[25] and of Saul's son Ishbosheth, claimant of the throne after his father's death.[26] He gave burial to seven sons of Saul after he had surrendered them for slaughter,[27] and he spared one crippled son of Jonathan.[28] Understandably, the Chronicler[29] substitutes a different name, *Dani'el*, "God has vindicated," perhaps in allusion to David's words as he hears of Nabal's death: "Blessed be the Lord who has fought the cause of my insult from the hand of Nabal.")[30]

(I had thought for years that it was a marvelous stroke of the Jewish—and Christian—religious genius to make David into the prototype of the pious king and, indeed, the pious soul in general, rather than the fundamentally decent Saul. Frail men need the example of one whose sins were really as scarlet yet became as white as snow, who acted atrociously, and not once only but again and again, yet again and again was capable of true repentance and found his way back to the light. Only recently did I discover that the Rabbis anticipated me. According to a Midrash,[31] when the Psalmist—King David—exclaims, "Against you have I sinned, that you might be justified," he means that his terrible crimes will help God when calling on transgressors to return: by reaccepting David, God has given proof that the road to forgiveness is open to all.)

The story of Nabal is not the only one where a drunk is duped, or at least an attempt is made to dupe him. Isaac is given both to eat and to drink by Jacob before mistakenly bestowing on him the blessing meant for Esau,[32] and Jacob in turn no doubt participates in the wedding feast thrown by Laban before mistakenly spending with the latter's elder daughter the night meant for Rachel.[33] No reason, however, to assume that either is actually drunk.

It is different with Joseph's brothers when they visit him in Egypt the second time—still not knowing that the high official entertaining them is Joseph: they do get drunk. The passage is sometimes said to show that, in the Old Testament epoch, even excessive drinking was not commonly disapproved.[34] But this is to be misled by the medieval arrangement of the text, which makes a chapter terminate at just this point. In the very next two sentences, however, we are told how Joseph has all sorts of things placed in the luggage of his brothers, and in particular, his own cup into Benjamin's sack in order subsequently to arraign him as thief. Evidently, this section must not be split off from what precedes: as is indeed recognized by many commentators,[35] Joseph takes advantage of the state his guests are in. After their awkward experiences in connection with their first visit,[36] but for their potations they might have watched too carefully for him to execute his design.[37]

An unsuccessful attempt to deceive a man in his cups is recorded of David. He commits adultery with Bathsheba while her husband Uriah is at the front. She becomes pregnant. He orders Uriah to come back and bring details of the campaign. After receiving the report, he encourages Uriah to see his wife: the child on the way would then be thought to be legitimately conceived. Uriah, however, declines to have intercourse while his comrades are on the battlefield, and he sleeps at the gate of the palace. David now invites him to his table and makes him drunk, hoping that in this state he will forget his scruples. Yet, even so, Uriah does not visit Bathsheba. He thus narrowly escapes belonging to the category of drunks fooled. True, had he succumbed, David would not have found himself driven to engineer his death. Nor, incidentally, would there have been a Solomon. But this sequel is not here relevant.[38]

In several instances, a drunk is sexually violated. The very first planter of a vineyard, Noah, overcome by drink, exposes himself and is shamelessly looked at by his son Ham.[39] Maybe there is a hint at even worse treatment in the description of his "awaking from his wine and knowing what his youngest son had done to him."[40] Then there is Lot, made drunk by his two daughters in successive nights, and in this state begetting two sons—the ancestors of Moab and Ammon.[41] Whether the legend is designed to extol these nations or to discredit them (or whether it did one thing at one stage and another at another), Lot, of whom we hear both times that "he knew not when she lay down nor when she arose,"[42] is definitely a sorry butt of abuse.

In a sense, the narrative of Hannah belongs here. She visits the sanctuary during a festival, when there is much merrymaking, and moves her lips in silent prayer. Eli, the priest, thinks she is drunk and reproves her. She is not, far from it; but if she were, she would very likely—as Eli sees it—attract base company and allow herself to be defiled.[43]

Lastly, Ahasuerus and Belshazzar. The book of Esther opens with a giant banquet at the former's Persian court. On the seventh day, "when the heart of the king was merry with wine," he orders Vashti, his lovely queen, to show herself before the guests. She, however, refuses, to his public disgrace.[44] Whether the Babylonian monarch Belshazzar qualifies for this list is doubtful: he may have been quite sober when, at a splendid feast, he remembered the sacred vessels plundered by Nebuchadnezzar from the Temple and had them brought in to drink from them. Two words in the original are susceptible to different interpretations. According to the traditional, Jewish one, he acted "under the influence of the wine." But the more common rendering "on tasting the wine"—in the sense of "on commencing the drinking"—is equally tenable; one might also translate "in connection with the wine," "when it came to the item of the wine."[45] (Heine, in his early poem "Belsatzar," follows the Jewish exegesis: *Des Königs Wangen leuchten Glut; Im Wein erwuchs ihm frecher Mut* [The king's cheeks glow with luster; in wine he found bold courage]. No allusion to intoxication occurs in Byron's "Vision of Belshazzar," a piece in his Hebrew Melodies.) Whichever line we adopt, his contempt for God brings about his death and the fall of his dynasty the very same night.[46]

Surely, this is selective reporting; such concentration on the misfortunes of the drunk, to the exclusion of what he may do others, cannot be accidental. True, there was no motorized traffic in those times, so what is today the commonest danger of drunkenness to the outside world did not exist. Nevertheless, Talmudic law does deal with a drunk guilty of a crime or sin,[47] and a glance at other ancient cultures suffices to show what was possible. Aristotle mentions a lawgiver doubling (instead of reducing) the penalty for offenses committed in drunkenness.[48] Demosthenes delivers a speech against a ruffian who, intoxicated, half-murdered a man he disliked.[49] From Alexander's biographers we hear how, inflamed with wine, he killed his friend Cleitus.[50]

Very likely, the peculiarly limited biblical presentation is due to two influences which, though generally quite different, for once happen to produce the same result: the nomadic attitude and the Wisdom attitude. Nomads wandering from place to place, ever encountering unknown perils, must not even temporarily take leave of their senses. Furthermore, both for them and for people hankering after a nomadic past, vinegrowing, representing an advanced stage of settled life, is an activity to be discouraged, which means to be depicted as doing no good to him who engages in it. Again, Wisdom's aim is to steer away its devotees from pitfalls and help them to well-earned prosperity. Hence, in dealing with impious or immoral conduct, it will appeal primarily to your own concerns; it will point out the undesirable consequences that will befall you.

A typical Wisdom sermon runs:[51] "Who has woe? Sorrow? Contentions? Babbling? Wounds without cause? Redness of eyes? They that tarry long at wine, they that go to seek spiced wine ... You shall be as he that lies down in the midst of the sea or upon the top of a mast. They have struck me (you shall say) and I was not smarting, they have beaten me and I did not notice." The neglect of violence emanating from the drunk becomes all the more striking when we compare a tribute to the power of alcohol in an anecdote of Greek provenance, preserved in 1 Esdras[52] and Josephus.[53] Here, "when they are in their cups, they forget their love both to friends and brethren, and a little after draw their swords."[54]

The Rabbis recognized this feature of Wisdom when they declared[55] that the chief sanction with which it threatened wrongdoers was expressed in the maxim from the book of Proverbs:[56] "Evil pursues sinners." Modern scholars agree, only many of them deplore it. "In spite of this high standard of ethics," laments an annotator of Proverbs,[57] "... goodness is almost always motivated by personal interest or success.... In the numerous warnings against illicit dealings with the strange woman, the man is told to abstain because he will be impoverished, or he will be physically weakened, or he will die prematurely. There is no comment on the sinfulness of the act...." He does not seem to be sensitive to the wisdom—and honesty—of Wisdom.

An inspection of the incidents listed supports my twofold explanation. We shall see, however, that the Wisdom factor far outweighs the nomadic one. Let us follow the order of the Bible.

That the ill fate of Noah, the inventor of grape culture, reflects nomadic prejudice is widely accepted.[58] It is directed especially against the depravity of the Canaanites inhabiting Palestine: Ham, it should be recalled, is introduced as the father of Canaan.[59] Whether there is a connection with non-

Jewish myths and cults—celebrations of vegetation deities and emascula-
tion or self-emasculation of zealots on such occasions—may be left open;
also, whether a nomadic element perhaps plays a part even at the inception
of these non-Jewish phenomena. Of more relevance is the possibility that
the tale has gone through some Wisdom editing. The elaborate account of
how Shem and Japheth manage to cover their father without setting eyes on
him smacks of the subtlety expected of a sage—"Good understanding gives
favor, but the way of the treacherous is rugged,"[60] or "A prudent man sees the
evil and hides himself, but the simple pass on and suffer for it"[61]—and even
their smooth, brotherly cooperation accords with the Wisdom ideal: "Two
are better than one, because they have a good reward for their labor."[62]

Cooperation between two sisters is conspicuous in the coming into existence of Moab and Ammon, and the counseling of the younger by the elder
and the latter's showing the way are also suggestive. It may not be enough
to postulate a Wisdom hand at work, but at least this saga would be savored
and sponsored by Wisdom circles.

The narratives of Isaac's elevation of Jacob, whom he mistakes for Esau,
and Jacob's marriage with Leah, whom he mistakes for Rachel, are not, we
saw above, strictly in point since, though there has been drinking, neither
Isaac nor Jacob are said to be in a drunken state. Still, it may be worth observing that the contribution of Wisdom to this cycle is considerable. It is evident precisely in the superbly fitting retaliation meted out to the over-clever
deceiver; Jacob, having obtained an advantage by impersonating his elder
brother, is himself outwitted by Leah's impersonation of her younger sister[63]—a grand illustration of Wisdom's slogan that "a man is repaid according to his works."[64]

The Wisdom bias of the epic of Joseph is well known; no need here to
enlarge on it.

Less attention has been paid to such traits in the story of Hannah. The
boorishness of her fellow wife Peninnah bears out the assertion in the book
of Proverbs[65] that "the unloved woman" in a polygamous setup belongs
to "the three things under which the earth trembles." She taunts—literally, "vexes"[66]—the as yet childless Hannah, who suffers grievous anguish.

"A stone is heavy and sand is weighty, but a fool's vexation is heavier than both";[67] "It is better to live in the wilderness than with a woman of contentions and vexation."[68] Hannah's meek response conforms to the ideal: "The vexation of a fool is known at once, but the prudent one covers insult."[69] Particularly significant is the happy ending when Samuel grows up "good with the Lord as well as with men"[70]—the true follower of Wisdom who is encouraged in Proverbs[71] to "find favor and good understanding in the sight of God and man."

A formal detail may be added. Hannah's husband Elkanah comforts her: "Am I not better for you than ten sons?"[72] In Wisdom guidance, we often find the comparison "such-and-such is better than such-and-such." We learned above that "Two are better than one,"[73] and presently we shall adduce a eulogy of Wisdom which "is better than corals."[74] Elkanah's words seem to echo this style. Who knows, there may have been a proverb (whether anterior to this tale or later): "A kind husband—or relation or friend—is better for a woman than a multitude of sons." At the end of the book of Ruth, it may be recalled, the people felicitating Naomi refer to Ruth as "your daughter-in-law who is better for you than seven sons."[75]

It is just conceivable that the names Hannah and Peninnah are meaningful opposites. (Both, of course, figure here for the first time.) The former is connected with "grace" or "favor"—Hebrew *hen*—a major aspiration of Wisdom. It occurs in the line just cited, "favor in the sight of God and man," and it is "to be preferred to silver and gold."[76] The latter, Peninnah, signifies "coral." Corals are mentioned in Wisdom literature five times,[77] invariably to be declared worthless compared with Wisdom or with a woman who comes up to the Wisdom pattern.[78] This name, then, may allude to its bearer's glamorous position as a mother of many children, yet devoid of the most precious quality. Nor should we overlook the fact that, in the outcome, in accordance with Wisdom teaching, quality triumphs: Hannah gives birth to the nation's leader. It has been found remarkable[79] that, though Peninnah plays a minor role, her name should be transmitted; on the basis of the foregoing conjecture, this is readily explicable. How far it may affect the question of historicity lies beyond the scope of my inquiry.

The chapter about Nabal virtually advertises its affinity with Wisdom. His name means "fool," more precisely, the kind of fool given to unconscionable actions. His wife expressly calls attention to it when she confides to David:[80] "As his name is, so is he; Fool (Nabal) is his name and folly is with him." He is wealthy and domineering, the type singled out for condemnation in Proverbs; another of the three things under which the earth trembles (besides the unloved woman) is "a fool when he is filled with food."[81] Moreover, "Overbearing speech becomes not a fool."[82] He is described as "hard and evil in his doings."[83] As for "hard," we read in Proverbs that "He who hardens his heart will fall into calamity,"[84] and "He who is cautioned but hardens his neck shall suddenly be broken."[85] "Evil" is the danger most to be avoided by a sage, as the Wisdom writers never tire of proclaiming.[86] By contrast, his wife is "of good understanding and of beautiful form,"[87] the embodiment of excellence from the point of view of Wisdom. We may recall the advice to "find favor and good understanding in the sight of God and man."[88] The combination of intelligence with looks recurs in Esther[89] and Judith,[90] each in her way representing Wisdom's perfect woman.[91] Of male sages who are handsome at the same time, Joseph is an early example.[92]

Nabal's wife is called Abigail, signifying something like "my father rejoices." Possibly the name is intended as a foil to her husband's. Whereas "the father of a fool has no joy,"[93] "the father of the righteous will greatly rejoice, and he that begets a wise child will have joy in him."[94] The latter saying is followed by an exhortation to choose the path that will bring about the blissful alternative: "Let your father and mother have joy, and her that bore you rejoice."[95]

Wisdom motifs abound in the account of David's adultery. He has clearly not "made a covenant with his eyes"[96] to refrain from being attracted by forbidden fruit. Both he and his accomplice Joab throughout act in the most wickedly devious fashion: "crooked in their ways and perverse in their paths,"[97] with "haughty eyes, a lying tongue, and hands that shed innocent blood."[98] Yet what commences by giving pleasure turns into a fearful embarrassment: "The treacherous shall be trapped in their own crafty device."[99] The historical analogy drawn in this narrative between Uriah's death and Abimelech's, both perishing under the walls of an enemy fortress,[100] also smacks of Wisdom, and even more, the prophet Nathan's parable. The Wisdom flavor of David's punishment, meticulously adapted to his crime, is generally appreciated:[101] "A man is repaid according to his works,"[102] "The Lord will pluck up the house of the proud,"[103] "A man that is laden with the blood of a person shall hasten his step unto the pit."[104] A detail deserves notice: David, guilty of hidden sin, is to incur public retaliation.[105] "There is no darkness," we learn in the book of Job,[106] "where the workers of iniquity may hide themselves; God strikes them in the open sight of others." Or "The murderer kills the poor and needy and in the night is as a thief; the eye also of the adulterer waits for the twilight, saying, No eye shall see us, and disguises his face; they are exalted for a little while, but are gone and brought low."[107]

The saga of Tamar illustrates Wisdom's inexorable law of retribution in more than one way. What she experiences at the hand of Amnon and he at that of Absalom is heaven's answer to David's appropriation of Bathsheba and disposal of Uriah. At the same time, Amnon has deserved his death by his cruel deed—called "folly," and he a "fool" for perpetrating it,[108] terms we came across in the tale of Nabal.[109] Jonadab, who first works out for Amnon the cunning method by which he may get Tamar into his bedroom and then becomes the confidant of Absalom in the planning of Amnon's murder, represents pernicious companionship, evil inspiration, perverted intelligence. He is introduced as Amnon's "friend,"[110] but is plainly of the false, hurtful kind of whom Wisdom writers warn us.[111] He gives advice, but it is the counsel of the wicked in which not to walk, according to the Psalmist.[112] He is labeled as "very wise,"[113] but what might be a positive quality is turned into a negative one by being divorced from the fear of the Lord.[114] (Tyre and Sidon are characterized as "very wise" in the same sense by Zechariah.[115]) A detail reminiscent of Wisdom is Absalom's admonition of Tamar to suffer in silence—so he can prepare his revenge on her behalf: "A man of discernment holds his peace."[116] Just so, Jacob, when Dinah was dishonored, kept silent until his sons returned from the field.[117]

Neither nomadic nor Wisdom ingredients are detectable in the reports of Elah's assassination and Benhadad's discomfiture. In view of the link between Deuteronomy and Wisdom, however, it is worth observing that the negotiations between Benhadad and Ahab contain a sophisticated allusion to a Deuteronomic ordinance. It lays down[118] that if you require a pledge when making a loan, you may not shame the borrower by entering his house to get it but must wait outside for him to bring it to you. Benhadad demands that Ahab become his tributary and, by way of security for good behavior, surrender members of his family as hostages and valuable objects as pledges. Ahab consents; but he decides on resistance when Benhadad adds the humiliating term that his men be admitted into the Israelite capital and its palaces to select and carry off the hostages and pledges.[119]

That the book of Esther owes much to Wisdom categories has been established by Shemaryahu Talmon.[120] He may indeed be going a little too far.

Again, it is an avowed design of the tale of Belshazzar's last night (in which drunkenness may or may not play a part) to commemorate Daniel as a sage superior to his Chaldean rivals who practice at court.

As for the book of Judith, the heroine is expressly lauded as the most accomplished wise woman.[121] Besides there are: her theological argumentation, at times reminiscent of Job;[122] her invocation of historical precedent;[123] her use of ambiguous formulation;[124] and, above all, her supreme self-discipline and resourcefulness in the service of a worthy cause.

Broadly, then, the scenes we have examined are either formulated by Wisdom or transmitted with its approval, hence the one-sided message. If it be objected that I am making Wisdom a very pervasive force in Old Testament literature, the answer is an admission: it was. At any rate, it is safe to conclude that, long before the Middle Ages, Jewish feelings about drunkenness were shaped by the scriptural approach which, it may be added, remains much the same in the New Testament as in the Old.

JEALOUSY, ZEAL (QIN'A)

Jealousy as a religious-political concept has an interesting history. The emotion is essentially momentary. However, while it may break out in spurts, it *au fond* refers to a person tending to break out of an ordinary state of mind and hence given to a tense, wholehearted dedication to a cause. True, the verb "to be zealous" mostly refers to action, so it is better to speak of "a display of zeal." In the canonical Old Testament we read of those who are zealous on God's behalf. Phinehas, a grandson of Aaron, when Moses seemed passive in the face of the men beginning to introduce heathen women into the camp, speared one of the detestable couples. This was a spontaneous outburst of religious fury, ratified, however, by God, who informed Moses of his full approval. The incident occupied an important place in postbiblical Judaism, as showing that there comes a moment when extreme supralegal action is called for. He counted as the first zealot.[125] Elijah convinces the people of God's superiority when he has 450 priests of the heathen god Baal slaughtered for the purity of the cult of the one God.[126] Jehu wipes out Ahab's family and the followers of Baal. This last instance shows that it is not a sudden flare-up. Jehu invites the leader of the Rechabites to accompany him and "see my zeal for the Lord" and then proceeds to trap the followers of Baal.[127] The act is far from being a criminal one. The fact that it emanates from a strong impulse does not prevent a demonstration of imperturbability on the occasion. Quite the contrary, such an attitude is to be viewed as exceptionally meritorious, one that is to be cultivated.

The relation between worshipers of God and those seen to be their enemies is often warlike. There is no feeling of tension with the law. Jehu acts as a good king should. In all cases the act is against an alien world, but this aspect is not inherent in the concept of zeal. It is simply the result of the Hebrew religion fighting other cults. However, from Maccabean times, in regard to these incidents, the national aspect is stressed and the concept of zeal is itself affected.

Fierceness, inner and bodily, is represented in a chapter from Genesis fervently appealed to by Judith in her supplication before her venture to rescue her people: her and her husband's ancestor Simeon, who took horrendous vengeance on the ruiner of Dinah and his whole clan.[128] While Jacob and his family dwelled at Shechem, the chieftain's son slept with her and, earnestly in love with her, asked for her hand, supported by his father. They offered a rich bride-price and, on top of it, general intermarriage from then on, indeed, a merger into "one people."[129] However, Jacob's sons Simeon and Levi (the latter not figuring in Judith), full brothers of Dinah, held the outrage unpardonable. They declared they would accede to the proposal if all the men of Shechem underwent circumcision. The citizenry agreed. On the third day after the operation, the circumcised being incapable of fight, Simeon and Levi mowed them down and appropriated their wives, children, and goods.

Obviously, Simeon supports Judith's unbending stand. This is not to overlook a marked difference in accent between the two episodes. Simeon's is a more personal one, retribution for the dishonoring of his sister. Judith identifies with him, not the woman. What provokes his inexorable severity is a "thus shall not be done" to an Israelitess: Judith quotes this very phrase.[130] From a simple power-political standpoint, the implanting of Jacob's migratory flock into a flourishing settlement might actually be a gain. But Simeon deems the price too high: Dinah, no matter whether or how far she collaborated, emerged as a living corpse—with no subsequent history.[131] Judith, otherwise pretty expansive on the affair, does not give her name. Simeon will risk the whole world's rage[132] rather than acquiesce in this monstrous offense. Judith's mission is to combine both roles: to cut down the officer directing an assault on the nation, and to strike a blow, like Simeon, against abuse of a Hebrew woman.

Originally, Simeon's (and Levi's) action is willed self-help—Jacob and moderate Rabbis condemn it—and shows no trace of religious zeal. Judith does mention zeal in her victory over haughty foreigners. This is enough to put her action in line with those of Phinehas, Elijah, and Jehu. The book of Jubilees also attributes zeal to Simeon and Levi because they took a stance against intermarriage. Naturally, the Maccabeans are zealous. Indeed, the book of Judith may draw on Maccabean ideas. The scene depicting the outbreak of their revolt is modeled on Phinehas' deed, his name being mentioned, as it is again along with Elijah's in Mattathias' last words.[133]

In 1 Maccabees, Mattathias slays the Jew who offers the Syrian sacrifice together with the Syrian officer who told him to present it. This officer corresponds to the Midianite lady killed by Phinehas in Num 25:6–15. The Old Testament heroes are individuals. But Elijah also inspires all the people, and so Mattathias calls on his compatriots to join in being "zealous." What is to some extent new is the organization: a permanent band of men zealous for

God. Insurrectionist groups show no niceties for the legal process, but the Old Testament story of Phinehas is now interpreted as a lesson that, in critical times, in regard to certain offenses, there can be a trial. This is worked out in the rabbinic comment on Phinehas. The anti-Roman zealots among the Rabbis upheld the doctrine and, curiously, *Mishnah Sanh.* 9:6 legislates for it: "If a man stole a sacred vessel or cursed by Kosem [meaning uncertain] or made an Aramean [Syrian] woman his paramour, the zealots may fall upon him."

To some extent, then, the Zealots may fall upon one who has intercourse with a heathen, and upon those who commit two other mysterious crimes. The exemption is not on the ground of emotion interfering with self-control but that the action deserves praise, although in the Mishnah the permission perhaps represents a halfhearted political concession. For the opponents of the zealots, their crime, if anything, is worse. In the New Testament, in Acts 5:17, zeal is ascribed to the Sadducean Sanhedrin apparently in a question unconnected with the Gentiles. It is directed at Peter and the apostles to deter their activity of preaching and healing.

In other examples there is a national coloring, although we must remember that the defense of pure tradition often inevitably coincides with an anti-foreign bias. Twice those Jews not believing in the claims about Jesus are filled with zeal as multitudes of Greeks listen to Paul.[134] On a third occasion, traditional-believing Jews are zealous for the law, having been informed that Paul suggested to those Jews living among the Gentiles to give it up.[135] In Rom 10:2, Paul acknowledges the Jews' zeal for God in a chapter dominated by the problem of Jews and Greeks. In Gal 1:14, Paul contrasts his early zeal for the traditions of the fathers with his present preaching to the Gentiles.[136]

A writer may think of zeal without an express reference to it. The account of the Levites in the incident of the Golden Calf furnishes an illustration.[137] So too possibly does the account about Jesus, on the point of death, when he "cried with a loud cry." At some stage during the course of its transmission, might it have been the shout of a zealot and over time its intent been modified? In the time of the Maccabees, Mattathias "cried with a loud voice, 'I and my sons will continue to walk in the covenant of our ancestors.'"[138] In a rabbinic comment on Phinehas, Phinehas "began to cry out," but it was not anything specific, if Kuhn is right.[139] Prior to his saving deed, there is the killing of the couple, a demonstration of zeal. If Jesus' cry has been modified, the reinterpretation in the Gospels is understandable. In his Gospel, John has no cry at all but the statement of Jesus, "It is finished."[140] For some interpreters the declaration is a triumphant remark because they see it in combination with the shout in the Synoptics. However, as John contains "and he bowed his head," this is unlikely. John seeks to convey the fundamental devotion of Jesus. Yet John, alone of all the evangelists, in the programmatic cleansing of the Temple, associates zeal with the ministry of Jesus. Indeed, he introduces zeal as that which will cause Jesus' end.[141] John quotes Ps 69:9 as being remembered by the disciples: "the zeal of thine house hath consumed me." So despite the absence of the last cry from the cross in John, we definitely, though subtly, are invited to bear the attribute of zeal in mind when reading of his death.

MADNESS

There is no crime associated with madness in biblical sources. The nearest we come to it is with King Saul. Even here, although there are outbursts on specific occasions, the madness is a drawn-out affair. It is not sudden action that is followed by clearance.

The Latin juristic term for an "insane person," *furiosus*, literally meant "raging."[142] When I moved to the United States from England, I was struck by a contemporary American colloquialism, "mad" for "angry." As a matter of fact, American, as so often, carries on an old English usage—which does not make its continued prominence in the States any less significant. In Acts 26:11, in the translation of the Geneva Bible, Paul confesses that at one time he was "exceedingly mad against" the followers of Jesus. This sense is attested from around 1300, and it may well owe something to the influence of Latin.

The Romans had no doubt about the closeness of insanity and rage. Cicero declares wrath, *ira*, akin to insanity, *insania*, and he quotes Ennius as saying that *ira* is the beginning of *insania*.[143] It is, however, a very general approach. Greek *mainomai* denotes both, "to be furious" and "to be insane," and when

Heracles becomes insane, he is "like a bull in act to charge."[144] (Modern psychiatrists might think him better off for venting his feelings.) No wonder, then, the designations are interchangeable, either way: "raging" may come to mean "insane" as in Latin or Greek, particularly the American variety. In all this, the typical insanity is of the aggressive sort, not, say, quietly incongruous. Also, it seems to be conceived of as coming out of the blue, not, say, as a congenital, long-drawn-out development.

Furiosus describes an external, visible indication—you see the man raging—as does "mad," allied to *mutare*, originally meaning "changed"—the man appears different. By contrast, "insane" constitutes a rather general, abstract classification. Hence it is more subdued, more polite. Its negative form, "in-sane," "not sane," has a further mitigating effect, pointing to something less crass than the forthright "sick" or (in Latin) *morbosus*—just as, say, "unwise" is tamer than "silly" or "stupid." Cicero distinguishes *insania* from *furor*: the former includes all folly, *stultitia*.[145]

In about the earliest passage where *insanus* occurs, in a play by Plautus, a courtesan mixes up one twin brother with another and thanks him for a generosity he never showed her.[146] He remarks to his slave that she must be "either insane or drunk," *aut insania aut ebria*. Plainly, the insanity is of a very tolerable nature, quite unlike that of a *furiosus*. In modern English, as "insane" despite its intrinsic moderation ended up by expressing things quite unmistakably, a new way of toning down was introduced: its rendering by "unsound." "Of unsound mind" is even more detached, spares the feelings of those concerned still more. American tends to go in the opposite direction: "sick" is rapidly coming up in this field and may yet replace "insane." Hasting's *Encyclopaedia of Religion and Ethics* offers a characteristic arrangement. You will not find a heading "madness" at all. If you look up "lunacy," you are referred to "insanity." Under "insanity" there is a discussion of the prevalent psychiatric doctrines; nothing historical whatever. The historical stuff is all assigned to the entry "possession."

Hazard and Louisell some time ago published a fascinating article on the question of why in quite a few systems, if a criminal sentenced to death becomes insane, he is not executed.[147] They come up with various reasons, all of them worth noting; nowadays special importance is attached—rightly—to the thirst for vengeance which is not appeased if the culprit does not know what is done to him, does not suffer terror and pain. However, a major factor is mentioned neither by these authors nor any others who have gone into the subject, namely, the feeling that the insane man is somebody else. If you hanged him, you would be hanging the wrong man.

"Mad" initially denotes "changed." Admittedly, a person may be changed without becoming somebody else. But the notion that, in severe disturbance, the very identity is affected seems widespread and deep-rooted. From the seventeenth century we find "changeling" employed in the sense of "an imbecile." The earliest quotation in the Oxford Dictionary remarks that "a changeling is not one child changed for another, but one child on a sudden changed from itself." This comes rather near substitution of a different person. Incidentally, again, the kind of insanity contemplated is one coming on a man out of the blue in the course of his life.

In Latin, *mentem alienare alicui*, "to change, alienate, the mind to somebody," signifies "to render somebody mad," and *alienatus mente, sensibus, animo*, "to be changed, alienated, in mind, senses, spirit," signifies "to be mad."[148] The ease with which the reference to mind or the like can drop out, and one can say absolutely *alienare aliquem*, "to change, alienate, somebody," or *alienatus*, "to be changed, alienated," is suggestive.[149] The latter phraseology does smack of an inroad into identity. While in English one mostly adds a qualification, "alienation of mind," in French it is quite in order to speak simply of an *aliéné*, "one changed, alienated." (The English "alienist" comes from the French *aliéniste*.) German *verrückt*, literally "transposed," starts in the same way as Latin—Goethe's Gretchen laments, *Mein armer Kopf is mir verrückt*, "My poor head is transposed to me"—and here also it becomes usual to apply the attribute to the person as such, *er ist verrückt*, "he is transposed." *Demens*, "demented" or "out of your mind," may still leave the person in place, but when we declare that a person is "beside himself," *hors de soi, ausser sich*, it means that he has left, is no longer there, what is left is not him. The connection with "ecstasy," "a standing outside," is obvious.[150] So is that with possession, a highly influential and flexible concept. Sometimes the old person is still there; sometimes he is gone. In the New Testament narrative of the Gadarene swine,[151] while the devils are at work, where exactly is the man?

Modern writers may well not take these attributes seriously enough. King, translator of Cicero, regards the latter's *exire ex potestate*, "to step from one's control," as equivalent to Greek *existasthai heatou*, "to step out from oneself."[152] This is definitely to blunt the meaning of the Greek, which goes much further than the Latin;[153] or rather, Cicero, not comfortable with the idea of a man going outside himself, moderates the Greek.

Certainly, ecstasy, possession, substitution of one person for another may all be for good as well as evil. What I am suggesting is that we must not forget about them when dealing with people's instinctive approach to insanity. And, incidentally, the problem of identity which I think plays a role in this area is likely to play an even greater one in the future if surgical and chemical intervention increases. Anyhow, the situation discussed by Hazard and Louisell is not the only one where the law appears to pay tribute to the notion that the madman is a different person. Even in countries generally disapproving of divorce, it is sometimes admitted where your partner becomes afflicted by severe mental illness. He is no longer the same; he is indeed not there.

WRATH

Like jealousy, wrath is not necessarily a very temporary emotion. In his *Theologisches Wörterbuch zum Neuen Testament* 5 ([Stuttgart, 1960], 394), Gerhard Kittel distinguishes holy, just anger and selfish anger along modern lines, but this is unhistorical. Apart from throwing together all Hebrew terms, he simply applies one-sided, modern standards: whenever anyone's self is involved, this element makes it unholy. But poor Potiphar! He believed his wife. The Old Testament does not regard this as unholy at all, just unfortunate. This is also true even in Esau versus Jacob. The modern doctrine is to prepare for the New Testament, but here again old categories continued. Within the Christian community wrath is, of course, wrong; but to manifest it to the outside world is largely permissible. We must compare like with like. The New Testament story is about the rise of a sect, so the variety of human relations and the complications of the Old Testament are absent. It is surely questionable that in the New Testament community a man who finds out about the seducer of his wife might not be angry.

RASH VOWS

Vows are often made under pressure, and hence there is warning against them because, when the danger is over, there might be regret for having made them. But we should not exaggerate. Jephthah vowed not whatever, but whoever first meets him. It is neither rashness nor a slip. Rabbinic exegesis, bent on mitigating his ruthlessness, makes him vow not "whoever would first meet him" but "whatever"—thinking of a goat or a dog.[154]

The verb *bata'* is rendered "to vow rashly." But this is as if, because many marriages are rash, a foreigner renders the verb "to marry" as "to marry rashly." Leviticus 5:4 concerns someone who swears an oath (*bata'*) "to do harm or good," then forgets that he has done so and, realizing that he has forgotten, erroneously transgresses. It is not about doing certain acts for worse or for better. The Targum has *perash*, "to utter distinctly," and the LXX has *diastello*, "to pronounce." Would the prevalent view require investigation in an individual case? Even if not, why should it be rash?[155]

Numbers 30:7(6) has the noun *mibhta'*: a married woman binds herself in some matter. If her husband at once cancels the utterance (*mibhta'*), it is invalid; if he does not, the utterance is good. Here quite clearly her utterance is the equivalent of *shebbua'* (oath) of Num 30:4 (3) of the daughter. It would be terrible if a premeditated oath did not fall under this judgment. There is no trace of rashness. The Targum and the LXX read it the same way. In Ps 106:33 we have, "they provoked his [Moses'] spirit and he spake inadvisedly with his lips." But it is God who swears that Moses is not to enter into Canaan. There is no rashness. When Sirach speaks of glory and dishonor through speaking, he clearly means speaking in a neutral manner (Sir 5:13). Critics recognize this for Sirach, though not yet fully: one translator has "glory and dishonor through babbling"—so strong is the prejudice.[156] It would be quite extraordinary if ancient Hebrew law gave special treatment to rash undertakings.

CHAPTER 5

NEGLIGENCE

Negligence ordinarily falls between the deliberate and the faultless. But there are different kinds of negligence. In the religious sphere there can be negligent faith.

Neglect of God; His Will; the Hour. In certain areas of life—religion, for example—negligence constitutes a fundamental sin as when one is heedless of God's commandments or, in the New Testament, when one fails to recognize the decisive manifestation of the hour. A constant formula of Moses is that one must do according to all the commandments of the Torah. The Israelites are warned to love God with all their might, to think of him and all his commandments constantly, whether they are lying down or getting up. The foolish virgins of Matt 25:1–13 omit oil for their lamps, and the consequence of their negligence is terrible. When the bridegroom is delayed they run out of oil and go off to buy more. But then he does appear, admits the wise virgins who had taken extra oil along with them, and when the negligent ones seek admission to the wedding the door has been shut. "Watch therefore, for ye know neither the day nor the hour wherein the son of man cometh."[1] Attachment to God and doing his will is one's chief destiny, and any wavering is a deliberate choice of wrong. The duty is comparable to the all-embracing duty of a general or the commander of a ship.

"To Forget"; "To Sleep"; "To Guard"; "To Remember"; "To Watch." If one is forgetful in the arms of a paramour, it is not just negligence but worse, a dereliction of duty. The love of God is comparable. To sleep implies an inclination to spiritual death, laziness, darkness. On the other hand, to guard or

keep the Sabbath and to remember God and his deeds means to watch and to be awake. Sometimes, in later writings, metaphors acquire literal life: in the Dead Sea Scrolls to fall asleep in the assembly is a grave offense. A Passover company breaks up if one of its members falls asleep. The matter is dramatically illustrated in the scene in the Garden of Gethsemane when the disciples of Jesus fall asleep. That particular Passover fellowship breaks up at a crucial moment in its existence.

In general, however, sleeping and watchfulness are about one's entire attitude. To forget God is not just like forgetting to press a button, but is something active; it is about going a different way. To forget the slavery in Egypt or to forget to wipe out the Amalekites is not a lapse but a decision and an active rejection. Significantly, this use of "forget" in modern language is occasionally found in regard to women. For the man to forget her means not a lapse but a forsaking, usually for another.

Negligent Transgressions. Still, the loyalty required by God is far more stringent. However, once loyalty is given, negligent transgressions are not too serious, at least ultimately. A sacrifice can take care of the matter. This very fact—for example, that to forget the date of a festival happens easily—shows that forgetting God or the commandments or the hour is a far more active matter.

Law. In the Bible, negligence in law comes much nearer to our views today, though the convergence is far from uniform. (Even our views are less uniform than might appear from the textbooks.) In Roman law the development is said to be from objective to subjective standards of liability. But certain factors indicate that we must beware of simplification. One, *dolus* [fraud, deceit] is subjective. Two, even a subjective standard like *neglegentia* requires a minimum of external objective evidence. Three, subjective elements contribute to the formation of objective standards; for example, the idea behind *custodia* is that certain mishaps can ordinarily be prevented with care. Four, developments are slower or faster in different areas, say, the dangers of a pit and the role of deposit in Hebrew law, sale and deposit in Roman law. Five, hypercriticism makes some developments later than in fact. Still, as in most systems, the evolution is roughly from the objective to the subjective. A mandatory is originally liable for *dolus*, then also for negligence. Commodatory goes from *custodia* to negligence. There is a convergence of movement.

NEGLIGENCE

The subject of Exod 22:6–8 is deposit,[2] most important in ancient times with no banksafes and police: you might easily need a friend to whom to entrust your valuables—money and utensils above all. Verses 6–7 are confined to these.

Verse 8 mentions beasts. No doubt they were soon taken under the contract, but that they were not part of the original formulation is clear from several inconsistencies, one of them that in Exod 22:9 the handing over of a beast to care for automatically constitutes a distinct agreement. To begin with, where a beast is concerned, the law takes note only of the relation owner-shepherd, and it takes a while before it acknowledges the possibility of depositing a beast with a nonprofessional in the same way as an inanimate object. The raiment appearing after the beasts is a yet later addition, for the sake of technical completeness; in actual fact, once the case came up, it can hardly ever have been looked at differently from utensils.

If, when called on to return the object, a depository alleges that it got stolen, an oracle will determine whether he has embezzled it. That hurdle cleared, he is not accountable. He was doing a service to the depositor, hence is not, unless proved fraudulent, to be saddled with the loss.

Except for the substitution of an oath for the oracle,[3] Tannaitic law is basically the same. "The gratuitous guardian takes an oath about everything," says the Mishnah: so long as he can swear that he did not act dishonestly, none of the various ways in which the object might become unreturnable involves him in compensation. That in principle, in this period, his liability is still tied to breach of faith and not yet extended to negligence may be gathered from the interpretations put on the clause "for every matter of treachery."[4] For the Hillelites, it means that he is answerable not only if he misappropriates directly but also if he does so through a servant or agent; for the Shammaites, that he is answerable not only if he completes the offense but also if he displays the wrongful intent. Moreover, both Philo and Josephus represent *dolus* as the criterion.[5] According to the former, a depositary swears that he has neither misappropriated any part of the object nor acted in collusion with the thief nor told a lie when pleading theft by a third party; according to the latter, that he lost the object through no knavery and wickedness and used none of it for himself.

Nevertheless, already the Tannaites treat as breach of faith cases of gross carelessness—for instance, a depositary letting his small children look after the coins[6]—which nowadays would count as negligence. In this context, they make use of the notion of *derekh*, "way," "manner," which plays an enormous part in their thinking generally. He must pay up "if he did not guard in the manner of guardians"; he need not if he did.

In the Amoraic sources, we find a new term, *peshi'a*. While deriving from the biblical *pesha'*, "treachery," it has the wider meaning of "fault": a depositary is now liable for both fraud and negligence. In a well-organized society one would expect more of him than at the earlier stage. An Amoraic argument runs:[7] since a paid guardian is liable for theft by a third party, akin to "force" (robbery by an armed band), he is *a fortiori* liable for simple loss, akin to *peshi'a*. Its Tannaitic precursor is preserved in a Baraitha of R. Ishmael,[8] without *peshi'a*: since a paid guardian is liable for theft, akin to "force," he is *a fortiori* liable for simple loss, not akin to "force." The formation of *peshi'a* from *pesha'* underlines the observation made above: the main route leading from liability for "treachery" to that for "fault" was via an extension of the former category—more and more careless conduct was assigned to it, till at last the need for a fresh though related, more comprehensive criterion was recognized.

However, an oath "I have not been at fault" is problematic. A man knows whether or not he is guilty of fraud, "has put his hand unto his neighbor's goods"; he cannot really judge whether or not he is guilty of negligence. A fourth-century decision has it that a depositary's inability to remember where he placed the object constitutes fault.[9] A common case, however, would be where he believes he remembers and, as he cannot find it, concludes that somebody stole it.[10]

Maimonides, drawing on the Mishnah, prefers the oath "I have guarded in the manner of guardians." His reason may well be that awkwardness of "I have not been at fault."

Exodus 22:9–12 deals with the shepherd. Being a professional, he is treated with greater stringency: if a beast got stolen, he must replace it. However, if he can bring witnesses that a beast died a natural death, fell to its death, or was carried off by brigands, he is free; and even in the absence of witnesses, he is free provided he can swear that he has not misappropriated it. He is free also if a beast fell victim to wild animals, provided he produces some remnants as evidence.

This is the type of liability the Romans called *custodia*. The idea is to counter negligence as well as *dolus*. However, in this phase of societal structure, it would be impossible to establish the presence or absence of negligence on each occasion. Hence the law divides the pleas a shepherd might advance into two classes: one where, since negligence is as a rule committed, the beast must be replaced even if, in the particular case, reasonable precautions were taken; another where, since as a rule negligence cannot be charged, it need not be replaced even if, in the particular case, better precautions would have made a difference. In general, a shepherd, if careful, can prevent theft by a third party: accordingly, if such a theft occurs, he is liable. In general, a shepherd, even if careful, cannot prevent natural death, death by a fall, capture by an armed gang, attack by wild animals: accordingly, he is not liable for any of these. Liability for *custodia* is liability not for negligence—that would mean probing into each incident—but for objectivized negligence, for what is usually due to negligence—so that the individual incident need not be investigated.

Whereas the depositary's guilt or innocence is established by an oracle, the shepherd's is by an oath. For the latter, businesslike relationship the more advanced method is used sooner than for the former, noncommercial one. The Rabbis, as already noted, apply the oath to deposit as well.

In Tannaitic law, the regulation is extended from a shepherd to the hirer of an animal: in the latter case as in the former, the contract effects a balanced quid pro quo (whereas in deposit and borrowing the benefit goes to one party only). How early the rules are applied (mutatis mutandis) to inanimate objects as well as beasts it is difficult to say; doubtless they were before the end of the Tannaitic era. The very terms "paid guardian" and "hirer" indicate a generalizing trend.

A remarkable Tannaitic achievement is the comprehensive term 'ones, "force," which designates the accidents exempting from reparation. While some cases not envisaged in Exodus are subsumed under it—say, the beast is killed by a serpent—others at first sight falling under it are excluded because the mishap is due to the guardian's inadequacy or rashness—say, the beast is killed by a single wolf, or it falls to death from a precipice to which the guardian led it.

By Amoraic times, what looks like "force" by and large exonerates only in the absence of negligence. Somewhat incongruously, absence of negligence does not exonerate in the case of theft by a third party. It is the latter twist alone that now distinguishes the position of a paid guardian or hirer from that of a depositary, liable in Amoraic law for fraud and negligence; though doubtless, in judging what constitutes negligence, greater leniency will always be shown to the depositary than to the paid guardian or hirer.

Maimonides uses "force" of theft by a third party and "great force" of the accidents that normally release from compensation. It is possible that non-Jewish concepts contributed to this deviation from Talmudic terminology.

Lastly, in Exod 22:13–14, the borrower of a beast is declared obliged to restore even where a shepherd is not. He is free only if the owner is present at the mishap. Talmudic law introduces few major changes. Three may be mentioned. It extends the provision to the borrower of any object. Freedom from liability results not just from the owner's presence, but from his services being engaged in connection with the loan. And an Amoraic development is that the borrower is free also if the object is ruined in the course of being used as agreed.[11]

DAMAGE TO PROPERTY

The *Mishpatim*—like the XII Tables—omit the obvious and confine themselves to the settlement of doubts and reforms.[12] Hence, as regards damage to property, they regulate only damage done through an intermediate agency, pit, ox, cattle, and fire. That a man who does damage in person is bound to make it good goes without saying.

One may wonder why the ox does not come first, seeing that the case of an ox killing a person immediately precedes that of the pit:[13] the order, ox killing a person, ox killing an ox, pit would be far smoother than ox killing a person, pit, ox killing an ox. The explanation is that the paragraphs concerning an ox killing an ox are later and were appended when the two earlier cases already formed an established sequence. It will be noted that whereas the earlier section, about an ox killing a person, speaks narrowly of "goring," the section about an ox killing an ox uses the wider "pushing"; and that in the earlier section, full responsibility depends on the ox's ferocious inclination "being solemnly announced" to its owner, in the later, on its "being known"—a looser and more subjective criterion.

A similar development accounts for the fact that the pit and the ox on the one hand and the grazing and the fire on the other are separated by the section about theft. The second pair was added when the section about theft had become fixed in its place immediately after the first. Significantly, the earlier paragraphs concern damage to beasts, the later ones damage to land: private ownership of beasts antedates that of land. Again, in the earlier rules, a man is primarily held responsible as owner of a destructive agent, ox or pit; in the later ones, as indirect cause of the destruction, as mover of the agent, cattle or fire.[14]

To inspect the cases one by one—to him who leaves his pit uncovered is applied what may be called *Gefährdungshaftung*: if you maintain a hazard, you should bear the consequences. The realization that, as a rule, his omission to protect the pit constitutes gross negligence also plays a part. It would be incorrect to say that he is liable for negligence: the court will not scrutinize an individual defendant's circumstances and conduct. At this stage of evolution, there would not be the means of doing it. We may, however, speak of liability for objectivized negligence. It is negligence that the law intends to come down on when it requires reparation on facts normally the result of such a lapse.

In general, if one man's ox kills another's, the loss is shared. The owner of the ox that killed is responsible simply because he is the owner: the damage emanated from his domain. That he need make good only half of it is a limitation found also in the laws of Eshnunna;[15] it is probably laid down in view of the experience that the fight is just as likely to have been started by the victim as by the survivor. The machinery of reparation envisaged by the law involves sale of the latter to a third party. This buyer (if everything is done properly) will be aware that the ox he is acquiring is dangerous and consequently subject to special rules.

According to them, if your ox is known to have battled before and kills another man's ox, you must make full restitution. As in the case of the pit, the grounds of your liability are, first, your maintaining a hazard; second, objectivized negligence: your behavior on this specific occasion is not investigated. It is enough that, usually, a disaster of this kind can happen only because the owner of the dangerous ox most negligently omitted to exercise vigilance.[16]

Full restitution is owed also by him who allows his cattle to pasture on another man's land and by him who allows a fire to spread to another man's land.[17] While the main rationale is that he set the agent to work, objectivized negligence again should not be overlooked. When your cattle trespasses or when a fire spreads from your field to your neighbor's, that is nearly always due to carelessness on your part. The law does not ordain an inquiry into each case; it proclaims strict liability, liability even should a particular defendant be free from blame—but this strict liability is largely directed against the careless.

Unlike the *Mishpatim*, the provisions in Leviticus, of a sacred-priestly flavor, deal with a man doing damage directly. They consider, however, only one action: the killing of a beast. This is paired off with the killing of a person, a feat of systematization a modern Western reader must find strange. How the ideas behind it grew up and how, subsequently, they dropped out of the mainstream of Jewish thought would be worth exploring. The duty to replace the beast is absolute, independent of fault, though doubtless the fact that most direct killing springs either from intent or negligence helped to shape it.

Throughout the Tannaitic period, the elaboration of damage to property rests on the *Mishpatim*, the passage from Leviticus playing no part.[18]

One improvement of the arrangement of the *Mishpatim* is common to Philo, Josephus, and the Mishnah: the ox killing a person and the ox killing an ox are brought together; the pit no longer intervenes.[19] For the rest, their ways of grouping differ. Philo in his *Special Laws* distributes the various Pentateuchic rules over the Ten Commandments. The ox killing a person he assigns to "Thou shalt not murder." He annexes to it the ox killing an ox. He follows it up with the pit, seen by him as a danger to human life as well as to beasts (while the *Mishpatim* speak only of a beast falling into it); and he compares the Deuteronomic warning to make a railing around the roof.[20] "Thou shalt not steal" provides a home for the cases of grazing and fire,[21] both of them revealing contempt for your fellow man's property, arrogance, greediness.[22] He thus adheres to the sequence of the *Mishpatim*: theft, cattle, fire. Josephus' section about theft[23] comes well before that about killing and maiming.[24] The latter includes the ox killing a person, with a final paragraph concerning the ox killing an ox; the pit—as in Philo, a danger to persons as well as to animals; and tacked on to it, as in Philo, the roof.[25] Grazing and fire Josephus does not discuss. Philo, incidentally, in his note on an ox killing an ox, considers only the case where the attacker's wildness is known; Josephus, only that where it is not known.

The Mishnaic exposition of delict opens with damage to property.[26] Theft receives far briefer treatment and is relegated to second place.[27] Damage to property, after an enumeration of the four heads—ox, pit, grazing, and fire[28]—is presented in two portions. The first works out the principles of an ox killing an ox, grazing, pit and—an innovation, brought in in the sketchiest fashion—damage done by a man directly.[29] The second gives more detail about an ox killing an ox, pit, grazing, and fire.[30] Within the discussion of an ox killing an ox, excursuses deal with an ox killing a person.[31] By now the owner at most has to make a payment; he is never put to death: the case is no longer of major importance.[32]

Already at the time of the Septuagint there may have been the first questionings of strict liability. It may have been asked, in particular, whether "and he has not guarded it"—namely, the dangerous ox—might not imply exculpation of an owner who has taken appropriate precautions. Whether or not in reply to such a suggestion, the Septuagint distinctly insists on strictness: it translates "and he has not destroyed it."[33] So no precautions are good enough.

Philo, in the section about an ox killing a person, writes that if the owner, "knowing it to be savage and wild, neither ties it nor guards it shut up…, having allowed it to pasture freely he shall be guilty as the cause"; the same circumstances entail full restitution should the ox kill an ox. Here are described the typical lapses apt to end in disaster. It does not follow that if a ferocious ox of yours kills another man's ox despite reasonable measures on your part, you need make no amends. The outcome is still enough to condemn you: liability for objectivized negligence.[34] Similarly, an open pit is inevitably indicative of aberration, in Philo's view, and its owner must replace an animal falling to its death; quite likely, the fall is sufficient evidence that the pit was open. Anyhow, there is no probing into negligence in the individual case.

Neither is there in a case of grazing; the owner of the land intruded on is to be recouped.[35] The standard offense, as Philo sees it, consists in the beasts being deliberately driven onto another man's land. This, he comments, ought by rights to lead to heavy punishment; but the law is satisfied with restitution because the culprit, as soon as he perceived the damage they were doing, may have tried his best to get them out.

The element of objectivized negligence is particularly clear in the chapter on fire. Philo holds the one who started it unconditionally is bound to repair what loss ensues—"in order that he may learn to guard very well the first beginnings of things." Lack of care is taken for granted. Throughout the chapter Philo moralizes on the importance of circumspection in respect of so dangerous a force as fire.

According to Josephus, it is the duty of the owner of a vicious ox to slaughter him. Probably that is why he finds it unnecessary to mention an ox known to be vicious killing an ox: it ought to be a rare occurrence. He does mention such an ox killing a person: "if the owner is proved to have known its nature beforehand and not to have guarded it, he shall die." The "and not to have guarded it" is a reproach—harking back to the wording of the *Mishpatim*—not a condition. The fact that the ox was able to kill shows its owner at fault. Pits should be closed, Josephus declares, and the owner of an open one must pay up if an animal falls into it and perishes.

It is only from the middle of the second century AD that negligence gradually becomes a standard in a given case. Eliezer ben Hyrcanus, a disciple of Johanan ben Zaccai, still firmly upholds the strict position (in language somewhat reminiscent of the Septuagint and Josephus): for the ox known to be ferocious—now standing for any beast which may be expected to kill, such as a wolf, a lion, a snake[36]—"the only guarding is the knife." According to R. Judah ben Elai, however, no damages are payable by an owner who "tied it with a halter and shut it up properly." To be sure, R. Meir, a contemporary, rejects this innovation. On the other hand, R. Eliezer ben Jacob, another contemporary, would exempt a careful owner even from compensation for half the loss inflicted by an ox hitherto harmless.[37]

As we saw above, the regulation of the *Mishpatim* concerning a hitherto harmless ox appears to be influenced by the idea that one cannot be sure which of the two beasts involved commenced hostilities. Which means that, as for human failing, neither of the two owners can be assumed to be in the wrong. By the time of Eliezer ben Jacob, the hitherto harmless ox killing an ox has long become a paradigm for a wide range of cases—namely, any damage done by a beast in an uncharacteristic manner—in most of which the former is obviously the attacker; say, a cock has a string attached to its foot and thereby breaks a utensil, a cow devours clothing, an ox known to be vicious to other oxen kills a small animal.[38] Hence it does now make sense to inquire into the guilt or otherwise of the destructive beast's owner. To appreciate Eliezer ben Jacob's radicalness, it should be remembered that, in the *Mishpatim*, the words "and he has not guarded it" occur only in connection with the savage ox. So while Judah ben Elai has a ready basis for his requirement of negligence, Eliezer ben Jacob must maintain that they are meant to be extended to the harmless ox.[39]

With regard to pit, cattle, and fire, too, by the end of the second century AD the criterion of negligence is fairly established. The Mishnah lays down that,

if an animal falls into a pit, the owner of the pit is free or accountable according as he did or did not "cover it properly."[40] The pit now includes anything
in the nature of a trap, say, a jug left lying on the ground so that a man with a
jar stumbles and the jar breaks.[41] Again, if your flock grazes in another man's
field, you are free or accountable according as you did or did not "shut it up
properly."[42] Grazing now covers both eating and destroying things by tram-
pling upon as the beast goes along.[43] Of a fire we hear, for example, that there
is no claim if it passed over a fence seven feet high, a public road, or a river.[44]

The Tannaites coin the designation "diminished guarding," "minor custody," for the new standard. Previously, the fact that the law imposed on you
the "guarding," "custody," of ox, pit, cattle, and fire meant that you counted as
rendering possible any damage they did: strict liability.[45] "Diminished guarding" admits of exemption on proof of adequate care or—the same—confines liability to fault on the particular occasion.[46] Where it is contrasted with
the old standard, the latter is called not simply "guarding," but "heightened
guarding." No doubt "diminished guarding" made its entry more rapidly in
some areas than others. For a number of Rabbis, for instance, it was apparently easier to welcome it in connection with pit, cattle, and fire than with
ox:[47] unlike those three, the ox is depicted in the *Mishpatim* as a peril to human
life as well as to property, so there were more scruples against a relaxation.[48]

Exoneration of the careful is not the only inroad into strict liability.
Another one, probably of earlier origin and greater practical import, is exoneration of one within his rights or—the same—limitation of liability to
unlawful damage. If your ox is on my land and my ox kills it, or if you keep
fruit in the public domain and my cattle consume it, you have no remedy.[49]
A shopkeeper keeping a light outside, in the street, is liable if a camel laden
with flax passes and a conflagration ensues; but he is not liable, R. Judah
asserts, if it is a Hannukah light—which it is a religious duty to place near
the door, outside, as a sign of celebration.[50] The distinction between the lawful and the unlawful is especially prominent in the rules concerning damage
done by a man in person.[51]

It should not indeed be thought that there is a steady movement from
fixed, objective criteria to flexible, subjective ones. As noted above, in an early

layer of the *Mishpatim*, about an ox killing a person, the owner's responsibility is enhanced if its ferocious habits were proclaimed to him; in a subsequent layer, about an ox killing an ox, if its habits were known. The Mishnah reverts to formal testifying.[52] Moreover, even an ox whose wildness is attested may regain harmless status as a result of external circumstances, such as transfer into a fresh ownership.[53]

In the Amoraic period, the standard of negligence is systematically explored. The term *peshi'a*, "fault," first introduced (on the basis of Exod 22:8) in connection with deposit and the like, is employed also in damage to property.[54] Medieval and modern commentators,[55] reading back liability for fault into the earliest strata, are driven to strange constructions. The old use of "guarding," for example, as denoting the position of one in charge of a hazard who is strictly answerable for damage done by it is forgotten; instead, it is taken to signify the duty of vigilance, fulfillment of which releases. Accordingly, "diminished guarding" no longer denotes the position of one in charge of a hazard who is answerable only if the damage done by it is due to his negligence; it is taken to signify a lightened duty of vigilance, *leichte Bewachung*, "inferior precautions."

But these authorities cannot, of course, admit that the Rabbis advocating "diminished guarding" are satisfied with, say, a flimsy door to keep in a vicious ox or a few twigs to cover a well. The conclusion arrived at, then, is that by "inferior precautions" must be understood careful ones.

They are inferior in the sense that they will not avail against *force majeure*.

Really adequate ones, "heightened guarding," would stand up even to that—so even if the damage is due to *force majeure*, a measure of fault is imputable to the one in charge.

Whereas the sequence of the Mishnah is first, damage to property, indirect and direct; second, theft; and third, injury to a person,[56] Maimonides presents first, indirect damage—"damage by property" he calls it—second, theft; third, robbery and lost things; and fourth, injury to a person and direct damage.[57] The bringing together of theft, robbery, and lost things is a systematic advance.[58] The separation of indirect and direct damage is in a way a retrograde step, yet not without good reasons. Already the *Mishpatim*, though in the province of damage to property looking only at your responsibility for an intermediate agency, in that of injury to a person look also at your own, independent action; and a good deal of attention is given to the economic aspect of the matter.[59] By the time of Maimonides, Lev 24, too, has come into its own as a basic guide in direct damage to property, and the Bible here places such damage side by side with injury to a person and even the killing of a person. The book of Precepts shows these factors at work in his mind.[60] When it is recalled, in addition, that direct damage has a mere toehold in the Mishnaic section about damage to property, his taking it after injury to a person is understandable. What does bring out the power of tradition is the fact that even in this work indirect damage—ox, cattle, pit, fire—still stands at the head of delict: the archaic preoccupation of the *Mishpatim* with this type of case determines the arrangement of the material after some two thousand years of legal culture.

Liability for indirect damage is ordinarily limited to fault.[61] By contrast, damage done directly is to be paid for whether there is fault or "force," sheer accident—though in some cases at first sight belonging here the causal nexus between action and result is missing and the latter must be ascribed to fate.[62] Among the causes of the stricter attitude to direct damage, the rigid formulation of Lev 24 is evidently a far from negligible one.[63] Both with respect to indirect and direct damage, you are free if you are within your rights.[64] If, running along the street, you knock into a peaceful stroller and break his watch, you will have to compensate him; but if it is late Friday afternoon, you are exempt—you are bound to hurry in order to be ready for the Sabbath.[65]

THE HAPLESS CAT

Babylonian Baba Metsia 96b–c:

> It was asked by them, what if the beast borrowed became emaciated through its work? ... Raba said, You need not ask whether, if a beast became emaciated through its work, he is free: even if it died through its work he is free, for he can say to the lender, I did not borrow it to place it in a fourpost-bedstead.

A man who borrowed an axe from his friend and it broke. He came before Raba who said to him, Go and bring witnesses that you have not deviated from its proper use and you are free. And what if there are no witnesses? Come and hear: for a man borrowed an axe from his friend and it broke. He came before Rab who said, Go and restore him a good axe. R. Kahana and R. Assi said to Rab, Is this the law? And Rab was silent. And the Halakha accords with R. Kahana and R. Assi, that he returns him the broken axe and makes up its value.

A man borrowed a bucket from his friend and it broke. He came before R. Papa who said, Go and bring witnesses that you did not deviate from its proper use and you are free.

According to the Bible, the borrower of a beast is to replace it even if it falls to its death or dies from natural causes—what we label as *force majeure*. By the end of the Tannaitic period this unmitigated obligation is extended to the borrower of an inanimate object.[66] Yet around AD 300 an important reservation is introduced: no liability if the article borrowed perished in the course of its use in accordance with the contract.

Rab, who in AD 219 founded the Sura academy, still adheres to the earlier harsh ruling. But already a colleague—Assi I—and a pupil—Kahana—question the position, and he becomes at least doubtful, "silent." It is Raba, in the first half of the fourth century, who finally establishes the modification. The law is now not dissimilar to the Roman: "If I lend you a slave as plasterer and he falls from the scaffold, the risk is mine."[67]

The evolution is obscured by various distortions, two of which it is essential to notice. First, in the episode involving Rab, the concluding sentence misconstrues the debate and makes Assi and Kahana object, not to Rab's insistence on compensation, but to the form that compensation is to take. Rab thinks of replacement of the broken axe; Assi and Kahana—according to this final sentence—prefer return of the broken axe and payment of the difference. Second, the redactors of the Gemara also misunderstand Rab. For them, his law was the same as that of Raba. Consequently, they harmonize his verdict against the borrower with Raba's opposite one by postulating that in the former case the borrower had no witnesses to prove his proper use while in the latter case he did have witnesses.

R. Ashi, legend has it, was born the year that Raba died. He had to decide a difficult case.[68] Somebody borrowed a cat—obviously to rid him of his mice. However, it was the cat that died. According to one version, the mice had banded together and done it in; according to another, it had eaten too many and succumbed to the excess. The rabbi was not sure whether it could be held to have died as a result of its agreed work or whether the borrower would have to pay. His doubts were resolved by an elder colleague, R. Mordecai, who quoted a pronouncement that his teacher Abimi had heard from Raba: "A man whom women killed [that is, through excessive gratification]—there is neither judgment nor judge."

CHAPTER 6

INTELLECTUAL AUTHORSHIP

THE INSTIGATOR AND THE RESULT

The German code of criminal law has a special paragraph about the man who deliberately induces another man to commit a crime; if the crime is committed, he incurs the same punishment as the actual doer. In English law, where things are less rigorously analyzed, the *Anstifter* falls into the very large and heterogeneous class of accessories, or if we take the three subdivisions of this class—accessory before the fact, during the fact, after the fact—into the still large subdivision accessory before the fact. He is not fundamentally distinguished from, say, a man who lends a burglar a car for his exploit. In principle, an accessory before the fact is punishable like the doer. Canon lawyers tend to differentiate between two aspects of intellectual authorship. Seen as a contribution to the result, it is rather less damnable than the actual deed; it is preliminary, more indirect. But it is worse than the actual deed in that, besides being a contribution to the result, it constitutes a separate offense, namely, the ensnaring of a soul, the pushing of another man, the doer, into sin. It is significant that the *Codex Iuris Canonici* imposes on the *Anstifter* "punishment not lighter than that of the doer."

When we look into the presentation of the matter by the Bible, we might incline to expect a leaning toward the canon law approach, an emphasis on the dragging down of a soul rather than on the role in bringing about the result. But this expectation is, on the whole, disappointed. With the exception of three cases—the incitement to defection, seduction by a loose woman, and deception by undutiful political or religious leaders—the intellectual author is called to account as a cause, or the first cause, of the event, not as a misuser of a soul. This does not mean that the misuse invariably remains unnoticed; but even when it is noticed, it is not made the basis, or even partial basis, of the punishment.

To take a few chapters which might a priori be thought to support the other view, and first, the story of the Fall.[1] Certainly the serpent encourages Eve to defy the commandment. Moreover, when charged with disobedience, Adam defends himself by saying that Eve gave him the fruit and Eve that the serpent misled her. Nevertheless in punishing the three, God makes no reference to the particular wrong of involving an innocent person in crime. We must not, for that period, proceed from accustomed notions of the serpent as the arch-tempter of mankind, and of woman as the ever-dangerous siren-companion of man—notions, it is true, with the authority of a two-thousand-year-old tradition behind them, but not, we would here insist, three thousand years old. In the story as it stands, shorn of later reinterpretations, the serpent is somewhat comparable to Prometheus, helping man to knowledge against the will of a jealous God[2]—the God of the tower of Babel. The scheme succeeds, and all God can do is to exact fearful retribution. It is this successful execution of the scheme, the raising up of man to a level God would have reserved for himself, for which God punishes the serpent; this, and not the ensnaring of a person, is meant when he says, "Because thou hast done this thou art cursed."

Nor is there anything in the nature of the penalty to connect it with the specific wrong of corrupting a soul. The serpent will have to walk on its belly and eat dust, and there will be warfare between it and man. The etiological point is obvious: the curse explains the striking features of serpents and their relation to man. If the violence were one-sided, if there were only decimation of serpents by man, one might perhaps argue that here was, after all, some reply to what the serpent had done to the human character. But the two sides are in absolute balance: man will bruise the serpent's head, and the serpent will bruise man's heel. Man did not corrupt the serpent, so this element cannot determine the punishment. The fellow criminals, the helper and he that accepted the help, will be separated by eternal enmity; that is all.

Let us add that, in punishing Eve, God states no reason. It would be arbitrary to claim that it is the ensnaring of Adam. She is not made responsible for his depravation. There is no depravation; there is victory bought at a very high price. To judge by the treatment of the serpent, she is punished for listening to the serpent herself and for contributing to Adam's transgression, providing him with the fruit that God had forbidden him to eat.

Remarkably enough, though the original, "Promethean" trend of the story must soon have been lost sight of, there is only one passage in the whole of the Bible, Old Testament or New, giving full effect to a different approach, in Revelation;[3] nowhere else is the serpent punished for the crime of depraving Eve or Eve for that of depraving Adam. In Sirach,[4] for example, we read that "From a woman is the beginning of sin"—and now, surely, we are prepared to hear "and she was condemned for spoiling the innocence of man." But no; the text goes on, "and because of her we all die." All of us together, no discrimination between woman who seduced and man her victim. First Timothy[5] may come slightly nearer the idea of punishing the dragging down of a soul. Woman is inferior to man because "Adam was not deceived, but the woman being deceived has come into transgression." But even here, little more is meant than that woman brought sin with her—just as Paul says that sin entered into the world through Adam.[6] Rabbinic literature widely shares this conservative attitude in regard to the punishment of the intellectual author: in the comments of *Genesis Rabba* on the story of the Fall, neither for the serpent nor for Eve is punishment associated with the specific wrong of seduction. What is perhaps most striking is that some apocryphal writings, such as the book of Jubilees,[7] faithfully adhere to the old presentation in Genesis.

The picture emerging from this portion of our sources is only underlined by the fact that there is another. It is evident that, by the opening of our era, the idea of the serpent or Eve condemned for what they did to another being had long taken root. It is discernible in Philo, though as he gives it a particular twist we shall have to postpone consideration of him. But Josephus also has it.[8] God curses the serpent "angry about his malignity toward Adam," and he sentences Eve "because she involved Adam in the calamity into which she had been tripped." In the books of Adam and Eve,[9] the serpent is punished for "deceiving innocent hearts" and "ensnaring them in his malice." As for Eve, though she is punished for disobedience, with no reference to the specific offense of corruption, it should be observed that when Adam falls grievously ill, she offers to bear a share of his pain since it is her fault.[10] In Revelation, "the great dragon was cast out, that old Serpent called the Devil and Satan, who deceiveth the whole world."[11]

How the new way of construing the intellectual author's punishment came up we shall discuss below. For the moment it is enough to be clear that it is new compared with the account in Genesis. Indeed, though arguments from silence are risky, we would maintain that Ezekiel furnishes a definite *terminus post quem*. It is incredible that, had the new construction existed in his time, none of his various examinations of responsibility, and especially of responsibility where several persons are jointly implicated in wrongdoing, should exhibit the least trace of it.

Going on to a law about murder in Deuteronomy where,[12] possibly, intellectual authorship is contemplated—we are told that, if a murdered man is found in open country and the murderer cannot be traced, the elders of the nearest city are to perform a ceremony of expiation, in the course of which they avow: "Our hands have not shed this blood neither have our eyes seen it." By the first clause they declare themselves to be without knowledge of the murderer. It is possible, however, that what is meant is the absence of any indirect participation, aiding, abetting, condoning, and other schemes— including instigation. But if so, the emphasis is again on the role of all this in the bringing about of the result; the actual deed "our hands have not shed this blood" and any contribution "neither have our eyes seen it" are placed on exactly the same level. There is not the faintest allusion to the latter activity being objectionable not only as a factor in the murder, but also (insofar as instigation is envisaged) as an infliction of harm on the doer's soul.

Nehemiah's enemies bribed false prophets to counsel him to flee into the temple, which would have made him impossible [a transgressor of Temple law].[13] In his record he invokes the vengeance of God on the bribers and those that served them. But it is for their wicked plotting against him that the former are particularly guilty, not for depraving those prophets.

Finally, from the New Testament, we may quote the beheading of the Baptist. Herod swore to the daughter of Herodias to give her whatever she desired. According to Matthew,[14] he had long wanted John out of the way and had refrained from murder only because he feared the populace. So when the woman asked for John's head, Herod was sorry not about the immorality of what he was to do, but about its impolitic character. At least as far as Herod is concerned, then, Matthew cannot be thinking of any corruption by the intellectual author—not to mention that, in a sense, the legend looks on his action as unavoidable since he is bound by an oath. As for the woman, we learn that she put her terrible request "induced" or "pushed forward" by her mother. Here was corruption, obviously. But as the legend does not say whether or how God punished the various participants in the crime, we are hardly justified in asserting that Herodias would have had to answer specially for involving another person.

In Mark, Herod respects John;[15] so the woman's request makes him sorry about the wrong which that just man is to suffer. But again, apart from the fact that, in view of the oath, the legend may not regard Herod as really guilty, nothing is said about punishment. It is rather unlikely that, if we did hear about it, the woman's penalty would be based on the harm she was doing to the king in dragging him in.

THE INSTIGATOR AND THE AGENT

The question arises: why in these and other biblical cases is the intellectual author not punished as harming a soul, but exclusively for his contribution to the result? The principal reasons seem to be three.

First, in general, in crime, it is of course the result that is the starting point for any reaction, for investigation, for vengeance. The primary concern will be to discover and exact retribution from whoever is responsible. Secular justice may indeed not find it within its powers to go behind the doer at all: in a previous chapter on causation, on direct and indirect causation, I drew attention to the many practical obstacles—such as the difficulty of proof—which, in a society not highly organized, stand in the way of bringing the intellectual author to book. But even where he is called to account—and divine justice or ethical reflection is not hampered by practical difficulties—the starting point being what it is, for a long time little interest is taken in side issues on the way from him to the final outcome. That he may, in the course of his activity, have wronged another being by pushing him toward sin is a very secondary element measured by the main question. When God found the human couple possessed of knowledge he would have withheld from them, he directed his curses against them for their disobedience and against the serpent for his treachery in enlightening them as to what lay within their grasp. He was not concerned with any details of the methods used by the serpent on Eve. Herodias found a way of compassing the death of the Baptist. Compared with this fearful result, anything she might have done to her daughter by involving her recedes into the background.

Second, it is well to remember that the attempted crime as such plays a very small part in biblical doctrine. Sinful thought, yes: "Thou shalt not covet thy neighbor's house,"[16] "Thou shalt not hate thy brother in thy heart,"[17] "Whosoever gazeth on a woman to lust after her hath committed adultery with her already in his heart."[18] And then the crime carried out: murder, theft, adultery, and so on. But in between, the preliminaries of a crime, the preparations which might go as far as attempt, are not, except for a few peculiar cases, worked out into a situation of special significance. The intellectual author's activity, however, belongs to this preliminary stage. So long as there is no interest in this stage as such, irrespective of whether or not the crime is actually committed, we cannot expect any deeper treatment of the intellectual author's offense, any recognition that it might affect not only the victim of the final crime but also the person he is seeking to influence. We would not be misunderstood. The Bible is full of attempts, of misdeeds foiled—Pharaoh's command to the midwives to kill the male babies of the Hebrews,[19] Saul hurling his spear against David,[20] Adonijah trying to usurp Solomon's prerogatives (at least that is how Solomon interprets his request to have Abishag to wife),[21] several conspiracies to murder Paul[22]—

and quite a few of these actions (for instance, that of Pharaoh and that of the plotters against Paul) do involve pressure or persuasion on the part of the original mover on somebody chosen to be his agent. All we are saying is that this stage is not isolated, not given a status of its own in thought and analysis as compared with sinful impulses on the one hand and a completed offense on the other.

Third, the notion of the intellectual author being responsible not only for the first move toward the event, but also for the agent's downfall presupposes a measure of ethical and theological refinement and systematization not fully attained in biblical times. No doubt there is a case—an early one, too—like that of Abraham who, by giving out that Sarah was his sister, caused Abimelech to take her into his harem and who, when God threatened Abimelech with death, was reproached by that innocent man for "having brought on him and his kingdom a great sin."[23] But this is not *Anstiftung*. There is not here between the first mover and the result a conscious wrongdoing by the agent. It is not as if Abraham had suggested to Abimelech to commit adultery in defiance of law and morality. What we are arguing is that, had Abimelech acted on such a suggestion, he could not at that period have turned round and complained about "Abraham having brought on him a great sin." Biblical accounts, that is, do not as a rule assume that even where the agent makes a free decision, the instigator is guilty in respect of his soul. Apart from the fact that the principle may sometimes be a little unrealistic— for instance, the prophets bribed by Nehemiah's enemies were surely worthless anyhow—the Bible proceeds, perhaps, in a sense, primitively, from too high a degree of individual autonomy for this notion to become dominant.

EXCEPTIONS

The correctness of our explanation may be seen from the three major exceptions already mentioned: incitement to defection, seduction by a loose woman, and deception by political or religious leaders. In these cases, the intellectual author is definitely held answerable for what he does to the person to whom he addresses himself.

Incitement to Defection. For example, "These (Midianite women) caused the children of Israel to commit a trespass against the Lord, and there came a plague among the congregation"[24]—the instigators here sinned not only against God but also against those whom they stirred on. Similarly, "All this wicked congregation (complaining and doubting my ability to bring them into the promised land) in this wilderness they shall die; and the men whom Moses sent to search the land, and who returned and made all the congregation to murmur against him, they shall die by a plague."[25] Again, "If thy brother entice thee secretly, saying, 'Let us serve other gods,' thou shalt stone him that he die, because he hath sought to thrust thee away from the Lord thy God."[26] Or, "For such are false apostles, deceitful workers, whose end shall be according to their works."[27] Or, "There shall be false teachers who privily shall bring you heresies, even denying the Lord who bought them, and they will make a gain of you by their deceitful words, whose punishment threatened of old lingereth not."[28] Or, "And the devil that deceived them was cast into the lake of fire and brimstone where the beast and the false prophet were."[29]

Seduction. "The adulteress will hunt for the precious life."[30] (The primary meaning may be, quite literally, that she will not rest till the affair has cost you your life. Anyhow, her responsibility is clear.)

Deceptive leaders. "For the leaders of this people cause them to err, and those that are led by them are destroyed."[31] Or the description of the Pharisees as "blind leaders of the blind," with the consequence that "both will fall into the ditch";[32] maybe also the warning that "Whoso shall cause one of these little ones to believe in me to stumble, it were better that a millstone were hanged about his neck."[33]

Now that wicked and treacherous leaders should be punishable for the harm done to those entrusted to them is not surprising. Their very function is to give good guidance, and if they encourage or allow their flock to stray, they violate their special, distinctive duty. Ezekiel, appointed "watchman" unto Israel, is told by God: "When I say unto the wicked, Thou shalt surely die, and thou (the watchman) givest him no warning, he shall die in his iniquity; but his blood will I require at thy hand."[34] Some of this is novel, at least in its systematized presentation. But the concluding idea, the leader's accountability, is not. The point is that, in this case, the real crime is precisely the leader's conduct to the people, while the resulting wrongdoings of the latter are merely symptoms of this crime.

However, though the case of depraved leadership stands out as the easiest of the three to explain, there are two important features which all three have in common. For one thing, in all of them, it is a question not of instigating one isolated transgression, but of encouraging an entire perverse mode of life. If I get you to commit murder, that is that. But if I persuade you to apostatize, or if a loose woman induces you to form a liaison, or if the recognized leaders of the nation imbue you with their wrong standards, all your doing and thinking will be affected, infected. This is clearly realized by the ancient writers. The section just quoted about a man's nearest relation trying to make him worship other gods is preceded by one concerning a false prophet who preaches apostasy. He is to be put to death because "he hath spoken to thrust thee out of the way which the Lord thy God commanded thee to walk in."[35] "To thrust thee out of the way": you would radically leave the right path.

That Satan's temptation of Jesus is designed to prevent the entire ministry at the start is evident from its position in all three Synoptics.[36] Again, the counselor against illicit attractions well knows that such an affair is continuous and swallows up the whole person; and it is not accidental that the concept of "the way" reappears in this connection: "Let not thine heart decline to her ways, go not astray in her paths."[37] When Ezekiel blames his more influential rivals for "not going up into the breaches," he means that they have confirmed the people in a life totally corrupted by false hopes and lax morals.[38] Similarly, in the New Testament, the false apostles may utterly uproot a man from the saving community he has joined, and the Pharisaic leadership lowers the entire religious tone of the nation. Evidently it is to no small extent this feature to which the progressive treatment of the three cases is due. Here where the whole life of the offender is involved, where he has become a different man from what he might have been, the intellectual author's wrong vis-à-vis him comes to the fore.

The other feature to be noticed is closely connected with this one. In all three cases, the main purpose of the instigator is not the criminal result as such, but the winning over of a man into a union—an unholy union from the point of view of the authors before us. If I get you to murder somebody who is in my way, my aim is that person's elimination. Presumably, if it could easily be done without you, I should prefer it. By contrast, if I recommend other gods, what I principally desire is to have you in this community. A married woman trying to catch you is interested not in the achievement of adultery, but in your entering into an alliance with her. The wicked leaders mind far too little what their flock may do, so long as it is safely theirs. Here, then, is a further factor focusing attention on the effect exercised by the instigator on the agent. This effect, the establishment of a bond, is the instigator's chief end, and, equally, it is the really pernicious element in the eyes of the right-minded. Once again, the biblical writers are not unaware of the point. "If thy brother entice thee, saying, 'Let us serve other gods'"—"let us": you are to join in. "Come, let us take our fill of love," says the adulteress.[39] Those who worship the Beast receive a mark; they are members of a fellowship of damnation.[40]

With regard to incitement to defection, yet a third consideration is relevant. We remarked above that the intellectual author's activity by its nature belongs to a preparatory stage of the crime; he makes the first move, and hence, so long as this stage is not isolated, so long as attempt is not worked out, we cannot expect any emphasis on what he does to the person he is using. However, especially where it is a near relation of yours who advocates false worship, obviously, the matter will come before the courts only if he is unsuccessful. If he succeeds, if you succumb, you will not denounce him, and by the time it may all be discovered, both of you will simply be guilty of idolatry—no more questions being asked about how it happened. In other words, this variety at least of incitement will come before the courts only while at the stage of attempt, at the stage where the instigator's role is fully revealed. No doubt this also helped the realization, in this and related cases, of the intellectual author's offense against his instrument. It may be observed that the statute which we have already quoted expressly refers to the case as one of attempt: "Because he hath sought, attempted, to thrust thee away from the Lord thy God."

INTERPRETATION OF THE STORY OF THE FALL

We are now in a position to understand how, at some time between Eze-kiel and the opening of our era, the story of the Fall could be modernized in the sense that the serpent was no longer condemned only for thwarting God's plan to withhold knowledge from man, but also for depriving man of his pristine innocence; and that Eve was no longer condemned only for disobedience but also for drawing into sin her previously sinless husband. The explanation is that in certain circles the fall came to be looked on as an instance of defection from God, or even as the prototype of this crime—one of those exceptions—where the intellectual author's wrong to the agent is stressed from early times. In the story as originally conceived, God is up to a point defeated, and he wreaks vengeance for this defeat. The idea of a fall in the moral or theological sense is quite absent. But in course of time, with a purer and more mature notion of God, it was possible for this first transgres-sion, which led to the loss of Eden, to assume the character of a fundamen-tal turning from a good and wise Creator for the sake of low gain, a turning that would forever mar the natures of Adam and Eve, if not of their progeny too. Seen in this light, the serpent had most certainly preached false worship, had "spoken to thrust thee out of the way which the Lord commanded thee to walk in," and Eve had most certainly played the part of "the wife of thy bosom enticing thee secretly, to thrust thee away from the Lord."

As we saw, this aspect of the serpent's and Eve's roles is by no means uni-versally prominent: the Bible brings it out only in Revelation, and we do not get much of it in rabbinic literature. Very likely it is not merely conservatism, a mechanical adherence to the presentation in Genesis, which accounts for this phenomenon. We must also reckon with a widespread reluctance to attribute overmuch significance to the deed of the first couple.

Even when the "Promethean" element was long forgotten, a large school of thought preferred to see in the affair an ordinary sin, the isolated infringe-ment of one definite commandment, rather than a radical defection engulf-ing the whole person and maybe even his descendants. That is to say, just as the intellectual author's wrong to the agent comes to the surface where the eating of the fruit is interpreted as, so to speak, the first great apostasy, so we may conclude that in many cases, the absence of emphasis on that wrong indicates nonacceptance of this interpretation.

Philo, we pointed out, proceeds from a version of the story of the Fall where the intellectual author is condemned for wronging the agent. This may be inferred from his allegorical comments: the serpent symbolizes pleasure, the basic evil, which deceives the senses symbolized by Eve, and they in turn seduce reason, Adam.[41]

We omit complications not essential to our immediate argument. In principle, for Philo, the senses are neutral; that is to say, good so long as not corrupted by pleasure; and even when corrupted, not deliberately deceitful like pleasure, but merely passing on ("unwillingly" passing on, *Leg. All.* 3.60) to reason the mistaken picture they have weakly formed under pleasure's influence. However, Philo is not above speaking of the senses using persuasion to get reason to accept their offer.[42] The soul in the fall chose the wrong turning once for all: human nature was perverted. The serpent is judged unheard because "pleasure has no seed from which virtue might spring but is always foul."[43] "It shifts the standard of the soul and renders it a lover of passion instead of virtue."[44] Clearly, in connection with this story at any rate, the instigator's offense consists less in whatever wrong is ultimately committed by the agent than in the depravation of the agent himself.

INTERNAL INTELLECTUAL AUTHORSHIP

At this juncture we would stress the importance of a phenomenon, discussion of which would take us too far afield but which should here receive mention: it might be called internal intellectual authorship, instigation going on inside man, man being pushed toward or into wrongdoing by organs or impulses that are part of him. In Philo, we find this exemplified on a sophisticated level: the highest part of man, reason, is influenced by the senses, which in turn are preyed on by pleasure, the lowest instinct. But, in less elaborate forms, as a psychological experience, the phenomenon is prephilosophical, very old indeed. "And ye shall not go about after your heart and your eyes, after which ye used to go a whoring":[45] the heart and eyes are here thought of as seducers of their owner. "The pride of thy heart hath deceived thee,"[46] God says to Edom, but a time will come when the nation will no longer "walk after the stubbornness of their evil heart."[47] "If thy right eye causeth thee to stumble, pluck it out, if thy right hand causeth thee to stumble, cut it off,"[48] we read in the Gospels.

As these expressions unquestionably draw on the model of proper, external instigation, a thorough investigation would throw light not only on the expressions themselves, but also on their source. One would have to compare with a phrase like "your heart deceives you"; others like "you deceive yourself"[49]; or "you harden your heart."[50] One would have to establish which parts of man can play the role of author; it looks, for instance, as if the ear were far less prominent than the eye. It does not occur in the warning from the Gospels just adduced. One would have to consider afresh the ideas underlying the so-called mirroring punishments, as when a hand is cut off for a particularly vicious attack.[51] The Rabbis have illuminating discussions as to the relative strength of the organs. The passage "ye shall not go after your heart and eyes" leads to the question whether the heart or the eyes are predominant, and the answer is that it is the heart, your general disposition.[52] In Philo, what in Genesis appears as a case of external, proper intellectual authorship is represented as internal, placed inside man. But the opposite development also occurs: the evil impulse, the *yeṣer haraʿ*, is apt to be identified with Satan.[53] No doubt, in internal intellectual authorship, from the outset the corrupting effect of, say, the eye on the man must be strongly felt: the instigator is here never merely a factor contributing to the result—say, adultery. It is possible, therefore, that once internal intellectual authorship is an established mode of construing a deed, it in turn exercises an influence on the analysis of ordinary, external intellectual authorship, in the direction of canon law.

LEGITIMATE INSTIGATION TO AN OFFENSE

The rest of this chapter I propose to devote to two somewhat extraordinary situations. First, let us look at the death of Saul. There are two versions.[54]

In one, Saul, wounded and with the Philistines on his heels, asks his armor bearer to kill him. The armor bearer is afraid—namely, to kill the king—so Saul kills himself; the armor bearer follows his example. In the other version, Saul puts his request to be killed to an Amalekite, who complies and brings David the royal insignia. David, however, is horrified that he was not afraid (like the armor bearer) "to slay the Lord's anointed" and has him put to death.

I have argued in another study that, originally, the killer in the second version was not an Amalekite; he was an ordinary Israelite; and the whole summary trial and execution are an even later addition.[55] But even so, it is an early enough account as it stands, and it accentuates a curious problem that in a milder way already arises from the first version. In both versions, Saul asks to be killed. There is no sign that the storyteller sees any wrong in this request; on the contrary, in the circumstances it is the appropriate course to take. Yet the armor bearer fears to comply, rightly; and the Amalekite who complies is perpetrating a deed for which he must pay with his life. We have then, certainly in the second version, a man, Saul, properly demanding a service which, rendered, constitutes a capital offense. The intellectual author is free from any blame; the doer is struck down, and "his blood is upon his head."

It may be useful to look for some comparable cases in everyday life. If a very sick person asks to be given something to release him, many people would think he was doing the natural thing, though they might regard it as utterly wrong to accede. In this case, perhaps the feeling that he is not fully responsible plays a part: in principle he is mistaken, only he is excused by his suffering; he is under stress. No such reflection should, of course, be imported into the story of Saul. And we could easily eliminate it from the example of the sick person by assuming that he is asking for the drug, not because of pain or the like, but because he wishes to relieve his family of a burden. Even here many might think him right while at the same time they would severely condemn the man who did act on his suggestion.[56] Again, to hold that Lady X, whose husband is the last of his line, would do right to ask that her life should be sacrificed to that of their child is not inconsistent with the view that acceptance of her offer would be a crime. A workman may earn praise for high-mindedly urging his employers to let him start on a machine before the safety screen is installed, yet the employers may count as blameworthy if they did let him start. Or suppose two Fellows of a College are considered for the Mastership. A is excellent, as everybody knows, including himself; B is far less suitable. It would be in order for A to recommend—genuinely to recommend—the election of B,[57] though undutiful of the others to follow this advice.

What unites all these cases, including that of Saul, is that one person, by reason of overriding considerations, renounces—indeed, may be morally forced to renounce—his status or privileges or normal claims, may even have to try and get others to accept this renunciation, while they for their part must still treat his position as inviolable. It is, we might say, one of the numerous cases where the maxim *volenti non fit iniuria* [no injury is done to a consenting party] does not apply—but is a very special case. The person asking for the injury is so absolutely bound, and entitled, to seek that injury that he may justly induce another person to inflict it, and nonetheless the person called on may not comply. Saul is acting as he should in not letting himself fall, alive, into the Philistines' hands. Nor need he scruple to choose the easiest and surest method—that is, to request somebody to dispatch him. In one version, the armor bearer refuses and Saul must resort to suicide. In the other, the Amalekite does as requested and becomes guilty. The point is that the two parties involved are judged on entirely different levels; each must proceed from his own standards—so that Saul may or must ask to be killed, and the person he asks may not listen. There is an unresolved conflict, a real one—by which we mean that such situations do occur in human experience and should not be analyzed away.

Naturally, there are gradations. The two cases of the sick person wishing to rid his family of a load and of Lady X and the child are very close to that of Saul; that of the eager workman less close; and that of candidate A least close—he would be decidedly going too far, for example, if he forged the ballot papers in order to get B elected. Again, in the modern examples, the person instigating the injury against himself does so out of consideration for his fellow men who are to derive some benefit. From this point of view, the examples fall under the wider problem of how far it is proper to take any gift the making of which means a real sacrifice. In the case of Saul, this element is hardly present at all. His conduct is that befitting a king in defeat.

The story of Saul is not quite the only one of its kind in the Bible: one or two others deserve mention, though in them the altruistic element is notice-able. When Absalom's revolt compelled David to leave Jerusalem, one Ittai, an exile from Gath, offered to accompany him. David generously warned him off: he had better not commit himself to a cause that at the moment looked very much like being the losing one. Ittai, however, insisted and did fight for David.[58] In this case we can only conjecture what might have happened after David's victory had Ittai given in to the warning. It is surely not inconceiv-able that Ittai would have been condemned—at least he might have figured, together with Joab and Shimei, in David's last charges to Solomon.[59]

Another episode is more clearly to the point. As Joseph's cup is discov-ered in Benjamin's sack, formal proof of his guilt, the brothers declare: "God hath found out the iniquity of thy servants; behold, we are my lord's bond-men, both we and he with whom the cup has been found." To which Joseph replies; "God forbid that I should do so; only the man in whose hand the cup has been found he shall be my bondman; and as for you, get you up in peace unto your father."[60] To be sure, both the brothers and Joseph have here very peculiar motives. The brothers could not face their father without Benjamin. Joseph knows this; he knows that his proposal to enslave Benjamin alone renders things not easier for them but more difficult. Nonetheless, as the matter is presented by one party to the other, what it comes to is this—that the brothers generously offer to share Benjamin's fate; they urge Joseph to enslave them all alike for the theft; and this is the right thing for them to do. They would be guilty of abject perfidy if they acted otherwise. At the same time Joseph would be committing the most flagrant injustice by consent-ing. He expresses horror at the idea: "God forbid that I should do so." He will punish the thief and no one else. That the debate—universally assigned to J, the oldest narrative source—completely vitiates the prevalent opinion that individual responsibility is of relatively late, Deuteronomic origin we have observed elsewhere.[61] The point here to be made is that, much as in the story of Saul, what one person rightfully, nobly, urges another to do may be a crime if actually done by the latter.

THE INSTIGATOR SHOULDERS RESPONSIBILITY

The other situation I still wish to consider is first met in the tales of the patriarchs and then, surprisingly, in the Matthean passion story.[62] Rebekah suggests to Jacob the stratagem by which he is to obtain the firstborn's blessing. From the narrator's point of view, this is not instigation of a crime in the ordinary sense. If Jacob succeeds, his good fortune will be assured. Nevertheless it is realized (far more than commentators seem to be aware of) that a wrong is being done both to Esau and, indeed, to Isaac who loves him; and in the event of premature discovery, the result might be disastrous. "My father peradventure will feel me," Jacob says to his mother, "and I shall seem to him as a great deceiver and I shall bring a curse upon me and not a blessing." It is only when she declares, "Upon me be thy curse, my son," that he falls in with her scheme.

Two things may be noted. First, it is expected that Isaac's curse will be directed against the doer, not the planner behind him. No doubt, to some extent, this may be ascribable to the special circumstances—for example, Isaac would be enraged and go for the agent without making long inquiries into the genesis of the deception, and furthermore, the whole scheme is thought out in Jacob's interest, not in Rebekah's. Still, the fact is of more general significance. There is no sign that, say, Rebekah would have to fear a curse as well when Isaac had found out more about the affair. Second, Rebekah relieves Jacob of the risk. We cannot here go into the belief that considers such a transfer possible. The curse belongs to a strange, magic region. In the present connection, what interests is the intellectual author's readiness to expose herself to any untoward consequences in the place of the agent.

Let us go on to Matthew. As in Mark, the chief priests move the people to ask for the release of Barrabas rather than Jesus; and though Pilate cannot find that Jesus has done any wrong, the people vehemently urge that he should be delivered to the soldiers to be crucified, and Pilate gives in.[63] Matthew, however, adds that, before handing him over, Pilate "washed his hands before the people, saying, I am innocent of the blood of this righteous man, see you to it. Then answered all the people and said, His blood be upon us and our children."[64] This is not the place to discuss the historicity or tendency of the insertion. We are concerned with its affinity, after many centuries, with the deal between Jacob and Rebekah—an affinity all the more striking as the ancient case is certainly not in the author's mind. It is just an illustration of the tenacity of certain ideas and the way in which, having been kept out of high literature for a long, long time and condemned to live underground, they may yet suddenly surface again. The report clearly assumes that, but for the transfer, the primary responsibility for Jesus' death would rest on the governor who orders it. As a corollary, the instigators would be responsible only in the second place, if at all. They could feel fairly safe, that is, not having done it themselves. The ceremony of washing on the one hand, however, plus the acceptance of the shed blood on the other effectively alter the case. It would be mistaken to think that the author sees any dishonesty in Pilate's procedure. (The proverbial phrase "I wash my hands of it," incidentally, which derives from this text, need not reflect any ambiguity.) Pilate is completely relieved of the consequences, and they are shifted onto the shoulders of the people—the shed blood having the same magic potentialities as a curse. Once again the intellectual author becomes exposed, or fully exposed, to retribution by voluntarily stepping into the agent's place [see "Causation," chap. 1, section on crucifixion].

It may be of interest to add that, if one man's blood is on another's head, this means that the latter will be attacked by the evil emanating from that blood; and if the blood of a man justly killed is on his own head, it means that he himself, and no one else, will bear the evil.[65] Usually, of course, one man's blood is on another's head because that other is responsible for, the cause of, his death; and a man's blood is on his own head where, though at first sight another might appear responsible, the responsibility is excluded by the special circumstances, thrown back on the guilty victim himself. In a sense he is his own murderer.[66] At the latest in early postbiblical times, the latter case is analyzed (perhaps under Greek influence) to such a degree that the implication is made explicit: the victim is described in so many words as the cause of his execution. For example, in a Tannaitic discussion of the execution of a blasphemer recorded in the Bible, we learn that when the witnesses and judges lean their hands on his head they are to say to him: "Thy blood be upon thy head, for thou hast brought this about."[67]

CHAPTER 7

ATTEMPT

Most modern systems of criminal law operate with the concept of attempt, roughly, that stage where the doer has gone beyond mere contemplation or even preparation of the deed and has proceeded to perform it, but where he has not, or not yet succeeded. If I place a mirror in your barn in order that when the sun comes out a fortnight later the barn may go up in flames, this would be attempted arson; if I shoot at you in order to kill you but miss, this would be attempted murder. Biblical law has no such concept of attempt covering the entire field. Nor do we find it in other ancient laws. On the one hand, it is a major problem of ancient law to confine the punishment to the proven crime. Hence, even in the case of a successful criminal, the law will often require the most precise evidence as a basis for punishment. (That the need of and reliance on rigorous objective criteria on occasion leads to the punishability of a man who is morally blameless we pointed out above in chap. 3, "Error and Ignorance.") A general concept of attempt would mean a giving up of this precision. Indeed, a situation would have to be classified as standing in a certain relation to a specific crime, say, as attempted arson or attempted murder, though this interpretation might be very debatable, hinging principally on the mentality of the doer.

On the other hand, in some areas—for example, political loyalty or disloyalty—a crime may be understood so widely as to include not only definite action but even reprehensible thought insofar as it can be more or less established. In between there are all possible gradations. Mommsen remarked that in Roman law some cases that nowadays can be dealt with as attempts were crimes in their own right. Even nowadays we may make it illegal to carry a weapon, which is less than attempted murder or even preparation of murder. In Leviticus the mere possession of a "familiar spirit" is a capital crime.[1]

SELF-DEFENSE

If self-defense had not been largely taken for granted by ancient law and if its exact limits had received a general definition, we might meet attempt in this connection. For as a rule this right will obtain precisely where the attacker has entered upon the actual perpetration of the deed; so long as he has not, it is too early for legitimate defense, and once the deed is done it is too late, whatever other steps may still be permissible. An indirect reference to self-defense in the cases of murder and rape occurs in the Deuteronomic code,[2] which lays down that if a woman betrothed to one man has intercourse with another in the city, she is to be put to death because "she cried not for help"; whereas if she is "seized and lain with" in the field, she is guiltless, "for as when a man riseth against his neighbor and murdereth him, even so is this matter; she cried and there was none to save her." The law is thinking of a third party coming to the aid of the party threatened; but it is clear that as soon as anyone "rises up against his neighbor to murder him" or as soon as anyone "seizes a betrothed woman to lie with her," the person attacked is entitled to resistance. In these two cases at least, attempt, though not punishable, will exonerate the prospective victim if he or she wounds or kills the attacker.

An earlier code provides that a thief of cattle, detected in the act of breaking in, may be killed without fear of legal consequences.[3] The law assumes that the affair takes place at night and adds that the right to kill ceases with daybreak. It is noteworthy that, according to the original version of the code, theft of cattle is punishable only when the thief has slaughtered or sold the beast: before he has done so, the crime is not proven since the beast might have wandered onto his property or he might have found it straying and taken charge of it in the owner's interest. (Similarly, theft of a person, to be punishable, originally requires sale.[4]) Nonetheless, for the purpose of self-defense he is a thief from the moment of breaking in. He need not even have reached the object he is after. In modern analysis this would be the phase of attempt (leaving aside the independent wrong of illegal entry). In Roman law—at least from early classical times—a person is punishable for theft as soon as he has touched the object, *contrectare*. Yet to make a case on theft for the purpose of self-defense not even *contrectatio* is needed. The XII Tables allow the killing of one who commits theft by night: obviously he need not be asked to touch something before he can be tackled.

There is little more in the codes about self-defense. It was superfluous to allow it in the case of physical assault. The reason for an express provision—both in the Bible and other early laws—in the case of theft is that at some point doubts must here have arisen. We know that as time went on, both in Jewish and Roman law the conditions under which you might kill somebody who had come to steal became stricter and stricter, until the right disappeared.

INTERVENTION BY GOD AND PUNISHMENT

In the biblical stories, self-defense or the warding off of an attack on an ally is of course a common phenomenon. Where God intervenes before a crime is finally carried out, it is sometimes difficult to say whether it is primarily a case of arresting the action at the stage of attempt or one of punishment of attempt. The Sodomites who try to enter Lot's house are afflicted with blindness—clearly in order to prevent them from executing their immoral designs: "and they wearied themselves to find the door."[5] Pharaoh and his army are drowned both in order to save the escaping Israelites and by way of judgment. In the texts it is the particular situation envisaged and perhaps also the outlook of an individual author that determine the relative weight given to either of these ideas. The case of Jeroboam's withered arm is also ambiguous. A prophet condemns his idolatrous altar, whereupon he stretches out his hand and gives order to seize the man. However "his hand dried up so that he could not pull it in again," and he is reduced to having to ask the prophet to pray for him.[6] The miracle certainly saves the prophet. But it may also be punishment; though, if so, one might further ask whether it is punishment of a completed crime, a godless order, or of an attempt to lay hands on the prophet. Probably it is both.

A story may start as a case of self-defense and be reinterpreted as punishment of attempt. The legend of the tower of Babel[7] represents mankind as bent on preserving its unity and building one big city as high as heaven. God, enemy of civilization, and fearful for his power, in self-defense confounds their speech, so that different groups speak different languages and the grandiose, universalist plan must be given up. It is only in subsequent interpretation by developed Jewish and Christian theology that what the people intended becomes an overweening revolt against a good and just God; and, consequently, his reaction becomes punishment of an attempted wicked assault rather than self-defense. The phraseology of the narrative is interesting. "This they have begun to do," God says, "and now (i.e., if they are allowed to go on, if their faculties and facilities are not curtailed) nothing will prevent them from what they devise to do." "To begin to do, to act" might figure in a modern definition of attempt. "To devise to do," *zamam*, we shall actually find in a law to be inspected below, about a false witness who is to suffer "as he had devised to do unto his brother."[8]

Similarly, for developed theology, the expulsion from Eden is nothing but a punishment of disobedience, of the eating of the forbidden fruit. In the story as it stands, however, it is primarily self-defense again, or even a precaution taken before man has had time to think of further steps toward making himself the equal of God. God grudges man immortality and, having realized the ineffectiveness of a prohibition, resorts to preventive force: "and now (the same particle as above: if he is allowed to use his faculties) lest he put forth his hand and take also of the tree of life."[9]

THE HIGH PRIEST'S SERVANT

In one instance a story originally reports something in the nature of punishment and is then reinterpreted as envisaging the warding off of an attack. When the men sent by the Sanhedrin arrested Jesus, one of his followers cut off the ear of the high priest's servant. I have argued elsewhere that in Mark[10] this is a grave insult rather than resistance. In Matthew, however,[11] it is taken to be resistance; Jesus explains that if he so wishes, legions of angels would be at his disposal. The secondariness of Matthew is shown (among other things) by the fact that, as defense, the action comes somewhat late, after the men have taken Jesus. This defect is put right by Luke.[12] Here also it is resistance, but—as is almost overemphasized—at the right moment: "When they which were about him saw what would follow they said, 'Lord, shall we smite with the sword?' And one of them smote." In John,[13] the overemphasis is gone. Jesus meets the men who are to arrest him, and it is he—not, as in Luke, his disciples—who is said to foresee what is to happen. He starts by proving that his mere word could defeat the opposing forces. Next he asks that his disciples should be left unharmed. Then Peter proceeds to armed resistance and Jesus bids him desist. And now he is arrested.

Here is the place to refer to a righteous attempt to kill stopped short by divine intervention. Abraham was bidden to sacrifice Isaac; he had already bound him and taken up the knife when the command was revoked.[14] Insofar as God's response is concerned, in a way the attempt is equated with the completed action: "Thou has not withheld thine only son from me."[15] Yet the negative formulation is significant. "Thou hast not withheld"—not "thou hast offered, sacrificed." In the canonical Old Testament, as is well known, the whole event is alluded to nowhere else. It is alluded to in 1 Maccabees, Judith, and Sirach, where Abraham is described as faithful when tested.[16] In rabbinic literature the story plays a great part, but we never hear of a "sacrifice of Isaac"; it is always a "binding of Isaac" (namely, on the altar). That is all that Abraham did; it did not in fact come to a sacrifice however ready he was for it and however close even in actuality.[17] To be sure, one second-century rabbi, Judah, claims that Isaac was in fact killed and immediately raised, and that he then became the author of the benediction "Blessed art thou, O Lord, who revivest the dead."[18] The Gospels are as silent about the story as the Old Testament. In the Epistles, on the other hand, we find the expression that has become prevalent, "sacrifice of Isaac" instead of "binding": both in Hebrews and James "Abraham offered up Isaac."[19] Doubtless the change is due to the influence of Jesus' death, a sacrifice completed. This reacted back on the interpretation and formulation of the Old Testament story of a father willing to give his son and a son willingly yielding. Confirmation is supplied by a passage in Romans.[20] Paul says of God that "he withheld not his own son but delivered him up for us all." The negative phrase from the Old Testament is here expanded by the addition of the positive "and he delivered him up." It is easy to see how the positive might penetrate into the earlier story itself.

Let us note, in passing, that the jailer of Paul and Silas[21] who, believing that his prisoners had escaped, drew his sword to commit suicide, and who changed his mind when Paul exclaimed that they were all present, has no place in a discussion of attempted crime. There is no reason to suppose that the narrator disapproves of his intent.

PUNISHABILITY; CASES IN THE CODES AND NOT IN THE CODES; FALSE WITNESS

There are in the Old Testament very few laws rendering punishable an attempted crime, and it is hardly accidental that these few are all in Deuteronomy. One, which we mentioned in chapter 6 on Intellectual Authorship, is directed against a person trying to seduce another person to idolatry: he is to be put to death.[22] The law addresses the person on whom the seducer works: "If thy brother entice thee, thou shalt not consent neither shalt thou spare him." It is in the nature of the case that the criminal can be punished only if he was unsuccessful, if he whom he hoped to win over denounces him. That the lawgiver looks at the matter from this point of view, that he sees it as attempted seduction rather than as a completed crime consisting in the utterance of false doctrine, may be gathered from the justification of the death penalty: "because he hath sought to thrust thee from the Lord." This verb *biqqesh*, "to seek to do," is frequently used of intent that has not materialized at all. It has all the range from here to, say, Saul's endeavor to decimate the Gibeonites with which he made a good beginning.[23]

The law is preceded by a similar one, equally mentioned above, about a pseudo-prophet, able to furnish a sign though he advocates apostasy. Again it is a case of attempted seduction. This law does not use the verb *biqqesh*, but the element of attempt is nonetheless unmistakably brought out. The prophet, we are warned, must die because he preached "to thrust thee from the way thy God commanded thee": the infinitive of purpose, very common. And, evidently, he has not succeeded in his undertaking, else he would not be hauled before the court.

The next law here relevant is that which enjoins to do to a false witness "as he had thought to have done unto his brother."[24] Both the penalty and the way it is formulated, with emphasis on what the criminal *zamam*, "thought to have done," render it certain that the matter is conceived of not just as the completed crime of false testimony but also, and maybe primarily, as an elaborate attempt to get at an enemy, to have him killed or maimed by using the judicial apparatus of the community.

Whereas the Pharisees applied this law only where the falsity of the charge was discovered in time and the accused had not been executed, the Sadducees applied it only where execution had taken place. Some modern scholars conclude that, because the Sadducean position is the fairer and more rational and more consistent with the general reluctance of Old Testament law to punish attempt, it must accurately reflect the sense of the ancient regulation; or at least that regulation must have been designed for both cases, that where the witness did not succeed and that where he did. However, it is the interpretation of the Pharisees—less fair, less rational, and less reconcilable with the norm—that is historically correct. The law refers to attempt only, not to the case where the accused had in fact been killed or maimed. This is corroborated by Josephus.[25] It is supported by the absence of any record anywhere of a false witness being tried after procuring his victim's death or mutilation: in the case of Susannah and the Elders, these were put to death having failed in their plot. Above all, it is confirmed by comparative law. There is no getting around the fact that the Code of Hammurabi also prescribes talion only if the false charge remained abortive.[26]

As a matter of fact even the Pharisees changed the original regulation—a little only in theory, radically in effect: they required that, to be punishable, the false testimony must have led to a verdict of guilty against the accused, though the verdict must not yet have been carried out. This is a weakening of the original meaning, due to two factors: dislike even on the part of the Pharisees of punishment of a mere attempt, and dislike of the death penalty as such. The Pharisaic solution in effect confines punishability to the case of the falsity of the charge coming to light between the sentence and its execution. It is an unlikely case, though exemplified by the—Pharisaic—model story of Susannah and the Elders: here, there was divine intervention. It follows that, as far as practice, not theory, is concerned, the Pharisees turn out more lenient on the false witness than the Sadducees: a good illustration of how careful one must be not to be misled by the appearances of doctrine. The witnesses against Jesus whose charge, if we go by Mark,[27] collapsed could not have been prosecuted even under Pharisaic law: no sentence had been pronounced on the basis of their testimony. However, the Deuteronomic regulation, like Hammurabi's, knows no such refinement: any false witness exposed in time—though only one exposed in time—is punishable.

There are three reasons for restriction of punishability to attempt. First, there is in ancient criminal prosecution an element of single combat, duel, ordeal. Either the accused or the witness will go down, but not one after the other. (Under Hammurabi, a man charged with sorcery must leap into the holy river. If he drowns, the accuser gets his house; if he comes back, the accuser is put to death and his house belongs to the accused.)[28] Second, once the charge has succeeded and the penalty has been inflicted, resumption would lead to a tremendous upheaval. It would involve the judges, all members of the community who took part in the proceedings—impossible. Finally, it would not do for a code like Deuteronomy or Hammurabi's formally to make provision for a court being misled to the extent of sending an innocent person to execution. It is easier to admit that there may now and then be a corrupt judge than that a court may sentence a good man to death or mutilation from a well-intentioned error. Nor should we feel greatly superior. Even nowadays governments are reluctant to reopen cases of this kind, and some sound grounds for such reluctance are the same as in biblical times.

This does not mean that the possibility of a false witness succeeding was not seen. But for the intervention of a young prophet, Susannah would have lost her life. Naboth did lose his.[29] To be sure, his judges were no less corrupt than the witnesses, but there would be nothing surprising in a story that laid all blame on the latter. The false witnesses testifying against Stephen also seem to have carried the day, though the execution is depicted as somewhat irregular.[30] Again, we are far from contending that a false witness who has succeeded need go out scot-free. The fact that the code ordains no punishment does not prevent self-help or communal vengeance. Ahab and Jezebel were told by Elijah that God would exact retribution. True, no mention is made of the false witnesses themselves: they are regarded as of secondary importance compared with the queen who initiated the scandalous affair and the king who reaped the benefit.

Of a further law it is doubtful whether it is meant to deal with attempt.[31] A newly married man who wrongly claims that his wife did not come to him as a virgin is to be chastised, has to pay her father a sum of money, and loses the right to divorce her; on the other hand, if his charge is true, the woman will be put to death. At first sight that half which assumes the charge to be unjustified might appear analogous to the more general law about a false witness just discussed. That law, we saw, pays attention to what the accuser "sought to do unto his brother." However, in the present case the slander as such seems to be the crime, complete in itself, not thought of as an attempt to murder the woman.

The main reason is that the accuser here will normally be convinced, or at least more or less convinced, of the truth of his allegation. He is not basically a "witness of lie." Certainly he is described as "hating" the woman. That is indeed implied in his turning against her: he is angry, disappointed. But the law does not contemplate the case—unlikely, perverse, reminiscent of Amnon—of a man coolly deciding on the morrow of his wedding to rob his innocent wife of her life by means of a trumped-up capital charge. Hence no reference to intent to kill; hence also the relatively light punishment. The latter is indeed advisable on other grounds: it would be of no use to the wife's father—who receives primary consideration from the lawgiver—to prescribe execution of her husband. On the contrary, the latter will now never be able to rid himself of this status. That no account is taken of the fact that a union starting in such inauspicious conditions will hardly be a source of happiness to the woman gives the legislation almost a modern touch. We must, however, not forget that though once things have reached this pass hardship will ensue, the regulation has the beneficial overall effect of making a man think twice before preferring a rash accusation.

It might be asked why a husband should ever take recourse to an accusation, seeing that in ordinary circumstances divorce is extremely easy. To this the answer is first, that groundless divorce is usually accompanied by financial disadvantages, and second, that a man believing himself to be wronged—and we have just noted that it is of such a one that the law speaks—is out for vengeance. Mary's husband proved himself "righteous" in being "unwilling to make her a public example and resolving to divorce her privily."[32] It makes no difference whether he might have proceeded under the law here discussed or another one in the same section of Deuteronomy concerning a betrothed woman who gives herself to another man.[33]

(Strack-Billerbeck's antirabbinic interpretation of Matthew is untenable. They paraphrase "Joseph, though righteous, was unwilling to make her an example"; the implication being that "righteous, just" for the Rabbis meant to exact any retribution the law would grant you. Apart from the fact that, if we take the remark in this way, it would follow that Matthew accepts this notion of justice, in the Greek before us righteousness is palpably the explanation of Joseph's conduct, not a potential obstacle: *Iōsēph dikaios ōn kai mē thelōn autēn deigmatisai,* "Joseph, being righteous and not wanting to make her an example." That Strack-Billerbeck twist the natural meaning is understandable considering the time in which they wrote. Regrettably the New English Bible relies on them and mistranslates: "being a man of principle and at the same time wanting to save her from exposure." It is amusing to watch the slow dawn of truth. Schlatter[34] realizes that the text simply cannot be understood otherwise than "Joseph, being righteous, just": causal. But he still will not admit that the rabbinic "righteous, just" may mean "forgiving." So he contends that Joseph already knew of the miracle and wanted to divorce Mary because he felt unworthy. But we need only render the full remark along his line to see that it does not work; "being righteous, i.e., believing in the miracle and considering himself too small, he was unwilling to make a public example of her and resolved to put her away privily." Schrenk, in his paragraph on rabbinism in the article *dikaios* in Kittel's *Theologisches Wörterbuch*,[35] does not go beyond Strack-Billerbeck. Yet it would not even be necessary to know rabbinic literature to appreciate the liberal range of *saddiq*, "just, righteous." It is in the Old Testament that Saul says to David: "Thou art more righteous than I, for thou hast rewarded me good whereas I have rewarded thee evil. For if a man find his enemy and let him go away well and safe ..."[36] Lohmeyer[37] gives the correct interpretation of Joseph's conduct and does quote Old Testament evidence for *saddiq* and *dikaios* in the sense of *gütig*, falling within the area of *ḥesedh*, "kindness, mercy, grace.")

Our analysis of this law as concerned with slander, not attempt, is consistent with its position: it opens a section concerning adultery and so on, three chapters after the law concerning false testimony. In the Code of Hammurabi—where, incidentally, even the law concerning the false witness has no express reference to what "he thought to do" but simply imposes on him the punishment carried by the crime he imputes—there are several provisions dealing with defamation as a completed crime, without construing it as attempt. If you slander the chastity of a married woman or a priestess you are flogged and have half your beard shaved off, if you slander a friend to such effect that his prospective father-in-law refuses him his daughter, you are precluded from marrying her.[38] The latter rule is a neat foil to the Deuteronomic law that ties a slanderer to a woman for good.

While no other extant law makes attempt punishable, it is by no means certain that there were not more offenses where semilegal custom at least sanctioned the punishment of attempt. We are thinking, for example, of political crimes. Soon after Solomon's ascent to the throne his elder brother Adonijah asked for the hand of Abishag, the girl who had ministered to David in his last illness.[39] The appropriation of a deceased king's harem was the prerogative of his successor, and though David had no longer been able to make Abishag his mistress, Solomon put the worst construction on Adonijah's request and had him killed. Admittedly, when it is a question of rivals for a crown, their calculations peaceful or murderous will not be governed by the law. Nonetheless it was probably recognized as well within the privileges of a monarch to eliminate a person of rank who threatened to become a danger. The problem is whether we ought to speak of attempt or whether disaffection is not by itself a full crime. That an element of attempt does play a part in the present story is suggested by Solomon's angry exclamation to his mother who (with what loyalty we can only guess) acts as Adonijah's messenger: "Why dost thou ask Abishag for him? Ask for him the kingdom also." On the other hand, how wide a prominent subject's duty is and how the slightest deviation may constitute him a criminal is clear from the words with which Solomon spared Adonijah's life earlier on, when the former's superior claims were first acknowledged: "If he will show himself a worthy man, not an hair of him shall fall to the earth; but if wickedness shall be found in him, he shall die." From the moment that a man *cupit imperium*, Tacitus represents Vespasian as deliberating,[40] the alternative to success is ruin; there is no halfway house.

In a much later source, the book of Esther,[41] we are told how two of Ahasuerus' courtiers "sought," "plotted," to murder the king and were hanged. It is not necessary to inquire the system of which country is reflected in this book. A conspiracy against the king's life might be punished with death anywhere; and it would surely be felt to be in accordance with sound usage. It is stated that the two were hanged only after careful investigation. With this we may contrast the king's outburst when Haman had fallen from grace and, fearing for his life, embraced the knees of the queen who was lying on her couch.[42] The king, returning to the room at that moment chose to interpret the gesture as an attempt to overpower his queen and, at the suggestion of a courtier, ordered the culprit to the gallows, which happened to be available. No doubt an absolute monarch could do this, but the storyteller shows his awareness that it was an exercise of power in—justified—passion rather than application of law or custom. "Then was the king's wrath pacified," ends the chapter.

In international relations an illuminating example of the extent to which the careful, narrow evidence of internal criminal law is dispensed with is supplied by the treatment of spies. The crime is completed by mere entry of the country to be explored. Entry is not treated as attempt to explore and report. That would indeed be a highly academic approach since by the time the mission is carried out a spy will often be beyond the reach of the injured party. The very term for "spy" reveals the nature of the crime: *meraggel*, "one that goes about." (The English term also designates the activity from the first moment.) Moreover, a spy need not come from an enemy country; a potentially hostile one is enough.[43] Altogether an alien may easily be suspected. Here, then, we have an instance of the phenomenon referred to above; the law—international law—treats as a crime what we might equally well analyze as attempt or even preparatory steps. Joseph pretended to his brothers to believe that they were spies, which under the recognized usage of the time certainly entitled him to shut them up.[44] The king of Jericho made vain efforts to seize the Israelite spies harbored by Rahab.[45] On Hanun's accession to the throne of Amnon, David sent ambassadors to congratulate him. Hanun, however, formed the opinion that they were spies and inflicted grave public insults on them—with war as a result.[46] Conversely, the Babylonian ambassadors who came to pay a sick visit to King Hezekiah (or to inquire about an astronomical event for which Isaiah had prayed as a sign that the king would be restored) seem to have been looked on as spies by Israel.[47]

Within the family, again, custom presumably sanctioned the punishability of attempt. From Potiphar's point of view Joseph was guilty of attempt to have intercourse with his master's wife.[48] Imprisonment was a relatively mild punishment, explicable because an intelligent slave was too valuable an asset to waste without absolute necessity and also, most probably, because the deed had not in fact been carried out.

It is easy to account for the statutory punishability of the false witness. Besides the element of battle, ordeal—note that the law calls the witness and the accused "the two men between whom the controversy is" (*ribh*, "strife, litigation") and that the two "shall stand before the Lord, before the priests and judges"—there is the fact that in this one case the usual difficulty in regard to evidence does not arise. The attempt is committed under the eyes of the court, in fact, by misusing the court itself; and failure to substantiate the charge is almost sufficient to convict him who preferred it. By contrast, the attempt, say, of a wife to seduce her husband to idolatry must be very hard to establish, yet this is one of the two other cases of attempt singled out by statute. It is astonishing. No law about attempted murder, but one imposing the death penalty on an attempt consisting in words personally communicated. Then, the pseudo-prophet: even he may give his sign to an individual or a small circle, so even here the evidence will be precarious. The conclusion is that the stopping up of any source of heresy was so essential that the normal safeguards were thrown to the winds. Alas, history offers more examples of the sort in this and similar fields.

A remarkable historical point arises. At least the law against an ordinary person advocating apostasy, and possibly also that against a pseudo-prophet, must be assigned to a time before the minimum number of witnesses in a criminal trial was two. The former law assumes the most intimate procedure on the part of the seducer: "If thy brother, the son of thy mother, or thy son or thy daughter or the wife of thy bosom or thy friend which is as thine own soul, entice thee secretly." Moreover it is "thou" who must denounce him and "thou" whose hand shall cast the first stone. The law concerning the pseudo-prophet is less unambiguous in this respect, but maybe he too could originally be brought to justice by one witness. Even in much later times, incidentally, in these cases, it looks from rabbinic sources that exceptions were made to the normal requirements for conviction; but we shall not enlarge on this aspect.

We would, however, go further. The law against the false witness also most probably antedates the minimum number of two. It opens "If a false witness rise up," it goes on to speak of "the two men between whom the controversy is," and it ordains talion, "then shall ye do unto him as he had thought to have done." All this suggests a single witness. Actually, it would appear that the law was first formulated precisely against abuse of the law or laws against the seducer to idolatry—against abuse, that is, of the law or laws so dangerous in enabling a man to bring another man to death by a charge of heretical counsel. One indication of this narrow, early scope is the term *sara*. The false witness is described as testifying against a man *sara*, generally translated "that which is wrong." But the original sense was probably far more specific, "apostasy": the false witness testifies that the accused has tried to turn him from God. The word recurs in six more texts.[49] In five the meaning "apostasy" is universally admitted.[50] Indeed, one of these five is the very law imposing the death penalty on the pseudo-prophet because "he spoke apostasy"[51]—surely a most suggestive coincidence. That leaves only one verse in Isaiah,[52] and even here, there is nothing to rule out the meaning "apostasy." It does seem that the law against a false witness started by contemplating specifically the charge of attempted seduction to idolatry and was only extended in course of time. Needless to say, when the ending was written, "life for life, eye for eye," etc.,[53] the range was already generalized.

As already pointed out (chap. 2, "Intent," on p. 52), rabbinism and the New Testament give much prominence to mentality even where no crime or only the first step toward a crime has resulted. "Ye have heard, Thou shalt not kill, but I say, That whosoever is angry with his brother shall be in danger of the judgment. Ye have heard, Thou shalt not commit adultery, but I say, That whosoever looketh on a woman to lust after her hath committed adultery in his heart." It would be rash to infer that this meant a more liberal punishability of attempt. There is much confusion about owing to the comparison of like with unlike. Where it is a question of moral exhortation, even the Old Testament has a provision like "Thou shalt not covet." But the rabbinic or early Christian courts no more than the Old Testament fined or put to death a man for anger with his brother or for lust after a woman. Attempt is indeed a stage where the culprit has already proceeded to action. However, on the whole, the factors militating against general punishability in Old Testament times still operated by the beginning of our era.

LANGUAGE: *"To think"; "to seek"; "to speak"; "to prepare"; "to devise"; "to hope"; "evil"; the Infinitive*

As regards terminology, it is doubtful whether biblical Hebrew has a word signifying "to attempt." We find actions constituting attempt, the throwing of a weapon and the like; and we find the intent behind actions—for example, the false witness "devised" (*zaman*) to afflict an evil on the accused and God disliked what the builders of the tower of Babel "devised" (*zaman*) to do. But, with the very dubious exception of *nissa* to be analyzed presently, we do not find "attempt" as such.

The book of Esther is all about wicked or presumptuous plans thwarted, but "to attempt" does not occur. It begins with Vashti's recalcitrance, which, unless made an example of, might encourage other ladies to disobey their husbands. Here we would not expect "attempt" since she did not really act with a view to this dreaded consequence. Next come the conspirators against the king's life who "sought" to lay hands on him, *biqqesh*.[54] We met this verb in the law about the seducer to apostasy; it may refer to intent or wish from the moment it is formed through all phases of preparation and action to the full attainment of the object. In the present case it is associated with preparatory measures. We are told that Mordecai laid information, which would no longer have been necessary after a proper attempt, and even then the matter had still to be investigated. The verb recurs right at the beginning of Haman's anti-Jewish career. Offended by Mordecai "he scorned to lay hands on him alone but sought to destroy all Jews."[55] Here we are at an even earlier stage, in fact, where Haman makes up his mind. Three comparable passages: Joseph, not yet recognized by his brothers, "sought" to weep and therefore left the room;[56] Jonathan "sought," that is, planned, to get into the camp of the Philistines;[57] Hadad, an honored exile in Egypt, "sought," that is, decided and asked permission, to return to Edom;[58] Saul "sought," that is, resolved, to march against a city that would harbor David;[59] Joab "sought," that is, took energetic measures, to destroy one which harbored Sheba.[60] The verb is common where a man is in a general way out to eliminate an enemy: Pharaoh versus Moses;[61] with the echo in Matthew, Herod and his henchmen versus the young Jesus;[62] Saul versus David;[63] Solomon versus Jeroboam.[64] In the law concerning an advocate of idolatry the verb is connected with attempt. So it is in the story of the Lord "seeking" to kill Moses' firstborn son[65] as well as that of Saul's second assault on David: "And Saul sought to smite David to the wall with the javelin, but he slipped away."[66]

Haman, asked by the king to suggest a suitable honor for an unnamed favorite, "spoke in his heart," 'amar belibbo, that is, secretly deliberated, calculated, that only himself could be meant and accordingly came out with the most elaborate honor.[67] Such secret deliberation occurs in other unpleasant minds: "And Esau (defrauded of his birthright) spoke in his heart, 'The days of mourning for my father are at hand—then will I slay my brother Jacob.'"[68] Evidently, again a reference to intent. The word 'amar, "to speak," alone—that is, without "in his heart"—may signify the same, except that the emphasis on secrecy is absent. "And Saul cast the javelin, and he said, wayyo'mer, I will smite David to the wall,"[69] or a few verses further on, where Saul promises David his daughter if he defeats the Philistines, "He said, 'amar, Let not mine hand be upon him but the hand of the Philistines."[70] We have just seen that, at Saul's second attempt to kill David, instead of a monologue there is an objective report: "he sought, biqqesh, to smite David to the wall." The interchangeability (mutatis mutandis) of the two expressions is significant.

To go on with the book of Esther, as the king finds Haman urging the queen to spare his life, he exclaims, "To force the queen?" likhbosh, infinitive.[71] It is usually interpreted as "Do you (or, Does he) intend to force the queen?" Something like this is no doubt meant, but we should not exaggerate the element of intent. The infinitive here is rather an overall description of the situation; the nearest English equivalent might be "What? Forcing the queen!" Certainly the infinitive can convey purpose, especially after another verb, and we may adduce from Esther the summary toward the end where it is recorded that Haman "cast lots to destroy the Jews."[72] The pseudo-prophet, the law says, is to suffer death because "he hath spoken apostasy to thrust thee from the Lord."[73]

The verb hekhin, "to prepare, get ready, put up," denotes a measure taken by Haman for the ultimate dispatch of Mordecai. Haman was hanged on the gallows "he had got ready" for the other.[74] God, the Psalmist warns, "hath prepared" instruments of death for the impenitent wicked,[75] but the wicked "have prepared" a net for the steps of the just.[76]

Hashabh, "to think, reckon, devise," and the corresponding noun mahashabha, occupy a dominant position in the book of Esther. Esther entreated the king "to put away Haman's device which he devised against the Jews,"[77] "to reverse the letters, the device of Haman,"[78] and the summary declares that Haman "devised against the Jews to destroy them" and "his evil device which he had devised returned upon his head."[79] In the same way, for example, Saul "devised" to get David out of the way, when he promised him his daughter should he slay a hundred Philistines;[80] or Nehemiah's antagonists "devised to do him evil," or again insinuated that he was "devising to rebel."[81] "Evil" both as an adjective and as a noun is of course often associated with planning, intent, resolve. In a passage just cited, the fuller text is that Esther entreated the king "to put away the evil of Haman and his device which he devised."[82] Haman begged for his life realizing "that the evil was determined against him from the king."[83] There is a law defining an unwitting homicide as one who "did not seek his (the victim's) evil." ("To seek," biqqesh.)[84] And we may recall Solomon's warning, "If evil shall be found in him (Adonijah) he shall die."[85]

Finally, the day when the Jews overwhelmed their opponents was the one on which the latter śibberu, "hoped," to overwhelm the former: śibber, "to hope, wait for, anticipate."

MODERN HEBREW: *"to attempt"*

It is noteworthy that *nissa*, the root which in modern Hebrew law stands for "to attempt" and so on, never occurs in this legal application in the Bible. The explanation is that its original meaning at least is nearer to "to test." Whereas an attempt is made in order to achieve a certain result, a test is made in order to establish the nature and qualifications of an object, an affair, or a person. Evidently it is the former, not the latter, that may constitute a stage in crime. However, we shall go further: we shall submit that even in extralegal biblical language *nissa* probably never signifies "to attempt."

TESTING AND TEMPTING

On the verb in the sense of "to test a person" or "to tempt a person," so much has been written that we may confine ourselves to a few points. We take it that the chief difference is that "to tempt" implies a wish that the victim should succumb, whereas "to test" is essentially neutral. (Hence you can "tempt" only an animate being, but you may "test" anything.) A secondary difference is that "to tempt" implies the holding out of an allurement, whereas "to test" essentially tells us nothing as to method. Any "tempting" is a "testing," but the reverse is by no means true.

Taking "to tempt," then, as implying a wish to make the victim succumb, we can say that *nissa* is never used thus in the canonical Old Testament.[86] Mostly it is used not of one man "testing" another, but of God "testing" man and of man "testing" God. The idea of man "tempting" God would not be expected. But neither do we find God "tempting" man. When God wishes man to do wrong—for instance, Pharaoh whose heart was hardened[87] or David whom he moved to take a census[88]—man does wrong. (Unfortunately, God's wish for man to do right does not work the same way.) God may indeed allow others to see whether they can get a person to sin—a false prophet, Satan in the case of Job. But as far as his role in this is concerned, he is "testing" that person. We are told so expressly in regard to the false prophet: "thou shalt not hearken, for the Lord testeth you."[89] In the case of Job it is indeed doubtful whether we should even think of a test. God is so convinced of Job's integrity that his only purpose may be the refutation of the skeptical Satan and the exaltation of the hero. The word *nissa* is conspicuously absent, though the LXX smuggles in its Greek equivalent in several places. Perhaps more doubts should be expressed. It is uncertain even whether the author would have thought of Satan as trying to "seduce," "entice" Job. These notions usually include an element of allurement, something pleasant held out as reward—as does "temptation." Satan, however, simply inflicts on Job misery upon misery in order to make him or show him up as disloyal to God. Job's wife, by contrast, does refer to a reward—a quick, defiant death: "Curse God and die."[90]

Another story mistakenly classed by modern writers under "temptation" is the Fall. Seesemann (who makes no distinction between "to test," *prüfen*, and "tempt," *versuchen*) says that it is accidental that *nissa* does not figure in it.[91] He is somewhat troubled by such an early case of God's adversary "tempting" man; except for this case, in early times it is always God who does it, and only late literature knows of an adversary to separate man from God. As a matter of fact, the narrative as it stands tells neither of test nor temptation but of how man acquired knowledge against the will of a jealous God with the aid of a friendly being. We have repeatedly commented on the subsequent reinterpretation of the story. In the first century *Vita Adae* we do hear of "seduction."[92]

TESTING MAN AND TESTING GOD

It looks as if the idea of God testing man had first come up, and always remained prominent, in explanation of events that might prima facie militate against God's omnipotence, omniscience, truthfulness, or morality. Contrary to some promises, God for a long time after Joshua's death refrained from driving out the remaining heathen nations from Canaan: his object being to "test" the people—would they prove steadfast or follow their neighbors?[93] (Other explanations of the delay: God was angry with the wicked people,[94] or those generations which had not taken part in the main conquest of Canaan ought to learn the art of war;[95] or—in a similar context[96]—the enemy's measure of guilt is not yet full, or delay provides an opportunity for more and greater miracles.)[97] Again, the forty years in the wilderness were due not to any lack of power on the part of God, but to the need to "test" and educate the people.[98] (Other explanation: they were a punishment for the people allowing themselves to be misled by an unfavorable report about the promised land.[99]) The order that only one day's supply of manna should be collected might appear arbitrary, senseless; it served to "test" the people's obedience.[100] A false prophet may be able to furnish a sign: once more this happens only because God wants it to happen for the purpose of "testing" you.[101]

Even the great "test" of Abraham seems to belong here. Whether or not there was at one time a version of the narrative without this concept, its introduction answers the question of how God could make such a monstrous demand as that to sacrifice Isaac. A case with notable consequences is the summary of Hezekiah's reign by the Chronicler. This king prospered in everything, and even his one brief lapse into pride only brought out more shiningly his true humble nature.[102] The Chronicler explains why such a good king was left to stumble: "God forsook him to test him, to know all that was in his heart." When Jesus exclaimed, in the words of the Psalmist, "My God, why has thou forsaken me?"[103] he was displaying a feature of Hezekiah—whose role as a messianic figure in Judaism was far greater than is commonly supposed. Jesus, a greater Hezekiah, emerged triumphant.

Lastly, we should call attention to the widespread doctrine of the Rabbis that the sufferings of the righteous are "tests." (It may well go back to Old Testament times, but there is no clear evidence.) The origin here postulated for the idea of God testing man is still noticeable: the doctrine helps to uphold belief in God's justice.

We may still ask whether it is possible to account for the choice of this idea by those who had to explain God's doings. Probably familiarity with ordeal or oracle had to do with it: familiarity, that is, with the testing of a man, or an issue between two men, or even an issue between man and God, by means of some supernatural agency—which would soon be identified with God. We may recall the way Achan's crime was detected.[104] Two obscure texts are highly suggestive. One says that at the well of Marah God "set up for him (Moses) statute and ordinance and there he tested him."[105] The combination of law-giving and testing evokes the kind of ordeal or oracle anciently associated with holy centers. The second passage is from the blessing of Moses: "And of Levi he said, Let thy Thummim and Urim be with thy pious man (Aaron) whom thou didst test at Massah and with whom thou didst strive at Meribah."[106] Here the oracle is actually mentioned; and it is combined with testing and with "striving," the Hebrew for which signifies also legal contest. (There is of course punning on the place names: Massah "test," Meribah "strife, litigation.") When the queen of Sheba is represented as having come to "test" Solomon with riddles,[107] the verb may contain a vestige of the oracular meaning; and so, in a different way, it may in the utterance of the Preacher, "All this I have tested by wisdom."[108] The book of Daniel, late as it is, has a proper ordeal.[109] Four young Jews, destined to be pages of the king of Babylon, are unwilling to take the unclean food and wine provided for them, but the supervisor is afraid that their looks might suffer. Daniel proposes: "Test thy servants ten days, and let them give us pulse and water. So he tested them ten days, and at the end their countenance appeared fairer than all who did eat the king's meat."

By starting from ordeal or oracle, we shall also understand the background of man's "testing" of God. Naturally most texts disapprove, and one might almost conclude that it is a secondary arrogation by man of a right belonging only to God.[110] In reality it is as old as God's "testing" of man, and not at all inherently wicked. Ordeal and oracle serve not only to test man but also to test God. This is true even where it is primarily a question of judging a man or between two men: even here the verdict will reveal God's views and directives. It is obvious where it is a question of divine blessing of or opposition to an undertaking. Gideon wanted confirmation that he could rely on God's assistance: "Let me test with the fleece, let it be dry only upon the fleece and upon all the ground let there be dew."[111] In the call of Moses we do not hear of a "test" of God. Yet, on Moses displaying some doubts, God offered various "signs"—in Hebrew 'oth—without being expressly asked.[112] We do, however, find "tests" in the recurrent description of the way God delivered the nation from Egypt "with tests, signs, and wonders."[113] These "tests" (the AV, quite wrongly, renders "temptations") are invariably interpreted as worked by God on man: God, it is thought, in the exodus proved the people's character.[114]

But the pairing off with "signs ('othoth) and wonders" shows that it is "tests" supplied to man by God. In two of the passages we read of "the great tests which thine eyes saw": surely not provings of character, but events like the turning of the river into blood. In the third passage God is praised as "having taken him a nation from the midst of another nation, with tests, signs, wonders, war, a mighty hand, a stretched-out arm, great terrors, according to all that the Lord did for you in Egypt before your eyes"; the interpretation here rejected would produce a gulf between the first noun and all the rest. We may indeed assume that the triad "tests, signs, wonders" became current before the disapproval of man's testing of God was general. A "sign," 'oth, is associated with a "testing" of God in Isaiah.[115] Isaiah, having assured King Ahaz that his enemies will not prevail, offers him any "sign" he may request. The king refuses: "I will not ask neither will I test the Lord." To which Isaiah replies that God will give a "sign" unasked (namely, the famous birth of Immanuel). Whether the king refused from a hypocritical show of piety (as is usually held) or from fear or from indifference, Isaiah sees no wrong in the "test."

That ordeal and oracle are potentially ambivalent, a test of God as well as man, is illustrated by the treatment of Massah and Meribah. While in the passage quoted above, with the Urim and Thummim, these are places where God "tested" and "strove, litigated with" man; in others the people there "tested" and "strove, litigated with" God or his servant Moses. (We have already enumerated these passages as expressing disapproval of a testing of God by man.) In the story of Gideon we can observe the transition from a legitimate testing of God to one that is objectionable. Gideon first asks that the dew should be on the fleece only, with all the rest of the ground dry. This is granted. Then he asks for the opposite, and this time he opens: "Let not thine anger be hot and I will speak but this once." The coming back betrays a lack of trust, which might be taken amiss. When Moses hesitated too long to accept God's call, God did show anger.[116] Time came when the dominant theology at least rejected as faithless any "testing" of God: man must always have absolute confidence.

As by rabbinic times "to test God" had acquired the character of a wrong, the term is not used where, say, a rabbi asks heaven to intervene in a debate and decide a point. Nor would the corresponding Greek occur in the New Testament, say, in the election of a successor to Judas, though God is invoked to direct the lots.[117] As for *nissa* in the sense of "to attempt" in modern Hebrew law, the development may perhaps be summed up thus. In English, the two verbs "to attempt" and "to try" are more or less synonymous. Yet the two nouns "attempt" and "trial," both technical legal terms, denote very different things. It is only in "trial" that a trace of test and ordeal survives. In Hebrew, *nissa* primitively was no doubt connected with "trial"; but that stage is buried under so many layers—among them the old translations of the Bible—that by now it has entirely shifted over to "attempt."

We indicated above that even in extralegal biblical speech *nissa* perhaps never signifies "to attempt." Only two passages need to be considered. One is from Job.[118] Eliphaz, the first friend to reply to him, begins: "If we attempt a word to thee." However, apart from the dubiousness of the text,[119] at a pinch we could translate: "If we test the matter with thee."

The only text where *nissa* is followed by an infinitive we have already quoted: "Or hath any god assayed to take him a nation from the midst of another nation, with tests, signs" and so on.[120] Surely, in view of the tests and signs emphasized, it is far more plausible, instead of assuming a singular use of the verb, to translate: "Or hath any god displayed such a test, sign, as to take him" and so on. It is in any case difficult to understand the "assaying" here. In the preceding verse the rhetorical question is: "Did ever another people hear the voice of a god out of the midst of the fire?" The stress is on what actually happened. The Piel *nissa* is very suitable to express the "display of a test."

It might perhaps be claimed that there is another occurrence of *nissa* with the infinitive, namely, where terrible hardships are predicted for "the tender woman who would not adventure to set the sole of her foot upon the ground."[121] But the Hebrew has: "who would not test the sole of her foot—to set it on the ground." Not "to attempt to do," but "to test an object for doing." The shade of meaning is remotely similar to that in the story of David and Goliath.[122] Saul put his armor on David who "made ready to walk (or, who labored vainly to walk[123]) for he had not tested, and David said, I cannot walk with these for I have not tested." Here one is reminded of a particular nuance of Greek *peirao*, that is, where it coincides with Latin *experiri* and German *erfahren* (etymologically allied). The shepherd boy has never proved, experienced, knightly accoutrement. At any rate we may note that no infinitive follows *nissa* in this story.

CHAPTER 8

COLLECTIVES

There may have been fewer kinds of collectives in biblical times than today, but even so the number was large. A family, the children within a family, a city, a tribe, a people, a king's advisors, a guild of artisans, a sect, a band of prophets, a circle of master and disciples, a gang of freebooters, a caravan— these are among the most familiar examples of groups treated as entities. Some would be far more important than others; some would be more or less stable, others rather temporary; some might be collectives for certain purposes only, others for practically all purposes; not to mention the changes any one of them might undergo in the course of evolution. All these varieties must be borne in mind when we inquire into deeds done by a collective.

TYPICAL OFFENSES

When all members of a collective act—as approximately in the case of Jacob's escape from Laban, which he discusses with his wives, or a unanimous mutiny—one could not say such and such an individual acted and also the collective acted. Only the latter is correct, in a sense. "To make war," "to make a mutiny," or "to make a revolution"—are these actions necessarily collective? No. But there does exist a distinction between a real action by a collective and an action that we ascribe to it. In the case of Dinah in Gen 34, one man, Shechem, acts, yet the whole also can be said to act. As in other areas, such views are sometimes less literal. One test of the literalness is to note the legal consequence. In the case of Shechem, the entire male collective is killed.

But even here there is a demand for a subsequent excuse. Jacob's sons who did the killing make clear, albeit in a second explanation, why they acted as they did: "Should he deal with our sister as with a harlot?"[1]

Lack of literalness is not possible where all members of the collective wage war: only the whole acts (apart from the ruler who represents all). What is a typical offense of a collective varies with political-social change. So long as a political unit is small—a family, for instance—theft and rape are two examples of perfectly feasible offenses that can be ascribed to the collective. When the units are bigger, less personal offenses are in the foreground—war and revolts being examples.

There can be a personification of the collective so that by way of metaphor it acts as an individual: Israel "whores" and the faithless people "commit adultery." The case of personification is less interesting here than that of the attribution of an individual's act to the collective. I shall concentrate on the latter. In one sense, all human action is by individuals. Therefore, whenever a collective is the doer there is some twist, and we also have to note the role of gradation. The story of Shechem concludes by stating that the actual deed is done by one man. In the vicious attack by the Amalekites on the Israelites, all the references are to the group.[2] This is what happens today. Yet, who makes war? Is it the baby in its cradle? The citizen in his home? Is there conscription against the people's will?

ACTION OF A COLLECTIVE

Roughly, and conscious that there is overlapping, we might list a number of grounds on which an action is ascribed to a collective.

UNIVERSALITY

First, all members of the group participate equally in an action: say, all the Fellows of Brasenose College at Oxford, without exception, one night after dinner go out and set fire to the new Magdalen College building across the river. The two sons of Eli, priests at Shiloh, both were guilty of fraudulent and immoral conduct and the same curse and disaster overtook them. The disciples of Jesus all fled after his arrest. These cases are the least interesting and, in a sense, do not even belong to the subject under discussion. If there were no such collective as Brasenose or the sons of Eli or the disciples, it would make no difference. The persons concerned would be responsible as so many individual offenders, each of them having in fact committed a wrong—just as if some of you and I now joined to rob a bank. In other words, where it is literally the totality of a group that acts, the situation is not basically distinct from the simple action of one man. We shall nonetheless have to come back to this type of case because of a tendency in the Bible, and indeed in modern literature and politics, to construe other types artificially as falling under this one, precisely in order to simplify and get rid of the difficulties arising where only a number of the collective have acted.

EMANATION

As the second type we might mention emanation: a collective is credited with an action merely because it emanates from it. If universal cooperation is one extreme, this is the other. So long as the deed is done by anyone among the group, however insignificant, it is the group that counts as the doer. This category, where the most insignificant, the most subordinate acts, is the easiest to understand. If a slave or servant offends against an outsider, to call to account the group to which he belongs or its representative would often be natural if only because in general they could control his activity. Abraham reproved Abimelech whose men had deprived him of a well. (It is true that the wrong is not directly described as Abimelech's.) But not all cases are explicable in this way. When Isaac in Gerar surprised Abimelech by the fact that Rebekah was his wife, Abimelech, on discovering the truth, expostulated: "one of the people might have lain with thy wife and thou shouldst have brought guiltiness upon us."[3] Here also the deed as such is not expressly ascribed to the collective. The chapter telling of Achan's embezzlement of consecrated booty begins: "And the children of Israel committed a trespass in the accursed thing, for Achan took of the accursed thing; and the anger of the Lord was kindled against the children of Israel."[4] Here the collective is described as the sinner in so many words. Or when a Levite traveler's concubine has been murdered in terrible circumstances by a rabble at Gibeah, a city of the tribe of Benjamin, the rest of the tribes send an ultimatum to the tribe of Benjamin: "What wickedness is this that has been done among you?"[5] At a pinch one might translate "by you"; but "among you" is the more likely sense. There is no direct attribution of the action to the tribe.

GENERALITY

Between universal participation and responsibility on the ground of emanation, there are several further headings to be considered. A very frequent and, one would say, often reasonable basis for regarding a collective as doer is—third—the behavior of the generality, the overwhelming majority. "And the Egyptians made the children of Israel to serve with rigor":[6] this can at most refer to the generality in the sense that there must have been many Egyptians who were never in contact with Hebrews. Yet Egypt as such is the evildoer, and Egypt as such undergoes punishment. When we hear that "the children of Israel did evil in the sight of the Lord and served Baalim,"[7] again a prevalent trend is envisioned. Likewise, when we read that "An Ammonite or Moabite shall not enter the assembly of the Lord because they met you not with bread and water in the way when ye came forth out of Egypt."[8] Such judgments are dangerous but inevitable and still function as the basis of daily decisions.

CHARACTERISTIC PART

Somewhat allied to action by the generality is—fourth—action by a characteristic portion of the group. What the generality does is always characteristic; but even a tiny number may commit a wrong typical of the whole and, therefore, be treated as a wrong by the collective. It can have been only a fraction of the Midianite women that seduced Israelite men to idolatry and whoredom. When we hear in Num 25:18 that "the Midianites have beguiled you" and that a war was waged against Midian to avenge this crime, it means that the crime of a few characterizes the lot: any of them may have committed it, fundamentally they are the same, the crime is theirs. Jesus laments: "Jerusalem, Jerusalem, thou that killest the prophets."[9] None of the prophets killed in Jerusalem, including Jesus himself, was killed by more than a small minority. Jerusalem is collectively addressed as the doer because the deed is thought of as typical. A striking feature of many collectives is their extension in time. The Amalekites in Deut 25:17–19, the Ammonites, Moabites, Jerusalem, the Jews in Justin Martyr all offend in times past but future generations are affected. Family curses and, even nowadays, national character reveal this extension in time. We should be careful not to pooh-pooh this way of thinking. Our task is to observe and define proper limits.

PROMINENT PART

Fifth, the group may be considered the doer if it is the prominent members, those who count, that are guilty. "For three transgressions of Israel," says Amos, "and for four I will not turn away the punishment thereof; because they sold the righteous for silver and the poor for a pair of shoes."[10] Presumably the wicked wealthy are far less numerous than those they oppress. Yet it is said of Israel as a whole that they do these terrible things. Matthew extends to the Pharisees a number of charges preferred in Mark against the scribes: they love the chief seats in the synagogues.[11] That this would be a failing of the somebodies rather than the humble mass is obvious.

DOMINANT PART

A sixth type of case is close to this one—where the action is that of the dominant part of the collective.

EXCEPTIONS

In all cases, excluding that which comes under the heading of universality, there is, seventh, the problem of exceptions. According to the basis on which responsibility rests, the problem of the exception assumes a different form. In that the various grounds of responsibility in the main reflect various modes of behavior of the collective, various interpretations of such behavior present themselves. Where emanation is stressed, the mere fact of a misdeed proceeding from the midst of a group, it is usually the question of one member or a small minority acting—recall Abimelech's servants or Achan—with the vast majority innocent. In other words, the exception is the wrongdoer.

By contrast, where a group is called to account because of the conduct of the generality or the characteristic part, any not guilty would be exceptional. In the former case, at a comparatively early date, dissociation on the part of the majority—withdrawal of protection and comfort from the doer, surrender of the doer to the party wronged or direct punishment—would exonerate the collective. After all, it will generally be in the interest of the wronged party to avoid a major clash if satisfaction can be obtained without its involvement. In the latter case where most members of the collective offend, consideration of the exception will be less pressing from a practical point of view, though stories like that of Rahab and the golden calf show that we must not exclude entirely the factor of expediency. Rahab's action on behalf of the Israelite spies involves her own interest, and she is spared and rewarded.[12] In the case of the golden calf, the Levites go over from the criminal collective to legitimate relationships and are rewarded.[13]

COMMUNAL PUNISHMENT

Communal responsibility for a misdeed is not absolutely bad, or if bad, is not necessarily evil. It depends on the measures adopted, and these will change according to circumstances in both the same period and in different ones. A family, a school, a club, a nation is responsible for the conduct of its members. "One's deed is that of all" is, up to a point, true and meaningful. But there is a danger in demanding that fathers are not to die for their sons.[14] Some fathers wish to.

The great text regarding the problem of the innocent minority is the controversy between Abraham and God in the matter of Sodom.[15] God hears of that city's wickedness, which must mean that at least, if not all, the major or permanent part misbehaves. As God informs Abraham of his decision to destroy the city, Abraham protests. There might be righteous men in the city, and justice requires that "the righteous should not be as the wicked." This slogan—separation of the good and bad—leads one to expect a plea for sparing the righteous ones when the others are wiped out. But this is not what Abraham asks for. His plea is that if there are righteous men in the city, the city should be spared for their sakes. That is to say, though the objectionable consequence of indiscriminate destruction is that the righteous would be as the wicked, he does not fear; indeed, he advocates the result that the wicked should be as the righteous. To collective punishment he opposes not individual treatment but collective pardon. It is a fruitful idea. The individual's refusal to be spared alone suggests that all are, at least to some extent, pardoned.

At one time I concluded that when the narrative was written the collective idea was still so strong as to preclude the rational solution of individual treatment. It was possible to think only in collective terms; and as the inclusion of the good in wholesale disaster had become intolerable, the alternative was their pulling the bad along to wholesale salvation. There is probably a grain of truth in this view: the narrative carries a somewhat primitive element. But it is certainly not the whole truth. We must not overlook the fact that, while in the scholar's study, individual treatment may appear as the only right and modern thing; in actual life this will often be quite impracticable. The choice will be between two ways of dealing with a group: proceeding against it or not proceeding against it. The United States may attack Cuba or not attack her. The academically preferable possibility of confronting with hostile measures only those sympathizing with the regime simply does not exist. It is relevant to note that the crime of Sodom specifically reported is a grave violation of the *Gastrecht*, the law of hospitality. In another part of the Bible we hear of a war made on the tribe of Benjamin by the rest because of just such a breach (Judg 20). It was, then, the kind of offense that might lead to international conflicts; and it follows that the antithesis, collective punishment or collective pardon, is not just an archaic survival but corresponds to a permanent reality in the political field.

A curious feature of Abraham's request is connected with this aspect and supports our interpretation. Abraham starts by asking God to spare the city if there are fifty deserving men, and then by repeated bargaining goes down as low as ten; but there he stops. So God will refrain from destruction for the sake of ten: he is not asked to do so for the sake of fewer—five or three or even one. Ten make a body of men, a section of the city. Though the motto is not to let the righteous be as the wicked, this is not pursued in an abstract, theoretical way but in a way reflecting a certain not infrequent political setting. In that setting the decision would be in favor of peace, of giving into or putting up with a generally blamable collective, not if one good man might be found but if it contained a sound part, a part opposing the prevalent trend. That is why I said that the story of Sodom deals with the problem of the innocent minority—the minority, a group within the main group, not the one innocent individual keeping apart from the general sin.

Another realistic feature is the mode of reasoning by which Abraham arrives at his minimum number of ten. To begin with, he requests God to spare the city if fifty good men are in it, a sizeable fraction. When this is granted, he makes it forty-five, then forty, then thirty, then twenty, and, at last, ten. Each time it would be mean or arbitrary of God not to assent to a slight reduction. The argument is technically, and has an affinity with, that called *sorites* by the Greeks, *acervalis* by the Romans: the argument of the heap. At what point does a number of grains become a heap or cease to be a heap? Fifty grains are clearly a heap but twenty, yea, ten, yea, five, rather doubtful. The original setting in life of this logical puzzle is no doubt the marketplace. It is interesting, by the way, that, as in the story of Sodom, the puzzle concerning the heap has to do with a collective. So has that mentioned in Horace:[16] at what point, if I pull out the hairs of a horse's tail, does it cease to be a tail? Horace refers to another example from trade, not involving a collective: precisely how many years are needed for a wine to be styled old?

A little twist toward the beginning of the Sodom story points in the same direction. Having extracted the assurance that fifty just men will save the city, Abraham, with a view to reaching forty-five, urges: "Peradventure there shall lack five of the fifty righteous: wilt thou destroy all the city for five?"[17] It has been pointed out that this is a sophism, since God would be destroying the city not because of the five missing just, but because of the many who are wicked. Whether or not we call it a sophism, it certainly accords with notions common in everyday thought. If I set fire to a building and the fire brigade is slow in arriving, it might well be said that the building burned down because of the fire brigade. If a member of an occupying force is murdered and the commander threatens to exterminate the village where it happened, unless the ten leading citizens are handed over for execution, and only nine are handed over, he might well be entreated not to proceed to extreme measures because of the one who cannot be found. Where something that might be expected to prevent a disaster fails to occur, it is apt to be considered a cause. What makes it justifiable to regard Abraham's way of putting it sophistic is that he overemphasizes it with a purpose: that, of course, is what a good bargainer has to do.

In the end, Sodom is destroyed despite Abraham's intercession. For the narrator, this implies that there did not exist even as few as ten good men. In one quaint passage, we are given to understand that no injustice was done at all, not a single individual was of any decency. It will be recalled that when two angels visit Lot the inhabitants of Sodom gather in front of his house and demand the surrender of the two strangers for unnatural sport. "The men of Sodom," we are told, "compassed the house round, from young to old, the entire people from one end of the city to the other."[18] This is difficult to imagine: surely some must have been too young and some too old to desire to participate. The narrator cannot bring himself, in this leading case concerning collective punishment, to admit that even one innocent person perished. So it does become individual guilt. Gunkel cuts out "from one end to the other," which makes no difference. To empathize is to hide. We might compare Deut 29:10ff. where even the babes are to hear: "Ye stand this day all of you before the Lord your God; your captains of your tribes, your elders, and your officers, all the men of Israel, your little ones, your wives, and thy stranger that is in thy camp, from the hewer of thy wood to the drawer of thy water." Lot is different. He is not a Sodomite at all, although his sons-in-law may be. The women do not count. Most authorities declare that the controversy is late. The consensus is that the wrong in collective punishment was only perceived long after the early historiographers. But Noah, of whom everybody agrees that the story is Yahwistic, is saved because he is righteous, the same word as in the story of Sodom. True, the story is superimposed on an old myth where probably he is saved for arbitrary reasons. But this only underlines the ease with which the notion of the separation of the righteous and the wicked was ready for use.[19]

RULER PUNISHMENT

David and Bathsheba's babe dies for their (or rather, David's) sin. But the punishment is intended only for the parent(s): the babe is a nonperson. (David's baby is a nonperson for God as judge, but his judgment is effective because he knows how much of a person the babe is for David. What a tension! We might recall Saul's treatment of Michal.) At Shechem, the son of the ruler offends. The punishment is intended chiefly for the ruler, but also for all the others. Of course, in the Shechem story the son is named Shechem, so I suppose some might take the view that here also, originally, the father slept with Dinah.[20]

Gina Frye, in her essay, shows feminist bias (very understandable at this time, in the 1980s) when viewing Rebekah as a nonperson: "The next morning Rebekah is asked whether she will go with the men. Even though she consents, it seems that this consent is a mere formality." But her consent is noted as decisive not only here, Gen 24:57–58, but also in 24:5, 8, 39. Moreover, the whole welcoming conduct of Rebekah from 24:18 on—reported fully again in 24:46ff.—is meant to testify to her willingness, indeed, eagerness. So at least in the case of giving away a daughter to go abroad, her agreement was sought. In 24:5, the servant asks whether, should Rebekah refuse, he is to take Isaac to her place: the marriage would then be there and they would live there, as Jacob and his wives do for many years. Abraham will have none of this. The assumption is that, but for the expatriation, Rebekah would automatically fall in with her family's disposal of her.

She (Gina Frye) also, like many others, fails to see that, however terrible it is to be in a lifelong marriage with a rapist or a false accuser, it would be far worse if he could divorce her (or perhaps even if he were to put her to death)—she being exposed to permanent treatment as suspect by the community: Deut 22:28, 29, 13–21.

In "Two Notes on Communal Responsibility" (*Sociological Review* 36

[1944]: 39), I consider the possibility that communal responsibility now and then turned into ruler punishment when a democracy had been taken over by a dictator. Even today, I would add, after defeating a dictatorship by war, the victors, some of them, may incline to take it out on the head and his henchmen rather than on the people as a whole. Roosevelt, Churchill, Stalin had all sorts of feelings; even Hitler's death would not necessarily quench all desire for personal vengeance, ruler punishment.

As for p. 40 n. 1 of this article [which reads as follows: There is another passage in the Bible where God is asked to attack a man directly and not by striking at his subjects, Job 2:4ff. But the request there springs from a very different attitude. David asked God to punish him personally and not by slaying his subjects, because he no longer regarded his subjects like dead property. In Job, Satan asks God to torture the hero personally and not by slaying his family, because he knows that having one's body hurt is worse for most men than losing one's property, even the dearest: the idea that it is not right to treat free subjects as "property" and to hit the "owner" by damaging them is not here present at all.]

Daube adds: in Job 2:4–5, Satan wants Job to be personally tortured instead of, or in addition to, the slaying of his family—which latter is ruler punishment—not because it is unjust to kill the subjects of an offender but because direct affliction will hurt him more. We might compare the present tendency in the United States to take it out directly on the Philippine ex-dictator, Marcos, or his widow, and to make them pay restitution, and so on. Of course, in this situation the Philippines are no longer his subjects, so measures against them no longer affect him so much. But there is also a special animus against the (ex-) leader, so there is a somewhat unholy turn to individual responsibility, that is, to vengeance.

CHAPTER 9

WOMEN

In this chapter I propose to do four things. First, I shall illustrate the road from woman's servitude to the double standard by asking some less usual questions. Second, I shall say something about woman's role in bilingual marriages. Third, I shall draw attention to a major motive in the book of Ruth that has so far gone undetected. And, last, I shall comment on a few recent statements concerning a woman's position in biblical law which betray a dangerous tendency toward oversimplification.

I: FROM SERVITUDE TO THE DOUBLE STANDARD

The cultivation of illicit relationships is a typical woman's crime. Sarah was twice taken into a king's harem, once by Pharaoh, another time by Abim-elech.[1] Both times it happened as a result of her being represented and representing herself as Abraham's sister. Both times God struck at and threatened the king alone in order to enforce her restoration, without a trace of disapproval as to her own conduct. Even the king, while reproaching Abraham for misleading him, had nothing to say against Sarah. Abimelech, to be sure, did mention that she as well as Abraham had suppressed the relevant facts. But he did so only in explanation of his deed, in his controversy with God; at his subsequent meeting with Abraham and Sarah, he rebuked only the former. What is the explanation?

It cannot be said that Sarah was a mere instrument of Abraham. In both episodes a substantial proportion of the space is devoted to the speech by which Abraham persuades her to fall in with his plan and conceal her status. For example, he says in one of the two passages, "Say, I pray thee, that thou art my sister," "This is the kindness which thou shalt show unto me, say of me, he is my brother":[2] evidently she could have refused to oblige. Nor can we say with the Rabbis,[3] for whom this was a great problem, that whatever the prima facie sense of the text, Sarah did reveal her married status to the king when she was closeted with him. The Bible doesn't mention this at all. So why then is there no trace of disapproval of her own conduct? The correct answer is that when these stories were formulated, adultery was still in the main a crime by the adulterer against the woman's husband, or more precisely, a violation of his rights as her master.

This does not mean that it was not also a sin. God sends plagues on Pharaoh and Abimelech; Abimelech blamed Abraham in so many words for having brought on him and his kingdom a great sin,[4] and Abraham had to pray for him to be healed. After all, theft, which is misappropriation of a man's belongings, was a sin: it is paired off with murder and adultery in the Ten Commandments, and Joseph's brothers, when the cup was discovered in Benjamin's sack, declared "God hath found out the iniquity of thy servants." (It does not matter that there is a double meaning, "the iniquity" referring also to their previous treatment of Joseph.)[5]

What is meant by saying that adultery was primarily an attack on the husband's rights as his wife's master is that, from the public legal point of view, she, his subject, could not take part in it. Society did not yet see in adultery a joint upsetting of the established order by the adulterer and the adulteress, nor did religion in that period regard them both equally intolerable as defiling the community. Insofar as the law was interested, law in the public sense which would set communal remedies in motion, the offense was his. At that time the punishment of the woman was left to her husband: he might kill her, he might cut off her nose, or, if he was a gentleman, he might let bygones be bygones.

In the chapter about Abimelech we are told how he had to return Sarah together with an additional payment—highly reminiscent of later regulations in the event of robbery or embezzlement.[6] We have to do with a crime affecting property. Another point is significant. God threatens Abimelech in a dream, "Behold thou art a dead man for the woman thou hast taken, and she is married to a husband." I have argued elsewhere that this presupposes the existence of some such statute as may be met in Deuteronomy: "If a man be found lying with a woman married to a husband, then indeed both of them shall die, the man who lay with the woman and the woman."[7] But, of course, the author of the chapter in Genesis may well have proceeded from a version more primitive than Deuteronomy in certain particulars. One very likely difference is that, in his version, the death penalty was imposed only on the adulterer. "Behold thou art a dead man for the woman…": this verdict against the adulterer, without any corresponding one against the adulteress, strongly points to a statute, "If a man take a woman married to a husband, he shall die." The lady was in her master's hands. The state made it its business only to see to the punishment of the adulterer.

The Deuteronomic provision that we have just quoted displays a suggestive emphasis: "indeed both of them shall die." This emphatic "indeed," *gam*, corroborates our reconstruction: it is directed against that earlier law under which the adulterer alone was handled by the public authority. Deuteronomy includes the adulteress as well, "indeed both of them."

Professor Martin David believes that, when read in conjunction with the statute concerning interference with a betrothed girl, that about a married woman points back to a stage when the husband, if he caught the guilty couple *in flagranti*, was entitled to kill them at once.[8] However, if we accept this idea, and if at the same time we try, as we must, to do justice to the insistent "indeed both of them," we arrive at a more complicated development. First stage: a husband was entitled to kill the adulterer no matter what he did to his wife. Next stage, at which the emphasis "indeed both" came in: he might kill the adulterer only if he killed his wife too. Third stage, Deuteronomy: the state took over the punishment from the husband, and the emphasis, "indeed both," remained standing though out of date, no longer meaningful. This development is not impossible; each stage may be paralleled from other systems;[9] and our thesis explaining the absence from the biblical records of any reflection on Sarah's conduct could be squared with it. Nevertheless it is far more probable that, before the Deuteronomic statute, whereas the adulteress was in the hands of her husband, the state already took charge of the adulterer. The emphasis in this statute, where the death penalty is imposed on her also, is by no means obsolete; it expresses a principal aim of the lawgiver. (This is not to reject a certain major distinction postulated by Professor David between the case of a married woman and that of a betrothed girl—but we cannot here pursue this aspect.)

In the case of Sarah's adventures, naturally there was no question of a complaint against her on the part of her husband, who himself begged her to act as she did. Indeed it might be asked whether he had just complaint against the king from whom both Abraham and Sarah had studiously withheld the fact of her being a married woman. He had no complaint unless, with the Rabbis, we attach a great deal of weight to his fear that, as Sarah's husband, he might be put out of the way.[10] But here we enter a region where direct conclusions as to the legal background become risky. God would counter a threat to Abraham's well-being irrespective of the precise rights and wrongs of the situation.

Let us note, however, two things. First, the mere fact that a man did not know that a woman with whom he had intercourse was married was certainly not a full excuse at all times. The Assyrian compilation does recognize it as an excuse,[11] and the chapter about Abimelech advocates the same progressive solution—especially if we go back to the original version where reprieve was conceded after intercourse had actually taken place. But we must not take it for granted. Second, it is doubtful how far, at one time, even a man trapped into adultery by the husband was able to escape punishment. Ancient laws trying to protect the adulterer in these circumstances suggest that, prior to them,[12] he had little defense against an unscrupulous, blackmailing husband. We have already touched on the discovery of Joseph's cup with Benjamin, in many ways comparable: the brothers were convicted though Joseph had engineered the whole thing.[13] In Assyria, incidentally, a man charged with adultery might plead that the woman offered herself,[14] a plea conceivably playing a part in Abimelech's emphatic affirmation, "and she, even she said, he is my brother."[15]

Like Abraham, Isaac, when in Abimelech's country, introduced his wife as his sister.[16] But, at least in its present form, the episode is only a shadowy version of those involving Sarah. Nothing untoward happened to Rebekah; the king discovered her true relationship to Isaac by chance; and he immediately took energetic steps to protect both. It is significant that according to this version—the latest of the three—the wife took no part in the deception; at least her part is not mentioned. We hear nothing about Isaac explaining the scheme to Rebekah or about her confirming his misleading statements.

The story of David, Bathsheba, and Uriah supports our main conclusions.[17] The prophet Nathan thundered against David; not a word against Bathsheba. Had there been a statute in ordinary law decreeing death for both parties, that would be unintelligible. Once again it cannot be argued that, faced by a royal command, Bathsheba had no choice. She need not have been as obstinate as Naboth, but she might have put up a show: "Doth not my lord know that I am married?"; all the more as from later occasions we know that she was quite capable of looking after herself. (Remember how she extracted the crown for her son from the dying king, leaving him with the words "Let my lord king David live for ever."[18]) Yet she complied. Actually, she must have agreed even to the scheme by which Uriah was to believe that he was the father of the child from the adulterous union. The storyteller, with wonderful delicacy and economy, manages to preserve silence on the point, but David could not have urged Uriah to visit his wife without informing her first. The scheme failed, and Uriah was got rid of. David alone was called to account: the legal background was the same as in Genesis—the adulteress did not interest public authority. The man who could have dealt with Bathsheba was dead. (The fact that Uriah was a foreigner is clearly accorded no relevance in the story.)

As a matter of fact, the prophet's parable draws a close parallel between adultery and theft, theft of a lamb or maybe a daughter.[19] This is how adultery was looked at, at the time. One would not think of attributing the crime to the stolen lamb or daughter—not even if they had willingly followed the thief. The owner or father might take reprisals against a runaway, but that would be on a different basis. Similarly, in the main, it was Paris who was guilty of a crime in the public sense; Helen who consented had only to come to terms with Menelaus, her husband.[20]

Reprisals were by no means inevitable. In the wild closing chapters of the book of Judges, we are told of a concubine who was unfaithful to her master and left him to return to her father.[21] Whether her master knew with whom she had deceived him is not recorded; probably he did not know. Anyhow all he did was to fetch her back, using friendly persuasion.[22] To be sure, she was not a full wife. We need not here follow up the terrible sequel of the incident.

Again, after Saul's death Abner supported his son Ishbosheth. They fell out, however, when Abner took Rizpah, one of Saul's concubines.[23] No doubt Ishbosheth, claiming to be Saul's successor, looked upon her as his; we may recall that David, when established, appropriated Saul's harem and the rebellious Absalom David's, and that Adonijah's request of Abishag who had ministered to the aged king cost him his life because Solomon saw in it an attempt to pose as heir to David.[24] It is nonetheless far from certain that Abner's motives were political. In his retort to Ishbosheth's complaint at any rate he contrasted his generous services to Ishbosheth in his struggle for the throne with Ishbosheth's meanness in making a fuss about a woman. What is here worth mentioning is that, though Rizpah must have allowed herself to be conquered, Ishbosheth does not seem to have taken serious steps against her; he may, of course, have been unable to do so. She reappears for a brief moment later on, in a role moving in its heroism and pathos.[25]

Where the adulterer as well as the adulteress was a subject of the offended husband, the affair must have been completely internal to the family for a long time. Reuben seduced Bilhah.[26] We learn of no vengeance Jacob wreaked on her—though the notice "and Israel heard" gives the impression of incompleteness. Whoever has had to read this portion in a Sabbath service will be familiar with the subtle and paradoxical way in which the Massoretes have doubled the accentuation of the last word ("Israel" in the Hebrew), one accent being the usual one for the end of a sentence, the other for the middle, with something yet to follow. An earlier version may have enlarged on Jacob's reaction, in regard to both or either of the culprits. In a subsequent chapter we do come across something like a curse by him on his eldest son.[27] In any case, there is no trace of any intervention from outside, from society.

The case of Absalom belongs here, in a sense. When he visited David's concubines,[28] he was acting as the new sovereign: they could not be expected to resist; or we might say, if they or any of them had resisted on the ground of his defective title, it would have made a grand story of loyalty and courage (and perhaps also self-denial). By the time the king could deal with the matter, his rebel son was dead. The concubines were pensioned off in confinement,[29] not as a punishment, but on the one hand the king's concubines must not become anyone else's, and on the other there appear to have been the beginnings of the idea—which kept gaining ground as time went on[30]— that once your wife or concubine has been with another man, you may not resume relations. Needless to say, there were special reasons for abstention in the particular circumstances; for example, the fact that it was a son who had come between must have played a part. David's reunion with Michal after she had been given to somebody else shows that we must be careful not to generalize for that period.[31] We have also just seen that an unfaithful concubine was fetched back, and indeed, in the course of that return journey her master, in order to save himself, offered her to a scoundrelly rabble; he would have been prepared to have her again had she not been murdered.[32] Still, in the Absalom story, the beginnings of the idea are discernible, it seems.

There are two instances of the utmost harshness against an adulteress, or "adulteress" in quotes. Judah's daughter-in-law Tamar, widowed yet still his subject since destined for his remaining son, was convicted of immoral conduct—wrongly, as it turned out in the end—and Judah ordered her to be burned.[33] This was clearly domestic justice. It is true that, if we follow the prevalent and most plausible interpretation, a considerable measure of publicity attached to it: "Bring her forth and let her be burned." But that is not irreconcilable with a system under which the decision as to what is to happen to the woman is still left with the husband or whoever else may be her master. The ease with which Judah reversed the sentence on realizing the truth is revealing. She is at his mercy for worse or better. In fact it is quite possible that, according to the law of the time, even the punishment of the seducer still lay with the woman's master, though the community might lend support of various sorts. What may be fairly argued is that the kind of retribution which it was customary for a master to exact, and to exact publicly, would tend in course of time to become the penalty insisted on by the state; and also that the publicity of domestic justice is a step on the way to criminal law proper.

It is just conceivable, however, that the phrase "Bring her forth" should be understood differently. Certainly, the use of "to bring forth" in the sense of "to bring to a public place for punishment" is well evidenced. It occurs in the stories of the blasphemer in Leviticus, of the man who gathered wood on a Sabbath in Numbers, and of Naboth in 1 Kings; also in the Deuteronomic provisions imposing the death penalty on an idolater and on the seducer of a betrothed girl and the girl.[34] (One might perhaps add Joshua's command to "bring forth" for execution the five kings shut up in a cave, and Jehoida's command to "bring forth" Athaliah;[35] but the word looks like it is being employed here in a nontechnical fashion.) But "to bring forth" may also refer to the production of a person by one who is in legal charge of him or her, or maybe simply in physical control. When Gideon was to be put to death for destroying the altar of Baal, application was made to his father, "Bring forth thy son that he may die";[36] his father refused. Somewhat comparable is the message of the king of Jericho to Rahab, "Bring forth the men who are come to thee, for they are come to search out the country"; or even the demand of the rabble in Sodom and Gibeah that a host should "bring forth" and deliver up for unnatural sport the men or the man whom he was sheltering.[37]

Under the Deuteronomic statute concerning the incorrigible son, proceedings start by the parents "bringing him forth" to the elders.[38] In the statute concerning the newly married wife,[39] the clause "they shall bring her forth to the door of her father's house" probably means that she is to be led there publicly. But even here we must reckon with the possibility that the situation envisaged is where she is at home with her parents, perhaps sent back by her husband. After all, her parents are supposed to be in possession of the cloth which is to serve as criterion of the justice or injustice of the accusation: it is they who must display it before the elders. So even here the meaning of the clause quoted may be "her parents shall hand her over, take her out to the door by way of surrender." It is worth noting that where the statute enjoins the parents to display the cloth, it says, "They shall bring it forth to the elders": again "to bring forth," and here the verb unquestionably signifies "they shall produce." Considering that the widowed Tamar lived not in Judah's house but in that of her father, it is just conceivable—though unlikely—that "Bring her forth that she may be burned" corresponds to "Bring forth thy son that he may die" in the tale of Gideon: a request addressed to her family.[40]

The other instance of an adulteress receiving harsh treatment is in the Prophets, where they declaim against the people breaking faith with God. "And now I will discover her corruption in the sight of her lovers and none shall deliver her out of my hand," says Hosea; and Ezekiel, "I will gather all thy lovers, and I will judge thee according to the law of adulteresses and women that shed blood, and I will give thee into their hand, and they shall strip thee, and stone thee with stones, and thrust thee through with their swords, and burn thine houses with fire, and execute judgments upon thee in the sight of many women."[41] As in other prophets using the same simile, it is the husband, God, who speaks to his unfaithful wife, the nation. Now far be it from us to assert that there is anything in either of the two denunciations—and they are fairly representative of Hosea and Ezekiel—inconsistent with an adulteress falling under the criminal law proper. But, significantly, we think, Hosea contains no sign that that stage of evolution had in fact been reached: the husband is going to punish his wife, make an example of her, "and none shall deliver her out of my hand." By contrast, in Ezekiel, punishment will be inflicted on her by others, though at her husband's instance; he will give her over to punishment. The repeated references to "judging" and "judgments" are particularly indicative of a background of less arbitrary, more official proceedings. By now Deuteronomy was in force.

Or perhaps not quite? In Hosea the husband is prosecutor, judge, and executioner. In Ezekiel he is still prosecutor and, it appears, judge also; but execution lies with the community. In Deuteronomy at first sight it looks as if the community were in charge from the beginning, under a duty to take the initiative in prosecuting. But in practice, and perhaps even in the lawgiver's intention, it must be the husband who sets proceedings in motion. However, judgment will certainly be delivered by the elders, not by him. Ezekiel, then, reflects a stage which, if evolution were designed in the scholar's study, would come before Deuteronomy. Yet Deuteronomy is older. The explanation may be either that poetic or prophetic imagery is apt to lag behind the actualities of social life. (This may go for Hosea too; so that we cannot be sure that the law had not progressed somewhat beyond what one would gather from his similes.) Or the modern regulation of Deuteronomy, with the public organs pronouncing the verdict, was—or had by Ezekiel's time become—an ideal rather than reality.

Let us now leap over the centuries and glance at the *pericope de adultera* in John.[42] An adulteress was taken before Jesus in order for his antagonists to have a handle against him if, as was expected, he disapproved of stoning. We are informed that she was caught *in flagranti*. So commentators sometimes raise the question: where was her paramour? And one answer is that he had fled.[43] Probably he had. But the point we wish to make is that he is missing from the story because he was uninteresting. Whereas, as we have seen, at one time the state saw to the punishment of the adulterer only, by now we have reached a Hellenistic-Victorian-Edwardian climate of opinion: it was only the adulteress against whom the rage of the mob would be naturally directed. Remember that the mob on such an occasion, insofar as it was active, would consist exclusively of males, unlike today. (Compare, or contrast, the case of incest with the father's wife at Corinth:[44] excommunication is pronounced only against the male party. Possibly the woman was not a Christian at all. But equally likely she was, and the reason for the concentration on him is that his excommunication in practical effect would automatically entail ostracism of the entire household.)

According to Epstein,[45] in Ezekiel's time, a husband might send out an adulteress to be lynched by "neighbors and tribesmen, men and woman, young and old." In our opinion he overlooks the fact that, in this prophet's description, between the husband's accusation—admittedly accompanied by disgracing gestures—and the dreadful end there is a "judgment." Even if he delivers it, as is likely, he is not quite free. The end no doubt involves an element of lynching: stoning, burning, and the like belong to the type that Mommsen calls *Volksfesthinrichtung*. But this in itself is not decisive. Many secondary features of self-help survive when self-help is repressed. In the most modern countries, in the case of a serious criminal charge, archaic practices are apt to survive from the moment of indictment to that of punishment (or acquittal). An error, however, which in this connection we are particularly concerned to put right is the statement that "men and women" took part. Women would not thrust, surely, "with their swords." Epstein relies on the verse saying that the judgment takes place "in the sight of many women." But this picture speaks against him. The women look on—and are supposed to profit by the spectacle. In another, similar chapter the purpose is expressed, "that all women may be taught not to do after your lewdness."[46]

Anyhow, in John, the accusers were men, "scribes and Pharisees"; and this must be so plainly if Joachim Jeremias is right in holding[47] that they were not hauling the adulteress to court, but were coming from court where she had been sentenced and were on the way to the place of execution. They would then be scholars responsible for things being done properly.[48] When Jesus suggested that the first stone be cast by him without sin, he did not mean without sin in general; in the circumstances it was clear that he thought of one who had never been guilty of unchastity. It is to the credit of those to whose conscience he appealed that they slinked away. But it all goes to show that there were now two different standards, one for men, another for women, which on the whole have dominated Western social life ever since and are only just about to go out.

The legend of Susannah and the Elders, some two hundred years earlier, already belongs to this milieu. The aim of the legend is to inculcate the superiority of the modern method of hearing witnesses—in the absence of one another—over the previous method of a ceremonious, collective testifying.[49] Of course, the particular *sujet*—a virtuous wife wrongfully accused of adultery—had many attractions compared with others in connection with which that aim might have been achieved. But the wrongful accusation of a virtuous husband, we claim, would simply not have done: it would have been unrealistic.

This may imply a slight dissent from Büchler's approach in his study of the punishment of adultery in the postexilic era.[50] He appears to make too little distinction between the man and the woman. His chief concern is indeed with Proverbs and Sirach, and in the epoch of Proverbs at least things may not yet have been so advanced. But even for Proverbs, not all his arguments are convincing. This is not the place to review them, but we may perhaps mention one. In support of his view—or rather his hunch, for he again and again points out how little evidence we have to go by—that the adulterer was really exposed to the death penalty, he adduces the warning that the injured husband "will not regard any ransom."[51] He compares a case in the legal portion of Exodus,[52] where one person through gross negligence is responsible for the death of another: the law lays down the death penalty, but allows the guilty party to buy off his life if agreement as to a ransom can be reached. By analogy, he infers, the injured husband could insist on the adulterer being put to death though he might be satisfied with money. But for one thing, once the law admits ransom in lieu of the death penalty, the former tends to oust the latter; it did so in the case from Exodus.[53] For another, it is arbitrary to assume that ransom can develop only as a mitigation of a state-imposed death penalty. In Numbers the next-of-kin of a person murdered is prohibited from accepting ransom, and that prohibition was directed against treating the crime as a private one; it was a step toward making it the concern of the community.[54] The whole section in Proverbs gives the impression that it was primarily up to the husband to settle accounts with the adulterer. No doubt there were legal rules to help him; for example, he could not be prosecuted if he killed his man. Epstein,[55] if I understand him correctly, inclines to this interpretation, assigning the passage to "the unwritten law of the day." We doubt whether, as far as the adulterer was concerned, the written law was strictly enforced.

We ought presumably to discuss Philo and Josephus. But their accounts of adultery are notoriously difficult of interpretation, and we cannot offer any worthwhile contribution. In some sections is reflected the letter of the law, death to the adulterous couple; others are curiously vague. Certainly Josephus' version of the sin with Bathsheba is of a more modern character than the original.[56] While he explains that Bathsheba, when pregnant, sent to David that he should devise some way of concealing her fault because "according to the laws of the fathers she was deserving death as an adulteress,"[57] we get nothing equally precise about David. True, he was a king and so on. Another little difference: according to the Bible, "when the wife of Uriah heard that Uriah her husband was dead, she mourned for her husband and when the mourning was past, David sent and fetched her to his house and she became his wife and bore him a son"[58]—the fruit of their union. The reference is to formal mourning and, manifestly, to the minimum time within which a widow was not supposed to remarry. We might almost paraphrase: "and as soon as the mourning period was past." By contrast, Josephus has: "Bathsheba, the wife of Uriah, on learning of her husband's death, mourned for him many days; but when she had ceased from her sorrow and her tears for Uriah, the king took her to wife and had a son by her."[59] There was genuine grief, and who will say that that would not be possible?

II. BILINGUAL MARRIAGES

We would not let it be thought that the biblical women were capable of no other crime than an irregular alliance. Before leaving this province, however, we might note that three men, and three men only, are punished in the Bible for attempted adultery, and all of them were innocent; and that the only two men guilty of attempted adultery are not punished for it. Abimelech was plagued for attempted adultery with Sarah, but he did not know her to be married; Joseph was thrown into prison as a result of a trumped-up charge brought by the wife of Potiphar; and Haman was put to death when the king claimed he was trying to rape the queen, whereas in fact he had only fallen at her feet to beg for his life.[60] On the other hand, the two elders who had designs on Susannah were executed not for this reason, but because of their false witness. This is, of course, nothing but an amusing coincidence, but it may serve as a warning that, as storytellers must tell the unusual, we should be careful in drawing conclusions as to what daily life was like.

Female influence is often represented as the cause of man's evil-doing, and in particular of his apostasy. We all know what happens when a Scotsman marries an English woman. In a marriage with a foreign wife the danger would be increased. Ezra's and Nehemiah's measures are well known. In this connection an interesting point arises. Nehemiah was greatly incensed by coming across Jewish men who had married foreigners and whose children could not speak Hebrew.[61] (Nowadays we might find the father equally ignorant.) At a guess we should expect that, in a mixed marriage, the children will use the speech of the mother—unless there is a special, contrary, external thrust, for example, if the father's speech is socially preferable. Up to ten years or so ago, in South Africa a white child would grow up with English as his main language whichever parent spoke it. For Nehemiah, the adoption of a tongue like Ashdodite (Ashdodite—the very sound is sinister) was sure to lead to abandonment of the Jewish religion. Presumably he was right.

He did not try Ahasuerus' tour de force. This king, enraged by Vashti's insubordination, and advised by his counselors that her example might incite others to do the same, not only dismissed the queen but also issued a decree "that every man should bear rule in his house and that speech should be in the language of his people."[62] The final clause, concerning language, is widely emended. The Hebrew is awkward—but that would not be adequate reason. The real trouble is that this part of the decree comes as something of a surprise: there is no previous mention of mixed marriages. Above all, it is strange that the question of language should be made the criterion of rule in the home.

Yet an emendation is not justified: it would be too easy a way out of the real problem posed by this clause. It is not only that we find bilingual marriages causing difficulty in Nehemiah, which book, like Esther, has Persian affiliations. The book of Esther itself displays a profound interest in the coexistence of different languages, and, of course, a mixed marriage is the central situation. The very decree we are here discussing was published, we are told,[63] by means of letters sent "into every province according to the writing thereof and to every people after their language." So we do not, after all, arrive at the clause in question quite unprepared. Of the two subsequent decrees issued by the king, the first, ordering the destruction of the Jews, was also written "to every province according to the writing thereof and to every people after their language,"[64] whereas the second, granting the Jews the right to defend themselves, went out "unto every province according to the writing thereof and unto every people after their language, and"—here is an emphatic addition—"to the Jews according to their writing and according to their language."[65] How far there is a historical background to this kind of thing is irrelevant to the purpose in hand; we know of trilingual inscriptions of Xerxes. What matters is that the author attaches the greatest importance to the several languages, not least the Hebrew.

We come back to the real problem: what doctrine of language stands behind this clause enjoining male rule? And what doctrine of education? The author realizes that, normally, the mother's language would prevail: that is why, if the opposite is wanted, a decree is needed. Whether such a measure could ever be successful—especially if, as we are given to understand, the ladies of the land are only waiting to assert themselves—one may doubt. A further assumption of the author's, probably correct, is that, if a couple speak different languages, that partner whose language is adopted in the house will dominate. It is up to the wife to yield, to sacrifice, what, if things were allowed to drift, would be hers.

But in what epoch and what milieu would theories of this kind be formulated? There is not here the special motive we meet in Nehemiah, that loss of Hebrew will mean loss of religion. Or at least that motive is not avowed; we shall presently see that with an author so subtle one cannot be absolutely sure that it plays no part. As it faces us, the ruling makes no discrimination between languages and, needless to say, is as far as can be from the consequence drawn in Nehemiah, that intermarriage ought to be shunned; it is clearly thought of as acceptable in any civilized commonwealth. The doctrine behind it must be a quite general one of human nature, speech, family, society, plural society. It is very strange and puzzling. (A slight restriction should perhaps be made: the book of Esther concerns the marriage of a Jewess with a Gentile. There is no certainty that the marriage of a Jew with an alien woman would be regarded in exactly the same light.) We are unable to find a discussion of, or pronouncement on, dominant influence and education in a bilingual marriage anywhere in the classical writers. The passage in Esther is unique. Presumably, as far as the classics were concerned, the fact alluded to above, that in a union between a Greek-speaking or Latin-speaking person and a native, Greek or Latin would invariably have the social pull, rendered the matter unproblematic. It would be different where two minor languages within, say, the Roman Empire came together. But such a case was beneath notice.

However, Esther is a sophisticated work and a product of perfect craftsmanship, each part hanging together with and illuminating the other.[66] We must not forget that, as any reader would spot, Ahasuerus and Esther conversed in Persian, his language: he did not know, until informed in a crisis, that she was Jewish. The decree, then, is in conformity with their practice. There may indeed be more to it. I have tried to show elsewhere[67] that a major object of the book is to recommend a tolerant statesmanlike treatment of the Jewish minority as the policy most profitable from the point of view of the government. In developing his thesis the author stresses the reliability of the Jews—Mordechai saves the king's life—and their thought for the public interest—they do not, in defending themselves, touch the enemy's property. They fully combine good citizenship with loyalty to their own. The charge against them is that "that they do not keep the king's laws."[68] By giving prominence to the language decree, clearly acted on by the heroine, the author indicates that a Jewess married to a Gentile will know her duty. (His admission of or indeed insistence on a high degree of accommodation in such a marriage may partly account for the absence of any mention of God in this book.) If this reading of his intentions is correct, it becomes just a little easier to understand how, alone of all writers of antiquity, he has gone into the structure of bilingual marriages: his peculiar politics would lead him to the problem, and lead him to tackle it in the way he does. As already remarked, we would not deny that, at the same time, he wishes to impress the importance of Hebrew where the husband is Jewish.

Josephus, who otherwise gives a prolix account of the story of Esther, completely omits the decree establishing male ascendancy.[69] Because it would be laughed at by his public? In reporting the subsequent decrees, he makes no mention of their promulgation in various languages. Out of tact toward the Roman administration?

III: THE BOOK OF RUTH

The book of Ruth illustrates the methods available to women in difficult situations. It ought to be entitled "the book of Naomi." The story starts with her, is dominated by her, and finishes with her. Every single step of Ruth is taken under Naomi's direction. It is Naomi who emigrates with her husband and two sons, who returns alone except that her (formerly) foreign daughter-in-law comes with her, and who in the end is recognized, by means of what we would call a fiction, as the mother of the son born by her daughter-in-law and destined to become the ancestor of King David. (We disregard the genealogy appended in the last four verses of the final chapter.)

There is an affinity, remote but still worth noticing, with the book of Esther. In the latter, after the introduction explaining how they came to search for the new queen, the main story begins with Mordechai, as it ends with a description of his glory. (The centrality of his figure supports our thesis, that wise statesmanship in regard to the Jewish question is the principal argument of the book of Esther.) And just as Ruth undertakes her precarious visit of the sleeping Boaz in compliance with her mother-in-law's counsel—"All that thou sayest unto me will I do"[70]—so Esther suppresses her provenance, a somewhat questionable procedure, in trusting obedience to her guardian—"for Esther did the commandment of Mordechai as she was under his care."[71]

A major motif of the story of Ruth quite overlooked by its commentators is the relation of age and youth. Let us first look at Boaz. He is considerably older than Ruth. From their first meeting in the field he addresses her as "my daughter."[72] His language is dignified, almost solemn, his position and actions those of an established, respected, mature or elderly citizen. As Ruth visits him in the barn and offers to become his wife, he thanks her for her kindness—again calling her "my daughter"—for not having gone after any of the young men. Tamar, who is mentioned in the book as in a way Ruth's model, also had her sons from a man far senior to her, belonging to the previous generation: Judah, her father-in-law. We need not decide whether that narrative finds the difference in years interesting; it would certainly not escape the author of the book of Ruth. It should be observed, too, that no intercourse takes place during Ruth's nocturnal visit: Boaz is not an impetuous lover. She suggestively occupies the place of a spouse (we must not forget that she is a widow, not a trembling virgin). But that nothing happens beyond this may be gathered from the way he explains that there is a kinsman with a better title who will have to be dealt with before they can complete their arrangements. It would have been too risky to anticipate success in disposing of that prior claim. Indeed, Ruth leaves the barn before dawn in order that the strange meeting should not become publicly known; otherwise enormous suspicion would be aroused and they would be putting themselves very much in the wrong. A little remark by Naomi furnishes corroboration. Ruth tells her about the night and Naomi assures her that they will not now have to wait long: "the man will not be in rest until he have finished the thing this day."[73] There has been no fulfillment; but he is stirred. The wise mother-in-law knows the effect this will have—was it not all her doing?

With regard to Naomi's own role, the motif of age and youth is even more important. At the moment of her return she has passed the stage when remarriage might be normally envisaged and child bearing is entirely, or nearly, out of the question: "I am too old to have a husband. If I should say I have hope, if I should have an husband tonight and should also bear sons, would you tarry for them till they were grown?"[74] Say she is fifty. The figure can be doubly checked. First, her two sons married while in Moab. Say they were around twenty, Naomi around forty. We are told that there elapsed about ten years before the sons died and Naomi returned.[75] Second, toward the end of the book, when Ruth bears a son, the women wish Naomi joy because he will be "a nourisher of thine old age."[76] This is not the kind of felicitation extended to a woman with active aspirations.

Now Boaz meets Ruth at the beginning of harvesting time, and though he is immediately informed who she is and though he knows all about her touching loyalty to her dead husband's mother,[77] throughout the following weeks he makes not the slightest move toward a marriage. He could not be friendlier to Ruth, he is profoundly moved, attracted; yet the entire harvesting period passes—barley harvest and wheat harvest[78]—and he makes no allusion to any serious bond, to his rights or duties as a kinsman of Elimelech, Naomi's late husband. There would have been plenty of opportunities. But he uses them only to be tender and generous to, and concerned about, Ruth—in a noncommittal, cautious way. How are we to explain his conduct?

He assumes, rightly, that if he is to enter into a marriage as kinsman, it will have to be with Naomi, the dowager, who now has charge of Elimelech's estate in his place as well as of Ruth herself. We shall not at this point investigate the status of a head of family's widow. It will suffice to recall a widow with a son in the books of Kings who, dispossessed of house and land in the course of a famine and seven years' absence abroad, is reinstated at the king's behest.[79] Nor shall we go into the exact nature of a marriage like that expected of Boaz. It resembles levirate marriage in its purpose of supplying an heir to the widow's deceased husband: the first son (if that were a contingency to be reckoned with) would count as Elimelech's son, not as Boaz's. But levirate marriage, in Old Testament times, takes place within the closed family: chiefly if a married son dies childless in his father's lifetime—the widow goes to the next son. (There is another case: if, after the father's death, his sons remain together on the undivided estate and one of them, who is married, dies childless, again, the widow goes to the next without change of family.) Boaz is not a member of Elimelech's family in this sense, he is only a kinsman—not even the very nearest. By marrying Naomi he would be performing an act of "redemption"; that is to say, he would acquire a woman and an estate having belonged to a relative and threatening to get lost to the clan (or whatever name we choose to give the wider agnatic organization). Whatever the legal and social details may be, while he has to contemplate union with Naomi, fifty, his contemporary, he remains studiously evasive. His attitude changes radically and dramatically the moment Naomi sent him Ruth to "redeem." She is thirty, at most; it makes a difference. We shall see in a moment, however, that there is more to it than sex.

The day after Ruth's decisive visit the nearer kinsman, whose claim takes precedence of Boaz's, must be settled. Boaz, who is now as businesslike as previously he was merely sentimental, achieves it by means of a stratagem. Before a quorum of elders he asks the other one whether he wishes to buy, "redeem," from Naomi her late husband's, Elimelech's, land; otherwise he, Boaz, will buy it. Naturally the other one replies that he does wish to take it. Then Boaz goes on: "What day thou buyest the field from the hand of Naomi and from Ruth the Moabitess, thou hast bought the wife of the dead to raise up the name of the dead upon his inheritance."[80] The widow goes with the estate or the estate with the widow. But the point is that Boaz formulates in such a way—"thou hast bought the wife of the dead"—that the other one must think of Naomi (as Boaz had thought of her until Ruth was surprisingly substituted). It is her dead husband's land that is in question, so "the wife of the dead," to an innocent can only be she. Many commentators and translators emend the text so as to get rid of the ambiguity: "What day thou buyest the field from the hand of Naomi, thou hast bought Ruth the Moabitess, the wife of the dead" and so on. This is to destroy a highlight of the story, apart from the fact that it makes the emphatic refusal which Boaz's rival now utters most uncomplimentary to Ruth. (It is indeed possible that the words "from Ruth the Moabitess" are an interpolation,[81] dating from a time when the figure of Naomi lost some of its prominence in favor of Ruth. But they may be original. On no account should the principal and striking feature of the statement be tampered with—the misleading omission of the name of the woman to be bought with the estate.) The rival withdraws from the bargain because he does not want to marry Naomi (as Boaz had not wanted to do).

This becomes quite evident from the reason he gives: "lest I mar mine own inheritance." No passage in the book of Ruth has created more headaches, and no satisfactory explanation has ever been produced. How could marriage by way of "redemption"—whether with Naomi or Ruth—interfere with his own estate? As one of the purposes of the marriage is to create an heir to Elimelech, a first son would get Elimelech's field; but never anything else, never any portion of his actual father's possessions. So what does the nearest kinsman fear? The answer is that he has Naomi in mind—and Naomi is "too old to have an husband." She is very unlikely to have any more children, certainly she would not have more than one, who would belong to Elimelech's line. At this juncture it should be clear that her age, contrasted with that of Ruth, does not only lessen her attractiveness, though that is important enough. It is an essential disability in this narrative, which is to culminate in the procreation of King David's grandfather. If he marries Naomi, the nearest kinsman reflects, he will indeed have Elimelech's land in addition to his own, but he will probably die without an heir for either, assuredly without one for his own part. But, it might be asked, could he not marry somebody else on top of Naomi, younger, capable of childbearing? No: the narrative is set in a monogamous milieu. Again, could he not divorce Naomi if she turned out barren? He obviously could not without giving up the land she brought with her, and, just conceivably, not at all; there were restrictions on divorce, and "redemption" marriage may have carried some. In any case he does not need to find out; he knows her age and condition. Anxious to perpetuate his own name, he declines to "redeem" the land at the price of tying himself to the matron.[82]

Boaz does not immediately come out with the truth. His rival, enlightened, would change his mind; and, as Boaz's phrasing was plainly deceitful, the refusal that it provoked might be held void. Hence, Boaz first has the other one's surrender of his title solemnized in a form that puts it above any possibility of attack, makes it absolute, irrevocable, "confirms" it.[83] (Cicero tells of the owner of a villa on a lake who got a large number of people to row about pretending to be catching fish while he was entertaining a prospective buyer. His guest offered a high price. But a simple, informal sale would not have been good enough for the owner since sale gave a *bonae fidei iudicium*, where the judge could take account of accompanying circumstances. For this reason the owner suggested to the visitor at once to confirm the sale by a formal "literal contract." That gave a *strictum iudicium* under which, at the time, payment could be enforced even though there had been fraud.[84]) It is only after this ceremony is completed that he triumphantly announces: "Ye are witnesses this day, that I have bought all that was Elimelech's, and all that was Chilion's and Mahlon's [the two deceased sons], of the hand of Naomi. Moreover [here comes the climax] Ruth the Moabitess, the wife of the dead have I purchased to be my wife, to raise up the name of the dead upon his inheritance." So Ruth, the desirable, thirty-year-old one, is the "wife of the dead" whom the unnamed kinsman had foolishly renounced. He must be shattered; and the ancient audience present on the occasion or listening to the retelling of it would laugh and rejoice.

At some stage, the story of Ruth may have been of an etiological character, designed (among other things) to set forth the origin of, or to recommend, certain usages; one of them, perhaps, the usage, in the event of there being several candidates for "redemption" marriage, of according preference, irrespective of status, to one of childbearing age over one past childbearing. That problems of this type arose and were ventilated we can see from rabbinic codes and discussions. (With regard to virility, for example, we find a distinction between a man congenitally impotent and one impotent as a result of castration or old age. The former is excluded from levirate marriage; the latter is not, in principle, but even he must avoid it by giving the refusal originally described and very much disapproved in Deuteronomy.[85]) At any rate, Boaz's marriage to Ruth is definitely a novelty—that is why neither he nor, less happily, his rival contemplated it in the first place—and there are distinct remnants of the previous, unreformed custom according to which he would have married Naomi. The story, that is, presents a stage of transition. It is not only that the final acquisition is "from Naomi's hand." It is Naomi to whom, after Ruth's visit in the barn, a kind of bride-present (*Morgengabe*, *pretium pudicitiae*—though nothing has happened) is sent.[86] Let us note also that Naomi manifestly comes to reside with Boaz along with Ruth. Above all, it is Naomi in whose bosom the son born by Ruth is placed; and while this means—as we are told—that she becomes his nurse and guardian, it means something more as well. In a sense Naomi is the mother. The last sentence of the book of Ruth (discounting the appended genealogy) contains the congratulations of the neighbors, and what do they say? "There is a son born to Naomi."

Let me just remark in conclusion that the figure of Ruth plays a far greater part in the New Testament than is generally realized. Recall that Ruth visits Boaz in the barn at night before she is married to him. That was a problem for the early Rabbis, for whom Ruth, of course, was a heroine of the Old Testament. And the Rabbis in their usual way, from various allusions of the text conclude that Ruth, far from being forward, was really the purest of all women who ever lived. Now on the occasion of that visit, Ruth says to Boaz, "I am thine handmaid, spread thy garment over me." In the Annunciation story one of the difficult passages is one that uses the Greek word 'episki-azo—"the Holy Ghost will overshadow thee." The verb for the expression used in the Ruth story is *peribaleis* "to spread over, to overshadow," and just as Ruth, despite the apparently compromising situation, was the purest of all women, so, of course, Mary, despite the apparently compromising situation with child before marriage, was the purest of all women. "The Holy Ghost will overshadow thee" is a definite harking back to the Ruth story. Mary is here presented as a second Ruth, and even the handmaid motive comes in because Mary answers, "I am the handmaid of the Lord." This also comes from the Ruth story, "I am Ruth thine handmaid."

IV: FROM HYPERCRITICISM TO CREDULITY

Pirenne has recently published a survey of the status of women in biblical civilization.[87] This betrays an excessive reaction against the hypercriticism practiced at the beginning of the century. Then the presumption was that the record must be wrong. Now many scholars tend to accept the record without looking right or left. Pirenne says that while Amram, Moses' father, married his aunt, the son prohibited this degree.[88] But the codes containing this prohibition can be shown to have grown up in stages, and the aunt does not belong to the earliest. In Lev 20, for instance, the series starting with adultery and ending with intercourse with a beast must at one time have stood by itself; then the prohibition of marrying the sister from the same father and of approaching a woman in the menses were added; and still later some further prohibitions including the aunt. If all this development is pre-Mosaic, it becomes very difficult to see how in King David's time, Amnon's half-sister

Tamar regarded marriage with Amnon as not out of the question.[89] Again, it is unquestionably assumed by Pirenne that the laws called the *Mishpatim*, an extremely early legislation, are much later than the patriarchal narratives.[90] The proper thing to do is to scrutinize each detail in these narratives and establish its relation to the *Mishpatim*.

Pirenne propounds other strange theories. He thinks that the acceptance of *mohar* entitled a father to have his daughter back if the husband misbehaved.[91] He sees evidence for this custom in the Samson story and the David story; hence he ascribes Philistine origin to it, the Hebrews took it over. In reality Samson over a long time failed to visit his wife—the marriage was domiciled in her father's home. Her father, probably in the genuine belief that Samson had left and divorced her, gave her to another suitor. Samson chose to treat the affair as adultery. In the case of David, his father-in-law Saul also gave Michal to another man during David's prolonged absence. But here, of course, the enmity to David played a part as well. Anyhow, there is no trace of the custom alleged by Pirenne. The question of its origin and adoption does not arise; it was as unknown to the Philistines as to the Hebrews. From the ritual laid down in Numbers in the event of a husband suspecting his wife of adultery,[92] Pirenne infers that he was not entitled to divorce her without good reason.[93] Otherwise, why should he make her undergo the ordeal, instead of simply sending her away? But this argument is not absolutely conclusive. A jealous husband may think divorce too lenient; if she is guilty, she ought to incur the terrible things which the ritual, divinely directed, will bring on her. Finally, the story of Ruth seems to be completely misunderstood. Pirenne deduces from it (in particular from Boaz's declaration that he has purchased all Elimelech's possessions from Naomi[94]) that a widow could escape levirate marriage by abandoning her goods.[95] But, first, there is no question of levirate marriage in this book. Second, in levirate marriage the widow has no goods to abandon: she is in the same closed family as the levir. Third, it is not a question of Naomi escaping marriage. The point is that she allows Ruth to take her place as Boaz's wife. As pointed out above, both women follow the estate to live as members of his family.

CHAPTER 10

AFTER THE DEED

In treatises concerning the crime, the subject of the doer after the deed is usually not treated.

Escape. A frequent aim of the doer after the deed is to avoid detection or conviction. Rachel, having stolen her father's idols, manages to frustrate his search; Moses, having killed an Egyptian, would like the deed to remain unknown; Achan, having misappropriated some booty, buries it; David employs the most outrageous means of covering up his adultery.[1] When a public curse is imposed on categories of criminals, such as the person guilty of incest or the person who commits murder in secret, that is the community's way of dealing with those who are successful in not being caught.[2]

Denial. On being challenged, the doer may deny the deed even where this is foolish in the extreme; nor can it be said that such a reaction is not life-like. Cain claims that he does not know where his brother may be, Sarah denies having laughed at the annunciation of a son—"for she was afraid," the text explains—and Gehazi, having gone after the Syrian general whom his master Elisha had healed and having taken a huge gift, which his master had refused, pretends not to have left home.[3] All three must know that there is not the slightest chance of the denial being accepted. It is only fair to note that this kind of denial is confined to relatively early stories: for the later ones, it is presumably too unsophisticated.

Naturally, in many cases the lie is effective; and it should be observed that human nature and circumstances can be so complicated that denial of a deed and distress about it are not mutually exclusive (though, as we shall see, for a refined ethics true regret must lead to a giving up of all fruits of the deed). Potiphar's wife manages to pull the wool over her husband's eyes;[4] no remorse in her case. By contrast, Reuben is genuinely upset when he learns that his brothers in his absence have sold Joseph, yet he joins them in the scheme by which their father is to be persuaded that a wild beast devoured his son.[5]

Defiance. For the sake of self-preservation, a person may strive to remain undetected even though he or she is not convinced at all that what they have done was wrong. The Hebrew midwives in Egypt, we are told, "feared God" and therefore disobeyed the king's injunction to kill the newborn males. However, they feared the king sufficiently to tell him a fib; here we have denial of a deed that the doer considered her duty.[6] It is the earliest example in world literature of conscientious disobedience, and it is interesting that the order disobeyed is one of genocide. The Epistle to the Hebrews credits the parents of Moses with the same attitude, "when they hid Moses they feared not the commandment of the King."[7] Moses certainly regarded himself as justified in killing the Egyptian; nevertheless he would have kept it secret. Similarly, Obadiah concealed some of the true prophets from Jezebel, again fearing the law, but he didn't want his role to become known.[8] Jesus for some time kept his feelings secret.[9] In this case there are indeed special factors such as the gradualness of the unveiling of the Kingdom or Messiahship. Peter disclaims acquaintance with the arrested Jesus. Again, it is denial of conduct which the accused regards as anything but reprehensible. But this time the denial constitutes a sad lapse—not indeed because of any objection to lying as such but because of the disloyalty which in the peculiar situation it involves. There are indeed impressive Old Testament models of bravery where loyalty to God requires it; the three men in Daniel accused of refusing to worship the image set up by the king reply, "O Nebuchadnezzar, we are not careful to answer thee in this matter."[10]

Where the crime is known, or will surely become known, the criminal will often, as we saw, run away. Adam and Eve hide on hearing God approach.[11] Moses, we noted, as he realizes his secret has leaked out, flees abroad.[12] So does Absalom after killing his half-brother Amnon.[13] So does Elijah, after mortally offending Jezebel.[14] So, according to John, does Jesus several times; and he hides for a while even after his first return.[15] At his arrest, his disciples "all forsook him and fled."[16] Like denial, flight need not imply a bad conscience. Moses, Elijah, and Jesus are convinced of the righteousness of their cause. The Old Testament provides cities of refuge where the unwitting homicide may find safety.[17]

Plea for Mercy. The offender may throw himself on the mercy of his judge; he may simply ask to be let off or let off lightly. Cain requests a mitigation of his punishment.[18] The Israelites on numerous occasions pray for pardon, which is sometimes withheld, more often granted.[19] David beseeches God to spare the child born in adultery, in vain, and again in counting the people, with partial success.[20] Shimei, who gravely insulted David when he seemed ousted by Absalom, meets him on his victorious return and asks him to let bygones be bygones; David assents, though later he has second thoughts.[21] Haman, exposed, begs Queen Esther for his life.[22] In most cases of this class the offender feels remorse, more or less intense: but not necessarily in all— Haman is probably thought of as driven by sheer fright.

Obstinacy. At the other extreme there is the obstinate offender, impenitent and unflinching. Again there are degrees. In many warnings of the Pentateuch and the prophets the Israelites at large are assigned to this category.[23] Rebecca is willing to incur the consequences of any curse that Isaac may utter should he notice Jacob's disguise.[24] True, this is her state of mind before the deed, and fortunately it is never put to the test. Pharaoh displays great stubbornness, weakened only at moments of the most fearful pressure.[25] Aaron's silence when Moses explains why his sons had to die is open to several interpretations, one of them being that it is indicative of dissent.[26] Of an adulteress it is assumed that she may conceivably risk the direst effects of the bitter water rather than tell;[27] admittedly if she told, she would practically be signing her death warrant. A complicated case is where the people in the desert, having sinned and recognizing that they have sinned, and being told that at present God will not assist them, nonetheless go out to battle—and defeat.[28] The rebellious son who does not mend his ways even after chastisement and the man who, despite an admonition by the elders, refuses to marry his childless brother's widow in order to perpetuate the deceased's name both belong to a period of loosening family ties.[29] The tribe of Benjamin decline to give up to the other tribes some men guilty of a heinous crime against a Levite traveler.[30] Abner finds Ishbosheth, son of Saul, revoltingly ungrateful in reproaching him for an affair with a concubine of the dead king.[31] Amaziah silences the prophet come to rebuke him for his idolatry.[32] Matthew's machinery of settling an offense reckons with a wrongdoer impervious to private, semiprivate, and public admonition.[33]

Conviction. In crimes of conviction stubbornness may appear a virtue to those sharing the conviction; they may indeed consider the other party criminally obstinate. We have already mentioned the three men in Daniel who refuse to worship the image set up by the king, and who openly admit to their defiance. To the other side, this must admit of inexcusable stubbornness. There are many examples of this kind in the Old Testament—Korah, Dathan, and Abiram go under with flying colors, and the latter two even refuse to fall in with the debate and test Moses' purposes.[34] Gideon's father mocks the followers of Baal who request the surrender of his son for overthrowing the altar.[35] Mordecai is persistent in his disregard of the royal decree to bow down before Haman.[36] Jesus and his followers are as adamant in their activity as their opponents in their rejection of it.[37]

In the Talmud, one who commits a crime of conviction is given a special status, the *Überzeugungsverbrecher*. In an interesting passage, it is laid down that a man who eats pork from lust, because it smelled so nice, is not only, of course, a sinner, he is also excluded from giving witness in any lawsuit: he is regarded as unreliable. Whereas a man who eats pork in defiance of the law, a crime of conviction because he rejects the law, is also a sinner; he is capable of giving witness in a lawsuit: he is regarded as reliable.[38] This is a very early instance in the development of world law where the crime of conviction is given a special and higher status.

Excuses. Between the simple request for mercy and defiance, there is explanation, that is, excuses good or specious, and special pleas of various kinds. We have already touched on the cities of refuge where a homicide might stay if he could prove accident. Adam blames Eve and, obliquely, God himself—

"the woman whom thou gavest with me."[39] Eve blames the serpent. (The serpent gets no hearing.) Abimelech twice defends himself by pleading ignorance—the problem seems to have interested the author of this cycle. Once when God calls him to account because he took Sarah into his harem, his defense is that both Abraham and Sarah suppressed the fact that she was married.[40] Another time when Abraham reproves him because of a well that Abimelech's servants took by force from Abraham, Abimelech affirms that this is news to him.[41] When Joseph first reveals his identity to his brothers, they are struck dumb with perplexity, and even after gaining their speech they do not seem to try any explanation.[42] However, despite Joseph's kindness they are ill at ease and on Jacob's death fear that he may now strike at them. That such belated vengeance occurs is illustrated by the case of Shimei, to whom David swore that he would spare his life. Yet on his deathbed the king instructs Solomon to find a way of involving Shimei in some capital crime so as to justify bloody retribution.[43] Joseph's brothers, then, ask him to forgive them, and they invoke the authority of their father, his last wish.[44] Moses, on behalf of the sinful people, reminds God of his assurances to the patriarchs and also of what the Egyptians will say should they hear that the Israelites perished.[45] Aaron tries to shuffle off his guilt in the affair of the golden calf—the people made him act as he did.[46] Saul, too, urges fear of the people in defense of his failure to wipe out Agag,[47] while on a previous occasion he explains a burnt offering brought in Samuel's absence by the latter's delay in arriving, though battle might be joined any moment.[48] Michal, having helped David to escape, claims that she acted under duress: he had threatened to kill her.[49] Then, of course, there are those who, rightly or wrongly, maintain that what they did was in conformity with the law and their duties. Ahimelech is an example: he gave food to David without entering into or being aware of any plot.[50] Paul denies any infringement of the established rules of the community.[51]

Bad Conscience. That a bad conscience can plague a man is stressed in Wisdom literature: the man of discretion is assured of sound sleep, the sinner is not.[52] It is movingly clear from a number of psalms: "Enter not into judgment with thy servant, for in thy sight shall no living man be justified."[53] What the prophets do mainly for the nation at large, the Psalmist does mainly for the individual, to interpret misfortune as the deserved consequence of guilt: "He will not always chide."[54] There is early evidence of this attitude: the brothers of Joseph, as they get into trouble during their first visit to Egypt, feel that they are suffering on account of their cruelty.[55] Nor is this attitude confined to Israelites. The Canaanite king Adonibezek, defeated and brutally ill-treated, is made to exclaim, "As I have done so God hath requited me."[56]

A remarkable story is that of the king of Egypt's chief baker who, while under arrest for some offense, dreams of birds eating out of a basket on his head. The meaning (expounded by Joseph) is that he will be hanged, food for birds.[57] Again, there is the law concerning a wife suspected of adultery.[58] She is given bitter water to drink and cursed in a conditional form: if she is innocent no harm will ensue; if guilty, the most terrible diseases will befall her. Quite apart from supernatural intervention, a guilty woman might waste away from psychological disturbance. In this connection, the workings of a bad conscience, we must make at least passing mention of the fairly frequent occurrence of a sinner being struck by sickness or death either as an immediate consequence of his sin or because God or a prophet or an apostle gives him over to such fate: examples are the leprosy of Miriam, the withered arm of Jeroboam, the leprosy of Gehazi, the death of the couple Ananias and Sapphira in Acts.[59]

Blind revulsion may follow the crime. Amnon, a son of David's, falls desperately in love with his beautiful virgin half-sister Tamar: she is a full sister of Absalom.[60] By an elaborate strategy he gets her to be closeted with him in his bedroom, seizes her, and asks her to do his will. "Nay, my brother," she protests, "do not force me. Whither shall I cause my shame to go? And thou shalt be as one of the fools in Israel. I pray thee, speak unto the king, for he will not withhold me from thee." However, he does force her. And now comes a surprising turn in this story, which, with its combination of subtlety, even slight perversity, and elemental spontaneity, is one of the most powerful in ancient literature. "And Amnon hated her exceedingly; for the hatred wherewith he hated her was greater than the love wherewith he had loved her. And he said unto her, 'Arise, be gone.' And she said, 'This evil in sending me away is greater than the other that thou didst unto me.'" And he would not hearken unto her, and he called his servant and said, 'Put this woman out and bolt the door after her.'" Which is what happened. (The Hebrew terms here translated "to hate," "to send away," "to put out" can have the meaning "to divorce." They have not this meaning in the present context, yet they are used in a way that shows very clearly how the sense developed.)

The sequel does not concern me. Here we have an offender against a woman who, directly after the deed, turns from and on her in disgust. The basic reaction involved is known from wild life. A lion will growl at the lioness who keeps close when his mood for friendliness has passed: natural selection would favor the survival of those knowing when to be firm. In civilized society such conduct is in general limited to situations like the present beset by special difficulties, unpleasantness, bad conscience. But there it does occur.[61] The monstrous manner in which Amnon treats his victim—note that he does not even throw her out himself; he can no longer touch her even for this purpose—is perfectly credible. After the long, underhand, crooked preparations and the short moment to slake illegitimate lust—nausea and hatred. That by acting as he does he makes things even more difficult and unpleasant, that he acts destructively and self-destructively, is no argument against this analysis. His behavior is compulsive, not rational. The narrator's insight is profound indeed.

Repentance. Confession plays a very great part in this area, but I would rather go on and say something on repentance. So much has been written that I will confine myself to three points which are not usually stressed. First of all, in the vast majority of cases, the doer repents only when things go wrong, when he is threatened with ugly consequences. The historical scheme of the book of Judges is typical: the Israelites do evil, they are given over to their enemies, and then they cry to God and are delivered.[62] Certainly here and there, when a sinner is called to account by God or a messenger of his, in modern language we might substitute an inner voice. But this interpretation must not be overdone. It is a fact that, in general, remorse is stimulated by ill-success. That the Bible does not falsify this experience is a good thing: it is truthfulness to life that makes for lasting interest. There are exceptions.

David, who repents his adultery only on being reprimanded by the prophet,[63] in the case of the census evinces spontaneous remorse. His general Joab had indeed warned him beforehand of the wickedness of this undertaking.[64] At first sight, it looks as if the Chronicler had changed this feature, assimilating the case to the norm.[65] While in Samuel we read, "And David's heart smote him and David said, 'I have sinned,' and the word of the Lord came unto the prophet Gad, 'Go and say unto David, I offer thee three punishments, choose one,'" in Chronicles we read, "And God was displeased and he smote Israel, and David said, I have sinned. . . ." But it has been convincingly argued that the clause "and he smote Israel" summarizes what was to come in pursuance of David's repentance and choice of punishment.[66] That is to say, the meaning is, "And God was displeased so that he had to smite Israel. For after David had said, I have sinned, God spake unto Gad, Go . . ."—and it was the pestilence chosen by David that constituted the smiting. In the New Testament both Peter and Judas repent spontaneously. Paul's case is as complicated as any.

The second point I want to draw attention to is something that is akin to what in Germany is called *"tätige Reue,"* where the sinner immediately tries to undo his sin. A striking example is the case of the Levites after the incident with the golden calf. Moses comes back, finds the people worshiping the Golden Calf, and calls those who are for the true God to his side. The Levites come, and indeed they then decimate the rest of the people. It is generally assumed that the Levites had not taken part in this false worship. But it is much more likely that they did, for when Moses immediately brings the sin to the consciousness of the people, the Levites come to his side and make good by going against their own people and slaying many of those who worshiped.

The third point concerns the doctrine of repentance in Jeremiah and Ezekiel that it is the latest attitude which counts:[67] the wicked nation—Jeremiah—or the wicked individual—Ezekiel—that repents will be saved, just as the righteous nation or individual that takes to iniquity will perish. Ezekiel is emphatic that neither a righteous man's previous transgressions nor a wicked man's previous merits "shall be remembered unto him." We are used to an extreme variant of this teaching, the idea that the very last thought of a dying person determines his fate in afterlife.

The Old Testament doctrine is much narrower. For one thing, it is not a question of a quick thought but of a fresh departure, a concrete choice of a new road, in Jeremiah just prior to the catastrophe, in Ezekiel at a critical stage in the Babylonian exile. For another thing, it is necessary to recall the familiar distinction between repentance relating to a particular misdeed and repentance relating to a way of existence. Needless to say, there are countless shades. But when David repents his adultery or his census, or when Peter repents his denial, or Judas his betrayal, they are sorry for an isolated action; whereas when the Ninevites respond to Jonah's call so that "God saw their works that they turned from their evil way,"[68] or when the Judeans seek John's "baptism of repentance for the remission of sins,"[69] they dissociate themselves radically from their previous mode of living. Up to a point, your actions taken singly and your general attitude are—though they perhaps should not be—independent. Paul has difficulty with those who misbehave despite entry into the Christian community; and the good heathen is an old problem. Jeremiah and Ezekiel are concerned with a radical change in outlook and conduct, not with regret for, say, a specific murder or theft. They are concerned with conversion.

Conversion. It is in this area of conversion that the absolute decisiveness of the latest attitude originates. Where attention is concentrated on isolated actions, or even the sum of actions, what happened in the past is not wiped out so readily. The assessment of a person or group will tend to take the form of weighing up good and bad. The scales of justice would not do, however, for Jeremiah and Ezekiel. In Hannah's psalm it is said of God that "by him actions are balanced."[70] Ezekiel may be deliberately twisting a more popular notion when he represents the all-importance of the latest attitude as the right kind of weighing, balancing: "Yet ye say, The way of the Lord is not balanced. Hear now, is not my way balanced? Are not your ways unbalanced?"[71]

Certainly there are good practical reasons, apart from the setting of conversion, for assigning prominence to the latest attitude. After all, in life one has to deal with men as they are now; their past may influence one's opinion of them, but it is their present behavior that must chiefly guide one's reaction. Again, if we wish to move men in a certain direction, we shall tie their hopes and fears to what they are going to do—not, obviously, to what they did in the past. Some theories, too, would favor emphasis on the latest attitude apart from conversion. Such emphasis might not be expected where man is considered as a more or less static unit, the same always; here an overall judgment of his entire life seems appropriate. But it is different where he is regarded as growing toward his destiny, as gradually developing and displaying his true self. This view dominates several classical writers of history, some of them going so far as to conclude that, when a ruler starts out as a moderate and finishes up as a tyrant, he must have practiced deception in the earlier phase. In a way, this conclusion lands us in the other camp—the static nature of man. Anyhow, notwithstanding these and other considerations, it remains true to say that the exclusive attention to the latest attitude such as we meet in the prophetic passages under discussion is genetically and essentially associated with conversion.

In rabbinic Judaism a Gentile who becomes a proselyte is treated as a newborn child,[72] a penitent person forgiven by God as a new creature,[73] and a change of heart however late—a day before death may procure salvation.[74] Judah the Prince remarked, "One man acquires his world in many, many years, another in an hour";[75] to be sure, the remark was prompted by a last-minute repentance of exceptional intensity. We shall presently have occasion to inspect the legend of Jakim, a renegade who made good by his death. Early Christianity adopted these notions "except a man be born again he cannot see the Kingdom of God," "If any man be in Christ, he is a new creature."[76] Some parables are here in point: the two sons asked by their father to work, one of them said he would not but repented and did, the other said he would and did not; or the laborers in the vineyard, some of them hired in the morning, others in the course of the day, at the third, sixth, ninth, even eleventh hour—all received the same pay.[77]

As may be expected, the weighing of a man's good and bad deeds against one another plays a large part in Judaism and Christianity side by side with the doctrines derived from conversion. For judging a humdrum career the

weighing is more suitable than concentration on a final climax. Various rec-
onciliations between the two viewpoints may be met in religious literature,
but mostly the discrepancy passes unnoticed and is certainly not felt to be a
serious problem. This should not surprise considering the relaxed character
of Jewish theology. We may recall *m. Ab.* 3:15, which deals with a similar problem, and where some MSS read that divine judgment is "according to the
majority of the actions," some that it is "not according to the majority of the
actions" (not to mention yet further variants). Schechter has observed that
Jewish commentators are not at all bothered by the difference; they hardly
remark on it.[78]

Self-judgment. The doer may pronounce his own verdict, but this is not
necessarily associated with either confession or repentance. In a way, a man
invoking on himself heaven's vengeance should he commit a certain crime—
say, break his word—thereby in advance condemns himself in the event
of the condition coming about; and the same is true when a whole people
accepts with "Amen" a curse like "Cursed is he that taketh reward to slay an
innocent person."[79]

However, we meet with self-judgment after the deed is done. The prophet
Nathan, come to rebuke David for his adultery, begins by telling him a fictitious story of a wealthy man who robbed a poor man of his one and only
lamb. "And David's anger was greatly kindled and he said, As the Lord liveth,
the man that hath done this is a child of death. And Nathan said, Thou art
the man."[80] At the moment of judging, the king does not yet know of his own
involvement; indeed an open attack might have had a far weaker effect. There
cannot be at the moment any question of confession or repentance. Since he
is a good king, both are indeed to follow as soon as he realizes the full implication of the parable. What he does at the moment is to acknowledge the
principle applicable to his deed: such acknowledgment in itself is a tribute
to and helps to restore the order that has been violated. Moreover, he comes
very near using a form of imprecation which up to a point brings down the
punishment as he declares it. Up to a point, that is, he actually turns himself into a child of death: the prophet's parable got him into a state of excite-
ment where he expresses himself in these extreme terms. (To be sure, God,

moved by his remorse, averts the worst consequences.) It is noteworthy that in the peculiar circumstances of the case no earthly tribunal would be likely to intervene. Self-judgment, and self-judgment charging heaven with the execution, will here be very appropriate, though we shall find other equally significant settings.

The next incident to be considered concerns King Ahab.[81] Contrary to the will of God, he spares his defeated Syrian enemy, Benhadad. A prophet approaches him in the guise of a soldier with ashes on his wounded forehead where normally the mark of the prophet would be visible. Like Nathan he relates a fictitious story to elicit a judgment. There is this difference that the prophet—the soldier—plays a role in the story himself, the role of the person to be judged. He tells the king that a fellow soldier during the battle had entrusted a prisoner to him, on the terms that "If by any means he be missing, then shall thy life be for his life." In the tumult of the battle, the prisoner escaped. "And the king said, So is thy judgment, thyself hast decided it. And he took the ashes from his face and the king recognized him. And he said, Thus saith the Lord, because thou hast let go the man whom I appointed to destruction, thy life shall be for his life and thy people for his people."[82] Here again the king judges his own action without knowing. There is neither confession nor repentance and, unlike David, Ahab will be induced to neither: he was a bad king. Actually, though as the prophet or the biblical author interprets him, he acknowledges the principle governing his case; he himself would presumably reject this interpretation. He would presumably maintain that his position was not at all comparable to that of the soldier in the story: he owed no one a duty to wipe out Benhadad.[83] So his acknowledgment—unlike that of David—is really rather formal, "acknowledgment" in quotes, uttered only because of his complete ignorance of the implications which the other party attaches to it and which he would never knowingly accept. It is interesting that, for the prophet or the biblical writer, even so formal an acknowledgment is of value: it still somehow supports the order to which it refers.

As for the setting of the self-judgment, as in David's case, the matter is not one for an earthly tribunal, and the execution of the judgment must be left to heaven. Certainly Ahab does not use the form of imprecation. But the prophet bases on his admission—"admission"—a fateful announcement which, like a curse, to some extent already translates the judgment into reality.

However, in addition to the self-judgment of the king, there is another, namely, that of the man who, for the moment, appears to be a wounded soldier. The king stresses the fact: "Thyself hast decided it." In the context of the affair as a whole, the purpose is merely to add irony to the self-judgment of the king: while he believes another—the soldier—to deliver his own verdict, he is in reality doing so himself. (That the soldier's self-judgment has only a subordinate function is clear: the principal object of the parable, to get the king to convict himself, could be attained equally well without it. In the case of David, there is no self-judgment on the part of the rich man.) But it is justifiable to tear it from its context, seeing that the ancient public must have found sense in the encounter between the king and the soldier even apart from its bearing on the escape of Benhadad. We have, then, a soldier petitioning the king for remission of a penalty insisted on by his opponent; but the undertaking he recites is so definite that in reciting it he has—the king replies—uttered his own doom. This time it is not only a question of acknowledging a principle: the soldier pronounces not on a fictitious parallel, but directly on his case—though this is not, of course, his intention.[84] Moreover, this case is not of a kind left to divine retribution. Still, at the time, neither in all probability would the community see to or even aid the punishment; that, under a private treaty like this, would be entirely for the party. Such circumstances may constitute a further setting for self-judgment. A verdict delivered by the guilty person himself would protect his opponent who executed it from the charge of unlawful violence. Where an offense is capital, self-judgment is indeed desirable for yet a different reason. Even the shedding of a capital offender's blood is terrible, and in the Bible we come across special efforts to relieve the person who puts him to death from that terribleness and throw it back on the offender himself. The formula "his blood be on his own head" is an example,[85] and the eliciting of self-judgment doubtless also belongs here.

Support is furnished by the legend of Jonah. He, having confessed his sin (we shall say nothing about his repentance, a delicate problem), is openly challenged by the mariners to decide what they should do to him; he answers that they must cast him into the sea; they do so after some hesitation; and they pray that God may not "lay upon them innocent blood."[86] It might perhaps be argued that Jonah is not judging himself; he merely indicates the means by which to expel an evil influence and calm the sea. But we must not draw too sharp distinctions. No doubt the case has unusual features, but that there is at least an element of self-judgment is undeniable. This is far from being the only instance in the Bible where a misdeed as yet unexpiated brings about a calamity to be overcome by meting out the appropriate punishment; we may recall the defeat of the Israelites because of Achan's theft of consecrated booty or the famine because of Saul's slaughter of the Gibeonites.[87]

The Rabbis are quite familiar with the idea of unconscious self-judgment. Samuel b. Nahman considers it a rule that the wicked does not die before uttering his own sentence (the Greek word *apophasis* is used).[88] Pharaoh figures among the illustrations. He boasted, "I will draw my sword, my hand *torishemo*, shall destroy them."[89] But the form *torishemo* may also mean "shall cause them to inherit it."

Judas. The New Testament contains a striking deliberate self-judgment, taking place in very extraordinary circumstances, and I shall devote the rest of the chapter to it.[90]

I

The case is that of Judas through whom an unprincipled administration could lay hands on the one they feared. In Matthew[91] it leads to self-punishment, by hanging. In Acts[92] punishment is inflicted from above, he falls and bursts. (Similarly, Papias[93] has him bloated, inflamed, perishing in his filth.) Church tradition, setting out from Matthew, finds here the prototype of the very worst evildoer, adding to his outrage of selling the Savior the ultimate one of self-slaughter. This has become the dominant interpretation—though a different one from the early third century will be looked at below.[94] A representative German account runs:[95] "*Das Ende des Judas . . . entspricht jüdischem Empfinden, für welches der Satz gilt (Tobit 12.10), 'Die Frevler sind Feinde ihres eigenen Lebens,*'" "The end of Judas . . . reflects Jewish feeling, in line with the dictum

'The evildoers are enemies of their own life.'" But it is a misreading, it does no justice to Matthew at all. Let us go through the story.

II

Matthew starts by saying that Judas felt remorse. Right here, the church-influenced commentators move to get it their way—way out. The verb used, *metamelomai*, corresponding to Hebrew *niḥam*, "to repent," "to regret," is weaker, they claim, than *epistrephō*, Hebrew *šub*, "to return." There is, however, simply no evidence for such an overall ranking.

Niḥam, strictly, is more concerned with motivation, unhappiness about wrong, *šub* with result, re-adherence to right. Hence, the former perhaps tends to be more specific, alluding to the peculiar flaws renounced, the latter to concentrate on the general, positive outcome. Jeremiah complains that the people "refused to return," and however carefully he listened, "no man repented his wickedness."[96] "Repent and return," Peter admonishes the Jews who helped to bring about Jesus' death.[97] But the scheme is not rigid. In another part of Jeremiah, Israel is forced by God to return like an unteachable bullock and only then repent: "after I returned I repented."[98] In Exodus, God himself, having told Moses of his resolve to annihilate the worshipers of the golden calf and make Moses into a nation instead, is implored by the latter: "return from your fierce wrath and repent of this evil against the people."[99] Alluded to in a psalm, "a prayer of Moses": "return, o Lord, by when? and repent yourself concerning your servants."[100] Here are three more quotes showing up the futility of downgrading *niḥam*. God, according to Jeremiah, confirms an apocalyptic prediction thus: "and I will not repent and I will not return from it."[101] Joel, as a disaster threatens, appeals for a true change of heart so God "may return and repent."[102] And the king of Nineveh hopes: "who knows, God may return and repent."[103] To leave no room for an argument that where *niḥam* stands by itself, as in Matthew, it loses in force; here are a few instances, first, of *šub* without *niḥam*, then of *niḥam* without *šub*. Deuteronomy assures the nation that its captivity will end when "it returns" to God.[104] Isaiah must proclaim the judgment that the people are too impious "to return."[105] Achior, an Ammonite commander, warns Holofernes against an attack on the Jews who, formerly sinning, "have returned to their God."[106] Luke has Jesus predict at the last supper that Peter, though about to fall prey to Satan, "will return."[107] As for "to repent"—emphasizing the finality of God's rejection of Saul, Samuel adds that he "will not lie nor repent, for he is not a man that he might repent."[108] "The Lord has sworn and will not repent" in Psalms[109] envisages the triumph of "the priest for ever after the order of Malkizedeq." Job's very last words to the Lord are "I repent in dust and ashes,"[110] the fullest imaginable confession and renunciation of errancy. The result: Matthew chooses *metamelomai* because Judas was horrified by, and wanted to do something about, his particular lapse—for the moment allowing less concentration on the broader theological aspect. It has nothing to do with one being more or less serious than the other; it is the natural choice in the situation.

III

Here should follow a paragraph showing that to drop the tendentious treatment of *metamelomai* in Matt 27:3 is important not only for my thesis, that is, the proper understanding of the Judas narrative, but for a much wider territory. Why? The desire to reduce *metamelomai* to an inferior standing— quite off—has colored the treatment of the vocables involved in general and caused misinterpretation in any number of texts, however remote. The distorting effect on "innocent" passages is really amazing. It is carried furthest, of course, in scholarly dictionaries, especially such as are devoted to selected subjects and go into historical detail. These works will need major revisions in quite a few portions to get rid of the fallout of forced exegesis, all from the one text. No one would have dreamed of such violence to the other passages were it not for the need to assimilate them to the misunderstood Matt 27:3.

IV

Well, then, Judas repented.[111] He, when Jesus' way grew incomprehensible, had contacted the judges of the Sanhedrin and for a monetary reward enabled his arrest, keeping them informed about his movements and, as their troops came upon him and his at Gethsemane, pointing him out.[112] Now that they pronounced the death sentence on the ground of blasphemy, he once again approached them—to return what he had come to realize was a reward for enabling them to shed the blood of an innocent.

At this juncture, again, reservations are put forward to get over the positive evaluation an ordinary reading will convey. We are advised that his action meant little: he was only complying with a postulate in Jewish law that if you truly repent a wrong you must give up any gain gotten through it. No doubt there was such a postulate, traceable in many places.[113] It is found also of course in Shakespeare, where the King who murdered his predecessor concedes that he cannot really pray because "I am still possess'd / Of those effects for which I did the murder, / My crown, mine own ambition and my queen."[114] So Judas did certainly intend to satisfy this condition, but there is nothing in Matthew to warrant the "only," he was "only" complying, as if formalistic monetary readjustment was all he had in mind.[115] His change of heart was sincere. His acknowledgment "I have sinned" recurs in Luke in the mouth of the prodigal son[116] and from early on in the Hebrew sources may express genuine sorrow over one's straying.[117] Indeed, "Lord," a Midrash exclaims,[118] "doest thou ever require of a man more than that he utter, I have sinned?" The running down of Judas' avowal, incidentally, is far more prominent in German commentaries than English ones. German, in addition to commonplace designations for the confession of an offense, has *beichten* and *Beichte*, the official variety before a priest: and Judas, it is stressed, did not resort to that.[119] Agreed—but (leaving aside *Beichte*'s overall history) neither did the prodigal son or, a thousand years before, Abigail when admitting, taking upon herself, and seeking pardon for her husband's miserable conduct.[120] Anyhow, only desperate overtheorizing can turn the apostle's offer into empty ritualism—in total neglect of the reality that, proceeding as he did, he risked, hoped, to be executed instead of, or at least with, his master. A cynic like the present writer might actually be less impressed by a report to an understanding *Beichtvater*.[121]

V

What he confessed to was the grave misdeed of steering a fellow Jew into the hands of a power out for his life under its repressive policy. Even the little I know about it would take up too much space.[122] So I just note that its scope varied enormously in different circles and periods. For example, while the hostile regime was usually non-Jewish, now and then it was Jews of an objectionable variety—or, as in this instance, an unholy alliance; or while in general silence was the course to take, now and then it was lying; or yet again, in exceptional situations—say, with an entire group doomed unless a certain member was abandoned—betrayal might be legitimated.[123] Here, Judas, his confidence and loyalty broken down, delivered—in fact, sold—Jesus to the Jewish leaders threatened by the radical preacher and enlisting Roman officials for his elimination. Monstrous. However, the very next morning, by whatever dispensation his spirit recovered. He revoked his charge, pressuring the judges to let him take the place of the pure one whose capture he had engineered or at least to make him share the penalty as equally culpable. In all likelihood, in less singular circumstances, the Sanhedrin would have listened, with whatever outcome. But he not only did not interest them. At this stage, when they were just about to succeed in their plot against Jesus, they could brook absolutely no interference, and they rudely bade him be off. Utterly alone, engulfed by self-reproach, he made over the thirty pieces of silver to the Temple and, without even waiting for Pilate's decision and the crucifixion, killed himself.

This Judas manifestly died in extreme contrition; and to do what has been done now automatically for some seventeen hundred years, that is, side with his detractors—"what is that to us?" and so forth—is like falling in some thirty-five verses further on with "if you are the son of God, come down from the cross."[124] He was a more radical Peter. The latter, when the bulk of disciples fled, stayed around; yet even he, under duress, disavowed the arrested Jesus and wept bitterly about it as the day broke.[125] Within a few hours, Judas, who had gotten him arrested, sought to share his fate and, contemptuously dismissed, hanged himself. As his getting Jesus into the enemy's hands was far, far worse than Peter's denial, so it was paid for more dearly than by tears. There is an unmistakable fundamental cross-reference.

VI

He is mercilessly demoted in Acts.[126] In Acts: not worthy of having his exit recounted in Luke's Gospel. (I take Luke to be the author of both.) Judas was credited with no attempt to undo his treason, buying himself a field for the ill-gotten pay instead of returning it, struck down into an ugly heap by heaven instead of hanging himself, and getting his destiny summed up by two devastating lines from Psalms.[127] To be sure, a reader sharing the long-standing—seventeen hundred years—distortion of the profoundly pious suicide in Matthew ought to find the Lukan Judas far less culpable—as if Luke wished him into paradise. This was quite irreconcilable, however, with the whole tone in Acts. The explanation is that Matthew had Judas redeem himself by his ending, and that Luke would not grant him this redemption, hence had him felled by what is plainly a damning blow from on high.

Two questions arise at this juncture: one, what was the Jewish attitude to suicide at the time; the other, what made Luke oppose Matthew's reacceptance of the deserter? On question one, it is enough to recall that neither Testament contains a word against suicide, let alone an ordinance; that in Jewish law to this day it is far from universally rejected; that the Samson of the book of Judges[128] invoked God when he made the palace collapse on himself together with thousands of Philistines; that old Ahithophel was clearly taking the reasonable, respectable course when, realizing Absalom whom he supported was about to lose out, "he got himself home, put his household in order and hanged himself";[129] that Philo, bravely protesting against the threat of putting up a statue of Caligula in the Temple, explained that a planned mass suicide of Jews would have to be the response;[130] and that even Josephus[131] did feel at one with the garrison of Masada holding out after the fall of Jerusalem and, when it was to be stormed, killing first the women and children, then one another, and the last survivor himself—the very Josephus whom his special call did not allow to live up, or die up, to such heroism.[132]

Certainly there were authorities—he among them—opposed in principle, though hardly any who would not approve in a fair number of dilemmas.

Question two is accounted for by Luke's world being well beyond the breakthrough one that had room for the Matthean Judas. In *Ur*-Christianity enthusiasm—and the sheer need for support at any price—favored admission and readmission on relatively few tests. As the sect gained in recognition and settled down, a stricter selection developed. The Letter to the Hebrews states in so many words that with the founding years over, a more exacting regime must judge apostasy unforgivable.[133] Just so Luke, while pardoning (up to a point) Peter's lack of courage in a precarious situation, allowed no degree of regret or restitution to make up for a going over to the enemy. The renunciation of life, then, by the Matthean Judas in order to reunite with his victim was refused to the Lukan. He broke up in a mode unmistakably signifying perdition.[134] There are other episodes adapted by Luke to the increased stringency called for as organization advanced. Jesus' parents made a Passover pilgrimage to Jerusalem with the twelve-year-old son. Traveling homeward with their caravan, after a day or two they discovered that he was not, as they had assumed, among the company. They returned to Jerusalem and here comes the main bit, in a standard tripartite form:[135] (1) revolutionary action, Jesus had stayed behind in the Temple in discussion with the Rabbis; (2) protest, his mother asked how he could do this to his parents; (3) silencing of the remonstrants, did they not know that he had to attend to his heavenly Father? Thus far, obviously old tradition. The continuation, that he went back with them and "subjected himself to them," is no less obviously from Luke, writing when an orderly acknowledgment of boundaries had become a priority respected even by the young Jesus.[136]

VII

At this point, at the risk of distraction, I plan to call attention to a further factor making for the Lukan position: the growing influence of the more rationalist, Greek-descended culture. To this day, an educated Western public just cannot brook Asian irrationalism. For example, Cain utterly damned for a monstrous deed in Gen 4:11–12 and fully reelevated in 15ff. This was intolerable from pretty early on and bringing about to this day far-reaching misinterpretations, à la Dillman (as we shall note, distortion of the meaning of *miphnē*, "from"). In this sense, Cain is a precursor of Judas: full pardon intolerable. King David receives similar treatment, maltreatment, though less extreme. If it be objected that they did not, like Judas, abjure God directly, the worshipers of the golden calf did: at first rejected for good, welcomed back immediately after intercession.

It is not accidental that it is the same Luke who, instead of being satisfied with little modifications of the traditional gospel, takes the giant step to a new era: Acts.

Perhaps I should say something about the greater care required in using material. We should not, for example, press fantastic Oriental exaggerations as if they came from a painstaking Western thinker. Say, an exclamation like "it would be good for so-and-so never to have been" ought not automatically to be applied to its fullest logical potentiality. Poor Strack-Billerbeck have to falsify the meaning of "thou sayest" into a definitive "yes" because they cannot bear the less precise or less direct Eastern diction.

To have Acts as a new beginning is not by accident the achievement of the one evangelist with one parent originally non-Jewish. The whole base and exposition become more logical, orderly.

A curious result: it is the New Testament, not the Old, which imposes on a certain sin strict unforgivableness—from about AD 300. It is still upheld in large portions of the globe. One might almost say: serves them right for their looking down on Old Testament religion as less merciful, whereas in truth, however demanding, it does not, cannot, exclude anyone rigidly from divine fulfillment.

Fortunately, ways around barriers are found in many instances. I was struck by Tolstoy making use of one in Anna Karenina (no doubt this has been noticed before): half a sentence or so, just before she expires, is dedicated to the thought crossing her mind that she would prefer setting out afresh and positively instead of putting an end to herself—repentance saving her from eternal torture as she enters the next world. The view that regretting the act before expiring may make all the difference has, of course, a long history prior to Tolstoy—and after: compare Codex Iuris Canonici 1917, c. 1240, with 1983, c. 1184.

VIII

As one would expect, the collision of Matthew—where a guilt-laden Judas confidently sought a reconciling death—with Acts—where an outcast Judas was publicly demolished—was resolved by the church fundamentally in favor of Acts, geared toward its disciplinary needs. The pro-Judas version indeed came to be taken as anti, as describing how, bereft of all hope, he gave himself up to hell. With an effect not dreamed of by the evangelists, the anti-Judas exegesis was reinforced by seeing here a radical disapproval of suicide as such, stamping it as the route for one beyond redemption. Had there been a trace of this at the time of Luke, he need not have substituted some malefic outer force. With little exaggeration one can say that while for the past seventeen hundred years or so Judas committed suicide because he was beyond the pale, in historical truth suicide, for Christians, got beyond the pale because he resorted to it.

Amazingly, what is almost direct testimony to the authentic position in Matthew has survived. Origen, in his commentary,[137] devotes considerable reflection to Judas who, his loyalty restored, hurried to put things right as far as he could in this world and be in the next before his master, confident of a merciful response. In my Edinburgh presentation I touched on this only in passing, wondering what on earth could have led Origen to so appreciative an attitude. The obvious answer struck me only a few years ago:[138] he was, on the whole, still faithful to the Matthean understanding of the scene. Still faithful, not returning.

Even more recent is my appreciation of the hero's—yes, the hero's—name, "Judas," making him a successor of Jacob's famous son. Whether it was in fact his name in life or only posthumously I leave open. It fits to perfection. The Judas of Genesis, while dissuading his brothers from killing Joseph, maps out his sale to foreign traders which will equally rid them of him—in fact, lead to his end before long—and, above all, will provide them with cash, a rarity so long as you are under a *paterfamilias*. Their father will be shown fake evidence that the youngster has been devoured by a wild beast. Not a glimmer of sympathy for one deprived of the creature dearer to him than any other.[139] Similarly, Matthew's Judas, in horrendous distraction, takes cash for delivering Jesus to his enemies.[140] Years later, the brothers are captives of Joseph whom they do not recognize: he is by now the highest official in Egypt. He does recognize them and, in order to test them, declares that they may all return home save Benjamin, since his brother Joseph's disappearance inordinately treasured by Jacob.[141] This time Judah comes up to the sternest demands of piety. Having caused the loss of Joseph, he cannot see Jacob lose Benjamin too: so he pleads to be enslaved in his stead.[142] The Matthean Judas, too, finds his way back, in fact, within a much shorter time, ready to suffer in the place of or jointly with Jesus.[143] It is his subsequent diabolization by assimilation to the Lukan one that disconnects him from Genesis; might just as well be called Haman. In earnest: the English and German Bibles ought to refer to Judah and Juda in Matthew, to Judas in Luke and Acts.

IX

If I have not so far convinced you, it does not worry me: my main evidence is only coming now, antedating the New Testament by about two centuries.[144] It concerns the end of a prominent Jew who treacherously helped the occupying power in the annihilation of heaven-dedicated separatists, his saintly uncle the most outstanding. No earthly authority would have exacted retribution, but he did so himself and received miraculous pardon.

Yakim (Eliakim, Alcimus), from a distinguished family, was a Hellenizer, an admirer of the Syrians who rewarded him with powerful positions, including the high-priesthood. Of rare political talent—of sorts—he gained the trust of the *Chasidim*, extreme religious idealists on the opposite side—only to arrange an enormous slaughter among them. By contrast, his uncle Jose ben Joezer,[145] leading rabbi of the period, genuinely stood his ground, refused to cooperate with the administration in antitraditional measures, and was sentenced to die at the cross. While he was up there on the Sabbath, his nephew rode by on his steed, mocking him: "Look at the horse which my sovereign has me ride and at the horse which your sovereign has you ride." To which Jose replied: "If it goes so well with those who anger him, all the better will it go with those who do his will." And when Yakim asked, "Has any human done his will more than you?" Jose warned him: "If so heavy is the lot of those who do his will, all the heavier it must be for those who anger him."[146] Yakim was overcome by penitence, went home and proceeded to a gruesome self-execution, comprising all four Mosaic forms of capital punishment. His uncle, by now barely alive, in a doze saw Yakim fly heavenward and uttered these last words: "By a short hour he (Yakim) has preceded me (Jose) into the Garden of Eden!"

The similarity in both the setting and the unfolding is impressive. Setting: The superpower—Rome, Syria—capable of rewarding its collaborators, yet firmly resisted by the believers in a higher, if for now sadly held off, order; with the ugliest relations between the two camps, resisters and collaborators, as a result. This is not to overlook considerable differences owing to date, to social environment—classier in the early incident[147]—and so forth. Unfolding: one close to the leader of the resisters—Jose's nephew, Jesus' disciple—joins the enemies, in fact, lends decisive support to their unholy measures against him. The divulging of secrets of the resisters naturally ranks high in such a constellation. Judas is the "hander-over," "betrayer," of Jesus, and the first thing we hear about Yakim in Josephus is his communicating to the Syrian king subversive activities of the Maccabean chief.[148] No sooner is the result irreversible, however, than the defector is appalled by his error. So much so that, there being no earthly avenger, he takes his own life—and is restored to eternal grace, in unison with his victim.

Despite the resemblance, I see little reason to doubt the historicity, *cum grano salis*, of the this-worldly elements in the two reports. Indeed, caution recommends reticence even in the assessment of direct influence. To this day, once a fundamental idea about how a surprising result may emerge gains acceptance, we apply it very freely: so the Judas picture could have other precedents as well. Nevertheless, one detail surely does go back to the Yakim one, where it fits much better than in the later case. Yakim kills himself as Jose is beyond any this-worldly rescue, Judas when the last word about Jesus' fate has not yet been spoken: there is still to come the presentation before Pilate who would actually prefer to execute Barabbas, not to mention his wife's dream.[149]

This may be the place for a conjecture—it is no more—about the non-suicidal death of Judas in Acts.[150] Nonsuicidal but scarcely natural. In fact, it exceeds in frightening strangeness all the ghastly endings commonly offered as parallels.[151] He "falls down on the ground, bursts asunder in the middle, pours out his bowels . . . on the field of blood." Perhaps lurking behind this termination are the four modes of capital punishment Yakim succeeded in subjecting himself to—with the enormous difference that they are here inflicted by a superior power, it no longer being a suicide.[152] Exactly when and where this combination came up and how long it was appreciated, with consciousness of the allusion to and distancing from the Yakim precedent lasting, I dare not speculate on.

X

A number of problems arise—such as Jesus' ominous remark to Judas at the Last Supper, in Matthew and Mark: "Woe unto the man by whom the Son of man is betrayed; it had been good for this man if he had not been born."[153] Does this not exclude salvation, leave the monster to his deserts? The easy escape route would be Yes, it does, and to assign the passage—and maybe one or two similar ones—to a source not sharing the Gospel's prevalent positive outlook; left unamended by oversight or a late intrusion. It would be quite wrong. We had better acknowledge the enormous room in scripture for the unpredictable and, indeed, the contráry.[154] It is not, of course, quite absent from, say, Greek tradition but rarer and rarer as rationalizing trends prevail. In the Bible, it retains its hold from the start to almost the end (almost—definitely loosened in Luke, Acts, and some Epistles). A horrendous verdict against Cain is replaced, two verses later, by extravagant protection, the building of the first city, the founding of a long-lasting mighty family.[155] God himself, as the people defect to the golden calf, announces that he will destroy them and start a nation with Moses, to change his mind in no time at the latter's plea.[156] Again, he has Isaiah predict to a sick Hezekiah that he is about to die; when the prophet has left, the king prays and God, according to the version in Kings, "before Isaiah has crossed the court," sends him back to promise another fifteen years of happy rule.[157] The "woe" applicable while Judas is benighted has no unshakable validity.

Believers in sober, "Western" unfolding cannot take it. Hence, for example, in the clause "and Cain went out from before the Lord," the preposition *milliphnē*, "from before," is widely credited with indicating a permanent, punitive barrier, a never-mended exclusion of intimacy.[158] Certainly, the word being neutral, it could be used of a regrettable separation—as when Jonah,[159] disobeying God's order to confront the Ninevites, sets out to flee "from before the Lord" or when Aram flees "from before Israel."[160] But there are plenty of instances to the contrary, among them, in fact, most of those involving *yaṣaʾ*, "to go out." Surely, the closest parallels are Joseph and Mordecai. Joseph, made virtual dictator, "went out from before Pharaoh" to look after the entire realm.[161] Mordecai, appointed prime minister in the place of Haman and having secured the king's signature for the pro-Jewish ordinance, "went out from the King" in royal apparel and with a crown of gold.[162] If something like banishment were alluded to, one would expect not *milliphnē* but *miphnē*, analogous to the phrasing just before,[163] "and from your face I shall be hid."

The futility of making Matthew conceive of Judas as beyond redemption is shown up fully by the far more massive rebuttal he has Jesus administer to Peter: "Get thee behind me, Satan, you are an offense to me, for you see not the things of God but those of men."[164] This rebuttal does not keep Peter from within a week being one of the three chosen to witness the transfiguration.[165] Commentators try to get rid of Satan by pointing to occasions when the meaning is attenuated. Nothing in the text, however, points to attenuation. It is our discipline that insists on it.

Let me end this section with an observation on "Father, forgive them, for they know not what they do." Confined in the New Testament to Luke,[166] it surely owes its place to the evangelist or his school—with a decisive bearing on its meaning at this juncture. At first sight one might assume a generously pardoning attitude like that at the close of Jonah or in a Socratic teaching: "should I not spare Nineveh ... with more than sixscore thousand persons that cannot discern between their right hand and their left hand, and much cattle?" "nobody is wittingly evil." But while such a message would be reconcilable with Matthew, the traitor being reinstated on a sincere mending,[167] it is not with Luke, focused on the rational consolidation of a growing community and indeed one which, with its strong foreign admixture, is in special need of discipline. By now a Judas who, one of the Twelve, betrayed Jesus could never rise again. I have already cited the Epistle to the Hebrews' irreversible no to the one who has seriously strayed.[168] The theme plays a greater part throughout Luke-Acts than is generally realized. The fate of Ananias and Sapphira, for instance, makes it clear that downright apostasy is not the only unpardonable crime against this new world: certain machinations within it are no better. This couple take credit, claim privileged status, for a higher financial sacrifice in the community's interest than they made and, charged by Peter, drop down dead.[169] In the Lukan "Father, forgive them ...," then, we have before us no idealistic, universal embrace, carte blanche for any returnee, but an intercession solely for as yet unenlightened, groping outsiders, Jewish or Roman or what-not. They are welcome however worthless up to now[170] while, once inside under this regime, a serious breach of faith is no longer tolerable. In the history of Christianity, the roles assigned to the prayer in different periods, parts of the world, circles, and circumstances to this day are of profound significance.

XI

An excursus on H. L. Strack and P. Billerbeck's *Kommentar zum Neuen Testament aus Talmud und Midrasch* may be in order. Of rare learning and nobility, it enjoys the trust of the scholarly world—and it does so even on the, say, two dozen occasions when it bends the evidence to the advantage of treasured convictions. No historian dealing with major issues can avoid this failing— "failing" from the strict, scholarly point of view. In real life, often, the effect of "misinterpretation" is preferable to what a "correct" reading would produce: for example, in the United States, when a statute assigning a certain right to men is held to include—have included all the time—women.

Their treatment of Jose ben Joezer's faith[171] is a relatively simple illustration.[172] They declare it unlikely that he called the abode of the departed pious ones "the Garden of Eden," as also that he assigned immortality to them; the first rabbi to sanction these notions, they hold, was Johanan ben Zaccai, who died ca. AD 80. So when Jesus came upon the scene, ideology in those circles was rather undeveloped. Such is the prestige of these scholars—understandably—that, for instance, the *Encyclopaedia Judaica's* article "paradise"[173] by the liberal Rabbi B. J. Bamberger cites Johanan ben Zaccai alone for "Garden of Eden": not a word about Jose. For my main thesis it matters little if the latter expressed himself differently. But the report sounds quite coherent in itself, and Strack-Billerbeck offer absolutely no suggestion as to what it contained in the place of their cuts. Besides, Jose is precisely the profound eccentric to stand at the beginning, with Johanan ben Zaccai seeing it through.[174] Above all, the Dead Sea discoveries, from after the death of Strack and Billerbeck, contain enough material to strengthen one's confidence in the Jose tradition. The Community Rule, for instance,[175] assures the just ones of "eternal joy in life without end, a crown of glory and a garment of majesty in unending light."[176]

Here is a distortion not of date but of substance.[177] Three times Jesus answers a question by *su eipas* "you have said (it)," or *su legeis* "you say (it)": (1) to Judas,[178] (2) to the High Priest[179] or to him and others,[180] and (3) to Pilate.[181] (1) is about the destiny of Judas, (2) and (3) are about his own. According to Strack-Billerbeck, it is a straight confirmation: *du hast recht,* "you are right," *wie du sagst, so ist es,* "as you say, so it is." They do realize that the Hebrew equivalents will not ordinarily carry this sense. Still, they go on, *'amarta,* "you have said (it)," does in one passage,[182] enough to legitimize their contention. Wishful thinking. Even there, the meaning, far from a clear "yes, correct," is eminently ambiguous.

The passage concerns a dispute between two survivors of the war with Rome as to whether a certain entrance to the Temple had required a washing of hands and feet. Rabbi Simon the Modest, in the presence of Rabbi

Eliezer ben Hyrcanus, reports that he entered without washing. Where-upon Eliezer, a giant in learning and piety yet rudely domineering, asked him who was more esteemed, he or the high priest. Simon kept silent. Eliezer: "You are ashamed to admit that the high priest's dog was more esteemed than you."[183] Simon: "Rabbi, you have said (it)." Eliezer: "By the Temple service, they would break even the high priest's head with their clubs [were he to enter unwashed]; what would you do that the guard might not find you?"

To appreciate the scene, we must remember that Eliezer was an extreme adherent to rigorous tradition and so crassly contemptuous of the major-ity that in the end he was excommunicated. His opinion that the entrance in question was restricted is what one would expect. So is his offensive com-ment on Simon's worthlessness. The extraordinary bit—no doubt account-ing for the anecdote's survival—is the latter's respect for any word of that great man while holding on to the right to go his own way. Actually, in strict-ness, he was here referring not to the major conflict—washing requisite or not requisite—but to the comparative ranking of himself and the high priest's dog. He was humble enough to put up even with that, but to read it as an unqualified "you have hit the nail on the head," "laid down the valid route," is quite off. "I respect your stand" comes nearer. It was surely this con-cession that earned him his surname: he turns up in no other text. Indeed, he pays for his modesty to this day, not figuring in the complete register of Sages added to Strack-Billerbeck by J. Jeremias and K. Adolph.[184] I shall come back to this register again.

A glance at the Gospel references. (1) In Matthew, as Jesus predicts betrayal by one of the Twelve, they one after the other ask, "Surely, I am not him, Lord?"[185] Judas' participation in this interlude receives special notice. He asks the question (with "Rabbi" instead of "Lord") after Jesus' threat that it would be better for the traitor not to have been born; and is told "you have said (it)." To work out the complicated role of this response would lead too far afield; it is plainly miles apart from a bare, solid "yes, you will betray me."

(2) Again, in Matthew, as the high priest adjures Jesus to tell them whether he is the Christ, son of God—an assertion punishable by death—Jesus replies "you have said (it); yet (*plēn*) I say unto you, hereafter you shall see the Son of

man sitting at the right hand of power . . . ." He declines to provide the pros-ecution with an explicit "Yes," comfortable for them. At the same time, the continuation with "yet," to those ready to hear does make of the following pronouncement an implicit arrogation of that rank. The high priest, ignor-ing the finesse, reacts as if Jesus had simply admitted the charge. By modern standards, defensible. By the standards of some two thousand years ago, more geared toward literal interpretation, liable to count as overweening. In Luke, the dignitaries asking Jesus whether he is the Christ are refused an answer because they would not believe, and were he to ask them they would not answer. From now, he goes on, the Son of man will sit at God's right. As they all ask, "Are you then the Son of God?" he replies "you say (it)"—which they take as relieving them of the need for witnesses, "for we ourselves have heard it." As in Matthew, then, the evasion is ruthlessly rejected.[186]

To come back for a moment to Matthew, Strack-Billerbeck base on their misunderstanding an enormous idealization of the early strugglers: doubt-less the urge to do so helped on the faulty process. Jesus' "you have said (it)," let me recall, in answer to whether he is Christ, is far from a definite confir-mation. For Strack-Billerbeck, we have seen, it is—and they go even further. As it replies to an adjuration—"I adjure you that you tell us whether thou be the Christ"—it has, they contend, the force of an oath. More than this, it proves that Jesus himself recognized its imposition by the regime in power as a legitimate institution. This is not first-century Palestine; this is the dis-ciplined Prussia of the 1920s. I am a Badener.

In the corresponding Marcan pericope,[187] Jesus resorts to no ambigu-ity. A charge that he boasted of the ability to destroy the Temple and within three days replace it he disdains to attend to; even when admonished by the High Priest, "he kept silent and answered nothing."[188] By contrast, the lat-ter's question whether he is the Christ meets with "I am, and you will see the Son of man sitting on the right hand of power." One need only hold this mighty assertion against the Matthean and Lukan "you have said" or "say" to sense the disparity. Whichever comes first—I think almost certainly Mark, but even if not—the contrast between absolute, militant clarity versus cau-tion, reservation, is tremendous.

Strack-Billerbeck are inordinately uncommunicative as to this version.[189] Not a word about "I am" in the place of "you have said" or "say," and the most laconic listing of the Talmudic "to keep silent and say nothing";[190] no name associated with it, no hint at the occasion. Such reticence—less than one line—is all the stranger as they find room for generous accommodation of the quote apropos of two parables: the unmerciful servant in Matthew[191] and the forgiving of big debt versus small debt in Luke.[192] And this though what the quote contributes to the two cases is of no major importance.

As for the unmerciful servant—Rabh Saphra, around AD 300, cultivated contact with Jewish Christians. One day they challenged him to explain Amos 3:2, "You only have I known of all the families on earth, therefore I will punish you for all your iniquities": should anger be allowed to prevail over friendship? When he could not answer, *meṣaʿaru lē*, "they took him by the throat," tormented him. Strack-Billerbeck record the incident because the unmerciful servant in Matthew, himself forgiven a debt of 10,000 talents, nonetheless *epnigen*, "took by the throat," a poor guy who owed him 150 pence. While it is interesting to be reminded of a Hebrew verb that would fit,[193] no particular light falls thereby on the Matthean simile. An even fuller recital of the Saphra incident is attached to Luke's parable of a creditor who releases two debtors, one owing 500 pence, the other 50: the former will be more thankful. Strack-Billerbeck here add the portion where Saphra's Palestinian sponsor, R. Abbahu, explains to the Christians that they should not expect the former to be an adept at original biblical exegesis: his base being Babylonian, he needs to be abreast only of postscriptural development—whereas Abbahu must cope also with what the Christians appeal to, the ancient text as such, never mind what the Sages made or did not make of it. He, then, can provide the answer: it is from preference that God punishes the Jews more. Suppose you are a lender of money to a friend and to an enemy: you will keep demanding it back *peu à peu* from the friend—the situation in Amos—while having the enemy accumulate his burden to his destruction. Once again, a most interesting piece; but as a comment on the two debtors in Luke, both graciously let off, not in place. No more to the point than any other instance of two debtors.

What one senses is an enormous urge on the part of Strack-Billerbeck to play down Mark. Oversubtle? There is surprising evidence where, in fact, they come out as winners. The register by Jeremias and Adolph lists Saphra as referred to by Strack-Billerbeck on fourteen occasions, Matt 18:28 and Luke 7:41 among them. Unlisted is Mark 14:61, though Strack-Billerbeck direct us to the same Saphraic "keeping silent and replying nothing" (yes, *b. A. Zar.* 4a)—without spelling out his name. They are doing their duty, then, but in a fashion that the generally very painstaking Jeremias and Adolph miss out on it—relegating Mark to a safer distance. There are several analogous complications in Strack-Billerbeck. How far planned, how far instinctive, may be left open: in a sense tragically, the aim is throughout to serve truth and clarity.

(3) When proceedings have moved before Pilate, in both Matthew and Mark he asks Jesus whether he is the king of the Jews, to be told "you say (it)." A number of charges, not specified, are added by priests and elders. These Jesus ignores, nor does he give way even when the governor confesses himself puzzled. In Luke, the crowd leading Jesus to the governor allege that he perverted the nation, forbade tribute to Caesar, and declared himself to be Christ, a king. To Pilate's question whether he is the king of the Jews he answers: "You say (it)." Pilate advises the Jewish audience that he finds no culpability in him, upon which they accuse him all the more fiercely of agitation. The charges against which Jesus will not defend himself are transferred by Luke to the occasion (mentioned by no other evangelist) when he is tried before Herod.[194]

In John, notice that we do not find "you say (it)." Manifestly developed from it, however, is "you say that I am a king," at the end of a private interrogation of Jesus by Pilate in the course of which he spells out the otherworldly nature of his office. Pilate honors this right to the end when he has the cross inscribed: "Jesus the Nazarene the King of the Jews"—rejecting the protest of the priests who want "who said, I am King of the Jews."[195] This is an immensely simplified summary—remember that when Jesus, after "you say that I am a king," declares standing up for the truth his task, Pilate leaves with the words: "what is truth?"[196]

SUPPLEMENT TO WOMEN

The Language of Seduction in the Old Testament

There is a striking affinity between the vocabulary and style found in connection with instigation to idolatry or disregard of God and the vocabulary and style found in connection with sexual seduction. Four reasons. First, sexual seduction is such a general phenomenon, one-half of mankind habitually practicing it on the other half, that it is almost bound to color other kinds of pleading. On this ground alone, if on no other, we may take it for granted that it is the invitations to idolatry or a life of sin which borrow from invitations to intercourse, and not vice versa. Second, where the relation between Israel and God is thought of as a marriage, and defection to substitutes as adultery, incitement to defection may readily evoke the idea of incitement to an illicit union. How far this process can be carried is shown by Hosea, who represents God as "infatuating" his unfaithful wife in order to win her back—that is to say, he adopts to her the ways of a seducer.[1] Third, in the Old Testament, idolatry or disregard of God's will is often characterized by lewd practices or a ruthless striving after gain and pleasure: "And they built pillars and Asherim, and there were sacred sodomites in the land, they did according to all the abominations of the nations,"[2] "Thy princes are rebellious and companions of thieves, every one loveth gifts and followeth after rewards."[3] To this extent, encouragement of idolatry or neglect of God coincides in fact with encouragement of perversion, or of what even nowadays might be called prostitution of the person, the selling of the true values for luxury and ease. Lastly, for many Old Testament writers, foreign women are a prominent instrument of gaining adherents to foreign cults and notions. "And the people began to commit whoredom with the daughters of Moab, for they called them unto the sacrifices of their gods";[4] "Now King Solomon had many strange women, and they turned away his heart after their gods";[5] "Ahab took to wife Jezebel, the daughter of the king of the Zidonians, and went and served Baal,"[6] "Jehoram walked in the way of the kings of Israel, for he had the daughter of Ahab to wife, and he did that which was evil."[7] The legislation against intermarriage, with the express motivation "lest their daughters go a whoring after their gods and make thy sons go a whoring after their gods,"[8] and the measures of Ezra and Nehemiah in this direction are well known.

"To whore" (*zana*). The association of idolatry or rejection of God's demands with adultery, immoral rites, selfish luxury, and the lure of foreign women has left its mark on terminology quite apart from instigation. The metaphorical use of *zana*, "to whore," is interesting. It can be put absolutely—"When, for that backsliding Israel had committed adultery, I had given her a bill of divorcement, treacherous Judah also went and whored";[9] "They mingled themselves with the nations, and shed the blood of their sons and daughters whom they sacrificed unto the idols of Canaan, and went a whoring in their doings"[10]—or it can be followed by "after"—as in the passage already quoted, "lest their daughters go a whoring after their gods"[11]— or by "away from"—"for the land whoreth badly away from the Lord."[12]

Foote contends that in most passages with *zana* in the metaphorical sense the translation "to whore" is wrong: the verb by itself, he says, conveys no opprobrium; it is morally neutral, signifying only an intense devotion, and it is the context that must show whether the object of this devotion is good or bad.[13] This is untenable, however. He holds that, say, Ezekiel could not have used the language he did use if a feeling of shame had been connected with it: "Thou hast whored with the Egyptians, swollen of flesh."[14] Why not? The assertion is particularly implausible considering that in the verse immediately following the prophet maintains that even the daughters of the Philistines "were ashamed," *nikhlamoth*, on account of such licentiousness. (Foote also quotes Jeremiah, and there again Israel is told "thou refusedst to be ashamed," *hikkalem*.[15]) A point he makes much of is that once we find "to whore after strange gods" and once "to whore after other gods."[16] If, he argues, the verb as such expressed a wrongful attachment, the attribute "strange" or "other" would be superfluous. But, for one thing, it would not be superfluous. In Hebrew, the same word *'elohim* stands for the one true God and the many false ones. So "to whore after *'elohim*" would be ambiguous. In other passages, where the attribute "strange" or "other" is not added, clarification is achieved by alternative means, for example, by a possessive pronoun—"their daughters go a whoring after their (their!) gods and make thy sons go a whoring after their (their!) gods."[17] For another thing, suppose the attribute were superfluous; it would not prove that the verb is neutral. Take a parallel: *na'aph* means "to commit adultery"—"Thou shalt not commit adultery."[18] When, in Leviticus,[19] the death penalty is imposed on a man "that committeth adultery with his neighbor's wife," or when Jeremiah prophesies against those who "have wrought folly and committed adultery with their neighbors' wives,"[20] are we to conclude from the addition of "his neighbor's" or "their neighbors'"—exactly corresponding to "strange" or "other" in the case of idolatry—that *na'aph* is here neutral, that it might refer to legitimate intercourse just as well as illegitimate, and that we need the context to decide which it is? Live speech is not as rigid as that (nor, fortunately, do even philologists always display that unrelieved precision which they assume in the texts).[21] At any rate, the Ten Commandments enjoin, "Thou shalt have none other gods before me" though, on the basis of Foote's thesis, there ought to be no room for "other."

A further argument of Foote is that the expression "other gods," which is frequent, is never accompanied by a verb that could not be used *in bonam partem*, of God; so it cannot be "to whore after other gods," it must be "to be devoted to other gods." But there are three flaws in this. First, there are very few disreputable verbs like "to whore" which could be applied to idols yet not to God. Foote gives no example of a verb that one might have expected in any particular passage. Second, Foote has confined himself to "other gods" and has failed to note that the expression "strange gods"—which is rarer—is in fact accompanied by *hesir*, "to put away," several times[22]—by a verb, that is, which is obviously inapplicable to God: "Put away the strange gods that are among you." Third, it must not be forgotten that *zana* with "after" nowhere has God as object. The reason is simple: it would be blasphemous.

Of course, *zana* being employed metaphorically some twenty-five times, of all sorts of abject conduct, the original meaning may be less close to the surface on some occasions than on others. But it is never absent. The only passage which at first sight might look like an exception is one in Isa 23:17–18: "And the Lord will visit Tyre, and she shall return to her hire and shall whore with all the kingdoms on earth, and her merchandise and her hire shall be holiness to the Lord, her merchandise shall be for them that dwell before the Lord, to eat sufficiently and for choice clothing." In Foote's view, the verb here refers to absorption of a god-fearing city in mercantile alliances. But the verses are preceded by a sarcastic ditty about an aged whore (*zona*) walking around the streets, and playing, in order to be remembered again; nor should we overlook the fact that Tyre's prosperity will be restored for the sake of the Jews—all her gains will be paid over.[23] Evidently, it is Tyre's job "to whore," to prostitute herself by trading, in the service of God's people.[24] As Gray points out,[25] Revelation takes up the traditional disparagement of wealthy merchant nations as harlots: "The kings of the earth committed fornication with Babylon, and the merchants of the earth waxed rich by the power of wantonness."[26]

By now it will already be clear that the verb *zana* illustrates our thesis. But it is not only that we have the causative *hizna*, "to make whore," in the sense of "to seduce to idolatry"—"lest their daughters make thy sons go a whoring after their gods," "Jehoram made the inhabitants of Jerusalem go a whoring."[27] Even outside the causative, little details reveal the connection of seduction to idolatry with sexual seduction.

A law in the Pentateuch bids the Israelites provide their garments with a fringe, "and ye shall see it and remember the commandments, and ye shall not explore after your heart and your eyes, after which ye use to go a whoring."[28] This is in the first place a case of what in chap. 6 we called internal intellectual authorship: my own emotions and senses lead me into sin.

Needless to say, however, to succumb to the temptation of one's eyes is not very different from succumbing to the temptation of what one's eyes see, and the two ideas may merge.[29] Anyhow, here are a few texts which seem relevant. Ezekiel expresses defection in much the same terms:[30] "their whorish heart which hath departed from me and their eyes which go a whoring after their idols." Both heart and eyes recur also in Job's exclamation:[31] "If mine heart walked after mine eyes, then let me sow and another reap." Though this may primarily refer to unjust gain, the thought of adultery is not far off: Job goes on, "If mine heart have been enticed to a woman and I have laid wait at my neighbor's door, then let my wife grind unto another."[32] The role of the eyes is indeed known from a very early chapter: "And the woman saw that the tree was good for food and a delight to the eyes."[33] Ezekiel calls idolatrous objects "abominations of their eyes"; he declares that "their eyes were after their fathers' idols," and—here again we come to the sexual background— the whoring Oholibah, that is, Judah, attracted by the mere images of the splendid-looking Babylonians, "was inflamed for them by the sight of her eyes."[34]

"Ye shall not explore after your heart and your eyes" stresses the danger of curiosity. *Tur* is applied, for example, to spies "exploring" a country or to the ark going in front of the people in the desert and "seeking out" a resting place for them. Gesenius' *Handwörterbuch* postulates a different meaning for the passage quoted, "to follow" or "to be seduced by": "ye shall not follow, be seduced by, your heart and eyes."[35] But though the verb here undoubtedly has these connotations, there is no good reason to deny that the main idea is "to explore," "to seek out." Where false worship is concerned, to be interested is already to be half-lost; and the arousing of interest is among a tempter's most insidious devices. "Take heed," we are warned in Deuteronomy,[36] "lest thou inquire after their gods, saying, How do these nations serve their gods, even so will I do likewise." The verb is *darash*; it is paired off with *tur*, in a good sense, in Wisdom literature—"I gave my heart to inquire and search into wisdom."[37] It recurs in the story of David's adultery: that started by his "inquiring about the woman."[38] The mere looking at the sun, moon, and stars is apt to seduce a man to worship them,[39] and he who wishes to avoid sexual sin had better "make a covenant with his eyes."[40] When Deuteronomy enjoins "Thou shalt not learn to do after the abominations of those nations,"[41] it may mean not only "thou shalt not learn and do" but also "thou shalt not study these things at all"; the summing-up is "thou shalt be perfect with the Lord"[42]—that is, having no contact whatever with that evil.[43]

Frequently, what the seducer wants is a participant in wrongdoing, and the very fact that he can use the plural "we," offering companionship—be it that of an audacious band or that of a small conspiracy—is a help to him. The idolatrous group of citizens leading their community astray,[44] the false prophet,[45] and the idolatrous friend trying to influence you in private,[46] all say "let us go after other gods." The sinners against whose solicitations we are warned in Proverbs, call "Come with us,"[47] and indeed expressly promise full partnership, "Let us all have one purse."[48] The elder of Lot's daughters, originator of the scheme, even in the second night uses the plural, "and we shall preserve seed of our father."[49] Naturally, where a man desires a woman or vice versa, there is not only the "we"—"Let us take our fill of love," suggests the adulteress[50]—but also "with me," "to me," and so on.[51]

Encouraging particles like *lekha*, "come," *qum*, "arise," *'atta*, "now," are not uncommon. "Come, let us make our father drink wine,"[52] Lot's elder daughter; "And now, come, let us slay him," Joseph's brothers;[53] "Arise, make us gods," the people to Aaron as Moses tarries to return;[54] "Now tell me, I pray thee, wherewith thou mightest be bound," Delilah to Samson;[55] "Now make us a king," the people to Saul;[56] "Come, let us take our fill of love," the adulteress.[57] There are subtle differences between the various exclamations. "Now" is quieter than "come" or "arise"; it has an element of argumentation in it. This has a considerable bearing on the understanding of some passages. No doubt the authors of the narratives of the patriarchs were fully alive to the dubiousness of the method by which Jacob acquired Esau's blessing: the way he himself was tricked in his first wedding night constitutes as precise retaliation as can be expected in such a cycle.[58] Nonetheless, Rebekah, as she explains to Jacob how to obtain the blessing, is represented as beginning, "And now, my son, hearken unto my voice."[59] That is to say, her language is not that of an instigator of a wrong, but that of a good parent giving counsel to a child. In fact we have before us the live situation which appears stereotyped, formalized, in Wisdom: "My son, hear the instruction of thy father and forsake not the law of thy mother,"[60] or, with the phrase "and now," "And now, O children, hearken unto me."[61] Another example of specific, live advice in the family tendered in this language found stereotyped in Wisdom is furnished by Jethro's recommendation to his son-in-law Moses of the establishment of law courts: "Now hearken unto my voice, I will counsel thee."[62] In both cases, "come" or "arise" would introduce a slightly different nuance.[63]

Instigation may take place in the open, notably where the instigator despises or defies or revolts against the legitimate order. Jezebel took little trouble to conceal her designs,[64] and we may recall the people's demand that led to the making of the golden calf[65] and Jeroboam's proclamation of rival temples at Bethel and Dan.[66] Ordinarily, however, the instigator, like the doer, shuns publicity. Of the relative or friend who tries to convert you to other gods it is assumed that he acts secretly,[67] and Potiphar's wife proposed to Joseph when "there was none of the men of the house within."[68] It is a fundamental difference between the summonings to the innocent love in the Song of Songs and to those guilty in Proverbs that the former are pitched higher up in the scale, free, self-confident, in contrast to the latter, lower down, anxious, "in the twilight, in the evening of the day, in the middle of the night and in the darkness."[69] In Proverbs, the voice of free, self-confident invitation is also heard—but not from love, but from wisdom.[70] (Whether the pastorale of the Song of Songs is genuinely naive or pseudo-naive we need not decide.)

"To sin" (*ḥaṭa'*). It may be useful to survey a few verbs denoting seduction. The Hiphil of *ḥaṭa'*, "to sin," is *heḥeṭi'*. It may signify to make somebody sin, and one would expect there to be wide scope in the Old Testament for its application in this sense. (Other senses we shall discuss below.) Curiously this is not the case. That it should invariably refer to the instigation of idolatry is perhaps not surprising, considering the main interest of the Old Testament. What is remarkable, however, is that in twenty-five out of twenty-seven texts it refers, directly or indirectly, to Jeroboam's idolatrous establishments at Bethel and Dan.[71] (It is used thus also in Sirach[72] and the

Testament of Dan.[73]) Twenty-two out of the twenty-five have to do with the northern kingdom.[74] In the three remaining texts,[75] Manasseh, king of Judah, is compared to the wicked northern rulers, and Ahab in particular; and, significantly, these three texts appear in sections that emphasize that the same fate is in store for Judah as for Samaria.[76] Over against these numerous references to Jeroboam, there are only two passages where *heḥeṭiʾ* means "to make somebody sin," "commit idolatry," without envisaging that king. The Canaanites, Moses is told, may not dwell in the land "lest they make them sin against me,"[77] and Nehemiah recalls the warning example of Solomon whom his "foreign women caused to sin."[78]

No doubt it is arguable that the twenty-five texts (twenty-seven with Sirach and Testament of Dan) associated with Jeroboam should be treated as one unit. But though twenty-four occur in the books of the Kings, one does occur in Jeremiah. The probability is that *heḥeṭiʾ* in the sense of "to cause to sin" was from the outset more or less technical of Jeroboam's seduction of the people, and thereby less suitable for other cases. His altars, we read, "became a sin and the people went there," and again, "Jeroboam drove Israel from following the Lord and made them sin a great sin."[79] It was not just one of many instances of seduction to sin, it was the seduction *kat' exochen*.

The complete absence of *heḥeṭiʾ* from Chronicles calls for explanation. Maybe we need not look for any deep theological or historical reflections on the author's part. The Chronicler is not concerned with the northern kingdom—that accounts for twenty-two out of the twenty-four occurrences in Kings. (Certainly, where we are told how Josiah's reform extended even to the north, there would have been an opportunity to use the phrase, as it is used in Kings.[80] But as it does not occur in the earlier chapters, its sudden introduction here would have puzzled a reader.) The two verses in Kings where the phrase is employed in comparing Manasseh to Ahab[81] can have no parallel in Chronicles, since—as is well known—an entirely different story is there substituted (captivity and repentance of Manasseh) for that given in Kings.[82] On the other hand, we would not exclude the possibility of deeper reasons. It is noteworthy that *heḥeṭiʾ* is not found in the Dead Sea Scrolls.

Heḥeṭiʾ in other senses than "to cause to sin" is rare. About the bowmen in

Judg 20:16 we have said enough in chap. 2 ("Intent"). Deuteronomy prohibits remarriage with one's divorced wife if in the meantime she was married to someone else—"and thou shalt not cause the land to sin," continues the prevalent rendering. But this seems a mistranslation. Gesenius' *Handwörterbuch* is preferable:[83] *in Schuld bringen*, "thou shalt not cause the land to be in sin, to be guilty."[84] We hear of the *'awon*, "transgression," "guilt," of a land whose inhabitants commit sexual perversion.[85] Incidentally, it is conceivable that the Deuteronomic prohibition is directed against foreign customs, maybe even customs associated with certain cults; if so, it would be another example of coincidence of idolatry and sexual depravity.

Isaiah prophesies the destruction of those that "make a man sin by their word"—the probable sense being "that make a man out to be a sinner by false accusation or judgment."[86] That, in Hebrew, the same form which may signify "to cause a man to do" may also signify "to represent a man as doing" is familiar.[87] In English, "to make a person sin" might refer to an author who represents a person as sinning.

In Ecclesiastes,[88] we are warned against vows: "Suffer not thy mouth to make thy flesh sin." This may be taken either in the sense evidenced in Deuteronomy, "to bring thy flesh into sin, guilt" (thus Gesenius), or in that evidenced by Isaiah, "to make thy flesh out to be sinning"—the idea being that, if you vow and do not perform, your own mouth has given judgment against you.[89]

"To thrust" (*nadhaḥ*). Several verbs signifying "to seduce" presuppose the picture of the good or fortunate man walking straight and the right way, whereas the bad or unlucky one staggers or turns off or wanders off. *Hiddiaḥ*, Hiphil of *nadhaḥ*, "to thrust," is an obvious example. In one passage it denotes "to thrust": "He will thrust upon us the evil fortune."[90] More often it denotes "to scatter," "to drive away," the usual object being a nation or some other group of persons[91]—sometimes likened to a flock of sheep;[92] in Psalms it denotes the "driving out" or "thrusting out" of an individual.[93]

What interests here is that the verb may signify "to seduce," and that in nearly all cases the picture of pushing a person from the safe or proper path is very noticeable. Actually, of the false prophet it is said that he is out "to thrust thee from the way in which the Lord commanded thee to walk in";[94] very likely, in the sections immediately following, where the friend who tries to entice you to idolatry is described as "thrusting off the inhabitants of their city," the idea is not much changed.[95] In Kings, Jeroboam is declared "to have thrust off Israel from after the Lord," "from following the Lord":[96] the "from after" makes it evident that it is a question of the right or wrong road. In Chronicles, in the chapter about Jeroboam, there is no such express indication: "he made high places and made the inhabitants of Jerusalem to whore and thrust Judah off."[97] It is noteworthy that the verb is used also of sexual seduction, and that the picture of the way may again be traced. The adulteress "with the flattery of her lips thrusts him off"—that we have to supply "from the straight, prudent path" emerges from the continuation: "he goeth after her."[98] (*Hiddiaḥ* is here paired off with *hitta*, "to turn"—"with her much fair speech she causeth him to turn.")

In Jeremiah God threatens the selfish shepherds who "have scattered the flock."[99] This may refer to bad example and seduction, "to thrust off from the right pasture." Rudolph assigns the Hiphil a "tolerative" sense and translates "have allowed the flock to scatter";[100] the prophet, he thinks, is condemning neglect of firm, moral responsibility. Whichever line we take, there is this difficulty, that in the same chapter God promises to gather again those whom "he has scattered:[101] here *hiddiaḥ* has a more literal meaning, "to disperse in exile." The difficulty is not, perhaps, as troublesome as is usually supposed: Ezekiel, in his use of the passive *niddaḥ*, seems to oscillate between "led astray morally and theologically" and "exiled."[102] But it may be retorted that Ezekiel is dependent on Jeremiah and plays variations on him. At any rate, the prevalent view assumes that in the condemnation of the shepherds also the verb must refer to exile, "who have caused the flock to be dispersed in exile." Even on this basis, there remains some difference: the shepherds by their treachery "cause scattering, exile," God by way of punishment "scatters, exiles." Admittedly, however, it is a slighter discrepancy than on the alternative interpretations.[103]

We might perhaps add that the passive *niddaḥ*, the Niphal, is used in a way reconcilable with the foregoing analysis of the Hiphil.[104] The noun *madduḥim* in Lam 2:14 has been variously translated: the false oracles have been "seduc-tions" or "causes for banishment." There is no means of deciding. The former translation would correspond to "thrust off from the right pasture" in Jere-miah, the latter to "caused the flock to be dispersed in exile."

"To stray" (*ta'a*). *Ta'a* means "to wander about,"[105] with reference, say, to a traveler in the desert or a straying animal,[106] and, more frequently, "to stagger about," "to err about," in the spiritual sense. The Hiphil, as causative, means "to make wander" in a text speaking of God who caused the peregrinations of Abraham.[107] Mostly, however, it means "to mislead," spiritually. Isaiah uses a forceful paradox when he charges that "the leaders of the people cause them to stray":[108] the literal translation of *me'ashsherim*, "leaders," would be "those who lead straight."

As *ta'a* may denote a straying animal, the causative is suitable where the people are thought of as a flock and the wicked leaders as treacherous shep-herds.[109] But it is generally used of statesmen, false prophets, and so on, who steer the masses wrong politically or theologically—for example, Manasseh, who installed idolatrous worship in the Temple.[110] In Hosea, not surpris-ingly, "a spirit of whoredom hath caused them to err, and they have whored away from their God."[111] The context shows that the prophet has in mind illegitimate cults involving licentious practices.

Isaiah applies the verb to Egyptian statesmen: God confuses them so that they give harmful counsel, "misleading Egypt."[112] According to Isaiah too, the Assyrians will fail to conquer Jerusalem because God will intervene by means of "a bridle steering them wrong"[113]—which may well be an allusion to the spirit which, Isaiah was sure, God would put into the king of Assyria, so that he would listen to a rumor and return to his country.[114] It is notewor-thy that God *hit'a* in three more passages. In one of the last chapters of the book of Isaiah, in a prayer for reacceptance of a nation deep in sin and dis-tress, God is asked, "Why doest thou make us err from thy ways?"[115] Into the complicated question arising in connection with this kind of thought we shall not here go. Job, remarking on God's power to help or harm at will, says that "he causeth the leaders of the people to wander in the void where there is no way, he causeth them to stagger[116] like a drunken man."[117] Probably this is the source of a verse in a thanksgiving psalm where the times of distress are characterized by God "misleading the princes in the void."[118]

An example of internal intellectual authorship may be seen in Sirach,[119] deprecating speculation about things too difficult to understand: "For many are the conceits of man, and evil imaginings lead astray."

"To beguile" (*nasha'*). *Nasha'* as Qal of the Hiphil *hishshi'*, "to beguile," does not occur, though the Hiphil is not infrequent. The verb is thought to be connected with *shaw*, "vain." It seems to have a far more specific meaning than has been realized, namely, "to give a vain assurance of peace or safety." God may do so,[120] a king,[121] flattering prophets,[122] or allies;[123] also a nation's overweening heart may "assure" that nation[124] and people may "assure" themselves[125]—an influencing going on internally. Let us add that the use of the noun *mashsha'on* is consistent with the sense here postulated—it refers to the reassuring guile with which an ill-wisher covers up his intentions[126]—and that the use of the Niphal, *nishsh'*, is not inconsistent with it.[127]

So far we have not considered the only Pentateuchic text with *hishshi'*, Eve's defense: "The serpent beguiled me and I did eat."[128] Very likely, the verb has its usual meaning. The serpent, "Promethean" aider of mankind against a selfish tyrannical God,[129] had mentioned only the sublime faculties to be obtained by disregarding the prohibition, but not the fact that retribution would follow.

"To incite" (*Hesith*). *Hesith*, Hiphil of a Qal *suth*, which does not occur, signifies "to entice," "to instigate," "to incite"; and with the exception of one obscure passage in Job 36:16, it is always used in *in malum partem*. (The verb recurs in two more texts from Job; in one of them it definitely refers to a bad action;[130] the other is not very clear but, insofar as the sense can be made out, the action is also bad.[131])

We hear of seduction to idolatry,[132] of a king misleading his people,[133] of counselors misleading a king or prophet,[134] of wrath moving a man to mock God—internal intellectual authorship.[135] Of course, a verb may designate an evil without blame to the subject. The action or result which he who *hesith*, "instigates," tries to bring about is always wrong or disastrous, but this does not mean that the instigation must be an offense. David considers it possible that God has "incited" Saul against him.[136] According to the earlier account of David's census, in Samuel, God "incited" him to it; the Chronicler substitutes Satan—when it becomes a wrong.[137] Satan it is who "incites" God against Job[138]—here again the instigation itself is damnable.

Curiously, two different passages from Ahab's and Jehoshaphat's joint campaign have given unnecessary trouble to different scholars. The Chronicler informs us that Ahab "seduced" Jehoshaphat to join him,[139] a remark not found in Kings. To go by Gesenius' *Handwörterbuch*, the word has here no bad sense; we ought to translate "persuaded."[140] But in the Chronicler's eyes, the alliance is a most deplorable slip on the part of the otherwise pious Jehoshaphat, for which he was severely reprimanded by the prophet:[141] no parallel in Kings. Neither is there a parallel to the Chronicler's mention of Jehoshaphat's affinity with Ahab as the deeper cause of the former's slip—*chercher la femme*, as so often in the biblical writers—or to the description by the Chronicler of how hospitably Ahab treated Jehoshaphat in order to make him well-disposed. The pious king was indeed "seduced."

The other passage also occurs only in Chronicles,[142] not in Kings, at the point where the Syrians, mistaking Jehoshaphat for their main enemy Ahab, nearly finished him, but God "enticed," "lured" them from him. In this case, while Gesenius correctly accepts the bad sense, Driver and Gray distrust the text—chiefly because, they think, the verb is used neutrally, "God moved, turned, the Syrians from him."[143] But we have already noticed that moral blame is not an inevitable corollary of the use of the verb *in malum partem*. As God, in drawing the Syrians away, was acting to their detriment, the verb "to lure" is quite appropriate. In Kings, they ceased attacking Jehoshaphat simply because they realized their error. In Chronicles, though this rational explanation is retained, the exercise of a harmful influence on a person's or group's decision is by no means unique.

Finally, the verb occurs in an interesting episode recounted both in Joshua and Judges,[144] where quite unnecessary emendations are made. Caleb promised his daughter to whoever would capture a certain city. Othniel fulfilled the condition and obtained her. "And it came to pass when she came, that she moved him to ask of her father a field; and she lighted from her ass (or, and she clapped her hands from her ass, i.e., called for attention when ready to depart) and Caleb said unto her: "What wouldest thou? And she said, Give me a blessing, for thou hast set me in the land of the South (or, dry land), so thou shouldest give me springs of water. And he gave her the upper springs and the nether springs."

It is universally held that "she moved him to ask" cannot be right because—it is claimed—it is the lady, not Othniel who won her, who in fact asked.[145] Many commentators, taking their cue from the rendering of Judges in the LXX, emend into "he moved her to ask." But it is rightly objected that, if this had been the original reading, first, it would be hard to account for the fact that, in Joshua, the LXX follows this *lectio difficilior*, and third, the use of *hesith* would be strange since elsewhere the verb always denotes instigation to something improper or harmful. Accordingly, some critics propose more radical emendation, and some think the corruption is so thorough that the original cannot be conjectured at all.

The text is in perfect order, the whole problem is illusory. We need only realize the field and the springs are two different objects. The bride told her husband to ask for a field, a piece of land; he did so and got it. Then she herself extracted a valuable addition. To be sure, it is not stated in so many words that "he did so and he got it." This is one of those very economical historical-etiological notices where what does not call for explanation and elaboration is not explained or elaborated. But a careful analysis leaves no doubt that we must distinguish between a first transaction concerning the land and a second one concerning the water. For in requesting the latter, she says, "Thou has set me in the land of the South"; evidently, the field, the land must be Othniel's. And she continues, "So thou shouldest give me springs of water"—this is the climax of the narrative, which is designed to account for the springs being in the hands of the Othnielites to whose geographical portion they do not prima facie belong. It is because of the emphasis on this additional gift, the etiological point of the episode, that the narrative becomes here more circumstantial: "and he gave her the upper springs and the other springs."

Why is *hesith* used? Because the lady resorts to a stratagem, outwitting her father. She gets her husband to ask for the land, the principal dowry; at the last moment, she requests a farewell present,[146] which her father cannot refuse. It is not impossible, given the character of the episode, that the word "blessing," *berakha*, includes a pun on "pool of water," *berekha*.[147] Conceivably, too, the grant of a principal dowry and, in addition, some *Zugabe*, some further, subsidiary present, was once a customary institution: something like it seems to occur in the Assyrian laws.[148] Indeed, the episode under discussion may be meant not only to justify Othnielite possession of the springs, but also to explain the origin of this very custom of a twofold grant.

"*To entice*" (*Pitta*). *Pitta* in the Piel, the causative, of Qal *patha*, which— closely allied to the adjective *pethi*—signifies "to be simple, ingenuous, silly, unlearned, easily fooled, enticed." Whether the root is identical with the exceedingly dubious *patha*, "to be spacious, open," may be left undecided.

The Qal is met in a Deuteronomic warning against idolatry, "lest your heart be enticed";[149] similarly, in an oath by Job that "his heart was not enticed" in secret by sun and moon.[150] In the same oath we find the Niphal, *niphta*, synonymous with the Qal: "his heart was not enticed" to another man's wife.[151] One verb appears for enticement by sun and moon and enticement by lust. The Qal further occurs in Hosea's comparison of Ephraim to "a silly dove":[152] the nation, when in danger, instead of turning to God, flounderingly seeks help now from Egypt, now from Assyria (maybe there is also the more specific idea that it is easily lured into alliances of this kind). In Job, Eliphaz says, "Passion killeth a fool."[153] More pregnant is the use in Prov 20:19: "He that goeth about as a talebearer revealeth secrets, and company not with one that is easily enticed as to his lips"—that is, to talk where he ought not to. Commentators (including the dictionaries) have great difficulty here. Some introduce the rare meaning "to open"; others assume a very general sense, "silly chatterer" or the like. But we shall come across *pitta*, "to entice," in several stories where it is a question of getting a man to reveal secrets.[154] Moreover, Sir 8:17 contains a highly relevant line: "Take no counsel with a *pothe*, for he will not be able to keep thy secret." *Pothe* clearly: "one easily talked over." Two more texts from Sirach with the Qal may here be added: "The fool is ensnared by gold."[155] Sirach may be thinking not only of the peculiar sins to which riches are apt to lead, but also of the trust in material wealth which is a denial of God: Job declares himself free from this guilt in the same oath in which he clears himself of worship of sun and moon and adultery.[156] "Be not ashamed to correct a fool and a grayhead occupied with whoredom."[157] The association of *pothe* with one readily attracted by the opposite sex may not be accidental; we already had some instances, and there will be more.

The Piel occurs in an old law, imposing payment of a dowry on him "who entices a virgin":[158] plainly in the sexual area, and seduction of the inexperienced. A late text, with the passive, the Pual, without doubt depends on the old one for its phraseology: Sirach, in a description of the cares besetting the father of a daughter, remarks that, while she is a virgin, he worries "lest she be seduced."[159] (Other expressions in this section derive from Pentateuchic laws.) Samson's wife is enjoined by her fellow countrymen to "entice him" to give away the secret of his strength.[160] The translation by Gesenius,[161] *durch heuchlerische Worte betrügen*, is too narrow and too exclusively intellectual; *betören*, one of the meanings given by Köhler,[162] is good, but the English he offers, "to deceive," "to fool," is not really adequate. The women to whom Samson is attached are to use all means women in such a position have at their disposal. Of course, in the end, he will be a fool and he will be deceived, but *pitta* here means something like "to infatuate," "to work on a person so as to make him stupid, willing."

This is not to say that the verb is never without sexual overtones. Joab claims that Abner has come over to David "to fool thee and to know all that thou doest."[163] It is simply that infatuation is prevalent between the sexes, and that, more specifically, women are good at extracting secrets from men, as any intelligence service knows. Ahab's defeat and death are brought about by God authorizing a spirit "to deceive him," to encourage him through lying prophets to go to the fateful battle.[164] According to Ezekiel,[165] a prophet consulted by idolaters may give no advice: if "he is enticed" (Pual, passive of Piel) and does so, it is God who "has enticed him"—which, in this theology, not here to be analyzed, only underlines the abjectness of the sinner. (Punishment, incidentally, is meted out to deter the people from further *taʿa,* "straying off.")[166] In the Psalms, *pitta* refers to the "seductive talk" of those who, at heart insincere, ask God to rescue them from misery;[167] in Proverbs, to the "enticement" practiced by the wicked on the innocent.[168] In Proverbs, too, the Pual, the passive, occurs in an obscure line: "by long forbearance is a prince—or judge—enticed."[169]

In all cases considered so far,[170] there is something bad about *pitta,* be it that the action itself is wrong or improper, be it that the result is harmful—as when God "entices" the false prophet or sends a spirit to "deceive" an arrogant king. It remains to inspect Jeremiah, Hosea, and one line from Sirach.

Contrary to the opinion of some scholars, Jeremiah is no exception. No one doubts that the Pual, the passive, is used by him *in malum partem*: his enemies hope that "he may be enticed" into a wrong step which will enable them to get the authorities to finish him.[171] "Peradventure he will be enticed and we shall prevail against him and we shall take our revenge on him." It is very possible that the meaning is "Peradventure we shall succeed in enticing him and we shall take our revenge." In sending out a lying spirit against Ahab,[172] God says, "Thou shalt entice and thou shalt indeed prevail," that is, "succeed in the work of enticement." Not to mention the passage from Jeremiah to be quoted presently.

Controversy arises about the preceding verse but two,[173] where the prophet bitterly accuses God: "Thou hast enticed me (Piel) and I was enticed (Niphal), thou hast overcome me and hast prevailed." Translations, commentaries, and dictionaries alternate between "entice," "deceive" on the one hand and "persuade" on the other. The latter view has the support of Gesenius' *Handwörterbuch,*[174] claiming that the verb is here employed *in bonam partem*. Nonetheless this is *au fond* a theologizing interpretation. Köhler rightly disagrees,[175] though his "to make a fool" does not hit the precise nuance. An excellent discussion is found in Rudolph's commentary.[176] The words, almost blasphemous, might be those of a girl seduced and deserted. Whether the second half, "thou hast overcome me and hast prevailed," adds a slight variation on the theme, bringing in an allusion to rape or at least a degree of violence,[177] whether it introduces an entirely different picture, of a weak man overpowered by a strong one,[178] or whether it must be read together with the first half,

"Thou hast indeed succeeded in enticing me" (on the analogy of several texts just referred to, one of them in the immediate neighborhood of that before us), is immaterial. In support of the line here taken it should be noted that we must not, without the strongest reason, ascribe to the verb a good sense in a verse so close to that about the enemies hoping that "he may be enticed."[179] Moreover, it is of interest that the prophet goes on to speak of himself as "a laughing stock, everyone mocketh me." The two notions are coupled in Eze-kiel,[180] in the prediction of the terrible fate of the unfaithful Oholibah, Judah, when she is abandoned by her husband: "thou shalt be a laughing stock and mockery."[181] Jeremiah, of course, though seduced and deserted, cannot let go of the beloved. And, equally of course, he would admit the ultimate necessity and "goodness" of God's exploitation of his prophets. Nonetheless the verb has its full pejorative force. We do no justice to this chapter by emptying it of passion.

Hosea differs: God will *pitta* his unfaithful wife.[182] Gesenius and Köhler are right in separating this passage from the others.[183] But they go too far: they give the verb a completely neutral, intellectual sense, "to prevail upon," *überreden*. It is not as simple as that. The picture is still that of allure-ment, seduction. The same sentence goes on, "I will speak to her heart": of Shechem, when he seduced Dinah, we are told that "he spake to the heart of the damsel."[184] It is allurement of the young, innocent, inexperienced: the woman "shall make answer as in the days of her youth."[185] The point is that allurement, seduction, in this case is to lead the pure to just the right goal, into an ideal, legitimate union.[186] "To infatuate," "to allure," is the nearest version.

By the time of Sirach, the verb can be used more laxly. He has it in an exhortation to dismiss sorrow:[187] "Entice thyself and soothe thine heart." An example of internal influencing, a man getting himself into a good mood as he might do with a friend or a girl. However, there is not much left of the original atmosphere of the verb. As far as this passage is concerned, it might have always been used *in bonam partem*.

The adjective *pethi* is not very remote from the verb. The idea of readiness to be talked over appears in a saying in Proverbs:[188] "The *pethi* believeth every word." And it is the *pethi* who in the twilight hurries to a rendezvous with a loose woman.[189]

The *pethi* is paired off or identified with *kesil*, "a fool," *ḥasar-lebh*, "one lacking reason" (*lebh* literally "heart") and similar types;[190] also—in accordance with the basic signification—with a *naʿar*, "a young man."[191] His opposite is the *ʿarum*, "the prudent one," and other characters possessed of understanding.[192] However, the *pethi* is better than the *leṣ*, the scoffer: the latter is unteachable, he can only be punished.[193]

While in Proverbs the *pethi* lacks wisdom, in the psalms he seems to lack learning in the law and its interpretation.[194] In one psalm, however, God is represented as coming to the aid of precisely the *pethi*.[195] Whether this is a protest against the deprecation of the unlearned, or whether *pethi* here means "simple" in the sense of "helpless," there is no means of deciding. The *pethi* is paired off with the *dal*, "poor," which at first sight speaks in favor of the latter interpretation. But the "poor" is identified (more or less) with him who does not know the way of the Lord in Jeremiah.[196] According to Ezekiel, the sanctuary is to be cleansed "from the man that erreth and the *pethi*."[197] Evidently, a reference to sins in ignorance, and the *pethi* may well be he who sins through ignorance of the law and its interpretation. The noun *pethayuth* is paired off with *kasiluth*, "foolishness"; it is an attribute of an undesirable woman, but the exact meaning is dubious.[198]

Needless to say, in many of these texts the enticement causes the victim to depart from the straight or safe path: "Take heed, lest your heart be enticed and ye turn aside and seek other gods";[199] "The *pethi* believeth every word but the prudent man looketh well to his going."[200]

[Daube wanted to explore the following points but never did:]

(1) General remarks on how far there is different vocabulary for invitation to true religion or love and invitation to false. (a) Words (verbs, adjectives, nouns) describing invitation—some neutral like *qaraʾ*, "to call," though used of seduction (Num 25:2), others, like *hiddiaḥ*, "to thrust off," essentially evil. (b) Words describing more specific actions, attitudes, qualities, "to seize," "to be smooth," *heḥeziq*, *taphaṣ*, *ʾaḥaz*, *heḥeliq*, *debash* (?), *shemen* (?). (c) Words used by seducer in speaking. Some of this may have to go into lecture on

Intellectual Authorship—for example, the expression *haya liphalon: ha'asoth*, "to be the cause for someone to do," which, though its only occurrence is with crime is, I think, neutral. It illustrates the fact that causation is more deeply probed into in connection with the bad than with the good—for obvious reasons. No one is bothered by the good!

(2) The different emphasis attached to the various senses in seduction: sight, hearing, smell, touch. (Taste is out, for by the time kisses, for example, are tasted, the stage of action is reached. For similar reason, touching is nearly out.) This also may have to come under Intellectual Authorship.

NOTES

CHAPTER 1—CAUSATION

1. Sir 33:14–15 reads: "Good is the opposite of evil and life the opposite of death; so the sinner is the opposite of the godly. Look at all the works of the Most High; they come in pairs, one the opposite of the other."

2. There is also the sickness of Hezekiah (Isa 38).

3. "Not even a bird is caught without the will of heaven; how much less the soul of a son of man" (*Gen. Rab.* on 33:18).

4. [Wayne Narey writes (in www.clt.astate.edu/wnarey): "In classical tragedy, we find the gods bickering, fighting, and doing all that makes up their anger in the form of the *sylleptor*, meaning 'partner.' The term is ironic, for no human asks for the partnership of the god who possesses him or her. But possess they do, so that they find relief in their petty quarrels between themselves by means of the human chess pieces, which they move about by literal possession, becoming *daemons* and inhabiting the human form for whatever term they desire. All of these gods and their corresponding possessions we recognize today as basic, human emotions: love may turn to passion, which is far less stable than 'love,' more destructive, and has depth to it that no one may measure until it strikes. What indeed are we capable of? The *thumos*, or soul, was like the sea: depthless, always in motion, unknowable in what inhabits it, and, once turning into storm, unstoppable until destruction lies in its wake. Aphrodite could do this to one, as could other gods in similar forceful if uncontrollable ways by means of passion, desire, intelligence, hubris, artistic accomplishment, etc."]

5. Daube wrote up this part of his Gifford lecture and delivered it as a lecture at the Institute of Jewish Studies, London, and also at a meeting of the Society for Old Testament Study. He pointed out that it is partially based on his unpublished *Göttingen* doctoral dissertation. For modern English jurisprudence on the subject, he referred to "the monumental work of Hart and Honoré, *Causation in the Law* (Oxford, 1959)."

6. Exod 21:20.   7. Exod 21:33–34.

8. 2 Sam 12:9.

9. Wilhelm Caspari, *Die Samuelbücher* (Leipzig, 1926), 543.

10. 1 Sam 27:21.   11. 1 Sam 27:17.

12. 1 Sam 27:25.

13. "Of his brave words hark to the bravest: 'This the woman gave that thou gavest.'" Dante Gabriel Rossetti in *Eden Bower*.

14. Gen 3:11ff.

15. Gen 20:9. Cf. Daube, "Error and Accident in the Bible," *RIDA* 2 (1949): 193, 199;

NOTES

"Concerning Methods of Bible-Criticism: Late Law in Early Narratives," *ArOr* 17 (1949): 91ff.; and "Rechtsgedanken in den Erzählungen des Pentateuchs," *Festschrift für Eissfeldt*, eds. J. Hempel and L. Rost (Berlin, 1958), 38ff. [*BLL*, 362, 82ff., and 97–98].

16. Exod 21:12ff., see also 21:22ff.

17. Exod 21:19. I omit details.

18. Cf. Daube, "On the Third Chapter of the *Lex Aquilia*," *LQR* 52 (1936): 257 [*CSRL* 1:6].

19. Exod 21:22.

20. E.g., Georg Beer, *Exodus* (Tübingen, 1939), 110.

21. Exod 21:26–27.

22 Cf. *tiqne*, "Thou buy," in Exod 21:2, and *kaspo*, "the money from the sale of the ox," in Exod 21:35.

23. Cf. Daube, "Some Forms of Old Testament Legislation," *Oxford Society of Historical Theology* (1944/45): 37ff. [*BLL*, 343ff.].

24. Exod 20:13; Deut 5:17. 25. Lev 25:43.

26. Deut 27:24, 19. 27. Deut 21:7.

28. See E. A. Wallis Budge, *Book of the Dead* (London, 1889), 191.

29. Daube, "Error and Accident," 210 [*BLL*, 373–74]. See also chap. 3, "Error and Ignorance," 71.

30. Deut 22:8. 31. Exod 20:16; Deut 5:20 ; 19:16ff.

32. Exod 22:17; Deut 18:10. 33. 2 Sam 19:24; 1 Kgs 2:8–9.

34. Cf. Daube, *Studies in Biblical Law* (Cambridge, UK, 1947), 200 [*BLL*, 249].

35. 1 Kgs 2:36ff. 36. Deut 19:5.

37. Exod 22:5.

38. Benjamin Daube, *Zu den Rechtsproblemen in Aischylos' Agamemnon* (Zurich, 1938), 186–87.

39. Plato, *Leg.* 9.873 E; Aristotle, *Ath. pol.* 57.4; Demosthenes, 23,76.

40. Richard Maschke, *Willenslehre im Griechischen Recht* (Berlin, 1926), 64ff.

41. Exod 21:28–29, 32. 42. Deut 22:8.

43. Exod 21:13. 44. Num 35:22–23.

45. Cf., for example, 2 Kgs 4:27, "but Gehazi came near to thrust her away," or Ezek 34:21, "because ye have thrust with side and with shoulder and gored with your horns."

46. HL I 3–4.

47. See Johannes Friedrich, *Die Hethitischen Gesetze* (Leiden, 1959), 90.

48. Deut 25:11–12. 49. Second ed. (Stuttgart, 1925), 1, 270.

50. Num 35:23. 51. 1 Kgs 3:19.

52. Daube, "Error and Accident," 190ff. [*BLL*, 360 ff.]. See chap. 3, "Error and Ignorance," 54.

53. Exod 21:33ff., 22:4–5.

54. Lev 24:17–18, 21.

55. Daube, "*Nocere* and *Noxa*," *CLJ* 7 (1939): 27, 31–32 [*CSRL*, 1:71–102].

56. Exod 21:35 over against 36. 57. Exod 21:36.

58. Exod 21:33–34. 59. Exod 21:34.

60. Daube, *Studies in Biblical Law*, 138ff. [*BLL*, 231ff.]. 61. Cf. above, sect. II.

62. Gesenius=Kautzsch *Handwörterbuch*, 16th ed. (Berlin, 1915), 108, s.v. *b'r* II.

63. Georg Hoffman, "Versuche zu Amos," *ZAW* 3 (1883): 122. 64. Daube, *Studies in Biblical Law*, 85ff. [*BLL*, 331ff.].

65. Exod 22:6ff.

66. Cf. my remarks about the growth of this code in *Studies in Biblical Law*, 88–89 [*BLL*, 333–34].

67. See Hans Bauer and Pontus Leander, *Historische Grammatik der hebräischen Sprache des Alten Testaments* (Hildesheim, 1962), 281ff., 325, 329.

68. Jer 23:27.   69. Sir 11:25, 27.

70. *m. B. K.* 4:4 at the end. Cf. Samuel Rosenblatt, *Interpretation of the Bible in the Mishnah* (Baltimore, 1935), 10.

71. *Leg.* 9.873 D–E.

72. Gesenius = Kautzsch 2nd Engl. ed., ed. A. E. Cowley (Oxford, 1910), 141.

73. Bauer and Leander, *Historische Grammatik*, 283.

74. Sir 15:13.   75. Ps 91:10.

76. Prov 12:21.   77. 2 Kgs 5:7.

78. Judg 14:4.   79. Jer 2:24.

80. Gen 20:6; cf. Daube, quoted above, sect. I, in connection with Gen 20:9.

81. *Spec. Leg.* 3.21.120.

82. For instance, J. Z. Lauterbach, *Mekhilta de-Rabbi Ishmael*, vol. 3 (Philadelphia, 1935), 35.

83. Wilhelm Bacher, *Die Proömien der Alten Jüdischen Homilie* (Leipzig, 1913), 41.

84. *b. Sanh.* 58b. Similarly, according to Simeon, the Bible, in Job 24:15 calls "adulterer" him who only sins with his eyes: *Lev. Rab.* on 18:3, ch. 23 toward the end.

85. H. S. Horowitz, *Mechilta* (Frankfurt, 1928), 262.

86. Lauterbach, *Mekhilta*, 1 (Philadelphia, 1933), XXVI.

87. Editor's note: This final section returns to Daube's brief discussion of the topic in his original Edinburgh lecture. I will append at the end of it further musings about the topic I gleaned from personal acquaintance.

88. Acts 2:23.   89. 2 Sam 12:9.

90. 1 Sam 18:17.

91. Aeschylus, *Cho.* [Libation-Bearers], 923. My brother compares Isa 3:9: "the wicked reward evil unto themselves." See Benjamin Daube, *Zu den Rechtsproblemen*, 188.

CHAPTER 2 — INTENT

1. Num 19:11.   2. Num 19:14.

3. Exod 21:12.   4. Lev 24:17–18, cf. v. 21.

5. Num 19:15.   6. Num 5:2.

7. In judging the relative age of norms we cannot simply go by the age of the source—J, E, and so on—in which a norm appears, even if that were secure. A norm may be much earlier than the source containing it; hence the most complicated permutations are possible.

8. Exod 21:13. The continuation "then I will appoint thee a place . . ." is no doubt substituted for an older apodosis on the exact nature of which, luckily, there is no need here to speculate.

9. Num 35:16–17.   10. Num 35:22.

11. Deut 19:5.

12. *Sunday Times* [London], May 28, 1961: Sayings of the week.

13. Exod 20:13, 17; Deut 5:17, 21.   14. 2 Sam 12:9, 13.

15. Gen 4:5, 8.   16. 2 Sam 11–12.

17. 1 Kgs 21.   18. 1 Kgs 3:16ff.

19. Of J-like character; see J. A. Montgomery, *The Books of Kings*, ICC (New York, 1950), 110.

20. *Pauly's Real-Encyclopaedie*, 16 (Stuttgart, 1935), 280–81.

21. *Il.* 23.85.

22. Frgmt. 144 in Alois Rzach's edition, *Hesiodi Carmina recensuit Aloisius Rzach* (Stuttgart, 1958): Pausanias 9.36.6–7.

23. "Schuld und Sünde in der griechischen Religion," *Archiv für Religionswissenschaft* 20 (1920–21): 256.

24. *Il.* 10.332.

25. Gen 19:35. The Rabbis, in defining what does and what does not constitute insulting behavior giving rise to damages, lay down that it is not insult if I lift somebody's skirt in my sleep or by falling on him from a roof: *m. B. K.* 8:17.

26. Gen 34; 2 Sam 13.   27. Deut 22:23ff.

28. Num 25:7ff.

29. As remarked above, the mere fact of a rule appearing in, say, P instead of the earlier J or E would not be conclusive; we therefore rely on additional arguments, from substance, from comparison, etc.

30. Gen 9:4ff.   31. Lev 17:3–4.

32. 1 Kgs 5:3 vs. 1 Chr 22:8 and 28:3.   33. Exod 15:3; cf. Ps 24:8.

34. Deut 22:26; the formulation of murder draws on Deut 19:11.

35. Gen 12:11ff.   36. I 1ff.

37. Num 35:31, 32.

38. See Daube, *Studies in Biblical Law* (Cambridge, UK, 1947), 121ff. [*BLL*, 218ff.].

39. Exod 22:5.   40. Judg 15:4ff.

41. 2 Sam 14:30ff.

42. VIII 10, D. 47.9.9; Gaius IV ad 1, XII tab. That something like this is the original regulation I argue in *Formalism and Progress in the Roman Law of Delict*, Ph.D. dissertation (Cambridge, 1936).

43. Ludwig Köhler, *Lexicon in Veteris Testamenti Libros* (Leiden, 1958), 288.

44. James Barr, *The Semantics of Biblical Language* (London, 1961), 118.

45. Isa 65:20; Ps 25:8.   46. Job 5:24.

47. Job 7:18ff.   48. Job 8:6.

49. E.g., Isa 32:18; Prov 3:33. With Job 5:25, cf. Ps 72:16.

50. Prov 8:34ff.

51. Grammatically there is nothing to choose between them: the Hebrew, literally, is "my misser" or "my sinner." It should always be borne in mind that even those who advocate the meaning "to miss the mark" can find no text where ḥaṭaʾ takes an accusative.

52. C. H. Toy, *Proverbs*, ICC (Edinburgh, 1899), 180, while adopting the translation "to miss," does realize that, with "to hate" put as parallel, there must be "an element of conscious action"; so "to miss" equals "purposely fail to find." This virtually—and reasonably—concedes our point.

53. Prov 19:1ff.; cf. Sir 11:10.

54. *Thesaurus Linguae Hebraeae et Chaldaeae* (1835), 1, 464. But I have not searched whether he had a predecessor.

55. Prov 13:6.   56. Prov 21:4–5.

57. Prov 28:20.   58. Prov 29:20.

59. Eccl 5:5.   60. Judg 20:16.

61. S.v. *hamartano*, in Gerhard Kittel, *Theologisches Wörterbuch zum Neuen Testament*, I (Stutt-gart, 1933), 271–72.

62. Judg 11:27.

63. Gen 40:1.

64. This is not found in Ulrich von Wilamowitz, though he may tend somewhat in that direction: *Glaube der Hellenen*, 2 (Berlin, 1932), 120.

65. If there were—as there are not—a significant number of passages in the Bible with *ḥaṭaʾ* in the sense of "to miss," this assumption of a wide original potentiality would be preferable to that of a simple straight line from the objective to the subjective. Here we may perhaps note that at first sight Ethiopic is somewhat divergent from the other relevant languages: the root here means "to sin" only where there is borrowing from Aramaic, whereas in general it means "not to have." See Theodor Nöldeke, *Neue Beiträge zur semitischen Sprachwis-sensehaft* (Strassburg, 1910), 36. But from some forms of the verb—e.g., one signifying "to hide"—it appears that even in Ethiopic an element of wrongdoing is inherent in the root. Moreover, before assigning "not to have" to the earliest stage of the language, we ought to make sure that this meaning is not due to the influence of a few biblical texts where the root was interpreted thus.

66. Num 35:11ff.

67. As in Deut 19:3ff.; Josh 20:3ff.

68. Digest 18.1.16 pr. Pomponius IX ad Sabinum; 18.1.37, Ulpian III disputationum; Code 4.21.17pr., Justinian A.D. 528; 4.38.15.1, Justinian 530.

69. Exod 21:15, 12.

70. Exod 21:17.

71. Lev 24:17ff.

72. Deut 27:24.

73. Roman tradition ascribes a higher age to the rule *Si dolo sciens morti duit parricidas esto* than to *Si telum manu fugit magis quam iecit*, and so on. This would not, however, be irreconcil-able with the speculation here proposed, since it is very possible that the former rule was preceded by many occasions when a person accused of a killing defended himself by declar-ing that he had not acted *dolo sciens*.

74. Exod 21:13.

75. I 1ff.

76. Exod 21:14.

77. Deut 17:12–13; 18:20, 22.

78. Deut 19:11; 22:26.

79. Deut 19:4, of the unwitting homicide: "without forethought"; 19:11, of the murderer: "and he ambush him." If *ṣadha*, "to lie in wait," which is used in Exod 21:13, is linked with *sadh*, "to hunt," it is slightly less close to "guile" than is *ʾarabh*.

80. We are not arguing from the apodosis of Exod 21:14, "thou shalt take him from mine altar to die," since this need not be from the same hand as the protasis. In 21:13, it is most unlikely that the protasis was from the outset followed by "then I will appoint thee a place whither to flee."

81. Num 35:9ff.

82. Num 35:11, 16.

83. Num 35:16ff.

84. Num 35:20–21.

85. Exod 21:13; though here in Exodus it is only the verb which appears. Numbers has a noun derived from it.

86. Num 35:22–23.

87. Many examples in the dictionaries. The transfer of the attribute to salvation, however interesting, is not here to be investigated.

88. Num 6:9.

89. *Second Tetralogy* 4.7.

90. Deut 19:3ff.

91. *Rhet.* 1.13.16; *Eth. nic.* 5.8.7.

92. Gen 4:8, generally assigned to J. While Deuteronomy has *'al*, Genesis has *'el*, a little weaker.

93. Deut 22:25ff.

94. Gen 19:30ff.

95. Exod 20:14; Deut 5:17.

96. *Mekhilta de-Rabbi Shimeon*, 111.

97. Job 24:15.

98. *Lev. Rab.* 23, Resh Laqish.

99. *Kalla* 1.

100. Matt 5:27–28.

101. *b. B. M.* 58b.

102. *Derek Eretz* 10, R. Eliezer ben Hyrcanus.

103. Matt 5:21–22.

104. See Daube, "Greek and Roman Reflections on Impossible Laws," *NLF* 12 (1967): 49, 50; *CSRL*, 2:1129–1222.

CHAPTER 3 — ERROR AND IGNORANCE

1. The first part of this essay on error appeared as "Error and Accident in the Bible," *RIDA* 2 (1949): 189–213 [*BLL*, 359–74]. The second part on ignorance appeared as "Sin, Ignorance, and Forgiveness in the Bible," Claude Montefiore Lecture, Liberal Jewish Synagogue (London, 1960) [*BLL*, 375–89].

2. 2 Sam 1.

3. Deut 19:5.

4. *Rhet.* 1.13.16; *Eth. nic.* 5.8.7.

5. Gen 27.

6. Gen 28:16ff.

7. Gen 42:6ff.

8. Gen 44.

9. Exod 3:4.

10. Lev 10.

11. Josh 9:3ff.

12. 2 Sam 6:6ff.; 1 Chr 13:9ff.

13. 2 Sam 11:14.

14. 2 Sam 12.

15. 1 Kgs 13:7ff.

16. Esth 6:6ff.

17. Matt 13:10ff.; 24:24; Mark 4:10ff.; 13:22; Luke 8:9ff.; 1 Cor 1:18ff.; 2 Thess 2:10ff.

18. Luke 12:48.

19. Acts 3:17; 17:30.

20. Rom 1:19ff.

21. Acts 23:5.

22. Gen 19:31ff.

23. Die Marquise von O. See p. 38 for the suspicion Kleist expresses.

24. *m. B. K.* 8:1 and Gemara attached to it.

25. Gen 12:11ff.

26. MAL 13–14.

27. Gen 38.

28. Gen 29:20ff.

29. Judg 14:19ff.

30. 2 Sam 13.

31. Esth 2:20.

32. *Ant.* 12.4.6.

33. Gen 20.

34. 1 Kgs 3:19.

35. 2 Sam 4.

36. Judg 7:22.

37. 1 Kgs 22:34; 2 Chr 18:33.

38. 1 Macc 6:43ff.; *Bell.* 1.1.5.

39. Luke 23:34; Acts 3:17; 13:27; 1 Cor 2:8.

40. John 16:2–3.

41. Acts 7:57ff.; 1 Tim 1:16; Titus 3:3.

42. Chetham Strode, *The Gleam*.

43. Gen 4:2ff.

44. Gen 22.

45. Num 15:32ff.; 27:1ff.

46. Matt 12:9ff.; Mark 3:1ff.; Luke 6:6ff.

47. Gen 38:24; Lev 21:9.

48. Lev 24:14.

49. 1 Kgs 21:13.

50. Deut 19:18.

51. *m. Aboth* 1:9; *m. Sanh* 5:4.

52. Mark 14:59.

53. Herodotus 1.32; cf. 3.40, 7.10.5–6, 7.40.

54. *Poet.* 14.

55. Gen 27:33.

56. *Poet.* 10–11.

57. Aristotle, *On the Art of Poetry*, trans. Ingram Bywater, preface by G. Murray (Oxford, 1920), 14.

58. *Poet.* 13.

59. Ibid., 9.

60. 2 Sam 4:10.

61. Esth 6:6.

62. Titus 3:3.

63. Acts 26:9.

64. *Antigone* 10.23–24.

65. *Don Quixote*, trans. J. M. Cohen (London, 1950), 2.74.

66. Num 35; Josh 20.

67. Deut 24:1.

68. Exod 21:18–19.

69. Deut 22:25ff.

70. Deut 13:15; 17:14; 19:18.

71. Num 35:30; Deut 17:16; 19:15.

72. Lev 20:2ff.; Deut 13; 17:2ff.; 18:20ff., etc.

73. Deut 18:20ff.

74. Deut 13:2ff.

75. Lev 4:2ff.; 22:14, etc.

76. The following two paragraphs, on the extension of the Levitical system to accident and confusion, come from Daube's later essay on "Error and Ignorance as Excuses in Crime," in *Ancient Jewish Law* (Leiden, 1981), 49–70 [*BLL*, 391–407].

77. Gen 28:16ff.

78. Exod 3:5.

79. Num 35:9ff.; cf. Josh 20:1ff.

80. E.g., Lev 22:14.

81. Exod 22:27.

82. *Mek.* on Exod 22:27.

83. Cf. Judg 7:22; Demosthenes, *In Aristidem* 53 (637), quoting a statute of Draco.

84. Cf. *b. Ber.* 28b; *Derek Eretz Rab.* 3, toward end.

85. *Daily Prayer Book*, trans. Singer, 15th ed. (London, 1935), 46; Claude Montefiore, *Outlines of Liberal Judaism* (London, 1923), 363.

86. 2 Sam 6:1ff.

87. Exod 3:5.

88. Exod 19:12–13.

89. Exod 20:19.

90. Judg 13:22.

91. Isa 6:5.

92. 1 Sam 14:24ff.

93. Verses 28–29 might be taken as pointing that way.

94. 1 Kgs 13:7ff.

95. 2 Kgs 17:26.

96. Gen 28:16ff.

97. Lev 4.

98. Ps 19:12–13; see *Midrash Psalms ad loc.*; *Lev. Rab.*, sect. 5, on 4:15.

99. *Daily Prayer Book*, 259ff.

100. *t. Sot.* 15:10; for the original scope of the principle, see Daube, "Concessions to Sinfulness in Jewish Law," *JJS* 10 (1959): 8–9 [*TL*, 8–9].

101. MAL 14.

102. Cf. Daube, "Concerning Methods of Bible-Criticism," *Ar Or* 17 (1949): 91ff., and "Rechtsgedanken in den Erzählungen des Pentateuchs," *Von Ugarit nach Qumran, Festschrift für Eissfeldt* (Berlin, 1958), 38ff. [*BLL*, 82ff. and 97ff.].

103. Gen 12:11ff.

104. Cf. Deut 22:22.

105. Gen 26:7ff.

106. R. Levi, around 300; *Gen. Rab.* sect. 41, on 12:17.

107. *m. Ker.* 1:1–2.

108. Acts 22:30ff. See above.

109. Under Exod 22:27.

110. Deut 19:4–5.

111. See above.

112. Exod 21:13; Num 35:7ff.; Deut 4:1ff.; 19:1ff.; Josh 20:1ff.; *m. Makk.* 2:1ff.

113. *m. Makk.* 2:1.

114. *Spec. Leg.* 3.21.120ff.

115. Exod 21:13. See chap. 1, "Causation," p. 24–28.

116. Deut 22:8; *b. Shab.* 32a.

117. *Bell.* 2.8.14.163.

118. Or more precisely, brings about the bad thing that one person deserves through another who is bad, culpable, disobedient, in being the agent. Cf. also *t. Yom.* 5:12; *b. B. B.* 119b; *b. Sanh.* 8a.

119. Gen 44:16; see Daube, *Studies in Biblical Law* (1947), 253ff. [*BLL*, 289ff.].

120. Camus.

121. *Mek.* on Exod 21:13; *b. Makk.* 10b.

122. Hos 4:6.

123. Hos 7:11.

124. Isa 6:10.

125. Matt 13:14–15; Mark 4:12; Luke 8:10; John 12:39ff.; Acts 28:25ff. Cf. Daube, *The New Testament and Rabbinic Judaism* (1956), 149 [*NTJ*, 313].

126. Num 5:12; see *Num. Rab.*, sect. 15, *ad loc.*; *b. Sot.* 3a; and cf. Jacob Levy, *Neuhebräisches und Chaldäisches Wörterbuch*, 4 (Leipzig, 1889), 542, s.v. *sheṭuth*.

127. John 9:39–40.

128. "Though knowledge is not the highest element in religion," "though she must 'know her place,' though 'she is second, not first,' yet assuredly that second place is high" (Montefiore, *Outlines of Liberal Judaism*, 363ff.).

129. Plato, *Apol.* 13.25E–26A, e.g.

130. Acts 3:17, 13:27.

131. 1 Tim 1:13.

132. Luke 23:34; see Daube, "'For they know not what they do': Luke 23:34," *Studia Patristica* 79 (1961): 223–45 [*NTJ*, 847–56].

133. Luke 16:19ff.

134. Eusebius, *Hist. eccl.* 2.23.16, quoting Hegesippus.

135. Isa 53:6.

136. 1 Pet 2:25.

137. *b. Meg.* 31a, a *Baraitha*.

138. Claude Montefiore, *A Rabbinic Anthology* (London, 1938), 611.

139. Heb 5:2.

140. *Siphre* on Num 15:25.

141. Hermann Cohen, *Die Religion der Vernunft aus der Quellen des Judentums* (Frankfurt, 1929), 234, 255ff.

142. Rom 10:1ff.

143. *b. Sanh.* 27a; see the stimulating article, "*Mumar*—Study in Rabbinic Psychology," by J. J. Petuchowski, *HUCA* 30 (1959): 179ff.

CHAPTER 4—PASSIONS

1. Num 35:22.

2. Deut 19:5.

3. See Daube, *Sin, Ignorance and Forgiveness in the Bible*, Claude Montefiore Lecture 1960, 15–16; "Direct and Indirect Causation in Biblical Law," *VT* 11 (1961): 266ff. [*BLL*, 375–89 and 409–27]; also chapters in this volume, "Causation" and "Error and Ignorance."

4. *Leg.* 9.866dff. Plato recognizes that a passionate malefactor, though deserving less punishment than a deliberate, cold-blooded one, may in the long run be a greater danger to society—namely, if his fits have a knack of recurring.

5. Plutarch, *Alex.* 8.1.43ff.   6. Exod 21:20, 21.

7. Cf. Graham Greene, *The Complaisant Lover*.

8. Daube wrote up and expanded this part of his lecture on "Passions" for a talk he gave in 1966 in St. Paul's Cathedral, London.

9. For a less impressionistic orientation, see J. H. Tigay and L. I. Rabinowitz, s.v. "Drunkenness," *Encyclopaedia Judaica*, vol. 6 (Jerusalem, 1971), 237ff.

10. Richard Stookey, *A Still and Woven Blue* (Boston, 1974), 293.

11. 2 Sam 13:1ff.   12. 1 Kgs 16:9ff.

13. Jdt 12:12, 17ff.; 13:2, 4ff.; 14:1ff.   14. 1 Kgs 21:12, 16ff.

15. 1 Sam 25:17. In v. 25 Nabal is once more labeled as "a son of Belial": probably in a more general sense, though even here, his drinking may play a part.

16. 1 Sam 1:16.   17. 1 Sam 25:26.

18. 2 Sam 18:32.   19. 1 Sam 25:36.

20. 1 Sam 25:3ff.   21. 2 Sam 3:3.

22. 1 Sam 25:3.   23. 2 Sam 1:17ff.

24. 2 Sam 18:33.   25. 2 Sam 1:11ff.

26. 2 Sam 4:5ff.   27. 2 Sam 21:13.

28. 2 Sam 9:1ff.   29. 1 Chr 3:1.

30. 1 Sam 25:39.   31. *Midrash Psalms* on 51:6.

32. Gen 27:25ff.   33. Gen 29:22ff.

34. See, e.g., R. Rendtorff, art. "Wein," in *Die Religion in Geschichte und Gegenwart*, 3rd ed., vol. 6 (Tübingen, 1962), 1573.

35. E.g., S. R. Hirsch, *The Pentateuch*, vol. 1, trans. Isaac Levy, 2nd ed. (Durham, 1963), 612.

36. Gen 42:25ff.   37. Gen 43:34ff.

38. 2 Sam 11:2ff.   39. Gen 9:20ff.

40. Gen 9:24; see *b. Sanh.* 70a.   41. Gen 19:31ff.

42. Gen 19:33, 35.   43. 1 Sam 1:12ff.

44. Esth 1:10ff.

45. See N. W. Porteous, *Daniel* (Philadelphia, 1965), 78.

46. Dan 5:1ff.

47. *t. Ter.* 3:1, *b. Erub.* 65a; see Reuven Yaron, *Gifts in Contemplation of Death in Jewish and Roman Law* (Oxford, 1960), 149–50.

48. Aristotle, *Pol.* 2.9.9.1274b.   49. Demosthenes, *Con.*

50. Plutarch, *Alex.* 8.1.51; Arrian, *Anab.* 4.8–9.   51. Prov 23:29ff.

52. 1 Esdr 3:18ff.   53. Josephus, *Ant.* 11.3.3.38ff.

54. 1 Esdr 3:22 (trans. S. A. Cook, in *The Apocrypha and Pseudepigrapha of the Old Testament*, ed. R. H. Charles, vol. 1 [Oxford, 1913], 30), cf. Josephus, *Ant.* 11.3.3.41.

55. *y. Makk.* 31d.   56. Prov 13:21.

57. C. T. Fritsch, "The Book of Proverbs," in *The Interpreter's Bible*, vol. 4 (Nashville, 1955), 777.

58. See, e.g., C. A. Simpson, "The Book of Genesis," in *The Interpreter's Bible*, vol. 1 (Nashville, 1952), 555.

59. Gen 9:22; cf. 9:18, 25–26.

60. Prov 13:15.

61. Prov 22:3; 27:12.

62. Eccl 4:9.

63. See Daube, *Studies in Biblical Law* (Cambridge, Eng., 1947) (repr. 1969), 191ff. [*BLL*, 242ff.].

64. Prov 24:12.

65. Prov 30:21, 23.

66. 1 Sam 1:6–7.

67. Prov 27:3.

68. Prov 21:19.

69. Prov 12:16.

70. 1 Sam 2:26.

71. Prov 3:4.

72. 1 Sam 1:8.

73. Eccl 4:9.

74. Prov 8:11.

75. Ruth 4:15; cf. also Isa 56:5.

76. Prov 22:1.

77. Prov 3:15; 8:11; 20:15; 31:10; Job 28:18. Only one occurrence outside: Lam 4:7.

78. Prov 31:10.

79. See H. W. Hertzberg, *I and II Samuel*, trans. J. S. Bowden (Philadelphia, 1964), 22.

80. 1 Sam 25:25.

81. Prov 30:21–22.

82. Prov 17:7.

83. 1 Sam 25:3.

84. Prov 28:14.

85. Prov 29:1.

86. Prov 1:33; 2:12; and often.

87. 1 Sam 25:3.

88. Prov 3:4.

89. Esth 2:7; cf. Job 42:15.

90. Jdt 8:7–8, 28–29.

91. See p. 106.

92. Gen 39:6; cf. 1 Sam 16:18; Dan 1:4.

93. Prov 17:21. The Hebrew verb is *śamaḥ*, synonymous with *gil*.

94. Prov 23:24, using *gil* in the first and *śamaḥ* in the second.

95. Prov 23:25, *śamaḥ* in the first half, *gil* in the second. Cf. 10:1; 29:3.

96. Job 31:1.

97. Prov 2:15.

98. Prov 6:17.

99. Prov 11:6.

100. 2 Sam 11:21; Judg 9:50ff.

101. See Hertzberg, *I and II Samuel*, 314.

102. Prov 24:12.

103. Prov 15:25.

104. Prov 28:17.

105. 2 Sam 12.

106. Job 34:22, 26.

107. Job 24:14–15, 24. Cf. Prov 6:31ff., on which see my remarks ["To Be Found Doing Wrong"] in *Studi in onore di E. Volterra*, vol. 2 (1969), 11–12, and ["The Culture of Deuteronomy"] in *Orita*, vol. 3 (1969), 50 [*BLL*, 992–93, 1012].

108. 2 Sam 13:12–13.

109. See p. 104.

110. 2 Sam 13:3.

111. Prov 13:20; 18:24; 28:7.

112. Ps 1:1.

113. 2 Sam 13:3.

114. Prov 3:7; 21:30; 26:12; Eccl 7:16; Job 5:12–13.

115. Zech 9:2; cf. Ezek 28:2ff.

116. Prov 11:12.

117. Gen 34:5; cf. 1 Sam 10:27.

118. Deut 24:10–11. See my comments ["The Culture of Deuteronomy"] in *Orita*, vol. 3 (1969), 34 [*BLL*, 1000].

119. 1 Kgs 20:2ff. See excursus to my chapter "The Shame Bias of Deuteronomy," in the

forthcoming *Ancient Jewish Law* by David Daube and Reuven Yaron [not published, but see *BLL*, 955–1013].

120. Shemaryahu Talmon, "Wisdom in the Book of Esther," *VT* 13 (1963): 419ff.

121. Jdt 8:28–29.

122. Jdt 8:13.

123. Jdt 9:2ff.

124. Jdt 11:6, 16; 12:4.

125. 1 Macc 2:26, 54; *Jer. Targum* on Exod 6:18; *b. Sanh.* 82a–b; *b. Sot.* 22b.

126. I Kgs 18:40.

127. 2 Kgs 10:15–28; cf. Jer 35:6–10.

128. Gen 34; Jdt 9:2ff.

129. Gen 34:16.

130. Jdt 9:3 from Gen 34:7.

131. See Daube on *Esther* (Oxford Centre for Postgraduate Hebrew Studies, 1995), 59 [*BLL*, 845].

132. Gen 34:30.

133. 1 Macc 2: 26, 54.

134. Acts 13:45; 17:5.

135. Acts 21:20.

136. cf. Acts 22:3; Phil 3:6.

137. Exod 32:26–29.

138. 1 Macc 2:20.

139. See K. G. Kuhn on Num 25:6–15 in *Sifre zu Numeri* (Stuttgart, 1959).

140. John 19:30.

141. John 2:17.

142. It is connected with Greek *thoreo*, "to rush," "to dart," and *thorybos*, "noise," "tumult."

143. *Tusc.* 4.23.52.

144. Euripides, *Herc. Fur.* 869.

145. *Tusc.* 3.5.11.

146. *Menaechmi* [The Twin Brothers] 373.

147. Geoffrey Hazard and David Louisell, "Death, the State, and the Insane: Stay of Execution," *UCLALR* 9 (1962): 381–405.

148. Livy, 3.48.1, about a *decemvir* crazed with lust; 25.39.4, about an enemy surprised by attack; 2 Macc 5:17 (Vulgate) about an overweening pagan oppressor.

149. Seneca, *Nat.* 5.53.2, *sulfa alienat*; *Ep.* 8.5.24, *demens alienatusque*.

150. See Daube, "Ecstasy in a Statement by Rabbi Joshua ben Hananiah," *Niv-Hamidrashia* (Tel Aviv, 1972), 60–62 [*TL*, 455–57].

151. Mark 5:1-20.

152. *Tusc.*, Loeb Classical Library, 236.

153. [Editor's note: regarding the problem of synonymous meaning, the literary critic William Empson reported how when teaching English in Japan one of his students translated the idiomatic phrase "out of sight, out of mind" as "invisible, insane." *LRB* 27 (2005): 5, *Among the Mandarins*, vol. 1, John Haffenden.]

154. Judg 11:30–40. See Daube, *Appeasement or Resistance: And Other Essays on New Testament Judaism* (Berkeley, 1987), 109 [*NTJ*, 111].

155. [Editor's note: in his recent commentary, *Leviticus 1–16*, AB 3 (New York, 1991), 299, Jacob Milgrom states, "The verb *bitte* and the noun *mibta* connote an impulsive statement (see Num 30:7; Prov 12:18; and especially Ps 106:33"). See Daube's following comments on Num 30:7 (6) and Ps 106:33.]

156. See R. H. Charles, *Apocrypha and Pseudepigrapha of the Old Testament* (Oxford, 1913), 1:333, note z.

NOTES

CHAPTER 5—NEGLIGENCE

1. Matt 25:13.

2. For more details on what follows, see Daube, "Negligence in the Early Talmudic Law of Contract," *Festschrift Fritz Schulz*, vol. 1 (Weimar, 1951), 124–47, and "Josephus on Suicide and Liability of Depositee," *Libro Jubilar de Victor Andrés Belaúnde*, Mercurio Peruano (Lima, 1963), 231–41 (repr. *JR*, 9 n.s. [1964]: 212–24) [*TL*, 305–32; *EOW*, 245–53].

3. See Daube, "Zur frühtalmudischen Rechtspraxis," *ZAW* 50 (1932): 149–50, 155 [*TL*, 381–96].

4. *b. B.M.* 44a; *y. B.M.* 9b; *b. Shebu.* 38c.

5. Philo, *Spec. Leg.* 47.30ff.; Josephus, *Ant.* 4.7.38.285ff.; *Bell.* 3.8.5.362ff.

6. *m. B.M.* 3:10.   7. *b. B.M.* 94b.

8. *y. Shab.* 38b.   9. *b. B.M.* 42a.

10. An oath denying fault recurs in the Codex Euricianus, in consequence of a development not dissimilar to the Jewish one. See W. Kunkel, *ZSS* 45 (1925), Rom. Abt., 347–48.

11. See below on the hapless cat, p. 128.

12. See Daube, "Das Sebstverständliche in der Rechtsgeschichte," *ZSS* 90 (1973): 1–13; *JR* 85 (1973): 126–34 [*CSRL*, 2:1277–86].

13. See Daube, *Studies in Biblical Law* (Cambridge, 1947), 85ff.; "Direct and Indirect Causation in Biblical Law," *VT* 11 (1961): 257ff. [*BLL*, 331ff., 417ff.].

14. "Owner" is a poor rendering of *ba'al*. "Lord," "master," "controller" are alternatives, but none is satisfactory.

15. Par. 53.

16. See Daube, "Zur frühtalmudischen Rechtspraxis," *ZAW* 50 (1932): 153 [*TL*, 391]; *Roman Law* (Edinburgh, 1969), 160.

17. Possibly in an earlier version of Exod 22:4 the vineyard did not figure; it is missing from the portion "and it graze in another's field." In Exod 22:5, the words "or the field" may be secondary.

18. See Daube, "The Civil Law of the Mishnah: the Arrangement of the Three Gates," *TLR* 18 (1944): 351–407 [*TL*, 273–77].

19. Philo, *Spec. Leg.* 3.144ff.; Josephus, *Ant.* 4.281–82; *m. B. Q.* 4, 5:3f.

20. Philo, *Spec. Leg.* 3.144ff.   21. Ibid., 4.20ff.

22. Philo, *Decal.* 171, *pleonexiai*.   23. Josephus, *Ant.* 4.271–72.

24. Ibid., 4.279ff.   25. Ibid., 4.281ff.

26. *m. B. Q.* 1ff.   27. *m. B. Q.* 7.

28. *m. B. Q.* 1:1.   29. *m. B. Q.* 1:2ff.

30. *m. B. Q.* 3:8ff.   31. *m. B. Q.* 4:4bff., 5:3b–c.

32. The stoning of the guilty ox is referred to in *m. Sanh.* 1:3, concerned with criminal law.

33. Possibly assuming Hebrew *yashmidennu* instead of *yishmerennu*—in unvocalized script a mere substitution of *d* for *r*; see Isaac Heinemann, in *Die Werke Philos von Alexandrien*, ed. Cohn, vol. 2 (Leipzig, 1910), *Über die Einzelgesetze*, 228. If so, the translators would, of course, be convinced that *d* was the correct reading.

34. However, in the case of an ox killing a person, Philo seems to suggest that though the owner, if aware of its ferocious nature, always incurs some penalty, its severity will vary according to his degree of care.

35. By whoever was in charge of the beasts, whether or not their owner; cf. *m. B. Q.* 6:2.

36. *m. B. Q.* 1:4.

37. *m. B. Q.* 4:9; *b. B. Q.* 45b. Instead of Eliezer (ben Hyrcanus) occasionally we find the reading Eleazar (ben Shammua). The two figure as alternatives also in 1:4, as fathering the statement that wild animals, when tamed, count as harmless (except the snake). The rigid opinion in 4:9 and the liberal one in 1:4 cannot go back to the same authority. The former belongs to Eliezer, early and generally rather rigid; the latter to Eleazar, of the same period as Judah, Meir, and Eliezer ben Jacob. The last-mentioned, incidentally, should not be—though he sometimes is—mixed up with a namesake his senior by some fifty years.

38. *m. B. Q.* 2:1; 2:2; 4:2.

39. He seems to have invoked the fact that, in the case of an ox killing a person, the *Mishpatim* use "to gore" of a hitherto harmless ox as well as of a ferocious one. By this (he argues) they are conveying that just as the owner of a ferocious ox is free if he has taken proper measures against the activity causing the upset, so also must be the owner of a harmless ox.

40. *m. B. Q.* 5:6.

41. *m. B. Q.* 3:1. Following the Amoraic interpretation in *b. B. Q.* 27a, the usual rendering is "He who leaves a jug in the public domain, and another came and stumbled over it and broke it, he (the other) is free; but if damage was suffered through it by him, the owner of the jar (jug) is liable for his damage." The change of the jug into a jar is so jarring that I prefer to assume the Mishnah is thinking of one party with a jug, the other with a jar—as it is in 10:4 ("This one came with his jar of wine and this one with his jug of honey"). Hence: "He who leaves a jug in the public domain and another came and stumbled over it and broke it, he (the other) is free; but if damage was suffered through it by the owner of the jar (the other), he (the owner of the jug) is liable for his damage." It must be admitted, however, that in 3:5 a jar indisputably turns into a jug. The main thesis of the text is not affected by this problem.

42. *m. B. Q.* 6:1.

43. *m. B. Q.* 1:4; 2:1–2.

44. *m. B. Q.* 6:4.

45. *m. B. Q.* 1:1–2.

46. *b. B. Q.* 40a, 45b, 55b.

47. *b. B. Q.* 55b: "Four things, the Torah has reduced their guarding, and they are these—pit and fire, tooth and foot."

48. Cf. *b. B. Q.* 46a, with reference to Deut 22:8.

49. *m. B. Q.* 1:2; 2:2; except that in the latter case I must pay for benefit I may have derived.

50. *m. B. Q.* 6:6; *b. B. Q.* 21b.

51. *m. B. Q.* 3:4ff.

52. *m. B. Q.* 1:4.

53. *b. B. Q.* 40a.

54. *b. B. Q.* 56a; cf. *b. B. M.* 36b.

55. See Rashi ad *b. B. Q.* 40a, 45b, 55b; L. Goldschmidt, *Der babylonische Talmud*, vol. VI.1 (Berlin, 1905), 142, 165, 205–6; E. W. Kirzner, Baba Kamma (*The Babylonian Talmud*, ed. I. Epstein, Nezikin I) (London, 1935), 223–24, 259–60, 323; and—very telling—the treatment on p. 28 of *m. B. Q.* 1:2: it is rendered "Whenever I am under an obligation of controlling [anything in my possession], I am considered to have perpetrated any damage that resulted," and a footnote adds "from neglecting the obligation to control." Goldschmidt no doubt thinks along the same lines: *Wenn mir die Bewachung obliegt, so habe ich den Schaden verschuldet* (28).

56. Damage to property in *m. B. Q.* 1–6, theft in 7, injury in 8.

57. Indirect damage in 11:1, theft in 11:2, robbery and lost things in 11:3, injury and direct damage in 11:4. The remaining chapter 5 deals with murder and preservation of life.

58. In the Mishnah, robbery and lost things follow injury, in *m. B. Q.* 9–10 and *m. B. M.* 1–2.

59. Exod 22:18–19.

60. Precept 236.

61. 11.1.4.1; 7.1 (where, however, the half-compensation in the event of a harmless ox doing damage is excepted from this principle), 12.2; 14.2–3; 11.4.6.4.

62. An illustration from indirect damage—fire—in 11.1.14.2.

63. 11.4.6.1. Maybe this influence is already discernible in the second half of *m. B. Q.* 2:6.

64. 11.4.6.3; 6.5ff.

65. 11.4.6.9, going back to R. Isi ben Judah, *b. B. Q.* 32a.

66. See p. 127.

67. D. 13.6.5.7, Ulpian XXVII *ad edictum*. Decision by Aufidius Namusa, toward the end of the Republic. Ulpian, in the early third century, adds the reservation that the risk is mine only if it is understood he will have to work on a scaffold.

68. *b. B. M.* 97a.

1. Gen 3.

2. It is indeed possible that the Prometheus myth contains Oriental components, ultimately descending from the same source as the Fall. It is widely held that the combination of the theft of fire and the gift of Pandora is relatively late. But, if there is substance in our suspicion, this is questionable, since, in the story of the Fall, the capture of the fruit is followed by Adam calling his wife "Eve, because she was the mother of all living." The original meaning of "Pandora" may well be the same. What is very remarkable is that this naming (together with the clothing of Adam and Eve by God) comes in the course of Adam's punishment, i.e., between the curses pronounced against him and his expulsion from Eden. This curious position has caused commentators great difficulty (e.g., John Skinner, *Genesis*, ICC [Edinburgh, 1930], 85ff.). In view of the Greek parallel it is doubtful whether we ought to assume either misplacement or the intrusion of a fragment from a different account. More probably, some of the original motivation is missing: one could think of many reasons for that.

3. Rev 12:9.	4. Sir 25:24.
5. I Tim 2:12ff.	6. Rom 5:12.
7. Jub 3:23ff.	8. *Ant.* 1.1.4.

9. R. H. Charles, *Apocrypha and Pseudepigrapha of the Old Testament* (Oxford, 1913), 2, 147–48.

10. Ibid., 142–43.	11. Rev 12:9.
12. Deut 21:1–9.	13. Neh 6:10ff.
14. Matt 14:1ff.	15. Mark 6:14ff.
16. Exod 20:17; Deut 5:21.	17. Lev 19:17.
18. Matt 5:28.	19. Exod 2:15ff.
20. 1 Sam 18:11.	21. I Kgs 2:13ff.
22. Acts 23:15ff.; 25:1ff.	23. Gen 20:9.
24. Num 31:16.	

25. Num 14:35–36. Cf. Deut 1:28; Josh 14:8, where we are told that the spies "made the heart of the people faint." The verb is the same as in Deut 20:8, according to which law the officers, before a battle, must request anyone who is "afraid and softhearted" to depart "lest he make his brethren's heart faint like his heart."

26. Deut 13:6ff.

27. 2 Cor 11:13ff.

28. 2 Pet 2:1ff.

29. Rev 20:10.

30. Prov 6:26.

31. Isa 9:15.

32. Matt 15:14; cf. Luke 6:39.

33. Matt 16:6; Mark 9:42.

34. Ezek 3:16ff.; 33:1ff.

35. Deut 13:5.

36. Matt 4:1ff.; Mark 1:13; Luke 4:1ff.

37. Prov 7:25.

38. Ezek 13:5; 22:30.

39. Prov 7:18.

40. Rev 13:16.

41. E.g., *Opif.* 165ff.; *Leg. All.* 3.1ff.

42. *Opif.* 165.

43. *Leg. All.* 60.

44. Ibid., 107.

45. Num 15:39.

46. Jer 49:16.

47. Jer 3:12.

48. Matt 5:29–30; cf. 18:8–9; Mark 9:43ff.

49. Jer 37:9.

50. Exod 8:28.

51. Deut 25:12.

52. *Siphre* on Num 15:39.

53. E.g., Resh Laqish, about AD 250, *b. B. B.* 16a.

54. 1 Sam 31:3ff., with which 1 Chr 10:3ff. is in general agreement, and 2 Sam 1:6ff.

55. Daube, "Death as a Release in the Bible," *NT* 5 (1962): 85, 86 [*BLL*, 515, 516].

56. Incidentally, it is strange that not one of the modern advocates of euthanasia has thought of an inevitable consequence of such a reform. Even with all safeguards, legal and medical, what could not be prevented would be a patient who qualifies for the drug asking for it, not because he himself prefers death, but for the sake of his wife or friends looking after him. In fact, once euthanasia were established, it would be precisely the more considerate, high-minded who would feel called on to cease being a trouble. It might conceivably be argued that this is in order. A man who is a trouble of this nature ought to have the necessary public spirit to desire to be put out of the way. After all, in war many a decent man voluntarily sacrifices himself for the well-being of his group. Maybe. What I am here pointing out is only that none of those writers has seen this aspect and dealt with it—no matter with what result.

57. This leaves out of the account a state of affairs where the college could only be saved by A. In 1940, it would not have been right for Churchill to support Chamberlain.

58. 2 Sam 15:18ff.; 18:2.

59. 1 Kgs 2:5ff.

60. Gen 44:16–17.

61. Daube, *Studies in Biblical Law* (Cambridge, UK, 1947), 244–45 [*BLL*, 282–83].

62. Gen 27:6ff.; Matt 27:20ff.

63. Mark 15:11ff.

64. Matt 27:25.

65. E.g., Lev 20:9; Josh 2:19.

66. See my brother's book, Benjamin Daube, *Zu den Rechtsproblemen in Aischylos' Agamemnon* (Zurich, 1938), 188–89.

67. *Siphra* on Lev 24:14, p. 104b in Weiss' edition.

CHAPTER 7—ATTEMPT

1. Lev 20:27.

2. Deut 22:26–27.

3. Exod 22:1.

4. Exod 21:16, where "or if he be found in his hand" is interpolated. Cf. the theft of Joseph by his brothers, Gen 36:27ff.; 40:15.

5. Gen 19:11.

6. 1 Kgs 13:4ff.

7. Gen 11:1ff.

8. Deut 19:19.

NOTES

9. Gen 3:22.

10. Mark 14:47. *Civil Disobedience in Antiquity* (Edinburgh, 1972), 110–12 [*BLL*, 649–50].

11. Matt 26:51.   12. Luke 22:50.

13. John 18:10.   14. Gen 22.

15. Gen 22:12, 16.

16. 1 Macc 2:52; Jdt 8:25; Sir 44:20. The verb "to test" occurs in the opening line of the story, Gen 22:1.

17. 4 Macc 16:19 is no exception to the usual Jewish way of describing this affair.

18. *Pirke de R. Eliezer* 31.   19. Heb 11:17ff.; James 2:21.

20. Rom 8:32.   21. Acts 17:26–27.

22. Deut 13:7ff.   23. 2 Sam 21:2.

24. Deut 19:19.   25. *Ant.* 4.8.15.219.

26. CH 1ff., 11, 126.   27. Mark 14:59.

28. Dan 6 shows the influence of such notions.

29. 1 Kgs 21.   30. Acts 6:11ff.

31. Deut 22:13–21.   32. Matt 1:19.

33. Deut 22:23–24.

34. Adolf von Schlatter, *Der Evangelist Matthäus*, 2nd ed. (Stuttgart, 1948), 13ff.

35. Gerhard Kittel, *Theologisches Wörterbuch zum Neuen Testament*, 2 (Stuttgart, 1935), 187ff., esp. 191.

36. 1 Sam 24:17.

37. See Ernst Lohmeyer, *Das Evangelium des Matthäus*, 3rd ed. (Göttingen, 1962), 14.

38. CH 127, 161. Cf. Assyrian Laws, 18–19.

39. 1 Kgs 2:13ff.   40. *Hist.* 2.74.

41. Esth 2:21ff.

42. Something like this is meant by Esth 7:8. Max Haller, *Die Fünf Megilloth* (Tübingen, 1940), 130, emends *'al* into *'el*. Haman, he argues, must have "fallen before the divan," not "on the divan." But the text as it stands sounds far more plausible, especially in view of the king's reaction. The queen was lying on the divan and Haman threw himself on—not in front of—it.

43. Cf. also a case like 2 Sam 3:25.   44. Gen 42:9ff.

45. Josh 2.   46. 2 Sam 10:1ff.

47. 2 Kgs 20:12ff.; 2 Chr 32:31.   48. Gen 39:7ff.

49. Not counting *bilti sara* in Isa 14:6.

50. Deut 13:6; Isa 1:5; 31:6; Jer 28:16; 29:32.

51. Deut 13:6.   52. Isa 59:13.

53. Deut 19:21.   54. Esth 2:21; 6:3.

55. Esth 3:6.   56. Gen 43:30.

57. 1 Sam 14:4.   58. 1 Kgs 11:22.

59. 1 Sam 23:10.   60. 2 Sam 20:19.

61. Exod 2:15; 4:19.   62. Matt 2:20.

63. 1 Sam 19:2.   64. 1 Kgs 11:40.

65. Exod 4:24.   66. 1 Sam 19:10.

67. Esth 6:6.

68. Gen 27:41. To be sure, his feelings came to Rebekah's knowledge: Gen 27:42. No

doubt, while trying to keep them from Jacob and his parents, he did express them to his circle.

69. 1 Sam 18:11.   70. 1 Sam 18:17.

71. Esth 7:8.   72. Esth 9:24.

73. Deut 13:6. In 13:4 a good purpose: "the Lord testeth ye to know whether ye love the Lord."

74. Esth 7:10. The passive *mukhan* means "ready" in modern Hebrew at sport events, for firing squads, etc.

75. Ps 7:14.   76. Ps 57:7.

77. Esth 8:3.   78. Esth 8:5.

79. Esth 9:24–25.   80. 1 Sam 18:25.

81. Neh 6:2, 6.

82. Esth 8:3. The word recurs in v. 6, "For how can I endure to see the evil that shall come unto my people?"

83. Esth 7:7. It is conceivable that the definite article alludes to the extreme evil, death, but there is no certainty: see, e.g., 1 Sam 24:17.

84. Num 35:23. In 1 Sam 24:10 David asks Saul, "Wherefore hearest thou man's words, Behold, David seeketh thy evil?"

85. 1 Kgs 2:52.

86. See S. R. Driver, *Deuteronomy*, ICC (Edinburgh, 1895), 95.

87. E.g., Exod 9:12.   88. 2 Sam 24:1, *contra* 1 Chr 21:1.

89. Deut 13:3.   90. Job 2:9.

91. *Theologisches Wörterbuch*, ed. Kittel, 6:25.

92. E.g. 10, *seducta es*.

93. Judg 2:22; 3:1, 4.

94. Judg 2:20. This may be combined with the explanation just mentioned.

95. Judg 3:2. Why, one may ask, if everybody had been driven out?

96. Gen 15:16.   97. Exod 7:3–4.

98. Deut 8:2, 16.   99. Num 14:34.

100. Exod 16:4.   101. Deut 13:3.

102. 2 Chr 32:31. We follow Wilhelm Rudolph, *Chronikbücher* (Tübingen, 1955). The usual interpretation assumes an unmitigated antithesis: the king prospered in everything—but on one occasion things went wrong. (The occasion is touched on in 2 Chr 32:25–26; for more details, see 2 Kgs 20:12ff., but it is far from certain how much of the account in 2 Kings would be accepted by the Chronicler.) Rudolph rightly maintains that the second half is intended to support the first and to show that the seemingly unfavorable episode in reality does not detract from the praise. He would therefore paraphrase: the king prospered in everything—and as for that one occasion, there God wanted to test him and (this the reader is expected to supply, on the basis of 32:25–26) in the end he emerged victorious and forgiven. That Rudolph is right is clear, above all, from the particle that opens the second half: *wekhen*, "and so," suggesting support, not antithesis. Even if one disagrees with Rudolph, his must be the interpretation relied on wherever Hezekiah's messianic status was emphasized.

103. Matt 27:46; Mark 15:34; Ps 22:2.

104. Josh 7:10ff.

105. Exod 15:25. Details are quite uncertain. One might hold that Moses set up for the

people statute and ordinance and tested them. The translation here chosen pays much attention to Deut 33:8, to be quoted presently. Anyhow all that matters is that law-giving and testing are combined.

106. Deut 33:8. Again details are shaky. Most commentators refer the passage to Moses.

107. 1 Kgs 10:1; 2 Chr 9:1.   108. Eccl 7:2.

109. Dan 1:12, 14.

110. Exod 17:2, 7; Num 14:22; Deut 6:16; Ps 78:18, 41, 56; 95:9; 106:14.

111. Judg 6:39.   112. Exod 3–4.

113. Deut 4:34; 7:19; 29:2.   114. Driver, *Deuteronomy*, 75, 95.

115. Isa 7:12.   116. Exod 4:14.

117. Acts 1:24.   118. Job 4:2.

119. See Gustav Hölscher, *Das Buch Hiob* (Tübingen, 1952), 18.

120. Deut 4:34.   121. Deut 28:56.

122. 1 Sam 17:39.

123. If we read *wayyele'*, as favored by Gesenius, *Thesaurus Linguae Hebraeae et Chaldaeae* (1835), 1, 326, instead of *wayyo'el*.

CHAPTER 8 — COLLECTIVES

1. Gen 34:31.   2. Exod 17:8–16; Deut 25:17–19.

3. Gen 26:10.   4. Josh 7:1.

5. Judg 20:12.   6. Exod 1:13.

7. Judg 2:11.   8. Deut 23:3–4.

9. Matt 23:37; Luke 13:34.   10. Amos 2:6.

11. Matt 23:6; Mark 12:38, 39.   12. Josh 2.

13. Exod 32.   14. Deut 24:16.

15. Gen 19.   16. *Ep.* 2.1.45–46.

17. Gen 19:28.   18. Gen 19:4.

19. The remaining comments come from notes attached to this Gifford lecture.

20. Cf. or contrast Eli's sons, Samuel's sons. Sextus Tarquinius may be original. I wonder what reason for the transfer is assumed by those who say it was Superbus.

CHAPTER 9 — WOMEN

1. Gen 12:11ff.; 20:2ff. See Daube, "Concerning Methods of Bible-Criticism: Late Law in Early Narratives," *Archiv Orientální* 17 (1949): 91ff.; "Rechtsgedanken in den Erzählungen des Pentateuchs," *Von Ugarit nach Qumran, Festschrift für Eissfeldt* (Berlin, 1958), 38ff.; "Sin, Ignorance and Forgiveness in the Bible," *Claude Montefiore Lecture* (London, 1960), 7ff. [*BLL*, 79–89, 91–99, 375–89].

2. Gen 12:13; 20:13. Chap. 20 is full of subtle, legal allusions. We would not have put it beyond the author to have intended the double meaning "this is thy kindness" and "this is thy villainy": *ḥesedh* has the latter sense, apparently borrowed from Aramaic, in Lev 20:17, the prohibition of taking a sister to wife. True, it would presuppose that when chap. 20 was written, incest, or more particularly intercourse with the sister from the same mother (that is what Sarah was urged to represent herself as), had already attracted the Aramaic term.

3. *Gen Rab* on Gen 12:17.

4. Gen 20:9.

5. Gen 44:16; see Daube, *Studies in Biblical Law* (Cambridge, UK, 1947), 248ff. [*BLL*, 285ff.].

6. Lev 5:23ff.; Num 5:5ff.

7. Gen 20:3; Deut 22:22.

8. Deut 22:23ff. See Martin David, "Overspel Volgens Deuteronomium 22:22 v.v.," *Jaarbericht van het Vooraziatisch-Egyptisch Gezelschap, Ex Oriente Lux* 8 (1942): 650–54.

9. Cf. CH 129; Assyrian Code I 13ff.; Hittite Code II 83–84, taking account of the state of the law that must have preceded these provisions; and see for Greek law, Kurt Latte, *Paulys Real-Encyclopädie* 15, 2 (Stuttgart, 1932), 2446ff.

10. *b. B. Q.* 92a.

11. Par. 14.

12. See Latte, *Paulys Real-Encyclopädie*, 2447–48.

13. See chapters in this volume, "Error and Ignorance," p. 70; "Intellectual Authorship," p. 137.

14. Par. 16.

15. Gen 20:5.

16. Gen 26:7.

17. 2 Sam 11:2ff.

18. 1 Kgs 1:31.

19. 2 Sam 12:3.

20. See my brother's book, Benjamin *Zu den Rechtsproblemen in Aischylos' Agamemnon* (Zurich, 1938), 110ff.

21. Judg 19–20.

22. Judg 19:3.

23. 2 Sam 3:6ff.

24. 2 Sam 12:8; 16:21–22; 1 Kgs 2:13ff.

25. 2 Sam 21:8ff.

26. Gen 35:22.

27. Gen 49:4.

28. 2 Sam 16:21–22.

29. 2 Sam 20:3.

30. E.g., Deut 24:1ff.

31. 2 Sam 3:14ff.

32. Judg 20:25ff.

33. Gen 38:24.

34. Lev 24:14, 23; Num 15:36; 1 Kgs 21:10, 13; Deut 22:24.

35. Josh 10:22–23; 2 Kgs 11:15; 2 Chr 23:14.

36. Judg 6:30.

37. Josh 2:3; Gen 19:5; Judg 9:22.

38. Deut 21:19.

39. Deut 22:21.

40. The following sentence, "She was brought forth, and she sent to her father-in-law," is neutral as far as this question is concerned. On the basis of the traditional interpretation, Judah gave orders to lead her out to execution, but did not personally attend the ceremony. On the interpretation here conceivable, he asked for her production, but was not personally there when she was delivered up. We have made no use of Hos 9:13 in this discussion of the two meanings of "to bring forth." The passage is too obscure.

41. Hos 2:10; Ezek 16:39ff.

42. John 8:3ff.

43. Bernard Weiss, *Das Johannes-Evangelium*, 8th ed. (Göttingen, 1893), 317.

44. 1 Cor 5:1ff.

45. L. M. Epstein, *Sex Laws and Customs in Judaism* (New York, 1948), 195.

46. Ezek 23:48.

47. Joachim Jeremies, "Zur Geschichtlichkeit des Verhörs Jesu vor dem Hohen Rat," *ZNTW* 43 (1950–51): 145ff.

48. *b. Sanh.* 42bff.

49. See Daube, "Error and Accident in the Bible," *RIDA* 42 (1949): 200–201; "Texts and Interpretation in Roman and Jewish Law," *Jewish Journal of Sociology* 3 (1961): 3–28 [*BLL*, 366–67; *TL*, 173–204]; also chapter in this volume, "Error and Ignorance" (p. 62).

50. Büchler, "Die Strafe der Ehebrecher in der nachexilischen Zeit," *Monatsschrift für Geschichte und Wissenschaft des Judentums* 55 (1911): 196ff.

51. Prov 6:35.   52. Exod 21:30.

53. *Mek.* on Exod 21:30.   54. Num 35:21–22.

55. Epstein, *Sex Laws and Customs in Judaism*, 195–96.

56. *Ant.* 7.7.1.130ff.   57. *Ant.* 7.7.1.131.

58. 2 Sam 11:26ff.   59. *Ant.* 7.7.1.146.

60. Gen 20; 39:7ff.; Esth 7:7–8.   61. Neh 13:23ff.

62. Esth 1:22.   63. Ibid.

64. Esth 3:12.   65. Esth 8:9.

66. On its ending, an integral part of it, see Daube, "The Last Chapter of Esther," *JQR* 37 (1946): 139–47 [*BLL*, 797–801].

67. Ibid.   68. Esth 3:8.

69. *Ant.* 11.6.1.184ff.   70. Ruth 3:5.

71. Esth 2:20.   72. Esth 2:8; 3:10–11.

73. Ruth 3:18.   74. Ruth 1:12–13.

75. Ruth 1:4.   76. Ruth 4:15.

77. Ruth 2:11.   78. Ruth 2:23.

79. 2 Kgs 8:1ff.   80. Ruth 4:5.

81. Max Haller on Ruth 4:5 cuts them out: *Die fünf Megilloth: Ruth, Hoheslied, Klagelieder, Esther* (Tübingen, 1940). In Ruth 4:9 only Naomi is mentioned.

82. The root *shḥt*, "to mar," occurs also in the story of Judah and Tamar. Judah's second son Onan was ordered by his father to take the widow of his elder brother who had died childless, in order that the firstborn from this union might take the place of the deceased: levirate marriage. Onan did not like this. He did not want a new elder brother by whose existence, on Judah's death, his share would be considerably reduced. So when he came together with the widow, he practiced *coitus interruptus*, "he marred (his seed) to the ground" (the verb in the *Piel*). Naomi's nearest kinsman is fearful lest, by marrying an elderly woman, he should remain without children and "mar his inheritance" (the verb in the *Hiphil*).

83. *Leqayyem* (Ruth 4:7).

84. *De Off.* 3.14.58–59. For a biblical parallel, see Daube, *Studies in Biblical Law*, 196 [*BLL*, 246].

85. Deut 25:7ff. See *t. Yeb.* 2:6. For the setting of the Deuteronomic refusal, see Daube, "*Consortium* in Roman and Hebrew Law," *JR* 62 (1950): 71–91 [*BLL*, 919–31].

86. Ruth 3:15, 17; cf. Gen 24:22, 47, 53—in this last verse both bride-present and *mohar*, purchase price, are mentioned, as they are in Gen 34:12.

87. Jacques Pirenne, *La Femme dans la Civilisation Hebraique, Recueils de la Société Jean Bodin*, vol. 2, *La Femme* (Paris, 1959).

88. See Pirenne, *La Femme*, 112; see also Exod 6:20; Lev 18:12–13; 20:19.

89. 2 Sam 13:13.   90. See Pirenne, *La Femme*, 115.

91. Ibid.   92. Num 5:11ff.

93. See Pirenne, *La Femme*, 123.   94. Ruth 4:9.

95. See Pirenne, *La Femme*, 121.

CHAPTER 10 — AFTER THE DEED

1. Gen 31:34–35; Exod 2:12 ff.; Josh 7:18 ff.; 2 Sam 11:5 ff.

2. Deut 27:20 ff.

3. Gen 4:9; 18:15; 2 Kgs 5:25.

4. Gen 39:14 ff.

5. Gen 37:29 ff.

6. Exod 1:19.

7. Heb 11:23.

8. 1 Kgs 18:4.

9. For example, Mark 1:44.

10. Dan 3:16.

11. Gen 3:8 ff.

12. Exod 2:14.

13. 2 Sam 13:37.

14. 1 Kgs 19:3.

15. John 7:1, 10; 10:39 ff.

16. Mark 14:50.

17. Num 35:9 ff.; Deut 19:1 ff.; Josh 20:1 ff.

18. Gen 4:13–14.

19. Deut 1:45; Judg 4:3.

20. 2 Sam 12:16 ff.; 24:10 ff.

21. 2 Sam 19:18 ff. The subsequent development will be mentioned presently.

22. Esth 7:7.

23. Lev 26:14 ff.; 2 Kgs 17:13 ff.; Ezek 3:6–7.

24. Gen 27:13.

25. Exod 5 ff.

26. Lev 10:3. He does speak out in Lev 10:19.

27. Num 5:16 ff.

28. Num 14:40 ff.

29. Deut 21:18 ff.; 25:5 ff. [Editor's note: On Jesus coming under the rule, see Daube, *Appeasement or Resistance* (Berkeley, 1987), 23–26 (*NTJ*, 54–56).]

30. Judg 20:13.

31. 2 Sam 3:8.

32. 2 Chr 25:16.

33. Matt 18:15 ff.

34. Num 16:12. Contrast, for example, the readiness of the prophets of Baal to accept Elijah's test in 1 Kgs 18:19 ff.

35. Judg 6:30–31.

36. Esth 2:3 ff.

37. Mark 11:28 ff.; Luke 6:8 ff.; Acts 4:19–20; 5:29; 7:51.

38. *b. Sanh.* 27a [*BLL*, 653].

39. Gen 3:12.

40. Gen 20.

41. Gen 21:25–26. It is often the servants who dig and quarrel about wells: Gen 26:15, 19 ff., 32. (In v. 18 Isaac himself reopens his father's wells.) From v. 32 it is clear that the master might be informed only after the event.

42. Gen 45:3, 15; cf. 44:16, primarily referring to the theft of the cup but in the second place to their real, graver misdeed, which had come to their mind in the similar situation in 42:21–22.

43. 2 Sam 19:23; 1 Kgs 2:8–9, 36 ff.

44. Gen 50:15 ff.

45. Exod 32:12–13.

46. Exod 32:22.

47. 1 Sam 15:24.

48. 1 Sam 13:11–12.

49. 1 Sam 19:17.

50. 1 Sam 22:15.

51. Acts 24 ff.

52. Prov 3:24–25.

53. Ps 143:2 ff.

54. Ps 103:9.

55. Gen 42:2.

56. Judg 1:7.

57. Gen 40.

58. Num 5:11 ff.

59. Num 12:10; 1 Kgs 13:4; 2 Kgs 5:27; Acts 5:1 ff.

60. 2 Sam 13.

61. A much mitigated degree is natural. Love wants unending embrace. As morning approaches and Romeo thinks of leaving Juliet because if he is discovered there he will be slain, she tries to convince him—and herself—that the bird he hears is not the lark, herald of the light, but the nightingale. A god has no problem. When Zeus visited Alcmene he bade the sun not rise the next day. The insatiability of human desire comes out in the gradual extension of his meeting by successive narrators: from two nights to three, to five, to seven—with, of course, all the days between them, the sun keeping away. The longest term is found in the church fathers: nine nights. Innocence allows free rein to fantasy.

62. Judg 2:1ff.; 3:7ff.; cf. 1 Kgs 8:38ff.   63. 2 Sam 12:1ff.

64. 2 Sam 24:3ff.   65. 1 Chr 21:7ff.

66. Wilhelm Rudolph, *Chronikbücher*, HAT 21 (Tübingen, 1955), 142–43.

67. Jer 18:7ff.; Ezek 18:21ff.   68. Jonah 3:10.

69. Mark 1:4.

70. 1 Sam 2:3. The text is uncertain, and so is the exact meaning of the verb. In support, however, we note that a noun connected with the verb figures in Ezek 45:11, where there is talk of scales.

71. We are not implying that its specific occurrence in 1 Sam 2:3 must precede Ezekiel.

72. *b. Yeb.* 48b; 62a.

73. *y. R. Sh.* 59c.

74. *m. Ab.* 2:10; *b. Kidd.* 40b; *Eccl. Rab.* on 1:15.

75. *b. A. Zar* 17a.   76. John 3:3; 2 Cor 5:17; cf. Gal 6:15.

77. Matt 21:28ff. and Matt 20:1ff.

78. Solomon Schechter, *Some Aspects of Rabbinic Theology* (New York, 1961), 15–16, 306.

79. Deut 27:25.

80. 2 Sam 12:5ff.

81. 1 Kgs 20:38ff. We might also bring the anecdote in 2 Sam 14:2–20 under the heading of self-judgment if the notion is taken in a liberal sense, and even a case like Esth 6:6ff.

82. 1 Kgs 20:40–42.

83. To a modern reader, the soldier's offense must look not more but far less serious than the king's: the soldier lost the prisoner unintentionally, indeed, very much against his will and interests, whereas the king flouted his instructions in pardoning Benhadad. At first sight, then, the prophet deprives himself of effectiveness by the weak parallel. As if he had said to Hitler, after the invasion of Poland: "Thy servant at night-time lost his way and stepped into his neighbor's garden." The explanation is that, under the law of the time, the strict undertaking, "If by any means he be missing, then shall thy life be for his life," renders the distinction between willfulness, negligence, accident, and so on immaterial: either you produce the man or your life is forfeited.

84. More precisely, it is not his intention insofar as he acts this role of soldier. In reality, the prophet knows exactly what he is doing. Pirandello's characters could not be more onion-like, one layer after another.

85. 1 Kgs 2:32; Lev 20:11ff.   86. Jonah 1:11ff.

87. Josh 7; 2 Sam 21:1ff.   88. *Lev. Rab.* on 16:3.

89. Exod 15:9.

90. Daube published his work on Judas in *CLR* 82 (1994): 95–108; *RJ* 13 (1994): 307–30; and *ILR* 29 (1995): 9–31 [*NTJ*, 783–99].

91. Matt 27:3ff.

92. Acts 1:16ff.

93. See Karl Bihlmeyer, *Die apostolischen Väter* (Tübingen, 1924), fragment III.

94. VIII below on Origen.

95. Ernst Lohmeyer, *Das Evangelium des Matthäus*, 3rd ed. (Göttingen, 1962), 376.

96. Jer 8:5–6, *'ēn 'iš niḥam-mē'anu lašub*. Septuagint: *epistrephō—metanoéō*, the latter equivalent to *metamelomai*. In an entirely nondoctrinal context, a somewhat analogous relation comes through. God led the freed slaves through the desert rather than the nearer Philistine territory "lest they repent when they see war and return to Egypt" (Exod 13:17, *niḥam, metamelomai—šub, apostrephō* equivalent to *epistrephō*).

97. Acts 3:19, *metanoēsate kai epistrepsate*.

98. Jer 31:18, *'aḥarē šubi niḥamti*. The Septuagint 38:19 simplifies: "after my captivity I repented," *ústeron aikhmalōsias mou metenoēsa*.

99. Exod 32:12, *šub—wehinnaḥēm*. The Septuagint simplifies: "cease, *pausai*, from the wrath of your spirit and become kindly, *'ileōs genou*, about the evil of the people."

100. Ps 90 (Septuagint 89):13, *šubah—weḥinnahēm, epistrepson... paraklēthēti. Parakaléō* in this sense, e.g. Judg 21:6, 15; 2 Sam 24:16.

101. Jer 4:28, *welō' niḥamti* (*metanoēsō* in Septuagint) *welō' 'ašub mimennaḥ* (*apostrepsō 'ap' autēs*).

102. Joel 2:14, *šub—niḥam*, Septuagint *epistrephō—metanoéō*.

103. Jonah 3:9, *yašub weniḥam*, Septuagint *metanoēsei kai apostrepsei*.

104. Deut 30:2, *šub*, Septuagint *epistrephō*.

105. Isa 6:10, *šub, epistrephō*. Quoted in Matt 13:15.

106. Jdt 5:19, *epistrephō*.

107. Luke 22:32, *epistrephō*.

108. 1 Sam 15:29, *niḥam*. The Septuagint reverently substitutes "to return" for "to lie" in the first half: *ouk apostrepsei oude metanoēsei óti oukh ōs anthrōpos esti tou metanoēsai autos*.

109. Ps 110:4. Septuagint 109:4, *ou metamelēthēsetai*.

110. Job 42:6, *niḥam*. Mitigated in the Septuagint: *égēmai de emauton gēn kai spodon*, "I consider myself dust and ashes."

111. C. H. Dodd, who took to my opinion, translated "was seized with remorse," hinting at extraordinary quality: *The New English Bible, New Testament* (Oxford, 1961), 52.

112. Matt 26:14ff., 45ff.

113. E.g. Lev 5:20ff.; Num 5:5ff.; *Exod. Rab.* 14:31, referring to texts like Ps 24:4–5. ("He who hath clean hands shall receive the blessing"); Job 16:17 ("No ill-gotten gain in my hand and indeed my prayer is pure"); *b. Tann.* 16a; *m. Gitt.* 5:5; *t. B. K.* 10:14; *t. B.M.* 8:26.

114. *Hamlet*, III.iii.53–55.

115. Even formalistic compliance is of considerable diversity; see my reference to "The Charge of the Light Brigade" in "Three Footnotes on *Civil Disobedience in Antiquity*," *Humanities in Society* 2 (1971): 76 [*BLL* 694].

116. Luke 15:18.

117. Exemplified by Saul, 1 Sam 15:24, 30; 26:21; by David, 2 Sam 12:13; 24:10, 17; 1 Chr 21:8, 17; by Hezekiah, 1 Kgs 18:14; by Mic 7:9; Pss 41:5; 51:6; Job 7:20. Abimelech, in Gen 20:9, stresses his manifest integrity of intent vis-à-vis Abraham by the rhetorical question, "What have I sinned against you?" See also below, n. 121, on Achan.

118. On 1 Sam 7:6.

119. See Lohmeyer, *Das Evangelium des Matthäus*, 375.

120. 1 Sam 25:24, 28.

121. Confession's history is immensely complicated from Gen 3 on. Joshua is told by God (7:10ff.) that a military venture miscarried because one of his men appropriated some of the accursed treasures of destroyed Jericho. A magical procedure identifies Achan as the criminal, dooming him and all his family and possessions to extermination. However, he is still needed to reveal exactly where the booty is hidden and at Joshua's behest—addressing him as "my son"—he gives glory to the Lord and cooperates without reserve. By talmudic times, he thereby gains atonement (*m. Sanh.* 6:2): as he and all his are being put to death, Joshua exclaims, "Why has thou troubled us? the Lord shall trouble you this day"—for the Rabbis "this day, but not in the next world."

122. I shall be reproved, rightly, for not at least citing the Hebrew, Aramaic, and Greek terms for the offense. But that would be about two dozen, with major problems never so far tackled. So I let sleeping dogs lie rather than get awake ones to embark on too complicated a truth.

123. Cf. John 11:50; 18:14. I last discussed this subject in *Appeasement or Resistance*, 75ff. [*NTJ*, 99].

124. Matt 27:4, 40.   125. Matt 26:75.

126. Acts 1:15ff. The demotion sets in already when, in Luke 22:47–48, his kiss is rejected. Or indeed in 22:22 when the synoptic record is shortened: see below, n. 153.

127. Acts 1:20; Pss 69:26; 109:8.

128. Judg 16:27ff.

129. 2 Sam 17:22. It is widely held that the Judas episode is influenced by this one; see e.g. Lohmeyer, *Das Evangelium des Matthäus*, 375. Does not conflict with what I say but strikes me as rather improbable.

130. *Embassy to Gaius*, 234ff.

131. *Bell.* 7.8.6.320ff.

132. See my "The Linguistics of Suicide," in *Philosophy and Public Affairs* 1 (1972): 410; repr. in *Suicide and Life-Threatening Behavior* 7 (1977): 155 [*EOW*, 84].

133. Heb 6:1ff.; 10:20ff. In my lifetime, on two or three occasions, when the ruling coalition in Germany was opposed by a radical party, you might join and leave and be welcomed on rejoining the latter. Growth in number, however, diversity, and self-confidence were apt to turn a leaving into irremediable desertion.

134. Why did Luke not retain the suicide and explain that, in this case, because of the preceding desertion, it did not work in Judas' favor? Would have been too complicated, too academic, at that stage. Up to a point, it became the dominant understanding, say, from AD 250; see just a little further on.

135. Ten applications from the Gospels are cited in my *The New Testament and Rabbinic Judaism* (1956; repr. 1973), 170ff. [*NTJ*, 389ff.], starting with Matt 9:1ff.; Mark 2:1ff.; Luke 5:17ff. where (1) Jesus declares a paralytic's sins forgiven, (2) the scribes declare it a blasphemy, and (3) he makes the paralytic walk and carry his bed.

136. Luke 2:41ff. "The verb is '*upotassein*, which is technical in the rules of behavior, the codes of community discipline, fashioned as the primitive Jewish-Christian sect began to crystallize": my *Civil Disobedience in Antiquity* (Edinburgh, 1972), 48 [*BLL*, 602].

137. J. P. Migne, *Patrologia Graeca*, 13 (Paris, 1857), 1766ff.

138. Shows how long it takes to shake off all the fallout of a long-entertained major misconception.

139. Gen 37:26ff., 31ff.; 44:18ff.

140. Matt 26:15.

141. Gen 44:14ff.

142. Gen 44:33–34.

143. Matt 27:3.

144. *Gen Rab.* 65 on Gen 27:27; *Midrash Psalms* 11:7; 1 Macc 7:9ff.; 9:54ff.; Josephus, *Ant.* 12.385–86, 391ff., 413; 20.235.

145. See on him I. Broydé, *Jewish Encyclopedia* (New York, 1907), 7:242, and on Alcimus A. Büchler, 1:332–33. Jose has a place among the rare early stars commemorated in the Mishnah's *The Fathers* (1:4). Apparently he is not meant to be forgotten: this tract still figures in the traditional Sabbath afternoon service between Passover and New Year.

146. I wish I had thought of these two *a fortioris* when I wrote on rabbinic argumentation.

147. Comes out in many ways: e.g., Yakim is the leader's nephew, Judas a disciple, Yakim "sells" him in quotes, Judas for cash.

148. I advisedly keep quiet about his name in the text. The few readers who consult footnotes are hopefully experienced enough not to get too confused by its, too, being Judas. N.B.: Neither 1 Maccabees nor Josephus records the drama of Jose and Yakim.

149. Matt 27:1ff.

150. Acts 1:18–19.

151. The deaths of Agrippa I, Herod the Great, and Antiochus Epiphanes, e.g., by Johannes Munck, *The Acts of the Apostles* (Garden City, NJ, 1967), 10, 114–15.

152. While dubious, then, about the *Verharmlosung* [downplaying], the treatment as amply paralleled, of Judas' death in Acts by commentators like Munck, I am no happier with its dismissal as silly, say, G. Bardy speaking of an *écho de fables assez puériles* [echo of rather childish fables] in *Dictionnaire de Théologie Catholique*, 11:2 (1932), 1946.

153. Matt 26:24; Mark 14:21. Luke 22:2 omits the second half, "it had been ...," relegating the main treatment of an evil figure to Acts 1:15ff.; see above n. 126.

154. Only underlined by its pronounced exclusion at certain junctures, like 1 Sam 15:29: "The Strength of Israel will not lie nor repent, for he is not a man that he should repent." Another proviso ought to be recorded here: superior, guiding factors are even behind the contráry—Cain's reinstatement, for instance, to be cited presently. I might inquire into all this if I were assured of another fifteen years; see n. 158. I am aware that the OED, 2nd ed. (1989), 3:841, ranks this use of "contráry" as colloquial and dialectical.

155. Gen 4:10ff.

156. Exod 32:9ff.

157. 2 Kgs 20:1ff.; Isa 38:1ff.

158. See, e.g., August Dillman, *Die Genesis*, 4th ed. (Leipzig, 1886), 95.

159. Jonah 1:3, 10.

160. 1 Chr 19:18.

161. Gen 41:46. His father Jacob, too, honorably received by the ruler, departed in this fashion: Gen 47:10.

162. Esth 8:15—possibly echoing the Joseph elevation.

163. Gen 4:13.

164. Matt 16:23; Mark 8:33.

165. Matt 17:1ff.; Mark 9:2ff.

166. Luke 23:34; cf. above at n. 133. See my *Sin, Ignorance, and Forgiveness in the Bible*, Claude

Montefiore Lecture, *Liberal Jewish Synagogue* (London, 1960) [*BLL*, 375ff.]; "For they know not what they do," *Studia Patristica* 4 (1961): 58ff. [*NTJ*, 847ff.]; *Ancient Jewish Law* (Leiden, 1981), 49ff. [*BLL*, 391ff.]; and "Jonah: A Reminiscence," *JJS* 35 (1984): 36ff. [*BLL*, 871ff.].

167. I am not saying that Matthew does have the full argument in mind.

168. See n. 133.

169. Acts 5:1ff. When Munck, *Acts of the Apostles*, 40, calls the case of Achan in Josh 7:1ff. (above n. 121) "a just parallel," he misses a great gulf between the two.

170. Though overextended hesitation could be a problem. Paul may have felt guilty of it: see my "Onesimos," in *Christians among Jews and Gentiles: Essays in Honor of Krister Stendahl*, ed. G. W. E. Nickelsburg with G. W. MacRae (Philadelphia, 1986), 42–43 [*NTJ*, 555].

171. See on him above, IX.

172. Vol. 4, pt. 2 (1924), 1130–31.

173. Vol. 13 (1973), 831.

174. Even he reaching back further than a superficial look might indicate: he lived well over one hundred years.

175. 1 QS 4.7–8, see G. Vermes with the collaboration of P. Vermes, *The Dead Sea Scrolls—Qumran in Perspective* (1971), 137.

176. I am indebted to the Community Rule in another context. In 1946, E. G. Selwyn, publishing a commentary on the First Epistle of St. Peter, included an appended note by me, "Participle and Imperative," 467ff. I argued that "a strange use of the participle in Romans, Ephesians, Colossians, Hebrews and 1 Peter must be the participle of Hebrew rules, of Mishnah, Tosephta and so on." There was strong support but some opposition as well, based on the post–New Testament date of the final Mishnah and Tosephta. A weak argument seeing that not a few rules in question are truly archaic and, indeed, that this application of the participle becomes much rarer as Tannaism comes to an end around 200. Well, the Community Rule does testify to the pre–New Testament origin of the phenomenon: "All that enter are saying, Amen.... The priests are recounting the just exploits of God ... and all that enter are confessing after them," 1.18ff. See my *Ancient Jewish Law*, 79ff. [*NTJ*, 192ff.].

177. Vol. 1 (1926), 990–91, 1006, 1031.   178. Matt 26:25, *su eipas*.

179. Matt 26:64, *su eipas*.   180. Luke 22:70, *úmeis legete*.

181. Matt 27:11; Mark 15:2; Luke 23:3; John 18:37, *su legeis*.

182. *t. B. K.* Kelim 1:6.

183. Strack-Billerbeck, 990, take it as a rhetorical question: "*Du schämst dich wohl zu sagen, daß (selbst) der Hund des Hohepriesters beliebter ist als du?*" "You are ashamed, are you not, to admit...?" Quite possible. Makes no difference.

184. *Verzeichnis der Schriftgelehrten* (Munich, 1961). The Simons are on 139–40.

185. *Mēti* comes near "surely not," for example, in Mark 4:21: "Surely, a candle is not brought to be put under a bushel or under a bed? Is it not [brought] that it may be set on a candlestick?"

186. J. M. Creed in his *The Gospel according to St. Luke* (London, 1930), 279, anticipates the essence of my interpretation. While *su eipas*, *su legeis*, and *úmeis legete* were "understood to imply assent ... the personal pronoun, *su*, *úmeis*, must be significant: the statement is yours, i.e. a certain protest against the question is implied." He cites Euripides, *Hipp.* 352, where Phaedra, Theseus' second wife, is about to reveal to her nurse her love for Hippolytus, Theseus' son from an Amazon. She cannot bring herself to openly name him, so says "whoever haply he is,

the Amazon's." The nurse: "You mean Hippolytus?" Phaedra: "From yourself you hear this, not from me." A certain protest against her own confession.

187. Mark 14:57ff.   188. Mark 14:61.

189. 2:51.

190. *b. A Zar.* 4a. Not the only place where the expression is met but pretty representative.

191. Matt 18:28; 1:799.

192. Luke 7:41; 2:163.

193. There are others; *hinnēq* seems favored in nineteenth-century translations.

194. Luke 23:9–10.   195. John 19:19ff.

196. John 18:38.

CHAPTER 11—SUPPLEMENT TO WOMEN: THE LANGUAGE OF SEDUCTION IN THE OLD TESTAMENT

1. Hos 2:16 (14). On the exact nuance of *pitta*, here translated "to infatuate," see below.

2. 1 Kgs 14:23–24.   3. Isa 1:23.

4. Num 25:1–2.   5. 1 Kgs 11:1ff.

6. 1 Kgs 16:31.   7. 2 Kgs 8:17; 2 Chr 21:6.

8. Exod 34:16; cf. Deut 7:4.   9. Jer 3:8.

10. Ps 106:35ff.   11. Exod 34:16.

12. Hos 1:2.

13. T. C. Foote, "The Old Testament Expression *zanah aḥrê*," *Journal of the American Oriental Society* 22 (1901): 64ff.

14. Ezek 16:26. German translations have *mit dem grossen Glied*.

15. Jer 3:3.   16. Deut 31:16; Judg 2:17.

17. Exod 34:16, repeatedly quoted above.   18. Exod 20:14; Deut 5:18.

19. Lev 20:10.   20. Jer 29:23.

21. We must be constantly prepared for unexpected variation. In 1 Sam 26:19, the phrase "other gods" occurs with no thought of idolatry. David complains to Saul about his enemies trying to drive him from the country or community and telling him "Go, serve other gods." No doubt the "other gods" are conceived of as inferior to the Lord, but all the same David's enemies are not exhorting him to a sin: the meaning does not go beyond exile, compulsion to join an alien group. The verb *zana*, "to whore after," could not, without major alteration of sense, replace "to serve."

22. Gen 35:2, 4; Josh 24:23; Judg 10:16; 1 Sam 7:3; 2 Chr 33:15.

23. Cf. Isa 45:1, 49:22–23; 60:6ff.; Hag 2:7ff.; G. B. Gray, *The Book of Isaiah*, 1 (Edinburgh, 1912), 396.

24. Correct Bernhard Duhm, *Das Buch Jesaia* (Göttingen, 1922), 171.

25. Gray, *Book of Isaiah.*

26. Rev 18:3.

27. Exod 34:16; 2 Chr 21:11, 13. Lev 19:29—"Profane not thy daughter to make her a harlot"—certainly contemplates actual prostitution; but from the context it is plainly prostitution connected with heathen rites. So condemnation of idolatry plays a part even here. Wilhelm Gesenius' *Hebräisches und aramäisches Handwörterbuch über das Alte Testamen* (Berlin, 1949), 202, goes too far in entirely separating this law from Exod 34:16; 2 Chr 21:11, 13. On the other hand, Ludwig Köhler, *Lexicon in Veteris Testamenti libros* (Leiden, 1958), 261, is slightly

misleading in giving the simple meaning "to commit fornication" for all the texts. In Exod 34:16; 2 Chr 21:11, 13, while idolatry is thought of as associated with sexual misconduct, it is nonetheless the idea of idolatry that is in the foreground. That is to say, there is here a metaphorical element in the use of *zana*.

28. Num 15:39.

29. G. B. Gray, *Numbers*, ICC (Edinburgh, 1903), 185, and others object to the clause "after which ye go whoring," on two grounds. (1) It is superfluous—a very subjective judgment: why should the people not be reminded of their propensity to fickleness? (2) Elsewhere the object of "to whore after" is regularly a false cult, not, as here, an organ tempting a man to go wrong—but this is the same attitude as Foote's, an unwarranted restriction of the potentialities of a phrase: Gray himself notices that the whole passage, "and ye shall not explore..." may well be concerned about idolatrous uses which the fringe in question had once served; surely, "to whore after" heart and eyes which are keen on those uses is not too remote from "to whore after" the cult itself. The point is not very material, since at least the final redactor must have approved of the clause.

30. Ezek 6:9.   31. Job 31:7–8.

32. In Eccl 11:9 the young man is told: "Walk in the ways of thine heart and in the sight of thine eyes"—no doubt here, too, it is largely the pleasures of love that are contemplated. Whether the approval is genuine or ironic depends on whether or not we reject as spurious the continuation: "but know that for all these things God will bring thee into judgment." The insertion of "and see," "and take delight," before "in the sight of thine eyes," proposed by Karl Budde and accepted by Kurt Galling (*Prediger Salomo*, HAT 18 [Tübingen, 1940], 88), is quite unnecessary. If one can "whore after one's eyes," one can "walk in the sight of one's eyes." The style of Ecclesiastes is free, imaginative, poetical.

33. Gen 3:6.

34. Ezek 20:8, 24; 23:16.

35. See Gesenius, *Handwörterbuch*, 874. Köhler, *Lexicon*, 1023, seems to overlook the passage altogether.

36. Deut 12:30.   37. Eccl 1:13.
38. 2 Sam 11:3.   39. Deut 4:19; Job 31:26–27.
40. Job 31:1—the same chapter as that quoted in the preceding footnote.
41. Deut 18:9.   42. Deut 18:13.

43. Of course, "to learn" need not imply the receipt of instruction in the literal sense; one may, for example, learn from experience. On the other hand, no doubt in many cases Jews were actually taught by heathens, or vice versa, especially where it was a question of initiation into specific customs or practices, say, how to exorcise witchcraft. Exactly what "to learn" signifies in a given passage must be decided from the context—if possible. In Jer 12:16 actual instruction seems to be contemplated.

44. Deut 13:13.   45. Deut 13:21.
46. Deut 13:6.   47. Prov 1:11.
48. Prov 1:14.   49. Gen 19:34.
50. Prov 7:18.

51. The finest love duet ever written, in Don Giovanni, begins by one strophe for the man and one for the lady; then comes half a strophe for him and half a one for her; then a line for him and a line for her; then they flow together.

52. Gen 19:32.   53. Gen 37:32.

54. Exod 32:1.

55. Judg 16:10.

56. 1 Sam 8:5.

57. Prov 7:18.

58. Daube, *Studies in Biblical Law* (Cambridge, 1947), 193–98 [*BLL*, 243–48].

59. Gen 27:8.

60. Prov 1:8.

61. Prov 5:7; 8:32.

62. Exod 18:19.

63. In Gerhard Lisowsky's *Konkordanz zum Hebräischen Alten Testament* (Stuttgart, 1958), the occurrences of *'atta* are not listed. The word is reckoned among those "which lack significant content," p. XIII.

64. 1 Kgs 21:5ff.

65. Exod 32:1.

66. 1 Kgs 14:28.

67. Deut 13:6.

68. Gen 39:11.

69. Prov 7:9.

70. Prov 8:1ff.

71. 1 Kgs 14:16; 15:26, 30, 34; 16:2, 13, 19, 26; 21:22 (with this verse the emphasis shifts from the criminal appropriation of Naboth' s vineyard to the worship of idols, a shift completed in v. 26), 22:53; 2 Kgs 3:3; 10:29, 31; 13:2, 6, 11; 14:24; 15:9, 18, 24, 28; 17:21; 21:11, 16 (the last two references a bit indirect, but clear enough if we compare, for example, 1 Kgs 21:22–26); 23:15; Jer 32:35 (a bit indirect, but cf. 2 Kgs 21:2ff., with the phrase in question in 21:11 and 21:16; Jeremiah has Manasseh in mind also in 7:30–31).

72. Sir 47:23.

73. Testament of Dan 5:6, connecting Dan with the antichrist and surely alluding to the objectionable sanctuary at Dan, 1 Kgs 12:29; see R. H. Charles, *The Apocrypha and Pseudepigrapha of the Old Testament* (Oxford, 1913), 334. The Testament of Dan is preserved in Greek, but we need not hesitate to see *heheti'* behind *poiein autous exhamartanein*.

74. We include 2 Kgs 23:15, where Josiah, king of Judah, breaks down the altar Jeroboam had erected at Bethel. Sirach and Testament of Dan may be added to the twenty-two.

75. 2 Kgs 21:11, 16; Jer 32:35.76. See above all 2 Kgs 21:10.

77. Exod 23:33, generally ascribed to the Redactor.

78. Neh 13:26.

79. 1 Kgs 12:30; 2 Kgs 17:21.

80. 2 Chr 34:6–7; 2 Kgs 23:15.

81. 2 Kgs 21:11, 16.

82. 2 Chr 33:10ff.; 2 Kgs 21:10ff.

83. See Gesenius, *Handwörterbuch*, 223.

84. Köhler, *Lexicon*, 289, reverts to the signification "to cause to sin," "to mislead to sin," a retrograde step, we think.

85. Lev 18:25.

86. Isa 29:21. Again Köhler, *Lexicon*, 289, prefers "to mislead to sin." In this case he may be right: there is a good deal of obscurity.

87. See the grammars on the Hiphil and Piel. Examples near *heheti'* are *hirshi'a*, "to find, condemn as, unrighteous" (this Hiphil in fact never means "to cause to be unrighteous"), *hikhzibh*, "to prove a man false"; and also *hisdiq*, "to find just."

88. Eccl 5:5.

89. Köhler, *Lexicon*, 289, again assumes the meaning "to cause to sin, to mislead to sin." But this is palpably wrong, it makes no sense. Köhler in this article is too much guided by the desire for a uniform interpretation. Live language is oscillating, variable.

90. 2 Sam 15:14. Cf. the Qal in Deut 20:19 and the Niphal in Job 6:13, "Aid is thrust away from me." Sirach's use of the Hiphil in Sir 8:9, "Thrust not away from upon thee the good fortune" derives from the uses in 2 Sam 15:14 and, above all, in Job 6:13.

91. E.g., Deut 30:1; Jer 8:3; 2 Chr 13:9. It is difficult to see why Köhler, *Lexicon*, 597, accords the last-quoted occurrence a heading of its own.

92. Jer 23:2 (on which passage see also below); 50:17.

93. Pss 5:11; 62:5.   94. Deut 13:6.

95. Deut 13:11. Admittedly there is some moving away from the original picture; but Köhler, *Lexicon*, 597, goes too far when he gives these two verses under a different heading from 13:6.

96. 2 Kgs 17:21. Only the Qeri has *hiddiaḥ*. The Kethibh has *hiddi'*, the meaning of which may well, however, be identical.

97. 2 Chr 21:11.   98. Prov 7:21.

99. Jer 23:2.

100. Wilhelm Rudolph, *Jeremia* (Tübingen, 1958), 133–34: *auseinanderlaufen lassen*.

101. Jer 23:3, 8.

102. Ezek 34:4, 16.

103. Rudolph regards Jer 23:3, 8, as interpolated, but this may be too violent a solution.

104. So is the Niphal noun *Niddaḥ*, "outcast," "exile."

105. Or *ta'a*, not found in the Qal; but the Hiphil is used of false prophets in Ezek 13:10.

106. Gen 21:14; 37:15; Exod 23:4.   107. Gen 20:13.

108. Isa 3:12; 9:15.   109. Jer 50:6.

110. 2 Kgs 21:9; 2 Chr 33:9.   111. Hos 4:11.

112. Isa 19:13–14.   113. Isa 30:28.

114. Isa 37:7; 2 Kgs 19:7; cf. Isa 37:29; 2 Kgs 19:28, with the picture of a bridle, though the word—*methegh*—is different from that in Isa 30:28—*resen*. As is well known, in the end, though there is mention of a rumor of an attack on Assyria by Ethiopia (Isa 37:9; 2 Kgs 19:9), the Assyrians withdrew because of a pestilence (Isa 37:36; 2 Kgs 19:35).

115. Isa 63:17.   116. Same word.

117. Job 12:24–25.

118. Ps 107:40; see the commentaries. It is indeed conceivable that both Job and Ps 107 draw on a commonplace. The drunken man recurs in Ps 107:27.

119. Sir 3:24.

120. 2 Kgs 19:10; Isa 37:10; Jer 4:10.

121. 2 Kgs 18:29; Isa 36:14; 2 Chr 32:15. A comparison with 2 Kgs 18:32; Isa 36:18; 2 Chr 32:11 will show the closeness of *hishshi'* to *hesith*; in 2 Chr 32:15 the two occur side by side. Yet *hishshi'* has a nuance of its own.

122. Jer 29:8, apparently referring to the promise by some of immediate restoration; as has often been pointed out, the verse may be misplaced.

123. Job 7.   124. Jer 49:16; Job 3.

125. Jer 37:9.   126. Prov 26:26.

127. Isa 19:13, of the confused princes of Egypt. Nouns possibly connected with *nasha'* are met in Pss 62:5; 73:18; 74:3, but there is too much obscurity.

128. Gen 3:13.   129. See chap. 6, "Intellectual Authorship."

130. Job 2:3.   131. Job 36:18, very close to 36:16.

132. Deut 13:7; 1 Kgs 21:5.   133. 1 Kgs 18:32; Isa 36:18; 2 Chr 32:11, 15.

134. Jer 38:22; 43:3.   135. Job 36:18, uncertain.

136. 1 Sam 26:19.   137. 2 Sam 24:1; 1 Chr 21:1.

138. Job 2:3.   139. 2 Chr 18:2.

140. See *Lexicon*, 540. Köhler is faultless in his treatment of *hesith*, p. 564; similarly Wilhelm Rudolph, *Chronikbücher* (Tübingen, 1955), 252ff., follows the correct interpretation.

141. 2 Chr 19:2.

142. 2 Chr 18:31.

143. S. R. Driver, *The Book of Job* (New York, 1921), 277, commenting on Job 36:16.

144. Josh 15:16ff.; Judg 1:12ff.

145. Carl Steuernagel, *Das Buch Josua* (Göttingen, 1923), 266; Martin Noth, *Das Buch Josua* (Tübingen, 1953), 62; G. F. Moore, *Judges*, ICC (Edinburgh, 1895), 28; C. F. Burney, *The Book of Judges* (London, 1930), 13.

146. For this nuance of blessing, see Steuernagel, *Das Buch Josua*, and Johannes Hempel, "Die israelitischen Anschauungen von Segen und Fluch im Lichte altorientalischer Parallelen," *Zeitschrift der Deutschen Morgenländischen Gesellschaft* 79 (1925): 25.

147. Used in 2 Sam 4:12 of a pool at Hebron, not far from the waters of the Othnielites.

148. Par 29: "her dowry and whatever she brought from her father's house."

149. Deut 11:16.   150. Job 31:27.

151. Job 31:9.   152. Hos 7:11.

153. Job 5:2. Cf., though the general argument is different, Sir 30:24.

154. Judg 14:15; 16:5; 2 Sam 3:25.   155. Sir 31:7.

156. Job 31:24.   157. Job 42:8.

158. Exod 22:15.   159. Sir 42:10.

160. Judg 14:15; 16:5.   161. See Gesenius, *Handwörterbuch*, 666.

162. See Kohler, *Lexicon*, 786.   163. 2 Sam 3:25.

164. 1 Kgs 22:20ff.; 2 Chr 18:19ff.   165. Ezek 14:9.

166. Deut 13:14, usually compared by commentators (also by Gesenius' *Handwörterbuch*), is not strictly parallel. Certainly, a false prophet is here described as a means by which God tests the people's faith. But there is no mention of God enticing him to sin. Nor is there any mention of a test in Ezekiel.

167. Ps 78:36.

168. Prov 1:10; 16:29. 24:28 is obscure; maybe "and shouldest thou entice—*scil*. the judge—with thy lips?" cf. 25:15, to be quoted presently in the text.

169. Prov 25:15.   170. Disregarding the puzzling Prov 25:15.

171. Jer 20:10.   172. 1 Kgs 22:22; 2 Chr 18:21.

173. Jer 20:7.   174. See Gesenius, *Handwörterbuch*, 666.

175. See Kohler, *Lexicon*, 786.   176. See Rudolph, *Chronikbücher*, 120.

177. Thus A. J. Heschel, *Die Prophetie* (Krakow, 1936), 92–93, quoted by Rudolph.

178. Rudolph inclines to this view.

179. True, this is no argument if vv. 7–9 are considered a different prophecy from 10ff. But there is little to be said for such separation: see Rudolph, *Chronikbücher*, 119–20.

180. Ezek 23:32. The change from *śeḥoq* to *ṣeḥoq* is negligible in this connection.

181. Modern critics are agreed in bracketing these words, missing in the cod. Vaticanus of the LXX; see, for example, G. A. Cooke, *The Book of Ezekiel*, ICC (New York, 1937), 255; Georg Fohrer, *Ezechiel*, HAT 13 (Tübingen, 1955), 135. But they overlook the associations called up by the phrase.

182. Hos 2:16.

183. Gesenius, *Handwörterbuch*, 666, Köhler, *Lexicon*, 786.

184. Gen 34:3.   185. Hos 2:17.

186. Academically, one could argue that even in Exod 22:15 the impropriety attaches only to extramarital intercourse, not to the preceding enticement. But in reality the two belong together. Where a man correctly asks a woman's hand from her father, we do not in general regard him as "having enticed her"—even should he have gained her consent beforehand. Yet in exceptional situations, we do so regard him, and certainly, while he is seeking her consent, he may be said to be busy "enticing," "seducing," "alluring" her.

187. Sir 30:23.

188. Prov 14:15.

189. Prov 7:7.

190. Prov 1:22, 32; 7:7; 9:4, 16; 14:16.

191. Prov 1:4; 7:7.

192. Prov 1:4, 22, 32; 8:5; 9:4, 6, 16; 14:18; 19:25; 22:3; 27:12.

193. Prov 19:25; 21:11.

194. Ps 19:3; 119:30.

195. Ps 116:6.

196. Jer 5:4.

197. Ezek 45:20.

198. Prov 9:13.

199. Deut 11:16.

200. Prov 14:15.

INDEX OF SOURCES